Ethics and the History of Indian Philosophy

ETHICS AND THE HISTORY OF INDIAN PHILOSOPHY

SHYAM RANGANATHAN

MOTILAL BANARSIDASS PUBLISHERS
PRIVATE LIMITED • DELHI

First Edition : Delhi, **2007**

ISBN : 81-208-3193-4

MOTILAL BANARSIDASS
41 U.A. Bungalow Road, Jawahar Nagar, Delhi 110 007
8 Mahalaxmi Chamber, 22 Bhulabhai Desai Road, Mumbai 400 026
203 Royapettah High Road, Mylapore, Chennai 600 004
236, 9th Main III Block, Jayanagar, Bangalore 560 011
Sanas Plaza, 1302 Baji Rao Road, Pune 411 002
8 Camac Street, Kolkata 700 017
Ashok Rajpath, Patna 800 004
Chowk, Varanasi 221 001

PRINTED IN INDIA
BY JAINENDRA PRAKASH JAIN AT SHRI JAINENDRA PRESS,
A-45, NARAINA, PHASE-I, NEW DELHI 110 028
AND PUBLISHED BY NARENDRA PRAKASH JAIN FOR
MOTILAL BANARSIDASS PUBLISHERS PRIVATE LIMITED,
BUNGALOW ROAD, DELHI 110 007

For Maggie

~:~:~:~:~:~:~~:~:~:~:~:~:~

"Are good and evil of importance to the universe or only to [hu]man[s]? Such questions are asked by philosophy, and variously answered by various philosophers." — Bertrand Russell, *The Problems of Philosophy*

"Now, therefore, we shall explain Dharma." — Kaṇāda, *Vaiśeṣika Sūtra*

Foreword

Shyam Ranganathan's book, *Ethics and the History of Indian Philosophy,* persuasively presents a detailed and comprehensive account of ethical theories in Indian philosophy. It is a significant addition to works on this topic and must be welcomed with enthusiasm and seriousness. Very few works are available on Indian ethics, and this book sumptuously contributes to the progressively dwindling list of recent studies in the area.

The first distinguishing feature of this work lies in the way it situates its task against the received wisdom in Indology and comparative philosophy that has systematically expressed misgivings regarding the very existence of the concept *ETHICS* in Indian philosophy. Stalwarts such as B.K. Matilal have maintained that Indians, except for cursory forays into the subject, have "seldom discussed" moral philosophy. In refuting this claim, Ranganathan refuses to take modern, positivistic Western ethics as canonical and escapes the limitations of trying to locate ethics in Indian philosophy in terms of this loaded comparison. On his account, Indian ethics is not reduced to what could, at best, be seen as a derivative discourse. Instead, he rejects the approach of treating modern, positivistic Western ethics as a formidable universal benchmark, and situates the recent Western incursions into the discussion as merely one instance of ethics. Rightly so.

The strength of this volume lies in Ranganathan's efforts at the very outset in identifying the *meaning* of moral concepts and of "ethics". By asking for a substantively neutral ground of what ethics is, he redresses the limitations posed by extant literature on comparative philosophy and ethics, which often reduces ethics everywhere else to a poor cousin of the Western canon. In identifying the definition of moral philosophy, he rejects the orthodoxy and the prevalent conservatism in Indology that invariably disqualifies anything ethical from the purview of Indian philosophy. Instead, he makes a case for a reformist view, one that allows us to reconsider contemporary practices of interpreting the meaning of "dharma" by depicting it both as a moral phenomenon but also as designating an arena of moral discourse that the use of the concept might envelop. Moreover, accepting the reformist view makes it possible that a term like "dharma" stands for *one* concept with a clear moral meaning.

In order to establish that "dharma" is a moral term in the language of Indian philosophy, Ranganathan begins by delineating what a moral term means rather than embarking on a specific discussion on dharma. The necessary external reference for arriving at this definition is found in the Anger Inclination Thesis, which he claims is inclusive and captures the essential nature of moral statements. After making a case for the Anger Inclination Thesis in order to arrive at an accurate definition of a moral statement, according to which morality is always related to an inclination to get angry over the violation of the evaluative import of a statement, he goes on to prove that "dharma" of classical Indian thought qualifies as a moral term. Specifically, he demonstrates that "dharma" possesses a singular meaning and is the equivalent of "ethics" or "morality" in the context of Indian philosophy.

Having discussed the views on dharma of philosophers from the major schools of Indian philosophy, and having convincingly demonstrated that they have a clear and unambiguous idea of the ethical, he concludes that the majority of Indian philosophical schools have, indeed, affirmed the reality of morals as a sphere of values. He also points out that there are many accounts of the subject matter of ethics in the West that have failed to track the historical domain of ethics. This conclusion is premised on the deft philosophical move of asking for an independent definition of ethics, or even philosophy, and a plea for not getting ensnared by recent fashions, however important they might seem at the present moment.

The second distinguishing feature of Ranganathan's work becomes clear when we recall the already existing, though not always evident, comparative axis in the realm of intellectual activity in India, particularly the philosophical one. In the prevailing comparative mode, popularised by philosophers like Matilal, J.N. Mohanty and others, classical India is invariably compared with contemporary Western philosophy creating an imbalance of time, temporality and category. Ranganathan corrects this imbalance by his brilliant and magisterial use of Western and Indian sources across the relevant continuum of time and geography. The writer's sensitivity to methodology and his provocative thesis go a long way in making this book indispensable to any study of Indian ethics. It also opens new vistas in the arena of ongoing philosophical debates and its salience will not remain limited to the study of Indian ethics alone.

Professor A. Raghuramaraju

Department of Philosophy
University of Hyderabad

Preface

This book is based on my MA Thesis in South Asian Studies at the University of Toronto. I began the degree in 1997 and finished it by the fall of 2002. The idea for the thesis was conceived and formulated early on in my pursuit of the degree, but I wrote the bulk of it between 2001 and 2002. The motivation for this project then was my dissatisfaction with accounts of ethics in the history of Indian philosophy in the literature—accounts that either marginalized the importance of ethics in Indian philosophy or did not properly identify the locus of Indian moral philosophical thought. My overarching concern then and now is how we as scholars represent non-Western traditions in the modern academy—particularly under the rubric of "philosophy."

While the arguments presented here are in no way incomplete, I consider this book as a slice of a work in progress that will engage me for the rest of my life.

The strengths of the arguments I present here, I believe, are to be found in the global criticisms of the Orthodox and Conservative views of Indology, my criticisms of the various accounts of Indian ethics in the literature, the positive arguments for an Intentionalist approach to defining moral concepts (and the associated criticisms of Extentionalist accounts), the positive views on how to find and interpret Indian moral philosophy, and finally the explications of Indian moral philosophy. My firm conviction continues to be that "dharma" is the term that Indian philosophers and thinkers in classical times used to denote the concept of *MORALITY* and *ETHICS*, and that morality and ethics, as an intellectual space of inquiry, surpasses the positivistic, Humean conception of it that many Indologists seem to have inherited. The corollary of this is that the scope of ethics and morality in all traditions—Western and Eastern—is far wider than the narrow anthropocentric domain that scholars on South Asia have traditionally assigned to it. I am now equally convinced, as I was when I wrote my thesis, that the view of Indian moral philosophy that one often gleans from scholarship on South Asia is the result of a straw-man conception of ethics in the Western tradition, against which the Indian stand on ethics is conceptualized.

I wrote my thesis at a difficult time in my life and I thus cannot thank enough my family and friends who supported me then. Special thanks go to my sister, Yashoda Ranganathan, my mother, Saroja Ranganathan and my uncle, N. Rajagopalan, for proofreading the drafts of previous incarnations of this work. I need to particularly recognize my father, Dr. Narasimhan Ranganathan, whose learning in Sanskrit and Hinduism was of great help to me. I am also especially indebted to my cousin, Dr. Sudhakshina Rangaswamy, whose counsel, support and encouragement in seeing this book to publication was invaluable.

Special thanks are due to Prof. Joseph O'Connell, who supervised my thesis. His patience and the intellectual freedom he afforded me to pursue leads as I saw fit, made the book possible. I would also like to thank Prof. Leonard Priestley who sat on my committee and gave me much constructive feedback on my arguments. Many of the criticisms of Profs. O'Connell and Priestley motivated me to defend my position more vigorously and have thus enriched the book.

Prof. N.K. Wagle's instruction in the historiography of traditional Indian law was extremely important in the development of my thoughts. He taught me that the *dharmaśāstras* were never Indian law. The very idea that such texts functioned as law is the scholar's (Brahmanical and academic) fantasy. But if they were never texts of Indian law, then what? Readers of this book will recognize, I believe, that they constitute a type of Brahmanical practical anthropology (in Kant's sense).

I would like to thank Prof. Danny Goldstick of the Department of Philosophy of the University of Toronto for reading an early draft of Chapter 2: his keen criticism prevented me from making some grave terminological errors (I suspect he may still disapprove of some of my wording, but had I not heeded his criticism, things would have been much worse). I also wish to thank Prof. Kenneth Dorter of the Department of Philosophy of the University of Guelph for his comments on an early draft of the thesis, and for answering the numerous questions that I put to him about Ancient, Western philosophy, and Plato in particular.

More recently, Prof. R. Balasubramanian (former Chairman of the Indian Council of Philosophical Research) was very supportive of my efforts to see this manuscript to publication. Later, as this book was under production, I received encouragement and support from the political philosopher and author, Dr. Jyotirmaya Sharma. I thank both of them. I also owe a special debt of gratitude to Prof. A. Raghuramaraju of the University of Hyderabad for writing the foreword to my manuscript.

I would also like to thank Prof. Emeritus Bishnu Sanwal of the University of Western Ontario and Mrs. Madhu Sanwal, for graciously allowing me to include, on the cover of this book, a picture that they had taken, and Mr. N.P. Jain, director of Motilal Banarsidass, for his patience in seeing this book to completion.

I would also like to thank my long-time friend, Christy Jackson, for helping me format the present work in FrameMaker and my friend, Alex Davis, for pulling me away from my books on occasions. My partner, Andrea Yandreski, deserves special recognition for her love and support while I prepared the manuscript for publication. And finally, I would like to acknowledge the unconditional love and support of my dog, Maggie, whom I adopted from the Toronto Humane Society during the course of my degree in South Asian Studies, two years before I began writing the first draft of this text. Her presence in my life has made me intimately aware of the great scope of ethical thinking in the Indian philosophical tradition. It is a great tradition of moral thought (perhaps the greatest) that has in many forms defended the moral importance of all creatures and even constituents of reality! It is a treasure-trove of inspiration to combat those who would reduce ethics to the norms of the market place, and the considerations of the socially expedient. In this age of untold levels of environmental degradation and unfathomable levels of cruelty inflicted on innocent animals in factory farms and laboratories, Indian moral philosophies shine the way out of this course to hell that we have set ourselves on.

Shyam Ranganathan

Department of Philosophy
York University, Toronto
Spring 2006

web: http://shyam.org/
email: *author@shyam.org*

References

References are included in the text in parentheses, after the quotation. Generally, references are cited by including the author's name first, year of publication of the work cited and an additional piece of information, which enables the reader to locate the reference—most always this additional piece of information is the page number, but on occasion, it is the chapter number, or sometimes it includes a volume number. (References to pages or sections within this work are cited without mention of the author's name or date.) For bibliographic information, please refer to the bibliography. The bibliography is organized around the name of the author, or anonymous canonical work and the year of publication.

In the case of canonical works in philosophy, like Plato's *Republic*, or (Ādi) Śaṅkara's commentary on the *Brahma Sūtra*, a different referencing convention is employed. In these cases, the canonical pagination is cited, after the name of the canonical work. If translations are quoted, then it is the translation of the work listed in the bibliography which is reprinted, unless otherwise specified. If two translations of the same work are quoted, then the name, year and page number of the translation are included in the reference to distinguish the translations.

In most cases of citations of canonical works, the canonical pagination is preferred, for then the reader may verify a reference without having to procure any particular edition or translation. If the canonical pagination is not sufficient to aid the reader to locate the quotation or opinion cited—if, for instance, the canonical pagination refers to a very long passage—then additional information, like the page number of the edition or translation listed in the bibliography, is provided, along with the name of the author and year of the publication.

For certain frequently cited canonical works, abbreviations are employed. They are listed below.

Ac	*Ācārāṅga Sūtra*
An	*Aṅguttara Nikāya*
B	Bādarāyaṇa's *Brahma Sūtra*,
DN	*Dīgha Nikāya*
MB	Madhva's commentary on the *Brahma Sūtra*
MN	*Majjhima Nikāya*
MS	Jaimini's *Mīmāṃsā Sūtra*
MT	Madhva's *Mahābhāratatātparyanirṇaya*
NS	Gautama's *Nyāya Sūtra*
S	*Sūtrakṛtāṅga*
ŚaṅB	(Ādi) Śaṅkara's commentary on the *Brahma Sūtra*
ŚriB	*Śri Bhāṣya*, or Rāmānuja's commentary on the *Brahma Sūtra*
SK	Īśvarakṛṣṇa's *Sāṅkhya Kārikā*
SV	Kumārila's *Ślokavārtika*
U	*Uttarādhyayana*
VS	Kaṇāda's *Vaiśeṣika Sūtra*
YS	Patañjali's *Yoga Sūtra*

It is customary in philosophical literature to distinguish between a term and a concept. A term is a linguistic and orthographic entity which stands for a concept. The distinction is important because two terms from different linguistic practises can, for all practical and theoretical purposes, bear the same concept. For instance, different numerals from different languages can stand for the same number: the concept thus is the semantic matter that is common to these numerals. To refer to a term, I shall use quotation marks—e.g. “100”, “१००”, “one hundred”—and to refer to a specific associated concept, I shall use italicized, small capital letters—e.g. *ONE–HUNDRED*. When a term stands for a certain concept, we can say that the meaning of the term is the concept. Adherence to this convention will not interfere with the use of quotation marks for their usual role, as indications of quotations, or idiosyncratic usage.

Contents

Chapter 3: The *Classical* Meaning of "Dharma" 113

Part III: Implications of the Moral
Meaning of "Dharma"

Chapter 4: Indian Axiology 181

Part IV: Moral Philosophy

Chapter 5: Ethics in Philosophy 189

Part V: Explication of Indian Ethics

Part I:
Introduction

Chapter 1

Introduction

1.1. Problem of Ethics in Indian Philosophy

(It is customary in philosophical literature to distinguish between a term and a concept. A term is a linguistic and orthographic entity which stands for a concept. The distinction is important because two terms from different linguistic practises can, for all practical and theoretical purposes, bear the same concept. For instance, different numerals from different languages can stand for the same number: the concept thus is the semantic matter that is common to these numerals. To refer to a term, I shall use quotation marks—e.g. “100”, “१००”, “one hundred”—and to refer to a specific associated concept, I shall use italicized, small capital letters—e.g. *ONE–HUNDRED*. When a term stands for a certain concept, we can say that the meaning of the term is the concept. When quoted authors fail to respect this convention, for the sake of clarity I introduce it in the reports of their writing. Adherence to this convention will not interfere with the use of quotation marks for their usual role, as indications of quotations, or idiosyncratic usage.)

I intend to show that ethics or moral philosophy constitutes an important part of the history of Indian philosophy. (The terms “morality” and “ethics” are regarded as synonyms in this study—their synonymity will be argued for in Chapter 2).[1]

The way to go about making this point, it would seem, is to simply proceed to an explication of ethics in Indian philosophy. However, the current state of scholarship presents problems for a learned and informed study of ethics in Indian philosophy.

Many scholars are of the opinion that Indian philosophy neglects ethics altogether. Bimal K. Matilal writes:

> Professional philosophers of India over the last two thousand years have been consistently concerned with the problems of logic and epistemology, metaphysics and soteriology, and sometimes they have made very important contributions to the global heritage of philosophy. But, except some cursory comments and some insightful observations, the professional philosophers of India have very seldom discussed what we call "moral philosophy" today. It is true that the *Dharmaśāstra* texts were there to supplement the Hindu discussion of ethics; classification of virtues and vices, and enumeration of duties related to the social status of the individual. But morality was never discussed as such in these texts. (Matilal 1989 p.5)

N.K. Devaraja makes virtually the same point:

> [My] remarks about Indian philosophy are not intended to belittle its achievements in the spheres of logic, epistemology and aesthetics. While these compare well enough with cognate achievements in the European philosophical tradition, it must be admitted that the contributions of Indian thinkers in the fields of ethics and socio-political philosophy seem to be very poor indeed when viewed against those of the European philosophers, e.g. Plato and Aristotle, Kant and Hegel .... (Devaraja 1962 p.v–vi)

Similarly P.T. Raju comments: "There is a general lack of interest in ethical problems as such in Indian philosophy" (Raju 1949 p.27). Finally, Eliot Deutsch adds his voice to this chorus:

> The criticism is often raised against Indian philosophy in general ... that it turns its back on all theoretical and practical considerations of morality and, if not unethical, is at least

> a-ethical in character. If by "ethics" one means a rigorous, independent inquiry into problems of, and questions concerning, the meaning of value, the justification of judgements, and the analysis of moral concepts and concrete existential modes of behaviour, then this criticism is justified .... (Deutsch 1969 p.99)

Then there is Albert Schweitzer's argument. According to Schweitzer, ethics is concerned with "world and life affirmation" while Indian thought is essentially bound up with "world and life negation" (Schweitzer 1936 pp.1–2). Hence, on this account, it is impossible for Indian philosophers to have views on ethics without abandoning the peculiar flavour that makes their philosophy Indian in nature. If an Indian philosopher has a view on ethics, the view is really uncharacteristic of Indian thought:

> [T]he greatest difficulty for the world-view of world and life negation comes from ethics. Ethics demands of man that he should interest himself in the world and in what goes on in it; and, what is more, simply compel him to action. So if world and life negation really becomes concerned with ethics at all, it is driven to make such great concessions to world and life affirmation that it ceases to exist .... In measures as the world-view of world and life negation becomes ethical, it necessarily therefore renounces itself. (Schweitzer 1936 pp.8–9)

1.2. The Problem of "Dharma"

The way to seeing ourselves out of the sceptical view regarding the presence of ethics in Indian philosophy is to grasp the term "dharma". If any term means the same thing as "ethics" or "morality" in the language of classical Indian thought, it is the Sanskritic term "dharma" or its Pāli equivalent, "*dhamma*". For example, the term is used in this fashion by the Indian Emperor Aśoka (272–223 B.C) in his Seventh Rock Edict at Topra: "King

Devanapiya Piyadasi speaks thus: ... [T]he world will be improved by this involvement in the noble activity of *dhamma*; that is, by compassion, generosity, truth, purity, tenderness and goodness".[2] If we were to look to Manu's summary of the content of dharma, it would be reasonable to presume that "dharma" simply means ETHICS; for according to Manu, dharma includes "abstention from injuring (creatures), veracity, abstention from unlawfully appropriating (the goods of others)" and "purity" (Manu X.63). If we could translate "dharma" into "ethics" or "morality", consistently, we would then be justified in viewing references to "dharma" in Indian philosophical literature as marking Indian thought on moral matters. With this approach to Indian philosophical texts, we would be in a position to evaluate how important moral matters are for Indian philosophers.

Yet, there are many objections issuing from the scholarly community to take into account. A major opinion among those who have written on the meaning of "dharma" is that it is untranslatable into English or any other language. Wilhelm Halbfass (1988) draws attention to this scholarly consensus:

> Numerous statements have emphasized the fullness of meaning and the complexity of DHARMA, as well as the difficulty of translating it or of even adequately paraphrasing it .... It has been repeatedly emphasized that the concept of DHARMA is so difficult to define because it ignores or transcends differences which are essential or irreducible for Western understanding—differences between fact and norm, cosmos and society, physics and ethics, etc. (Halbfass 1988 pp.311–13)

Halbfass later concludes that "We cannot reduce the meanings of DHARMA to one general principle; nor is there one single translation which would cover all its usages" (Halbfass 1988 p.333). P.V. Kane, a leading authority on the Hindu *Dharmaśāstra* literature, writes: "'Dharma' is one of those Sanskrit words that defy all attempts at an exact rendering in English or any other tongue" (Kane 1990, vol.1 p.1). R. Lingat, another authority on the same literature, writes: "DHARMA is a concept difficult to define because it disowns or transcends distinctions that seem essential to us, and because it is based upon beliefs that are ... strange to us ..." (Lingat 1973 p.3). Similarly, J.A.B. van Buitenen holds: "It is difficult to define *DHARMA* in terms of Western thought ..." (Buitenen 1957 p.36). K.V. Rangaswami Aiyangar states: "'Dharma' is used in so many senses that it eludes definition. It stands for nature, intrinsic quality, civil and moral law, justice, virtue, merit, duty and morality" (Rangaswami Aiyangar 1952 p.63). Echoing these thoughts, S.N. Dasgupta writes: "The word 'dharma' ... is used in very different senses in the different schools and religious traditions of Indian thought" (Dasgupta 1975, vol.4 p.2). Reflecting upon the use of "dharma" throughout Indian literature, G.J. Larson writes: "The term 'dharma' seems to be one impossible to reduce even to a few basic definitions. It is ubiquitous throughout the texts of the Indian tradition, ancient and modern, and has been used in a bewildering variety of ways" (Larson 1972 p.146). Finally, in his work *Dharma in Hindu Ethics,* Austin B. Creel concludes that "One looks in vain ... for a Sanskrit term equivalent to 'ethics'" (Creel 1977 p.20). Prior to this observation, Creel advises against narrowing the definition of "dharma" to one meaning. He writes:

> One must avoid identification of "dharma" as directly equivalent to any of the various components of its meaning, such as law, duty, morality, justice, virtue, or religion. All of these are involved, but we should cease looking for an equivalent for translation, inasmuch as premature identification with Western concepts tends to blind one to the particular multifaceted structure of meanings in the Hindu "dharma". (Creel 1977 p.2)

Let us call this strongly critical view of the translatability of "dharma" the "Orthodox View". According to the Orthodox View, "dharma", as it functions in classical Indian thought, is not capable of being consistently translated as one term in any other language; it is a term with a plethora of meanings, which must be determined on a case to case basis.

In contrast, there is a relatively more liberal view on the translatability of "dharma". We can call this the "Conservative View".

The Conservative View acknowledges that "dharma" has many different uses, but, holds that these are explainable by reference to a putative account of the etymology of "dharma". The prominent version of this theory holds that the Sanskrit term "dharma" comes form the verbal root "*dhṛ*"—meaning *TO–SUPPORT* or *TO–UPHOLD*. On this account, "dharma" is applied to matters that are (regarded as being) supportive or upholding.

There is a less popular version of the Conservative View where "dharma" is derived from the earlier Vedic concept *ṚTA*, which translates as "Truth, Law, Right, Order; the course of things" and derives from the root "*ṛ*"—"to rise, tend upward" (Grimes 1996 p.256). While it does appear that "dharma" supplants the concept *ṚTA* in later Vedic literature as the designator of cosmic principles, there appears to be no morphological similarity between the two words. In other words, this account of the meaning of "dharma" is a failure as an etymological explanation. This may account for its relative unpopularity.[3]

Most scholars who have elaborated on the meaning of "dharma" have found the Conservative View difficult to sustain. The failure of the Conservative explanation of "dharma" provides *prima facie* credence to the Orthodox View—that "dharma" is not capable of being consistently translated into one term in any other language; it is a term with a plethora of meanings, which must be determined on a case to case basis. If the Orthodox View is correct, it appears that classical Indian thought has no single, reliable, vehicle for the expression of moral convictions. With no such language at their disposal, it is difficult to imagine how Indian philosophers could have contributed to ethics.

1.3. Approach to the Problem

Frequently, the approach taken toward this kind of historical question is to explicate primary source material, in an effort to prove a thesis of clear historical relevance. However, I believe that the problem is not one of unfamiliarity with source material, but rather, an inability on our part to appreciate what our primary sources in Indian philosophy are trying to tell us.

Our assumption is that we have an adequate grasp of the language of Indian philosophy. In order to have such a grasp, we need to have an adequate grasp of the concepts of philosophy first. If we cannot distinguish between a particular philosophical view, and the meaning of terms and concepts used to formulate that view, we will likely believe that philosophers who radically disagree with us are not making claims of a contrary nature regarding some cherished philosophical view of ours.

The reason that scholars have frequently missed that Indian philosophers have written on ethics, I believe, is that they have failed to distinguish between their own, substantive views on morality and an account of the meaning of moral concepts. In making this fundamental assumption, scholars who conclude that Indian philosophers did not address moral issues draw an incorrect conclusion. In reality, Indian philosophers have written on ethics; it is just that their views on morality are frequently very different from many of ours.

In order to appreciate whether or not Indian philosophers wrote on ethics, we need to be clear on the meaning of moral concepts. To do so, we need an unambiguous account of moral meaning.

Thus, instead of rushing to an explication of primary texts and what they have to say about morality, a family of questions will be the cynosure of the first part of the investigation into Indian ethics—these questions include the meaning of the concept *DHARMA*, the terms "ethics", "moral", "philosophy" and the concept *MORAL–PHILOSOPHY.* The answer to these questions will not only help to settle the matter of whether Indian philosophers wrote on ethics or not, but they will furnish the tools that we require to explicate the moral philosophical content of Indian philosophies. Having questioned the meaning of those key terms and concepts, we will have the philosophical acuity to explicate Indian stands on morality, ethics, and the moral aspects of their philosophical projects; we will then have the concrete proof that Indian philosophers did involve themselves deeply in the task of moral philosophy.

Notes

1 The terms "ethics" and "moral" are used by various authors in different ways. However, both terms share a common history. "Ethics" comes from the Greek term "*ethos*" while "moral" comes from the Latin term "*mores*". Bernard Williams notes that both terms meant either something like "custom" or "disposition" in ancient times (1985 p.6). Both terms, moreover, have come to function in the title for one and the same discipline: "moral philosophy" or "ethics". Some authors insist on using these terms in different ways, but it is important to note that such regimented uses are not representative of any strong convention in the history of philosophy itself. We shall see that there is a reason that the history of philosophy has remained ambivalent about treating these terms as wholly different. They are the kinds of philosophical terms that abstract from any particular content. It is because these terms are formal in nature that they can be used as make-shift labels for items that philosophers want to bring attention to. In using these terms, philosophers communicate to each other that the items that they are designating under the heading of "ethics" or "moral" are morally or ethically important.

2 Seventh Aśokan Pillar Edict: Delhi-Topra. Translated by N.K. Wagle and Gibbons of the University of Toronto.

3 Halbfass provides a very informative exposition of the two varieties of the Conservative account of "dharma". While his account is packed with useful historical information, I cannot help but feel that the overall presentation lacks coherence. For not only does Halbfass appear to endorse the Conservative View in his account, but he favourably endorses Larson's expression of the Orthodox View, which is explicitly at odds with the Conservative View. See his chapter "Dharma in Traditional Hinduism" in Halbfass 1988 pp.310–333. Halbfass, in other words, seems to affirm and deny all the received positions on the meaning of "dharma" in his essay.

Part II: Dharma

Chapter 2

"Dharma" as a Moral Term

While the Orthodox View represents the dominant account of the meaning of "dharma" in the secondary literature on Indian philosophy, its thesis is vulnerable to serious criticism. Once we give due thought to the question of how to define moral terms, it becomes apparent that the Orthodox approach to the meanings of "dharma" is without justification and productive of a poor explanation. In contrast to the Orthodox View, I intend to make a case in the present chapter for what may be called the "Reform View". This view holds that (1) "dharma", in the language of Indian philosophy, stands for one concept with a clear moral meaning—the concept of *ETHICAL* or *MORAL*; and (2) the concept that terms like "dharma" and "moral" stand for furnishes the common, semantic ground for meaningful philosophical disagreement on the topic of ethics. The term "Indian Philosophy", for the purpose of this study is understood as referring only to the philosophical literature, indigenous to South Asia, authored prior to the modern period of history.

2.1. Extention and Intention

It is important to distinguish between *intention* and the concept I shall call "*extention*" (both spelled with a "t"). These two concepts must be distinguished from yet another pair of concepts, with a similar meaning and spelling: *INTENSION* and *EXTENSION* (both spelled with an "s").

The distinction between *intension* and *extension* has an apparently long history, but, like many notions in philosophy, its precise import has been a matter of debate. On many accounts, the distinction can be traced back to Aristotle. According to one historian of logic, the influence of this distinction in modern logic stems largely from Arnauld and Nicole's treatment of it in the *Port Royal Logic* (1962).[1] The *extension* of a concept was regarded by these authors as the individuals to which the concept applied, while the *intension* of a concept was thought to consist of the related, subsidiary concepts, attributes or qualities that constitute it (Swoyer 1995 pp.99–100).

The distinction between *intension* and *extension* resembles the distinction between the connotation and the denotation of a concept, and on one account, the distinction between *intension* and *extension* can be explained as this distinction (Nute 1995 p.379).

In recent times, fine distinctions between kinds of *extensions* have been drawn (differences between the *extension* of a concept; of a sentence; of an idea ...). However, there is a constancy to the use of these ideas. "*Intension*" generally refers to the conceptual fund of a concept, which is the idea behind a term and its rational connections to other ideas. We might say that the *intension* of a concept is its meaning. In contrast, the *extension* of a concept is the class of entities that falls under it. To make this clear, consider the question of who the next Prime Minister of Canada will be. Two people may disagree. One commentator says that candidate *A* will be the Prime Minister, while another thinks that *B* will occupy this office, and that *A* will never be Prime Minister. In this disagreement, both commentators are in agreement on what the *intension* of the concept *NEXT–PRIME–MINISTER–OF–CANADA* is: a person who comes to occupy a position in the lower chamber of the Canadian Parliament at a certain time, after having satisfied certain other conditions (must be a member of dominant party in Parliament, must have been elected by own party to be leader, must have been elected by regional constituents to be their representative in parliament, etc.). What the disagreement centres around is an account of the *extension* of the concept: the first commentator thinks that *A* is part of the *extension* of *PRIME–MINISTER–OF–CANADA* while the second commentator thinks that *B*, and not *A*, constitutes part of the *extension* of *PRIME–MINISTER–OF–CANADA*.

While "*intension*" and "*extension*" are technical philosophical terms, found mostly in works in logic and semantics, "*intention*", spelled with a "t", is a word that has a common usage. (1) In common parlance, "*intention*" refers to the purpose behind an action. (2) In philosophical talk, "*intention*" has a technical meaning: it refers to a feature of a person's mind (Bratman 1995 p.380). The technical sense of "*intention*" is related to a distinct use of the term, as it appears in (3) the Phenomenological term "*intentionality*".

Traditionally, the concept of *INTENTIONALITY* was applied broadly to anything that had the property of being *about something*. Examples of such items include representational models (maps, for instance), mental states and texts. The term comes from the Latin verb *intendo* and was used by the Mediaeval philosophers of the Western tradition to designate such phenomenon (Dennett 1995 p.391). The term was brought back into prominence by Franz Brentano, who postulated that *intentionality* differentiates minds from matter—only mental phenomena have *intentionality*, according to Brentano (1924). The concept comes to dominate the thought of Husserl (the father of Phenomenology)[2] largely through the writings of Brentano. However, the notion of *intentionality* also appears revived in the Analytic tradition of philosophy through the attention that R.M. Chisholm brings to *intentional* idioms. For the new wave, *intentional* idioms are used to designate mental states and events (Chisholm 1952). In this revival, it seems that the third meaning of "*intention*", as it appears in the term "*intentionality*", has coalesced with the second meaning of "*intention*": (4) now "*intention*" appears to designate both (a) mental phenomenon, and (b) its character of being *about* something.

In this study, I will use the term "*intention*" in this fourth sense. While *intentional* matters so conceived are about something, frequently this aboutness concerns something outside a person's mind (though not always)—an *intention* can only be fully comprehended as existing within the subjective sphere of an individual. In contrast, I will use the term "*extention*" (with a "t") to refer to the thing that is the target of *intentionality*, which usually is not in a person's mind.

INTENTION and *INTENSION* bear a certain similarity, as do *EXTENTION* and *EXTENSION*. The former two concepts refer to something that can exist, fully, within the subjective awareness of a person, whereas, *extention*, and *extension*, are things that are not necessarily mental in nature. This is arguably the extent of the similarity.

An *intention* that accompanies the use of a concept may be transient, whereas the *intension* of a concept (its conceptual meaning) is something common for all meaningful uses of the concept. Hence, an individual might have a grudge against postal workers, and would thus have an *intentional* state regarding postal workers that is negative. However, for that person, the concept of *POSTAL–WORKER* will have the same *intension* as it does for all people who employ this concept meaningfully: the *intension* of *POSTAL–WORKER* is: person who works for the postal service. Likewise, the *extention* of a concept is something that is possibly transient, though its *extension* is not. Hence, the *extention* of the employment of the concept of *POSTAL–WORKER* might be a certain individual on a particular day, but the *extension* of *POSTAL–WORKER* is the set of all persons (past, present and future) who work for the postal service.

It is important to note that while *INTENSION* and *EXTENSION* (both spelled with an "s") are fundamentally semantic notions concerned with the theoretical discussion of meaning, *INTENTION* and *EXTENTION* are not. *INTENTION* and *EXTENTION* are better understood as experiential categories. Yet, there is a semantic dimension to *INTENTION* and *EXTENTION*. Both *intention* and *extention* are, potentially, different kinds of linguistic referents. When either reference is consistent in meaningful use, it can help us define the term.

Some terms bear a remarkable constancy in the *extentions* that they pick up, in linguistic usages, and such terms can be defined in terms of these *extentions*. Examples of such terms are "cedar" and (ironically) "intention". In contrast, there are terms whose meaning cannot be comprehended as the typical *extentions* that accompany the use of the term. These terms can only be defined if we take into account the *intention* accompanying their use. An example is "remarkable". Terms of the former variety we can call "*extentional* terms", and terms of the latter variety, we can call "*intentional* terms". As concepts are the (cross-linguistic) semantic entities that terms stand for, and as it is the meaning of a concept—its *intension*—that is the meaning of a term, we can also distinguish between *intentional* and *extentional* concepts. An *intentional* concept is the concept that an *intentional* term stands for, as an *extentional* concept is the concept that an *extentional* term stands for; the *intension* of an *intentional* concept is defined with respect to an essential *intention*, while the *intension* of an *extentional* concept is defined with respect to an essential *extention*.

To highlight the distinction between terms and concepts that are definable by *intentions* and those that are definable by *extentions*, consider the following scenario of an anthropologist attempting to learn the language of natives that she is studying. The anthropologist has developed a certain level of proficiency in the language of the natives, but she is unsure about a term that seems to name scorpions. She knows that the term in question refers to scorpions because, when she asks clarification questions, she is told by the natives that what they are talking about is the small animal with a stinger on its tail. What she is not fully aware of is that the natives have an unusual phobia of scorpions—a phobia that is so powerful that they rarely ever directly refer to scorpions, and instead, exclaim a word that means *FRIGHTENING* or *FRIGHTENING–THING* when shown a scorpion, or when talking about a scorpion. (Hence, instead of saying, "then a scorpion came out of the hole" or "that is a scorpion" they say "then a frightening thing came out of the hole", or "that is a frightening thing".) Moreover, few things frighten these natives as do scorpions, so they rarely refer to anything else but scorpions as *FRIGHTENING*. As an outsider, the anthropologist has a choice: either she can hypothesize that the term that the natives exclaim when they are talking about scorpions is an *extentional* term, or she can hypothesize that it is an *intentional* term. On the former hypothesis, the anthropologist would be led to the conclusion that the term in question literally means *SCORPION*, which is incorrect. If she hypothesizes that the term is *intentional* in nature, her next move is to determine the *intention* that the term expresses or bears. She would thus eventually be led to the correct interpretation: that the term in question means *FRIGHTENING* or *FRIGHTENING–THING*. What helps confirm this diagnosis is that our anthropologist would eventually observe that the term meaning *FRIGHTENING* or *FRIGHTENING–THING* shows up in conversations about matters other than scorpions.[3]

As another example, take the case of a foreigner who attempts to learn English by immersion in an English speaking society. The foreigner does not know what the term "good" means. He has two choices. He could hypothesize that the term is *extentional* in nature. This would be an extremely unfruitful path, for the *extentions* of "good" are diverse, with no intrinsic property holding them together. Some people use the term "good" in reference to cars—others call ice cream "good". Perhaps (thinks the foreigner) "good" stands for things made of atoms. But then the foreigner confronts the statement "that is a good argument"—arguments are not made of atoms! In contrast, the foreigner could hypothesize that "good" is an *intentional* term. Then our novice would be led to investigate the *intentional* states that accompany the use of "good". He would eventually realize that, typically, "good" is used in the presence of positive *intentional* dispositions toward things, and finally, he would realize that things can be "good" in different ways, and for different reasons, but that "good" is applied to things that the author approves of in some fashion.

A sign of *extentional* terms is that they are typically used to refer to members of a class of entities, and that their meaningfulness depends largely upon the fact that they are consistently used as names for these entities. There are typically no intractable controversies surrounding the meaning of *extentional* terms. In contrast, *intentional* terms are deceptive proper nouns. They seem to function as names for things (and they do) but further observation reveals that they do much to reveal the opinions of authors as well. If we incorrectly presume that *intentional* terms are *extentional* in nature, we are bound to observe that their use violates our efforts to fix the class of entities that they stand for.

There is often controversy surrounding the proper use of *intentional* words—controversies not easily resolved to everyone's satisfaction. Take the word "pleasurable". Not only is it the case that people use this term to describe diverse things, but also we can find people in a given society that have conflicting and contradictory views on what *is* pleasurable. Most people tend to think that the absence of, or distraction from, pain is a condition of something being pleasurable; yet, masochists believe that pain is pleasurable. For the nonmasochist, the *extention* of "pleasurable" consists in the absence of pain while for the masochist, the *extention* of "pleasurable" consists in the presence of pain. If "pleasurable" were an *extentional* term, we would eventually be led to the conclusion that "pleasurable" does not mean the same thing for the masochist and the nonmasochist, for the *extentions* they join to "pleasurable" are mutually exclusive. However, this is not our normal reaction to this controversy. We tend to think that both the masochist and nonmasochist are talking about the same thing when they talk of "pleasure"—this is because we understand the term with respect to the *intention* that accompanies its typical use. The *intention* of "pleasure" has to do with a positive disposition toward the *extention* of the term—an interest in the continued existence of the *extention* of "pleasurable", and most importantly, a desire to maximize and prolong the experience of the *extention*.

In summary, the distinction between *extentional* and *intentional* terms concerns the *loci of consistency in the use of terms*. The distinction between *extention* and *intention* brings up two different loci around which usage can be consistent.

There are also parasitic uses of terms, which shift the loci of comprehendability from one pole to the other. There are parasitic uses of *extentional* terms that can only be understood if the *intention* accompanying them is taken into account. Take, for example, the word "Christian". This is an *extentional* term; applicable to anything (book, rite, person) that affirms or professes the belief that Jesus of Nazareth is the Messiah. There is, though, a secondary usage of this term that is *intentional*. It is not unheard of for some Christians to use the term "Christian" as a term of moral approval, as in the statement "that is very Christian of you". Similarly, one might imagine that an atheist or member of an alternate religion might repeat the same sentence and yet use the term "Christian" as one of criticism—either signifying something that is heretical (in the eye of the member of the alternate religion) or something that exemplifies religious superstition and dogma (in the eye of the atheist).

Such a shift from *extentional* to *intentional* meaning is also typical of metaphorical uses of terms. For example, someone might use the *extentional* term "scorpion" as a metaphor when they call some human a "scorpion". The only way that such a usage is comprehendible is if we look to the *intention* of the author. Perhaps the author's idea is that the person in question has the behavioural patterns of a scorpion; perhaps the author believes that the person in question is dangerous in a manner similar to a scorpion—capable of delivering a harmful blow with little effort or provocation. It is typically the mind-set of the author or speaker that we must speculate on, if we are to understand how some particular human being can be a scorpion.

Does the observation that *extentional* terms take on secondary *intentional* meanings falsify the view that there are terms whose meaning is reducible to its typical *extentions*? I do not believe so. In every case where the basis of the meaning shifts from one pole to the other, it remains that we continue to understand the secondary meaning as derivative and based upon a more fundamental meaning. It is the fundamental or primary meaning of a term that the notions of *extentional* terms and *intentional* terms attempt to address.

It will be helpful at this point to introduce some terminology that deals with philosophical views on the relationship between terms and their *intentions* and *extentions*.

There are two possible simple views, and combinations and variations upon these two views. One view holds that certain terms (and their concepts) are definable, at least in part, by their typical *extentions*. I shall call this view "Extentionalist", or "Extentionalism". Then there is the view that certain terms (and their concepts) are definable, at least in part, by their typical *intentions*. I shall call this view "Intentionalist", or "Intentionalism".

Intentionalism and Extentionalism are "isms" after the fashion of Platonism. Platonism is the view that a certain class of abstract entities exist. Hence, one might be a Platonist about numbers, and not, say, about interrogatives. Thus, both Intentionalism and Extentionalism must be specified with respect to the class of entities they are concerned with. Moreover, both of these views are contraries, but not mutually exclusive or contradictory. It is possible then, to regard some group of terms or concepts as definable by both their *intentions*, and their *extentions*. Such a view would constitute a mixed, Intentionalist–Extentionalist account. As a matter of taxonomy, however, such mixed views can also be designated simply as either "Extentionalist" or "Intentionalist"—no contradiction is involved in omitting mention of both views, as they are not inherently mutually exclusive.[4]

There are extreme variations on Extentionalism and Intentionalism. One extreme view that we will have occasion to note in our discussion on Indology (2.6. The Meaning of "Dharma" pp.91–95), is that all terms have their meaning in their *extentions*—and only their *extentions*. We might call this "Global

Extentionalism". The other extreme view is that all terms have their meaning in their *intentions*. We might call this "Global Intentionalism". Global Extentionalism is typical of Naturalistic philosophies (Semantic Holism appears to be a version of Extentionalism) and some postmodern theories (Derrida 1974 pp.62–63, argues a version of Global Extentionalism). Global Intentionalism is what Derrida identifies as Logocentrism (Derrida 1974 pp.11–18), which on his account is the traditional view of Western philosophy. Most people these days (philosophers and ordinary people, I think) tend not to buy into the Global views, and opt for flexible mixed views. One version of such a view is that there are some terms that are solely definable in terms of their *extentions*, as there are some terms that are solely definable by their typical *intentions*. Another version of this relaxed view is that many terms are definable by a combination of both their typical *extentions*, and their typical *intentions*.

2.2. Key Philosophical Terms

The previous discussion furnishes us with certain tools that can aid us in our inquiry into the meaning of "dharma" in Indian philosophy.

As noted, the most successful view on the meaning of "dharma" in secondary, Indological literature is the Orthodox View. The Orthodox View holds that "dharma" has many meanings in the language of Indian philosophy, and moreover, that the various meanings of "dharma" are to be determined on a case-to-case basis. What is significant about the individual cases of "dharma"? According to the Orthodox View, what we find is that "dharma" has several different *extentions*: at times, "dharma" stands for attributes; at other times, "dharma" stands for ritual; at other times, "dharma" stands for the constituents of reality. The Orthodox View's counsel is that we ought to take the various *extentions* of "dharma" as its meanings. The Orthodox View is thus a species of Extentionalism applied to the question of the meaning of "dharma" in Indian philosophy.

The unrestrained Extentionalism, applied to all uses of "dharma", is what is responsible for the Orthodox View that "dharma" is a bewildering term with no coherent and consistent meaning. For unlike "cat" which displays regularity with respect to its typical *extentions*, "dharma", in classical Indian thought, does not. The result is an account of "dharma" as a term with countless, unrelated meanings.

My suggestion is that it is incorrect to construe "dharma" as an *extentional* term in classical Indian thought. Rather, I will argue that "dharma", in classical Indian thought, is a term with one, *intentional* meaning. I will argue that all moral terms are fundamentally *intentional.* And moreover, I will argue that "dharma" in the language of Indian philosophy is a moral term with the same *intentional* meaning as "ethics" or "moral". I am urging this in part because dharma" is a *key philosophical term.*

A key philosophical term is a phonemic entity that stands for a concept, which serves as the grounds for meaningful disagreement between proponents of distinct philosophical views. The concept that such a philosophical term stands for is a *key philosophical concept.* The employment of key philosophical terms is the linguistic and orthographic flag that signals that a distinct perspective is being voiced within a philosophical debate. The particular philosophical debate they signal is one that is delimited by the question of the correct application of the particular key philosophical term or concept, or to the question of what the *extension* of the corresponding key philosophical concept consists in. Examples of key philosophical terms are the words "reality" and "knowledge" in English—as are the terms "moral" and "ethics". Hence, any introductory course to metaphysics will present its foundational question as "What is reality?" just as an introductory course to epistemology would portray its problematic as "What is knowledge?" and as a course on ethics will be limited to the question "What is ethical". The explication of these terms define the respective debates of metaphysics, epistemology and ethics; the question of what the *extensions* of the concepts *REAL*, *KNOWLEDGE*, and *ETHICAL* are, forms the substance of the controversies of metaphysics, epistemology and ethics. It follows from this that the *extentions* granted to these terms will vary according to philosophical perspective.

The meaning of key philosophical terms is broached in contemporary metaethical debate. Here, the question that is raised is not so much "What do all key philosophical terms mean", but rather, "What do moral terms mean; some of which are key philosophical terms, like 'ethical', 'good', or 'evil', and some of which are not so philosophically central, like 'kind', 'considerate', and so on". The issue of whether moral terms are fundamentally *extentional* or *intentional* is reflected in this debate. The prominent advocates for Extentionalism with respect to all moral terms—including key philosophical terms of moral debate—are Definitional Naturalists; those who believe that the meaning of moral terms can be cashed out in terms of their natural, empirical or physical *extentions*.[5]

A more complex Extentionalist position is that moral terms—including key philosophical terms like *MORAL*—or moral statements, are in part defined by their typical *extentions*. This is a widespread view, and it surfaces in accounts where there is a particular kind of content to moral statements and moral terms. This view does not state that the meaning of moral terms and statements are solely reducible to their *extentions*. It holds that all moral terms and statements, by definition, concern certain *extentional* matters (be they actions, virtues, social matters, and so on). These accounts of moral terms and statements are often offered in tandem with Intentionalist constraints on the meaning of these items. There is the view that moral terms concern social matters, and moreover that they issue from a "moral point of view". This is the view put forward by William Frankena (1973). Then there is the view of Schweitzer (1936) that "ethics" is predicated of the world and life and that moral statements issue from a positive perspective on these matters. Such views offer a mixed, Intentionalist–Extentionalist accounts of moral terms.

I think that there is more than one good reason for rejecting Extentionalist (including mixed Extentionalist –Intentionalist) positions that attempt to define all moral terms—including the key philosophical terms of "ethical" and "moral".

The problem of finding a consistent *extentional* equivalent for "dharma" in English makes a case against the claims of the Extentionalist about moral terms on *extentional* grounds. Extentionalism about moral terms holds that *all* moral terms are defined, at least in part, in terms of their *extentions*. Yet the best Sanskritic candidate for a key moral, philosophical term, from classical Indian philosophy, is a word whose list of *extentions* finds no match in the English language. In addition to being applied to matters that modern Westerners are apt to use moral terms to refer to, classical Indian philosophers have called such things as the constituent of reality—"dharma". Other Indian philosophers have used "dharma" to name the Principle of Motion. In the philosophical literature of India, "dharma" is also applied to the idea of a property or attribute. The untranslatability of "dharma" (from Indian philosophy) on *extentional* grounds is grounds for rejecting the (Naturalist or Non-Naturalist) Extentionalist's account of all moral terms. "Dharma" is the falsifying evidence against Extentionalism applied to all moral terms.

The Extentionalist with respect to key philosophical moral terms might argue that this objection against their view begs the question, for it presumes that "dharma" is a key, philosophical term meaning the same thing as *MORAL* or *ETHICS*. On what basis would such an Extentionalist be able to argue that "dharma" is not always such a key, philosophical, moral term in Indian philosophy? Based on its *extentions*: "dharma" has *extentions* that are not commensurate with the *extentions* of a key philosophical, moral term—says the Extentionalist about moral terms. However, such Extentionalists overlook that the question at hand is whether certain kinds of *extentions*, and only these, are moral in nature. The only plausible way that the Extentionalist could exclude considering "dharma" as a persistent moral term in

Indian philosophy is by having decided, in advance, what *extentions* are moral in nature, and what are not. Hence, if the Extentionalist decides that "dharma" is not always a moral term in Indian philosophy, they have begged the question, and their argument pertaining to the *extentional* foundation of key philosophical, moral terms is circular.

There is one decisive reason for abandoning the Extentionalist's account of all moral terms, which opens up our foray in semantics to metaphilosophical considerations.

An account of the meaning of foundational terms that define philosophical fields (key philosophical terms) has one important constraint. It must not intrude upon substantive debate within the field of philosophical concern that the defined terms delimit, for a philosophical field is wide enough to embrace opposing and contradictory opinions on what its disputed terms stand for. Extentionalist accounts of key philosophical concepts improperly intrude on such substantive questions by specifying what key disputed concepts can designate.

Consider the cases of "knowledge" and "reality". The concepts that these terms designate are the foundational concepts that respectively define the philosophical fields of epistemology and metaphysics. If we were to define these terms *extentionally*, we would do as commentators have done for "dharma": draw up a list of items that these terms are predicated *of*. Yet, if we travel down this path, we would end up with one or the other of two undesirable outcomes: Either we could take all the *extentions* of *KNOWLEDGE* or *REALITY* as, disjunctively constituting one single meaning of these respective concepts, or, we could take each *extention* of these terms as constituting a distinct meaning of these terms. On the first option, we end up with a list of items by definition that we may consider constitute knowledge, or reality. In other words, the first option ends up defining "knowledge" and "reality" in such a way that there is no room for real disagreement on what these terms designate. Such an approach would render all seemingly contrary philosophical views regarding what counts as "knowledge" or "reality" as equally valid, for the *extentions* that they attribute to these terms would already be built into the common definition of these terms. On the second option, it turns out that every different view on what "knowledge" or "reality" is constitutes its own meaning. Thus, on this Extentionalist approach, there was never any genuine philosophical disagreement between Rationalists and Empiricists, or Idealists and Materialists, for, on this latter approach, all of these philosophies meant something different by the terms "knowledge" and "reality".

Extentionalist accounts of key philosophical terms and concepts, thus kill philosophical debate.

In contrast, Non-Extentionalist, Intentionalist accounts of foundational subject-matter do not tell us what things we can think are epistemologically or metaphysically important. Rather, they provide accounts of the *attitudes* and *expectations* associated with these key terms as the focal point of their use. The Non-Extentionalist, Intentionalist account of these matters would thus leave the substantive question of what counts as knowledge or reality to epistemology or metaphysics, and importantly, to individual philosophers. They provide us a way to understand how opinions from divergent philosophical schools could be *talking about the same thing*, even though they are referring to distinct objects in their disputed claims. An Intentionalist account of key philosophical terms and concepts thus provides a grip on shared philosophical resources, independently of a substantive philosophical view.

If key philosophical concepts were defined in terms of their *extentions*, then it would follow that an acquaintance with their meaning would shut down philosophical debate. *CAT* is not a philosophical concept precisely because it can be defined in terms of its *extentions*. Because *CAT* is defined in terms of its *extentions*, we do not ask the question "what is a cat", or "what is catness" in philosophy. The dictionary can help us with these questions. The dictionary cannot help us with the questions "what is morality", "what is real" or "what is knowledge" because "morality", "reality" and "knowledge" are not *definable* in terms of their typical *extentions*. What the dictionary can do is to specify the *intentional* meaning of these terms, considered apart from the question of what the appropriate *extentions* of these terms are. The dictionary would thus provide clear definitions for these terms, without affirming any particular substantive philosophical view on the nature of reality, knowledge or morality—this would be exactly what we require, as an introduction to key terms around which the philosophical debates of metaphysics, epistemology and ethics revolve.

If "dharma" is a key philosophical term in classical Indian thought, it follows that we ought to abandon the Orthodox and Extentionalist approaches to defining it, for they are incapable of modelling the kind of meaningful disagreement that is characteristic of philosophy. We have already reviewed the evidence in favour of "dharma" being a key philosophical term in classical Indian philosophy in Part II Chapter 2: it is used to refer to many different items in Indian philosophy; it is ubiquitous in classical Indian thought and philosophical texts (1.2. The Problem of "Dharma" pp.5–9). At many junctures, it appears to have a salient moral meaning, as "ethics" and "moral" have—terms that are also key philosophical terms. The evidence thus points to "dharma" standing for the same concept that "ethical" and "moral" stand for, for "ethical" and "moral" are key philosophical terms with a moral significance.

2.2.0.1. Criticism and Discussion

A critic might argue that the Intentionalist approach to defining key philosophical concepts cuts short the possibility that their analysis can solve philosophical problems. For the kind of definition of key concepts being proposed here does not build into them the resources for answers to substantive philosophical questions.

This *might* be true, particularly if by "solve" one means *RESOLVE–DEBATE*. What choice do we have? The kind of definition of key philosophical concepts that we are after must leave room for philosophical disagreement, or else, it could not serve as a useful definition when we study the history of philosophy. For philosophical debate is unlike any other kind of disagreement—it is not simply about particulars, but about general and universal matters. If we do not carve out a definition of key philosophical terms allowing for meaningful disagreement on the import of universals—like "The Good"—we could not afford philosophers the room that they require to disagree philosophically.

The argument I have made here bears a resemblance to G.E. Moore's Open Question Argument. Moore argues in his *Principia Ethica* (1903) that any definition of "Good" leaves the question open as to whether what is defined as good, is in fact good. This has been called the "Open Question Argument" by posterity. This line of reasoning may seem similar to my argument, for both Moore and I attempt to reject Definitional Naturalism by appealing to the possibility of contrary moral opinions. My view differs from Moore's in some important respects. Moore was honing in on a feature that he took to be peculiar to moral subject-matter, and one of the theses that Moore attempts to establish in connection with his Open Question Argument is that the idea of *THE GOOD* is indefinable. My view is that terms like "good", and the corresponding concept *GOOD*, are definable according to their *intention*. My argument is not that moral questions are peculiarly open-ended, but that philosophy is a subject that by definition, embraces contradictory substantive views. Hence, our philosophical terms have to be amenable to such discussions.

The critic might argue that the *intentional* route of defining terms does not render them any more amenable to being employed in an open debate; for *intentional* definitions too can specify, in full, the *extensions* (with an "s") of a concept, and hence, they too can stop debate. For instance, consider the *intentional* term "game" that stands for the *intentional* concept of GAME. This concept is definable as, *an activity that presents both a challenge and entertainment to those who undertake it.* To determine the set of all games, we need the following information: what all persons find both entertaining and challenging. We may have trouble determining the *extension* of *GAME* because of our impaired ability to survey people's views on entertainment and challenges. However, our limits in knowing have nothing to do with whether the concept of *GAME* specifies its *extension*.

Note that the *intentional* concept of *GAME* has, within its definition, room for interpersonal variability on what individuals will consider its *extension*. What is challenging for me may not be challenging for another; what is entertaining for me is not entertaining for another. Hence, my personal account of the *extension* of *GAME* will differ from those of others. Moreover, I may have reasonable opinions on what we *ought* to appropriately consider entertaining or challenging. For instance, some persons think that hunting is entertaining and challenging (that it is a game); however, I think that it is inappropriate for humans to regard hunting as entertaining and challenging (particularly given our technological advantage) just as I feel it is inappropriate for a child to think that squashing insects is entertaining. None of these activities are *genuine* games. Rather, they are instances of cruel and callous behaviour. Others are bound to have differing opinions on the matter.

This explication of interpersonal differences with respect to interpretations of the purely *intentional* concept of *GAME* is a case in point: controversy is endemic to purely *intentional* concepts, for what counts as their *extensions* is a matter that we often have personal views on.

In contrast, accounts of the *extensions* of *extentional* concepts are not subject to the same interpersonal variability, and what controversy there is surrounding their *extensions* is theoretically resolvable to everyone's satisfaction. Consider the case of a disagreement over whether a bowl is filled with water. "Water" is an *extentional* term. My companion might think that a bowl, in plain sight of both of us, is filled with water, i.e., that the contents of a bowl is designated by the term "water" and that those contents are part of the *extension* of the concept of *WATER*. I do not see any water in the bowl: I disagree. This disagreement can be resolved by testing the contents of the bowl (sticking our fingers in it, pouring it out, and so on).

If this is illustrative of typical debates over *extentional* concepts—and I submit that it is—we can conclude that disagreements about *extentional* concepts can, in theory, be resolved decisively, once and for all. *Extentional* concepts are thus not inherently controversial. Controversy may surround them, but it is never, in theory, intractable, for we define such concepts with reference to a public orientation to things.

2.3. Definitions of Moral Statements

The previous section forwarded the view that "dharma" is a key philosophical term of classical Indian thought. The chief evidence in favour of this perspective on "dharma" is that it is ubiquitous in the texts of classical India—particularly those of philosophical importance—and that its *extentions* (what it is used as a name for) vary according to philosophical school; these are precisely the traits of a key philosophical term. Moreover if "dharma" is such a term, then it is a term with the meaning of "ethical" or "moral". The evidence adduced for this latter claim, up to this point, is largely intuitive in nature. Given the moral aura of "dharma" and given that its use displays the traits of a key philosophical term (i.e. it has a great variety of extentions in the context of philosophical works, which change according to philosophical perspective) it is reasonable to conclude that "dharma" means the same thing as "ethical" or "moral", which are also key philosophical terms. The actual moral meaning of "dharma" has not been secured by any argument of its own yet.

In order to positively establish that "dharma" is a moral term in the language of Indian philosophy (and not, say, a key term of epistemology or metaphysics), and that it can and ought to be consistently translated as a moral term from classical Indian thought, a general account of moral terms is required against which the term "dharma" can be appraised. To arrive at such an account, without begging any questions, we must suspend our discussion of "dharma" and procure a definition of moral terms.

No real definition consists in simply repeating the definiendum as the definiens: "cat means cat" is not a definition of "cat". Hence, in order to procure a definition of moral terms we need to define them in reference to something else. What could this something else be?

Moral terms are key ingredients in moral statements. If we could arrive at an account of moral statements that does not depend upon a definition of moral terms, we could then define moral terms in reference to their role in moral statements.

As a prelude to a definition of moral terms, I propose to embark on a quest for a definition of moral statements.

2.3.0.1. Theories of Moral Statements

Over the last several decades, a body of literature has developed dealing with the defining traits of moral statements. To make a long story not so long, I think that the literature presents nine basic views: (1) the Social Content Thesis, (2) the Conduct Thesis, (3) the Categoricality Thesis, (4) the Universalizability Thesis, (5) the Importance Thesis, (6) the Overridingness Thesis, (7) the Blame Inclination Thesis, (8) the Conformity Thesis, and (9) the Punishment Thesis. The view that I will argue for is a distant cousin of the Blame Inclination Thesis and the Conformity Thesis. I call this proposal (10) the "Anger Inclination Thesis".

By making a case for the Anger Inclination Thesis as the accurate definition of a moral statement, the groundwork is laid for what I would urge is an accurate definition of moral terms. Having procured an account of moral terms, we will be in a position to judge whether "dharma" of classical Indian thought qualifies as a moral term.

It may be an over-simplification to reduce the options in the literature to just nine, when in reality, many philosophers propose composite views on the definition of moral statements. The nine theses propose defining properties of moral statements that are like building blocks for composite views on the nature of moral statements. For instance, the Categoricality Thesis is the view that the property of *categoricality* defines moral statements, as the Importance Thesis is the view that the property of *importance* defines moral statements. Thus, for example, some philosophers advocate that moral statements are defined as having the properties of (i) *categoricality* and (ii) *importance*. Should such composite options not be considered?

By addressing them separately, we will be in a position to assess whether they are capable of being veridical building blocks in a definition of moral statements. After determining which of the minute theses make true assertions about moral statements, we can assess whether these basic accounts, in combination, or in isolation, are capable of yielding an accurate definition of moral statements.

Two accounts of defining features of moral statements, which are left out of the list above, are the positions of Cognitivism and Noncognitivism. Cognitivism is the view that moral statements are like statements of fact in one respect: they *declare* that something is so. Hence, on the Cognitivist's view, moral statements express judgements (they make an attributive claim about a subject). Because they express judgements, they are *cognitive*. Noncognitivism is the view that moral statements differ from statements of fact: they do not declare that something is so. Hence, they are *noncognitive*, as they make no attributive claim. (Often, Noncognitivists hold that moral statements are *imperatives*—they tell us that we ought to do something.) The debate over whether moral statements are *cognitive* or *noncognitive* is a staple of metaethical debate, and yet, neither of these options have been included in the list of theses from the literature. Is this not a major oversight?

The proposed properties of *cognitivity*, and *noncognitivity* are both properties that all parties agree are not unique to moral statements. If the Cognitivist is correct, not only do moral statements have the property of *cognitivity*, but also so do statements that are not explicitly evaluative in nature, like statements of the natural sciences. If the Noncognitivist is correct, not only do moral statements have the property of *noncognitivity*, but so do value-theoretic statements on the whole (by most accounts) and meaningless statements, which do not say that anything is so. Determining whether a statement is *cognitive* or not, in itself, will not determine whether or not it is a moral statement. Neither of the properties of *cognitivity* nor *noncognitivity* are said to define moral statements by themselves. The debate between Cognitivism and Noncognitivism is thus not a debate on the definition of moral statements.

Arguably, a correct definition of moral statements would include mention of whether moral statements are a subset of *cognitive* or *noncognitive* statements. There is a reason, however, to conclude that no adequate definition of a moral statement will include such information.

The issue of whether moral statements are *cognitive* or not fails to intrude upon our ability to identify moral statements. For instance, both the Cognitivist and the Noncognitivist can agree that the statements (i) "cruelty is evil" and (ii) "one ought not to be cruel" are moral statements. However, the first statement appears to be *cognitive* in nature, while the second is *noncognitive*. If there is any truth to Cognitivism or Noncognitivism, it is because they explain a deep-grammar of moral statements; not what is apparent on the surface of moral statements.

The debate between Cognitivism and Noncognitivism pertains to an esoteric side of moral statements—their deep grammar. Our concern is with a definition of moral statements. Definitions are not thorough inventories of the properties of an item. Definitions concern those properties of a thing that help us to identify them. It follows that definitions are not primarily concerned with esoteric properties of things. As the debate between Cognitivism and Noncognitivism is something pertaining to a hidden side of moral statements, we need not settle the debate in order to procure a definition of moral statements. Arguably, the Cognitivism–Noncognitivism debate is best understood not as a debate on whether moral statements are *cognitive* or *noncognitive*, but on whether moral statements, in addition to having certain defining properties, are also *cognitive* or *noncognitive*.

2.3.1. Social Content and Conduct

Out of the nine suggestions in the literature for a definition of moral statements, two approaches define them in terms of their *extentions*: the Social Content Thesis, and the Conduct Thesis. The Social Content Thesis holds that moral statements concern our relationship and treatment of other persons. The Conduct Thesis holds that moral statements are those that provide guidance for our conduct and behaviour. Both accounts of the nature of moral statements imply Extentionalist accounts of moral terms. The Social Content Thesis holds that moral terms are definable, at least in part, by their typical application to social matters. The Conduct Thesis holds the view that moral terms are definable, at least in part, by their typical application to matters of conduct or behaviour.

2.3.1.1. Social Content Thesis

A robust version of the Social Content Thesis has been put forward by William Frankena (1973) who argues that morality concerns itself with regulating our relations with others in a manner that is similar to law and etiquette, but is to be distinguished from prudence. Morality and moral statements, on Frankena's view, issue from a social circumstance, and concern social issues. It is for this reason, in part, that moral statements differ from statements of prudence, on Frankena's account. As well, Frankena holds that moral statements are authored from a particular "moral point of view", whereas prudential concerns, which are by nature more egocentric, issue from another corner (Frankena 1973 pp.6–9). The "moral point of view" is arguably an *intentional* restriction on moral statements. However, this restriction on moral statements is offered by Frankena to show how moral statements, as a subset of statements concerned with social matters, differ from other such statements, like statements of law, etiquette and prudence. Moreover, Frankena's "moral point of view" is defined in terms of its concern for a specific set of *extentions*: social *extentions*. While there is an *intentional* aspect to Frankena's account, it is logically dependant upon *extentional* restrictions on what moral statements and terms can be about.

I argued earlier that Extentionalist accounts of foundational philosophical terms, which limit the scope of a philosophical subject-matter, ought to be rejected because they improperly intrude on substantive debate (2.2. Key Philosophical Terms p.22–31). The same line of criticism applies to Extentionalist accounts of moral statements.

The Social Content Thesis intrudes on substantive moral debate by excluding the ethics of Plato from the realm of moral concerns. On the conventional reading, Plato's conception of The Good (as spelled out in the *Republic*) is a moral value. For Plato, The Good is the Form of Forms, concerned with regulating the behaviour of ideal objects—not people (*Republic* 506e–509a). Yet, the Social Content Thesis propounded by philosophers like Frankena would cut Plato's conception of The Good out of the purview of morality, for Plato's conception of The Good as laid out in the *Republic* has nothing essentially to do with persons (it is concerned with ideal objects). On this view, Plato's statements about The Good would not constitute moral statements. As well, the Social Content Thesis fails to adequately account for the moral significance of theoretical moral claims (e.g. "The Good ought to be maximized", "goodness is better than evilness", etc.). It also fails to make room for certain forms of Utilitarianism that do not define *utiles* or goodness in terms of moral agents or subjects—theories of morality that continue to have support today (Leslie, 1972). In various ways the Extentionalist, Social Content suggestion delimits the scope of morality in such a way that genuine, uncontroversially, moral doctrines are left out of the scope of moral debate. It follows from this observation that *social content* is not an invariable feature of moral statements and concepts, let alone an essential feature.

2.3.1.2. Conduct Thesis

A once popular *extentional* account of the subject-matter of ethics holds that moral statements are concerned with directing conduct. This is the Conduct Thesis that appeared in many textbooks on ethics in the early twentieth century. John S. McKenzie, for instance, in his *Manual of Ethics,* began by defining ethics as "the study of what is right or good in conduct" (McKenzie 1929 p.1). John Dewey writes, "Ethics is the science that deals with conduct, insofar as this is considered right or wrong, good or bad" (Dewey and Tufts 1929 p.1). James Seth defines morality as synonymous with conduct: "Ethics is the science of morality or conduct" (Seth 1928 p.1). In a similar vein, Surama Dasgupta in her *Development Of Moral Philosophy In India* defines *MORALITY* as "a system of practical rules of conduct of a man in the light of his religion" (Dasgupta 1961 p.4).

While the Social Content View is too narrow, an argument can be made that the Conduct Thesis is too wide. For on this view, seating arrangements, plans for music lessons or laboratory procedures would constitute moral statements, since all of these have direct import for how people behave and conduct themselves; all of these things can be done in a right or wrong fashion; they can be accomplished in a good or bad manner. In another respect, the Conduct View of moral statements is predictably narrow, as a version of the Extentionalist account of moral statements. Arguably, its main defect is that it cuts out of the breath of ethics theories of virtue and vice.

G.V.Y. Trianosky (1986) draws attention to the conceptual distinction between *deontic* matters—pertaining to action and behaviour—and *aretaic* matters—pertaining to mental and motivational states. When someone has the wrong motive for an action, their *aretaic* state is vicious; when they have transgressed a moral rule with respect to an action, they have done something *deontically* wrong. Trianosky lucidly points out that "not every judgement of viciousness presupposes a judgement that the agent has done wrong; and not every negative *aretaic* judgement of the person need also be a negative *deontic* judgement of the person" (Trianosky 1986 p.32). Trianosky's observation implies that we can criticize a person for doing the wrong thing, though their motives were praiseworthy, while in other instances, we might not be able to blame a person for doing anything wrong, though we think that their motives for actions—even good actions—are less than honourable. The implication of all of this is that ethical considerations regarding matters of character or virtue and vice are logically distinct from considerations pertaining to conduct.

A lesson to be drawn from Trianosky's observations is that the description of ethics, and moral statements, as something only concerned with conduct or behaviour, is false. Hence, the Conduct Thesis cannot be an accurate account of the nature of moral statements.

2.3.2. Categoricality and Universalizability

Two suggestions in the literature that proffer logical features of moral statements as their defining traits include the views that moral statements are those that are *categorical* and not *hypothetical* in nature, and the view that moral statements are those that are open to a universal interpretation, and are hence *universalizable*. The former is the Categoricality Thesis, and the latter is the Universalizability Thesis.

2.3.2.1. Categoricality Thesis

While perhaps no one has argued strongly for the feature of *categoricality* since Kant, philosophers have generally tipped their hats to Kant for identifying something necessary, if not sufficient, for moral statements (Kant appears to have regarded this quality as sufficient for a definition of moral statements). To my knowledge, Philippa Foot (1995) is the only one who has vigorously criticized the distinction, and she later recanted her criticism.

Generally, the *hypothetical–categorical* distinction has

been taken to represent the intuitively obvious difference between statements like "If you want your car to run, fill it with gas regularly" and "You ought to drive your car". Sometimes the distinction is taken to be an archaic way of expressing the instrumental–absolute value split. How are we to distinguish in principle between the instrumental–absolute distinction and the *hypothetical–categorical* distinction? Kant, in the *Metaphysics of Morals* suggests:

> All imperatives command either hypothetically or categorically. Hypothetical imperatives declare a possible action to be practically necessary as a means to the attainment of something else that one wills (or that one may will). A categorical imperative would be one which represented an action as objectively necessary in itself apart from its relation to a further end. (Kant II.82)

One problem with Kant's formulation of the distinction is that it seems to exclude from the purview of ethics Consequentialist moral statements; for a Consequentialist moral statement like "one ought to do *x* because it maximizes *y*" represents an action as necessary because of its relationship to a further end.

Perhaps Kant wishes to cash the distinction out in logical terms: *hypothetical* / instrumental statements are those that are expressible in conditionals ("if-then" statements) while *categorical* statements are not. The problem is that there seems to be moral statements that are expressible in conditionals, like, "if you want to do the right thing, you will marry her". Instrumental statements can be moral too.

John McDowell reads Kant as holding that *hypothetical* statements are those that do not, on their own, express the desirability of some thing. Rather, "the agent's belief about how things are [i.e. as expressed in the *hypothetical* statement] combines with an independently intelligible desire to represent the action as a good thing from the agent's point of view". In contrast, a *categorical* statement "suffices on its own to show us the favourable light in which the action appeared from the point of view of the agent" (McDowell 1995 p.23). McDowell and Kant's elucidations of the concept of *CATEGORICALITY* are unfortunately couched in *deontic* terms, and it was argued that moral statements are not simply those that concern conduct. If *categoricality* concerns conduct, then it cannot be an invariable feature of moral statements. However, I think that McDowell's reading of Kant's distinction does not depend upon the truth of the Conduct Thesis. McDowell's reading of the property of *categoricality* makes it out to be something that permits a statement a kind of value-theoretic sufficiency: a statement that is *categorical*, on McDowell's reading, is capable itself of saying that something is valuable. On this interpretation, the property of *categoricality* is no different than the property of a statement to express a value. Thus, on this reading, the property of *categoricality* is no different from the property of a statement to be a value-theoretic statement.

If the property of *categoricality* is construed as a property that all moral statements have, it is also a property that all value-theoretic statements have. On the plausible reading of the property of *categoricality*, the view that moral statements are solely defined by the property of *categoricality* is false, though the view that all moral statements have the property of *categoricality* is undeniable.

2.3.2.2. Universalizability Thesis

Many philosophers hold that moral statements are necessarily (though perhaps insufficiently) characterized by the logical criteria of *universalizability.* This is the Universalizability Thesis. For a statement to be *universalizable* is for it to be expressible in a form that makes no reference to individuals. Because it is possible to pick out unique objects by rendering one's universalized statement so thorough that it contingently applies only to one item, the *universalizability* requirement is thought to be too permissive to be objectionable.

The Universalizability Thesis rules out some

prescriptions—those that are meant to be relevant in principle to a particular person or state of affairs. The view that in principle moral judgements cannot be universalized is a key feature of some forms of Existentialism—particularly Sartre's (1975 p.354). What is the reason for ruling out such prescriptions as counting as moral? R.M. Hare relates the following conversation between a Kantian (who advocates the Universalizability Thesis) and an Existentialist to answer this question:

> E: "You oughtn't to do that".
>
> K: "So you think that one oughtn't to do that kind of thing?"
>
> E: "I think nothing of the kind; I say only that *you* oughtn't to do *that*".
>
> K: "Don't you even imply that a person like me in circumstances of this kind oughtn't to do that kind of thing when the other people involved are the sort of people that they are?"
>
> E: "*No; I* say only that you oughtn't to do *that*".
>
> K: "Are you making a moral judgement?"
>
> E: "Yes".
>
> K: "In that case I fail to understand your use of the word 'moral'".

Hare concludes from this that, "[m]ost of us would be as baffled as the 'Kantian'; and indeed we should be hard put to it to think of *any* use of the word 'ought', moral or nonmoral, in which the Existentialist's remarks would be comprehensible" (Hare 1955 pp.304–5).

I do not wish to dispute the *propriety* of Hare's thesis: moral statements *ought* to be *universalizable*, but I must ask Hare in what subject he would have us criticize the Existentialist's prescriptions? Clearly, this is not a matter for epistemology or metaphysics, but ethics. If this is so, it is odd to claim that the Existentialist's prescriptions are not moral. Within a philosophical subject, philosophers make competing claims. Given that the Existentialist's claims in question are those that are made within the subject of ethics, it follows that the un*universalizable* statements of the Existentialist are moral statements, subject to ethical scrutiny. In the face of this, to argue that *universalizability* is a defining feature of all moral statements is to improperly intrude on moral debate.

The defender of *universalizability* may retort that my argument here is inconsistent, for I grant that perhaps all moral statements ought to be *universalizable*, but that the Existentialist's moral statement is not, though it counts nonetheless as a moral statement. Is this an inconsistency? The point is that *universalizability* is something that is the subject of disagreement within the field of ethics: arguments can be made for and against it, within ethics alone. Because this disagreement is internal to the field of ethics, it is odd to say that one option correctly describes moral statements (formally) while another does not—as odd as saying that the Deontologist is correct about the nature of moral statements, and the Utilitarian is not; therefore, statements from Utilitarianism are not moral statements. They may be false or ill-formed according to some moral theory but they are not failures as moral statements. Based on this line of reasoning it cannot be sustained that *universalizability* is a universal feature of all moral statements.

Another objection can be raised against the Universalizability Thesis in that it does not uniquely pick out moral statements. Many aesthetic statements, pertaining to the production of good art, music, dance and drama are *universalizable* too: they can be formulated in such ways that do not specify individuals ("Violins ought to be played with good posture"). Such prescriptions are hardly moral.

Universalizability, unlike *categoricality*, is not a universal feature of moral statements or evaluative statements.

2.3.3. Importance and Overridingness

Wallace and Walker in their anthology, *The Definition of Morality* (1970 pp.1–25) identify and distinguish two suggestions for the defining characteristic of moral statements. These are *importance* and *overridingness.* The view that *importance* characterizes the nature of moral statements is the Importance Thesis, and the view that *overridingness* characterizes the nature of moral statements is the Overridingness Thesis.

2.3.3.1. Importance Thesis

According to Wallace and Walker, the Importance Thesis and the Overridingness Thesis are two distinct proposals for defining the nature of moral statements. In reality, however, those who argue for *importance* invariably cash it out in terms of *overridingness* (see Cooper 1970; Hare 1971, 169; Hart 1961, ch.8; and McDowell 1995 p.26). Is the Importance Thesis really a distinct thesis from the Overridingness Thesis? The Importance Thesis asserts that moral statements have the characteristic of being *important.* There are at least two ways to construe this thesis. On one reading, the Importance and Overridingness Theses are distinct. On the other reading, the two theses turn out to be identical.

On one reading, *importance* is construed as a property that is found in all moral statements, but is not unique to moral statements. According to this reading of *importance,* all value-theoretic statements have the property of being *important,* for values, by definition, are things of *importance.* As evaluative statements express values, they too share in the *importance* of their subject-matter. While *importance* so conceived is accurately predicated of moral statements, on this conception of *importance,* it is not the case that the Importance Thesis provides us the key to understanding the peculiar nature of moral statements.

If the property of *importance* is construed as something unique to moral statements, and hence, the Importance Thesis is read as describing a feature that is peculiar to moral statements, then the Importance Thesis turns out to be identical with the

Overridingness Thesis. For the only way to make sense of the claim that moral statements are important, while other value-theoretic statements are not (or that they are *more* important than other value-theoretic statements) is if we give precedence to the counsel of moral statements over other value-theoretic statements. This is the Overridingness Thesis.

2.3.3.2. Overridingness Thesis

Wallace and Walker (1970 p.1–25) argue that there are two ways to interpret the Overridingness Thesis, or rather, two versions of the same thesis. On one view, moral statements defined by the property of *overridingness* are those that in fact override other prescriptions. This is the *de facto* version of the Overridingness Thesis. On the second reading, moral statements defined by the property of *overridingness* are those that *ought* to override other prescriptions. This is the *normative* version of the Overridingness Thesis.

The Overridingness Thesis has a great following. It is not uncommon for contemporary philosophers to use the term "*akrasia*"—which means weakness of will—to describe any instance in which someone fails to do what is morally required. The presumption is that people, at least upon reflection, cannot fail to think that moral requirements must trump all other concerns, and hence, any failure to do the moral thing is necessarily a weakness; a failing with respect to a person's own values.

A counter example to the *de facto* interpretation of the Overridingness Thesis is that people in ordinary life often compromise their moral convictions for apparently nonmoral reasons. Case in point: the majority of Catholics who believe that abortion is murder still pay taxes to and support states that sanction or fund abortions. It would be a mistake, I think, to interpret such failures to act upon deeply held convictions as the true moral convictions of these individuals. An equal mistake would be to view the law-abiding Catholic as weak in will.

The *normative* version of the Overridingness Thesis—the

view that moral statements are those claims that ought to override other claims—seems implausible when we consider the possibility of religious demands and moral convictions conflicting. The classic example of such a conflict, which Kierkegaard (1985) brings to our attention, is the Old Testament story of Abraham who is faced with the choice of sacrificing his child, or failing to make the appropriate ritualistic offerings to God. Neil Cooper (1970) argues that we ought to interpret this scenario as consistent with the Overridingness Thesis:

> Kierkegaard talks at length of "a teleological suspension of the ethical" ... meaning, I suggest, by "the ethical" much the same as "positive morality", Hegel's "Sittlichkeit". If he was in fact maintaining that religious considerations overrode moral considerations, one would expect him to say of Abraham's intended sacrifice of Isaac that, although it was morally wrong, it was right from the religious point of view, and it was the latter point of view which had priority. What, however, he appears to be holding ... is that Abraham's faith is morally relevant and that because of it he was not guilty of sin in being ready to sacrifice Isaac. In this passage, then, Kierkegaard seems to be advocating a distinctive and monolithic morality, a "Put God first" morality. (Cooper 1970 p. 96)

Philip L. Quinn (1986) argues that such an interpretation overlooks the conundrum that Kierkegaard is trying to draw our attention to. To really understand Kierkegaard's dilemma, we must appreciate that Abraham is being asked to do something by God that is gravely immoral—"for what sin was more terrible?" (Kierkegaard 1985 p.47). Thus, Quinn's suggestion is that Kierkegaard is trying to get us to recognize the possibility of being *prima facie* justified in believing oneself to be in a situation where two distinct systems of values make contrary claims to one's compliance—a scenario that Quinn dubs the "Kierkegaardian conflict" (Quinn 1986 p.196 n.8). Quinn argues that the Overridingness Thesis presumes that there cannot be distinct realms of value that can come into conflict—or if it does allow for the differentiation of values, it is committed to the view that there is a greater standard of value against which another set of values can be ranked. Quinn's criticisms are insightful for they locate the Overridingness Thesis within a wider, substantive, Axiological debate: ought moral claims to override other value-theoretic concerns?

On consideration, the *de facto* version of the Overridingness Thesis is simply unsound, because it is a sociological fact that people either fail to live up to their own moral expectations, or because people decide to compromise their moral convictions for political reasons.[6] The factual property of *overridingness* so conceived does not constitute a property of all moral statements. The *normative* version of the Overridingness Thesis says that in order for us to have an adequate definition of moral statements we also have to be committed to the substantive axiological view that moral values ought to override other value-theoretic concerns. While this latter substantive thesis—that moral claims ought to override other value-theoretic claims—is a plausible, or at least, an interesting, axiological view, it seems to be just that: a substantive thesis regarding the relative importance of moral statements. It does not really describe a feature of moral statements. Rather, it attempts to prescribe to us how we ought to order our lives—around moral values. The *normative* version of the Overridingness Thesis is no definition of moral statements, but rather a substantive axiological and moral view.

There is one final hope for the Overridingness Thesis: to simply define the overriding conviction of a person as their moral conviction, regardless of whether they or others regard the conviction as moral. Hence, on this view, the Catholic who pays taxes to a state that supports or funds abortions is to be regarded as not having the moral conviction that abortion is evil. This Catholic might insist that her views on abortion are in conformity with the Church's position, but this final version of the Overridingness Thesis tells us to disregard such confessions as confused. I am not aware of anyone in the literature who has argued for this view. However, it seems that this approach to saving the Overridingness Thesis is a failure, for it completely disregards facts about the nature of moral statements; that they are things that we do not always heed, even when they are our own.

2.3.4. Blame Inclination

John Skorupski (1993) in his article "Definition of Morality" provides a rather complex conception of morality that promises to distinguish moral oughts form nonmoral oughts. On his account, there is a peculiar kind of criticism that attends moral matters.

What distinguishes moral criticism, from nonmoral criticism, on Skorupski's account, is that in the case of moral criticism, what we mean is, "x is morally wrong if and only if the agent ought to be blamed (by himself and others) for doing x ... in normal circumstances ..." (Skorupski 1993 p.126). Moral criticism thus involves the imputation of blame. Criticisms that do not employ the concept of *BLAME* are not moral criticisms.

Also, on Skorupski's account, blame is a feeling, or *intentional* criterion, that defines moral criticism. There are three criteria that define this kind of feeling:

> [O]ne constraint on the intelligibility of the blame-feeling is that its object must be a doing which is taken to be avoidable .... Another constraint on the intelligibility of the blame-feeling, of course, is that the doing must be thought to be wrong. But "wrong" here is still pre-moral .... A third constraint is that one must believe that the agent knew or could have known what he was doing. (Skorupski 1993 p.132)

Finally, Skorupski believes that blame is a kind of punishment or penalty (Skorupski 1993 p.126).

On Skorupski's account, what is peculiar about moral matters is that we employ the concept of *BLAME*, or what he calls a "blame-feeling", in moral criticism. Hence, on this view, we can define a moral statement as:

1) an evaluative statement, about which
2) one is inclined to *blame* someone—other things being equal—should they violate the evaluative import of the statement.

We could call the second condition of a moral statement the "*blame inclination*". On this view, moral statements are defined by having the property of the *blame inclination*. This is (7) the Blame Inclination Thesis.

I too think that there is a particular kind of negative emotional response associated with failed moral expectations that define moral judgements. This aspect of Skorupski's thought is to be commended, for it provides a way to distinguish between moral and nonmoral matters on intentional grounds. However, Skorupski's view of morality is skewed, as it is fundamentally concerned with *deontic* matters.

BLAME appears to be a highly *deontic* concept, concerned with criticizing failures to *do* the right thing. Hence, we only blame someone if they are responsible for some wrong-doing. If this were so, the suggestion that blame is an invariable feature of moral statements would leave ethics of virtue out of the scope of morality.

Some argue that blame is not only possible but also appropriate in certain cases where no wrongdoing has been committed (see Calhoun 1998 and M. Zimmerman 1997). Blame may be a concept wide enough to account for the nature of moral statements. On another front, Stephen Cohen (1977) argues that *BLAME* is not a distinctly moral concept: what makes blame moral in nature is the reasons we have for blaming (Cohen 1977 p.165). Common parlance supports Cohen's position: we blame the weather for ruining the parade, we blame dumb luck when things do not go our way, and we blame our genes for our health problems. On Cohen's account, *BLAME* cannot elucidate the nature of moral statements, for the moralness of moral statements is something separate from its connection to the notion of *BLAME*.

While there appears to be some disagreement in the

literature over the nature of *BLAME*, as it appears in Skorupski's account, it is a highly *deontic* matter. On Skorupski's own account, we only blame someone if they have *done* something wrong that they could have avoided doing. Skorupski's account of moral matters, and his conception of blame thus presupposes the Conduct Thesis. Skorupski seems to note the distinctly *deontic* nature of his theory of morality:

> As well as morality, whose emotive core is the blame-feeling, there is the system of ends whose affective core is liking or desire. Then there is a system of character-ideals, whose core is admiration .... Behind these systems of valuation lies the background framework of practical reason .... My division [of it] into morality, character-ideals and ends corresponds fairly obviously ... [to John Stuart Mill's] division [of it] into Morality, Aesthetics and Prudence. (Skorupski 1993 p.143)

As virtues are character traits, it seems that Skorupski believes that his theory of morality rules out theories of virtue as being moral theories. Yet, Skorupski asserts that his account of morality can embrace matters of virtue and vice:

> [S]omeone who could have done something to overcome his natural cruelty, but has not bothered, is blameworthy. A virtue is something narrower than the general notion of a character-ideal. It is a quality of character which we admire or can come to admire, and failure to develop it, which in oneself, where it is possible to do so, is, other things being equal again, blameworthy. (Skorupski 1993 p.143)

What if someone could not do anything to overcome their natural cruelty? Does this render the quality of cruelty any less vicious or morally criticisable? What if a person is in poor health and not in control of his faculties, but is yet cruel? Does cruelty in these circumstances cease to be morally criticisable? Skorupski's theory of moral criticism is unable to account for how we might morally criticize character flaws in circumstances when we are at a loss to blame a person or to say that a person could have done something otherwise.

The idea of *aretaic* moral criticism is not consistent with the overall thrust of the Blame Inclination Thesis. We must repeat the lesson from Trianosky (1986) once again: *deontic* and *aretaic* moral matters are logically distinct concerns; because of this, we can morally criticize a person's character, even if they have done nothing wrong, while we can praise another person's motives, while we criticize their actions. By asserting that *aretaic* and *deontic* matters are logically distinct, we are not committed to the view that persons can never alter their character. We are, however, affirming that criticisms appropriate to character flaws can leave aside questions of whether a person could have done otherwise. Cruelty is arguably a vice, and hence morally criticisable, whether or not a person could have been more kind.

Skorupski's Blame Inclination Thesis is thus a combined Intentionalist–Extentionalist account of moral statements. It recognizes blame as the *intentional* component of moral statements, yet it defines "blame" as being exclusively relevant to certain *extentional* matters—those things that are under volitional control. As a species of Extentionalism, Skorupski's account is unsatisfactorily narrow in failing to embrace genuine instances of moral statements such as statements of virtue ethics.

2.3.5. Conformity

There are a group of views in the literature converging on the idea that moral statements are defined by a desire for *conformity*. This is the Conformity Thesis. The theories adhering to the Conformity Thesis fall into two categories: those that understand conformity in terms of individual expectations, and those that understand conformity in terms of societal expectations.

The individualistic version of the Conformity Thesis is presented by T.L.S. Sprigg who argues that, "[i]n every application of an ethical term one indicates the presence of three features: an attitude of one's own, a wish to have that attitude shared, [and] a wish to have it supported by moral sanction" (Sprigg 1960 p.137). In a similar vein, Danny Goldstick (1998), who argues that a peculiarly "moralistic attitude" is essential to the definition of a moral judgement, holds that constitutive of this attitude is "not merely a desire for the incidence of such behaviour to be reduced, and preferably eliminated ... [but also] a desire that the attitude thus taken be shared by everyone else as well as oneself". According to Goldstick, the adoption of this attitude is psychologically what it is "to get up on a moralistic high horse" (Goldstick 1998 p.25).

The societal version of the Conformity Thesis holds that moral judgements are social institutions, enforced by strong social pressure and sanction. This is a view that is widespread in the social sciences and among philosophers H.L.A. Hart (1961 ch.8) argues for it.

The Conformity Thesis, in its various incarnations, has problems it seems to me.

The social version of the Conformity Thesis fails to describe moral statements, for it makes them out to be matters that people within the same society do not disagree about. Societies have moral controversies. If there is disagreement on moral issues within a society, moral statements are not social institutions. It is true that some moral statements are expressive of social institutions. However, the moral convictions of the social critic do not express the social institutions of the culture.

Sprigg and Goldstick's view that moral concerns are those that we individually desire a likeness of mind on fails to accurately map out moral concerns. In many areas of our lives, we want people to agree with us. For example, this does not make my recommendations here moral. Moreover, it strikes me as perfectly conceivable for someone to have moral opinions without the slightest concern for what anyone else thinks. Such a person might be pig-headed, irrational and extremely anti-social, but it may not be that they lack moral convictions (e.g., "I don't care what anyone else thinks: what they are doing is wrong!"). Desiring likeness of mind is neither unique to moral concerns nor is it an invariable feature of them.

While I think that the Conformity Thesis is wrong, I also

think that the live versions of the thesis are on the right track. What most versions of the Conformity Thesis have in common is the view that there is a peculiar kind of emotional response associated with failed moral expectations. This aspect of the suggestion, I believe, is correct. The view that a desire for, or the fact of, conformity is a feature of moral statements is excessive.

2.3.6. Punishment

Several of the theories examined so far assert that moral statements are defined, at least in part, by *punishment*. This is the (9) Punishment Thesis. There are two variations on this thesis.

On one version, moral statements are those that are in fact enforced by some kind of punishment. This view is expressed in Hart's societal version of the Conformity Thesis: that moral judgements are social institutions, enforced by strong social pressure and sanction (Hart 1961 ch.8). This also shows up in Skorupski's view, that blame, which constitutes moral criticism, is a kind of *penalty* (Skorupski 1993 p.126).

Another version of the Punishment Thesis holds that moral statements are those that we wish to enforce through punishment. This thesis is most clearly expressed by J.S. Mill, who argues that "[w]e do not call anything wrong unless we mean to imply that a person ought to be *punished* in some way or other for doing it; if not by law, by the opinion of his fellow creatures; if not by opinion, by the reproaches of his own conscience" (Mill 1965 vol.x p.246, my italics). This view is echoed by Sprigg, who argues that "[i]n every application of an ethical term one indicates the presence of three features: an attitude of one's own, a wish to have that attitude shared, [and] a wish to have it supported by moral *sanction*" (Sprigg 1960 p.137).

Not every punishment is a moral matter. For instance, we institute *punishments* or *sanctions* as a means of generating revenue (e.g., parking tickets), or deterring behaviour that may be morally praiseworthy but civically inconvenient (e.g., "one-hundred dollar fine for feeding the geese"). More importantly, it does not seem that we wish *punishment* or *sanction* to accompany every negative moral judgement or criticism.

Not every negative or harsh response to something we find objectionable is a punishment. *Punishments*, *sanctions* or *penalties* are consequences of *doing* something wrong. Hence, they are appropriate responses to *deontic* failings. While punishment may be an appropriate response to *deontic* moral failings, it is not an appropriate response to all *aretaic* moral failings. There would be something logically wrong about punishing someone who has done nothing wrong, though we find their motives and desires criticisable. We can morally criticize a person for having vicious and depraved desires, but our criticism can stop short of *punishment*, and still be moral, if they have actually done nothing wrong.

The Punishment Thesis, like the Conduct Thesis, and the Blame Inclination Thesis, sets its sights solely on *deontic* moral statements. Not all moral statements are *deontic* in nature—some are *aretaic* in nature. The fact of or the desire for *punishment,* in the case of moral failings, cannot be a defining trait of all moral statements, as such a response is only appropriate in the case of *deontic* moral failings.

2.3.7. Anger Inclination

My view is that moral statements are things that there is a tendency to get angry about, if the evaluative force of the statement is violated. Often, there are coexisting additional factors that offset the inclination to get angry. These are *mitigating reasons*. Mitigating reasons can include scruples that a person might have (e.g., "it is not nice to get angry"), or practical reasons for holding tempers (e.g., "losing my temper is not good for my blood pressure"). The view that I am proffering can be formulated thus:

1) a moral statement is an apparently meaningful claim with evaluative import, about which
2) there is, attached to it, an inclination to express anger,

> likely in the absence of mitigating reasons, should the evaluative import of the statement be violated.

The inclination to express anger if expectations regarding evaluative matters fail (the second condition) constitutes what I call the "*anger inclination*"; it is the ugly and offensive side of moral convictions—the side that comes out when people are being *moralistic*. The *anger inclination* is what makes an ordinary evaluative statement into a moral statement. Thus, I call this account the (10) "Anger Inclination Thesis".[7]

As a point of clarification, I would like to note that, on the Anger Inclination Thesis, an *anger inclination* may be hypothetical, that of a third party, or that of the speaker. Hence, if we mention, but not assert a moral statement, the *anger inclination* attached to the statement may be that of a third party, or a hypothetical *anger inclination* (if the moral statement is purely hypothetical and not held by anyone). Hence, the Anger Inclination Thesis is not committed to the view that any time we mention a moral statement meaningfully, we ourselves have an inclination to get angry over its evaluative import.

The presence of mitigating reasons together with the *anger inclination* is an important feature of this account. Mitigating reasons may be sufficient to so offset the inclination to get angry that a person who has the *anger inclination* may have no experience of anger, or even any strong sense of their own inclination. On this view, moral issues are defined by being potentially, if not actually, explosive.

2.3.7.1. Argument for the Anger Inclination Thesis

The Anger Inclination Thesis embraces instances of moral thinking in the history of ethics that other accounts reject. For instance, in not specifying the *universalizability* criterion, this account is able to accept the Existentialist's un*universalizable* claims as moral statements. In not specifying whether moral statements refer to things that people have control over or not, or whether they concern actions or character traits, the Anger

Inclination Thesis is equally amenable to ethics of virtue and *deontic* moral theories. This proposal also embraces and explains Plato's conception of The Good as a moral value. Plato, in the *Republic,* is seen to denigrate physical reality and representational art for being several steps removed from The Good. In short, Plato has the *anger inclination* with respect to the maximization of The Good.[8]

The Anger Inclination Thesis has other virtues. As an Intentionalist account of moral statements, it does not specify what *extentions* moral statements must be about, hence, it does not intrude upon substantive moral debate. This suggestion also does not intrude upon axiological debates as far as it does not specify which sphere of value-theoretic concern is more important than others.

How is the Anger Inclination Thesis different from the view that *punishment* defines moral statements? Not every expression of anger is a *punishment* or sanction. Punishments are instituted as deterrents, or as consequences for doing something wrong. Anger and kindred emotions have penal functions, but these are not essential to the experience or expression of these emotions. It is conceivable to have an inclination to express anger over some happening or thing, without the slightest regard for whether it could have been avoided, or whether the expression of anger will deter future occurrences of the thing we find objectionable. Our inclination to express anger can be purely cathartic. Moreover, our expressions of anger can also be private—anger need not be expressed at the thing responsible for violating our evaluative expectations. We can be angry with someone over having the wrong desires, while not punishing them if they have actually done nothing wrong. On this score, the Anger Inclination Thesis can embrace *aretaic* moral criticism, where the Punishment Thesis cannot. Even if anger were always a form of punishment, it is important to note that the Anger Inclination Thesis does not define moral statements as those that we do get angry over. It defines moral statements as those that there is an inclination to get angry over. Hence, one may never lose one's temper, though one has moral convictions, on the Anger Inclination Thesis's account.

The fact that the Anger Inclination Thesis does not intrude upon substantive moral debate is what we might recognize as a negative virtue of the account. What speaks positively in its favour? The positive data in favour of the Anger Inclination Thesis is our pre-reflective tendency to separate moral issues from nonmoral issues. Many of the preceding accounts of moral statements, which have been criticized for failing to capture the essence of moral discourse, are theoretical afterthoughts; attempts to rationalize our practise of ethics. If we forfeit this endeavour, I think that what we will find is that morality—what people say is moral—is always marked by its explosiveness. If anyone should doubt the connection between the *anger inclination* and a moral claim, I would invite them to consider their emotional response to those they consider to be moral monsters. The emotion that is triggered by persons like Hitler, rapists, and lynch mobs—persons that we take to be moral monsters—is anger in its many forms. Consider also the emotion surrounding such issues as abortion, homosexuality, same-sex couple rights, animal rights, globalization, the environment, taxation and property rights. These are paradigms of contemporary moral debate. These are also issues over which tempers flare.

The main reason that the connection between anger and moral claims is not always addressed by philosophers is that philosophers who make ethics their business tend to believe that moral matters are amenable to rational discussion. For persons with faith in reason's ability to mediate moral controversy, reason itself functions as a mitigating factor, holding in check the expression of anger.

The strength of the Anger Inclination Thesis, I submit, is not that it conforms to most academic speculations on the nature of morality. Rather, it conforms to our unschooled opinion about ethics—that ethics is a topic that is confrontational and potentially unpleasant.

There are certain points of contact between the Anger Inclination Thesis and relatively recent opinions in philosophy. These opinions are not part of mainstream moral thought, but are to be found in political philosophy.

Since Marx, there has been an increasing sense among political theorists that ethics is not the avenue through which significant social change can be achieved. Marx himself appears to have eschewed ethics as a matter of ideological mystification (Wood 1991). More recently, the Radical Feminist theorist Catherine MacKinnon suggests that ethics is of no help to achieving the goals of the women's movement: the struggle that feminism is involved is political; it seeks to recognize and confront unequal power relations among groups of people. Morality, in contrast, is concerned with the minimization of emotional unpleasantness (MacKinnon 1989 pp.195–214).

John Rawls (1996) in his second treatise, *Political Liberalism*, appears to recognize the divisive and private nature of ethics in distancing his account from morality, and calling it "political". Explicitly, Rawls affirms that political questions are a subset of moral questions (Rawls, 1996 p.11 n.11). Yet, at many points Rawls talks about moral doctrines as though they were all "comprehensive", and he emphasizes that what he in turn is arguing is something political, which is not comprehensive. The implicit view of his tract appears to be that ethical views belong to the world of private, comprehensive views of citizens, while political reasons are public, and can be reasonably accepted by all.[9] This, at least, is my Straussian reading of Rawls.

Finally, in his insightful article on the distinction between political philosophy and ethics, Anthony Quinton (1993) comes close to affirming the Anger Inclination Thesis. Quinton argues that politics or political philosophy is not, essentially, a part of ethics. While political matters can be evaluated from the perspective of morality, so too can matters of prudence. The distinction between politics and morals is instructively brought out by the difference in attitude between seasoned and nonseasoned politicians. According to Quinton, "[P]eople are not so indignant with those with whom they disagree politically as with those with whom they disagree morally. And the more professional political disagreers are, the less indignant they are" (Quinton 1993 p.101).

On the whole, there has been a tendency to distinguish political thought from ethics, and to identify ethics with emotionalism and private sensibilities. This accords with the defining role that the Anger Inclination Thesis attributes to emotion in moral statements.

2.3.7.2. Criticisms

A likely objection to the Anger Inclination Thesis is that it incorrectly construes every expression of anger as morally significant. I believe this is a mistaken criticism. To construe every expression of anger as the surfacing of the *anger inclination* is to unreasonably stretch the notion of an *inclination*. An inclination is a propensity of a person; a direction in choice that they lean towards. Not every expression of anger is a result of an inclination of a person. Sometimes, ill-health or extenuating circumstances can cause people to get angry about things that they are not *inclined* to get angry about. It is only the expression of anger consequent of an inclination that the Anger Inclination Thesis considers as a candidate for moral significance.

Likewise, a critic might argue that the Anger Inclination Thesis attempts to define moral statements in terms of one putative moral concept—*ANGER*—when *ANGER* is not properly a moral concept. Such a critic would be both correct and incorrect. It is true that anger is not a moral concept, and hence, the statement "I am angry with you" or "she is angry with me" are not moral statements. However, what is being asserted here is not that *ANGER* is a key moral concept, but that the *inclination* to express anger should the evaluative import of a statement be violated is the *intentional* core of both moral terms and moral statements. Later, I shall present an account of moral terms, like "ethical", "dharma", "right" and "wrong", which define these terms by their ability to refer to the *anger inclination*. I delay providing the account until the Anger Inclination Thesis is defended, and a determination is made as to which composite definition of moral statements is correct. For now, it can be noted that the Anger Inclination Thesis is not committed to the view that *ANGER* is a moral concept. This implies that the Anger Inclination Thesis is not committed to the view that anger is a good thing, any more than it is a bad thing, from a moral perspective. As *ANGER*, on this account, is not a moral concept, it follows that this account does not state that anger itself is the subject-matter of ethics.

Similarly, a critic may object that on the Anger Inclination Thesis's account, the statement "Anger is an evil" cannot be any person's moral conviction, for, in order for it to be a person's moral conviction, *ex hypothesi*, a person must have an inclination to express anger over its violation. If a person thinks that anger is an evil, how could they have an inclination to express anger over its violation? If the statement "anger is an evil" is not embraced as a moral statement on the Anger Inclination Thesis's account, how can this thesis claim to be a means of defining moral statements that does not intrude upon substantive moral questions?

In response, I would argue that a person who expresses or has an inclination to express anger over the statement, "Anger is an evil" would have a problem of consistency whether or not the Anger Inclination Thesis is correct. The belief that they formally affirm is contrary to their own behaviour or inclinations. In the Anger Inclination Thesis's defence, we ought to note that there is nothing psychologically impossible about people being inclined to express anger over the violation of the statement "anger is an evil". A person who is inclined to get angry over the violation of "anger is an evil" is likely suffering from a certain psychological incoherence, but this psychological incoherence does not prevent the statement from counting as moral, on the Anger Inclination Thesis's account. Nor does this incoherence prevent the moral statement "anger is an evil" or "anger is wrong" from being substantively true—for arguably, what renders an evaluative statement morally significant (the *anger inclination*) is distinct from what makes it true.

What then of a phenomenon like road rage? If we take the Anger Inclination Thesis seriously, road rage implies that statements like "people ought to signal before they change lanes" or "people ought not to cut me off on the road" are moral statements. According to the critic, this is an absurd conclusion. My feeling is that this conclusion is not absurd at all. If a person spends a lot of time on the road, scruples about how people are to conduct themselves on the road could take on moral dimensions.

One might object that on the Anger Inclination Thesis, temper tantrums of children define statements like "I need grape juice" or "Give me ice cream" as moral statements, for tantrums occur when such expectations are violated.

Technically, the child's statements, quoted here, are not evaluative statements. They do not express that anything is of importance, (though we might infer from them that the child thinks that grape juice or ice cream are important) and hence, they express no value judgement. According to the Anger Inclination Thesis, such statements could not be moral in nature. However, if a child had an inclination to get angry over the statement "I deserve ice cream on demand", this statement would, according to the Anger Inclination Thesis, be moral (*DESERVE* being a value-theoretic concept). I believe that this is not a counter-example to the Anger Inclination Thesis.

The better part of a child's education is moral in nature. Sometimes, when we are raising children, we impart to them mitigating reasons for holding their temper. However, most of the time we try to shake children of their innate moral convictions. In the place of the child's pre-reflective moral convictions, we attempt to impart *our values* to them. As children imbibe our moral convictions, ("it is not correct to vent anger upon failing to procure grape juice or ice cream") they leave off their inappropriate moral convictions (like "I deserve grape juice or ice cream on demand").[10]

Another objection against the Anger Inclination Thesis is

that it is too wide. This time, the objection is that the Anger Inclination Thesis fails to respect the boundaries between intellectual spheres of concern.

In not legislating what is morally important, the Anger Inclination Thesis tells us that people can have moral convictions about all sorts of matters. Some people have moral convictions about economic matters, while others have moral convictions about religious matters. But this is what life is like. People have moral convictions about all sorts of issues, and one of the eye-opening surprises in life's education is the discovery that some person or group of persons has the *anger inclination* about a conviction that one never gave a second thought to. The implication of such life lessons is that morality is an infectious sphere of concern that spills over into other facets of our lives. Hence, it is no fault of the Anger Inclination Thesis that it fails to define moral concerns in such a way that it cannot overlap with other areas of intellectual concern.

The following line of argument can be brought against the Anger Inclination Thesis:

> While it may be true that some moral matters are those that we get angry about, the domain of issues that we get angry about is not identical with the domain of moral issues. People get angry at themselves for making mistakes. They get angry at being on a slow check-out line at the supermarket and being the victim of other kinds of bad luck. They get angry when someone disagrees with them. They get angry when they explain something and the person doesn't understand. None of those things are moral. If there's any common denominator to what things make us angry, one might say it is whatever makes our life more difficult than we think it ought to be.

How could the Anger Inclination Thesis be defended against this line of criticism?

The critical issue for the Anger Inclination Thesis is not whether someone gets angry some time, or not. The critical issue is whether a particular evaluative statement is something that there is an *anger inclination* attached to. In the examples just considered, it is not the anger, in itself, that one feels because the cashier's line is too slow, that is moral: it is (a) the evaluative statement (b) about which one is inclined to get angry about, which is moral. Hence, if the impatient customer's anger is indicative of a moral conviction, the conviction would be something like, "I ought not to be kept waiting so long"; "as a paying customer, I deserve better service". If the anger expressed over a mistake that one makes is indicative of a moral conviction, that conviction would be something like, "I ought not to be making mistakes". If someone's anger at the inattentive interlocutor is indicative of a moral judgement, it is because the speaker has a conviction like "others ought to listen to me when I take the time to speak to them". If someone is angry at their bad luck streak, and if this anger is indicative of a moral judgement, that judgement would be something like, "life ought to treat one fairly"

I agree with the criticism that the domain of matters that we get angry over is not identical with the domain of moral issues. But, as a point of fact, the Anger Inclination Thesis is not committed to the view that all things that we get angry about are moral in nature.

What about the following scenario: (a) a person has an inclination to get angry over some evaluative statement; but (b) the person insists that the expectation, belief or issue is not moral for them. Such examples pose a considerable challenge to the Anger Inclination Thesis because it makes the claim that we do call evaluative statements over which we are inclined to get angry about moral issues. Hence, the counter example just mentioned constitutes potentially falsifying data for the Anger Inclination Thesis.

The Anger Inclination Thesis can withstand such counter examples on the following considerations. (A) The Anger Inclination Thesis need not be committed to the view that, every person calls evaluative statements that they are inclined to get angry over moral issues. It is possible for there to be cases of mistaken persons, who do not fully understand what a "moral statement" is. (B) It is possible that persons conform their use of language to the description of the Anger Inclination Thesis, and yet, they have a false understanding of their own inclinations. While the Anger Inclination Thesis is committed to the view that the meaning of moral statements (and derivatively, moral terms) is an *intentional* matter, it is not committed to the view that we all have accurate meta-conceptions of our own subjective states or dispositions.

2.3.7.3. Supererogation

A challenge to the Anger Inclination Thesis is the matter of *supererogation.*

"Supererogation" refers to a putative class of moral acts that are extraordinary. The classic article regarding this is J.O. Urmson's "Saints and Heroes" (1958) and, as the title of this article suggests, supererogation is what separates saints and heroes from the rest of us. Urmson relates the following scenario to elucidate the nature of supererogation:

> We may imagine a squad of soldiers to be practising the throwing of live hand grenades; a grenade slips from the hand of one of them and rolls on the ground near the squad; one of them sacrifices his life by throwing himself on the grenade and protecting his comrades with his own body. It is quite unreasonable to suppose that such a man must be impelled by the sort of emotion that he might be impelled by if his best friend were in the squad; he might only just have joined the squad; it is clearly an action having moral status. But if the soldier had not thrown himself on the grenade would he have failed in his duty? Though clearly he is superior in some way to his comrades, can we possibly say that they failed in their duty by not trying to be the one who sacrificed himself? If he had not done so, could anyone have said to him, "You ought to have thrown yourself on that grenade"? Could a superior have decently ordered him to do it? The answer to all these questions is plainly negative. (Urmson 1958 pp.202–203)

Urmson brings to our attention an act of heroism with a moral dimension. On Urmson's account, acts of heroism (like saintly acts) are not simply commendable (after the fashion of worldly accomplishments) but morally commendable. Yet, no one would be correct to criticize someone for failing to act heroically, or in a saintly fashion:

> In the case of basic moral duties we act to some extent under constraint. We have no choice but to apply pressure on each other to conform in these fundamental matters; here moral principles are like public laws rather than like private ideals .... But, while there is nothing whatever objectionable in the idea of someone being pressed to carry out such a basic duty as promise keeping, there is something horrifying in the thought of pressure being brought on him to perform an act of heroism. Though the man might feel himself morally called upon to do the deed, it would be a moral outrage to apply pressure on him to do such a deed as sacrificing his life for others. (Urmson 1958 pp.213–214)

Urmson is drawing attention to acts that are *above and beyond the call of duty.* On many accounts, these are exhaustive of supererogatory acts.

Alternatively, we could follow Gregory Mellema who argues that an "act of supererogation is standardly characterized as satisfying the following three conditions:

> 1) it is nonobligatory in that its performance does not fulfil moral duties or obligations,
> 2) it is morally good or praiseworthy or meritorious to perform, and
> 3) it is not morally bad or blameworthy to omit". (Mellema 1996 p.406)

On this account, supererogatory acts are those that are not simply above and beyond the call of duty, but also those that are not a means to fulfilling our duties.

Some philosophers, from the Kantian tradition, argue that

there are no such things as supererogatory acts, for all moral matters are obligatory, and hence, open to censure upon failure. Susan Hale (1991), for instance, argues that at best, supererogatory acts are a means of fulfilling imperfect duties. These are duties that Kant holds are geared toward fulfilling moral ideals (e.g. kindness, charity, altruism, and so on) that leave room for us to choose how we wish to fulfil them.

Hale, arguably in consort with the Kantian tradition, fails to recognize the important difference between matters of duty, or *deontic* matters, and matters of virtue, or *aretaic* matters. Properly speaking, the qualities of kindness, charity and altruism are character traits, which are distinct matters from obligations to be kind, charitable and altruistic to others. Hence, someone may act kindly, charitably and altruistically outwardly, and inwardly harbour desires that are contrary to these actions. Based on this distinction, Trianosky (1986) suggests that supererogatory acts are those that are not required as an obligation, but issue from positive *aretaic* dispositions that we find morally praiseworthy. These are actions that, in a strict way, are above and beyond the call of duty. On Trianosky's account, failures to do the supererogatory thing do not warrant *deontic* criticism, but they do warrant *aretaic* criticism. Hence, on this account, those of us who are not saints or heroes can be *aretaically* criticized for not being more like saints and heroes (Trianosky 1986 pp.26–33).

Having considered some views in the literature, what should we say are supererogatory matters? It occurs to me that there are two distinct conceptions of supererogation that need to be distinguished. One may be called "*weak supererogation*": this is an action that is not *deontically* required, but we might criticize someone for not doing any way, because it points to a short coming of character. This is the idea that Trianosky alerts us to. Then there is what we can call "*strong supererogation*": this is an action that is not *deontically* required, *aretaically* praiseworthy, and something that we would not criticize someone for failing to do, even on *aretaic* grounds. This is the idea that Urmson and Mellema highlight.

The idea of *strong supererogation* seems to pose a problem for the Anger Inclination Thesis. For the Anger Inclination Thesis defines a moral statement as one that there are inclinations to get angry over, should its prescriptive import be violated. However, statements speaking of *strong supererogatory* acts are those where anger seems inappropriate, should someone violate their prescriptive import. How can the Anger Inclination Thesis respond to this challenge?

The Anger Inclination Thesis is capable of recognizing statements of *strong supererogation* as genuine moral statements, via its stipulation that there are often *mitigating reasons* that offset our inclination to get angry. In the case of *strong supererogatory* matters, our mitigating reasons are so compelling, that much of us thinks that it is inappropriate to get angry over a failure of supererogation—yet, part of us is *inclined* to get angry over such failures. It so happens, that the divided self that is in charge of our emotions is that which holds that expressions of anger surrounding supererogatory matters are inappropriate. Thus, if we did not think that the pain and the practical consequences involved in *strong supererogation* were inordinate, and that it is something that, practically, no person can or should bear, we may get angry over a failure to *strongly supererogate*. *Strong supererogatory* statements, thus, are sharply delineated from nonmoral statements, in which there is no corresponding inclination to get angry.

Strong supererogation is a classic example of the role of mitigating reasons suppressing our very real *anger inclination*, with respect to an evaluative statement.

2.3.8. Composite Accounts of Moral Statements

We are now in a position to summarize the findings of the preceding investigations.

The mistaken views on moral statements include the views that they all have *social content*, concern *conduct*, are *universalizable*, *override* other value-theoretic concerns, are defined by the *blame inclination*, are those that we seek *conformity* on, and those that *punishment* enforces or that we wish *punishment* to enforce. No definition of moral statements that solely rely on these descriptions can be true. Definitions of moral statements that are wholly formed of these descriptions may only have a certain pragmatic facility to select out moral statements from nonmoral statements, but they will also lead us to overlook some examples of moral statements when we are confronted with them.

The views that moral statements are *categorical* and that they are defined by the property of *importance* are true, on certain readings.

The reading of *categoricality* that makes it out to be a genuine feature of moral statements is informed by McDowell's (1995) explanation of the concept. McDowell reads Kant as holding that *hypothetical* statements are those that do not, on their own, express the desirability of some thing. Rather, "the agent's belief about how things are [i.e. as expressed in the *hypothetical* statement] combines with an independently intelligible desire to represent the action as a good thing from the agent's point of view". In contrast, a *categorical* statement, defined by the property of *categoricality,* "suffices on its own to show us the favourable light in which the action appeared from the point of view of the agent" (McDowell 1995 p.23). As noted, McDowell and Kant's elucidation of *categoricality* are couched in *deontic* terms, and it was argued that moral statements are not simply those that concern conduct. If *categoricality* concerns conduct, it cannot be an invariable feature of moral statements. However, we can read McDowell's elaboration of *categoricality* in such a way that it does not depend upon the truth of the Conduct Thesis. McDowell's reading of the property of *categoricality* suggests that it permits a statement the ability to state that something is of value on its own. *Categoricality* is thus *the* property of an evaluative statement.

The view that *importance* is a unique feature of moral statements leads to the Overridingness Thesis. Often *importance* is cashed out in terms of *overridingness*. For the only way that we can make sense of the claim that moral statements are important, while other value-theoretic statements are not, or that they are more important than other value-theoretic statements, is if we give precedence to the counsel of moral statements over other value-theoretic statements. This is the Overridingness Thesis, which was shown to constitute a mistaken description of moral statements. If *importance* is construed as a genuine feature of moral statements, it is because all value-theoretic statements bear the feature of *importance*: values are by definition things of *importance*. Any statement that expresses a value thereby expresses something of *importance*. Hence, the quality of *importance*, like the revised reading of *categoricality*, turns out to be borne in all value-theoretic statements. (Arguably, "*categoricality*" and "*importance*", on this reading, are two words for the same property.) As *categoricality* or *importance* are found in all value-theoretic statements, in isolation or in combination with each other, they fail to produce an accurate definition of moral statements, which identifies moral statements from nonmoral statements.

A definition of moral statements that attempts to combine the descriptions of *categoricality* or *importance* with any of the remaining accounts of moral statements defended elsewhere would produce a definition that is ultimately false. For instance, to suggest that moral statements are defined by being *important* and having *social content* would be like defining a Canadian as "a North American who is left-of-centre of the North American political spectrum". While it is true that Canadians are North Americans, and that they are often left of the North American political spectrum, it is not true that all Canadians are like this.

The Anger Inclination Thesis is a composite definition of moral statements. It asserts that,

1) a moral statement is an apparently meaningful claim with evaluative import, about which
2) there is, attached to it, an inclination to express anger,

> likely in the absence of mitigating reasons, should the evaluative import of the statement be violated.

The first condition of a moral statement is intended to make clear two features of moral statements. First, they have the appearance of being meaningful. On this view, there are no moral statements that appear to be meaningless to the persons who hold them. The first condition of moral statements also attempts to make clear that moral statements are part of the set of evaluative statements. This feature of moral statements is important to draw attention to, for two reasons. First, frequently, we fail to explicitly notice that not all values are moral values. The definition of moral statements here draws attention to this fact about moral statements; that they are a subset, and not identical with, the set of all evaluative statements defined by the properties of *categoricality* and *importance*. Second, by drawing attention to the evaluative nature of statements that we have the *anger inclination* toward, the Anger Inclination Thesis makes it clear that it does not attempt to reduce value as such to an emotional response like anger. Nor does it attempt to enlighten us on the nature of value or evaluative statements, past specifying the properties of *categoricality* and *importance*. The definition of moral statements that the Anger Inclination Thesis provides, attempts to only state what makes an evaluative statement into a moral statement. It tells us that the *anger inclination* is what leads us to call an evaluative statement a moral statement: it renders the evaluative statement morally significant.

The second condition makes clear that moral statements are the kinds of claims that people are inclined to get upset about, if they do not have mitigating reasons that obscure such an inclination. Thus, moral convictions need not be always imbued with the colour of anger—though counterfactually, if such mitigating reasons were absent we would and do get angry about them.

Why should we accept the Anger Inclination Thesis? One of the objectives of the previous section was to argue that the

Anger Inclination Thesis does capture the essential nature of moral statements. To this end, it identifies the potential explosiveness of moral issues as definitive of moral statements. The Anger Inclination Thesis is also a purely Intentionalist account of moral statements. One symptom of its Intentionalist thrust is its inclusivism.

Because the Anger Inclination Thesis does not define moral statements in terms of *social content*, it is able to affirm Plato's statements about The Good as moral statements. Because it does not define moral statements as being concerned with *aretaic* or *deontic* matters, it is equally consistent with virtue theories of ethics, as it is with moral theories of obligation and duty. Because it does not specify *universalizability* as a feature of moral statements, it can affirm the moral nature of the Existentialist's un*universalizable* prescriptions. Because it does not stipulate a concern for *conformity* as defining moral statements, it can accept that anti-social people too have moral convictions. Because it does not commit itself to the Overridingness Thesis, it can accept the reality that we do not always oblige moral statements and moral values because other value-theoretic considerations (be they political, aesthetic or religious) make greater claims to our compliance.

Having examined the alternate definitions of moral statements, having assessed their draw backs, having noted the virtues of the Anger Inclination Thesis, and having responded to criticisms against the Anger Inclination Thesis, we can conclude, with confidence, that the Anger Inclination Thesis is the correct account of moral statements.

2.4. Definition of Moral Terms

The main reason for delving into an account of moral statements was to have the groundwork laid for an explanation of how some terms come to have a peculiarly moral meaning; terms like "moral" "ethical" or "dharma".

Against the backdrop of the Anger Inclination Thesis, I

contend that the *anger inclination* is what renders an evaluative statement moral in nature. How do terms become moral terms?

Just as a moral statement has two defining components—its evaluative component and its attached *anger inclination*—so must moral terms have two semantic components: the ability to refer to the *anger inclination*, and the ability to make clear that the accompanying statement is evaluative in nature. For moral terms are the key logical ingredient in the grammar of a moral statement: no moral term, no moral statement.

How does a moral term come to have the power to deliver these two pieces of information? The prime function of a moral term, if we follow the counsel of the Anger Inclination Thesis, is to *intentionally* refer to the *anger inclination* attached to an evaluative statement. Hence, minimally, moral terms are defined as *intentionally* referring to the *anger inclination*. Moreover, by delivering this *intentional* mode of reference, they also make clear that they are in a value-theoretic statement, for the *anger inclination intentionally* relates to an evaluative statement. Hence, moral terms clarify both the value-theoretic and the moral nature of the statement they are in, by virtue of *intentionally* referring to the *anger inclination*. As a summary description of moral terms, we may define them simply as those terms referring to the *anger inclination* attached to the statement that they appear in. This is their bare moralness.

The Anger Inclination Thesis is proffered against the background of the distinction between *extention* and *intention*, and the notion that some terms are definable with reference to one, or both, of these elements. If we combine these ideas, we arrive at a relatively detailed account of moral terms. The remainder of this section will be devoted to fleshing out what the Anger Inclination Thesis has to tell us about the nature of moral terms. With this, we will be in a position to evaluate whether or not "dharma" is a moral term, and if it is, what kind of moral term it is.

2.4.1. Subsidiary Features of Moral Terms

To say of moral terms that they refer to the *anger inclination* is to say very little about their particular meanings. Most terms have complicated lives with multiple referential relationships. Their specific meanings consist in these various relationships.

All moral terms refer to the *anger inclination*. Yet, most moral terms also refer to some other contextual, or *extentional,* matter when used. In the statement, "she is highly moral", "moral" not only refers to the *anger inclination*, but also to the person designated.[11]

In addition to having contextual *extentions* and referring to the *anger inclination*, some moral terms have the ability to *focus* on the circumstances eliciting the venting of anger. Moral terms that have this function are terms like "evil" "cruel" and "despicable". Such terms can be said, thus, to have the property of *focus.* In the statement, "He is very evil", the moral term, "evil", brings our attention to the thing that constitutes the disappointment of the evaluative import of the statement; the person who is being called "evil". Moral terms that lack *focus*, in contrast, are often regarded as evaluatively positive. Examples of moral terms that lack *focus* include, "ethical", "moral" and "kind".

Why should we regard the *focus* property, when there are the more traditional ideas of moral approval and moral disapproval? Traditionally, what is identified as *focus* is simply the property of moral disapproval.

The main reason for construing moral appraisal in terms of the presence or absence of one property, instead of the mutually exclusive occurrence of two properties, is that seemingly positive moral terms are evaluatively ambiguous. In some circumstances, "moral" is a term of praise, as in "he is highly moral". In other circumstances, the same term lacks the function of appraisal, as in "moral philosophy", "moral philosophy" is not philosophy that is morally praiseworthy; it is philosophy that deals with moral matters. *Evil philosophy,* however, is something morally criticisable. "Evil" unlike "moral" is always a term of criticism and appraisal.

Given the evaluative ambiguity of terms like "moral" and "ethical" it makes sense to conceive of positive moral appraisal in terms of a lack of criticism, or *focus*. In other words, "positive" moral terms are not really positive: they are just not negative.

Some moral terms have inclusive specifications regarding their *extentions*. Such terms have *substantive content*. Examples of moral terms with *substantive content* are *aretaic* moral terms, which always refer to motivations or characteristics—"virtue", "vice", "considerate", "conscientious", —or *deontic* moral terms, which always concern actions—"duty", "obligation". If a term lacks *substantive content*, it is *formal*. Prime examples of *formal* moral terms include "ethical", "moral", "good" and "evil".[12] The difference between *substantive* and *formal* moral terms does not reduce to whether a moral term refers to an *extention* or not, but to whether the *extention* of the moral term is specified in its meaning: *substantive* moral terms have *extentions* built into their meaning; *formal* moral terms do not.

While all moral terms refer to the *anger inclination*, not all moral terms enjoy the same success in communicating to others that there is an *anger inclination* regarding some statement. Those moral terms that enjoy maximum semantic success are understood as having a moral meaning throughout a linguistic community. Moral terms that are understood by a linguistic community at large as having a moral meaning, such as "evil", or "ethical", function *perfectly* as moral terms. Hence, such terms have the property of *perfection*, or, we could call them "*perfect* moral terms". Moral terms that fail to be *perfect* are *imperfect*.

A third variety of moral terms are *virtually perfect* moral terms. Such terms are ambiguous as to their moral import—though not their evaluative import—and yet, they are understood by the whole linguistic community as sometimes functioning as moral terms. Examples of *virtually perfect* moral terms in the English language are "good", "bad", "virtue", "ought", "must", "responsible" and "should".

2.4.2. Double Role of Some Moral Terms

Some moral terms have a double role. In some circumstances, they inform us of the author's substantive moral opinions, in other circumstances, they function to inform that the matters under discussion are morally ripe. What accounts for this difference? The double life of moral terms comes down to *which anger inclination* they refer to.

Where moral terms are used to express the moral convictions of the author, they point back and connect the *anger inclination* of the author with the sentence that the selfsame moral term appears in. In such circumstances, the moral term is employed *expressively.*

When moral terms function to simply designate moral matters, they are employed *nonexpressively.* Such uses of moral terms do not explicitly refer to the *anger inclination* of the author of the statement that the same moral term appears in. Rather, they may either refer to a third party's *anger inclination*, or likely to a hypothetical *anger inclination.* An example of a *nonexpressive* use of a moral term is found in the statement "this is a work on ethics".

2.4.3. Meaning of Moral Terms

Several properties of moral terms have been noted in this present section. Yet, the differences among moral terms are reducible to three important factors.

1. The pragmatic issue of a moral term's ability to communicate its moral significance comes down to whether the term in question has the property of *perfection*.

2. The issue of whether a moral term is one of criticism or is noncritical comes down to whether the term in question has the property of *focus*

3. The question of whether a moral term is *substantive* or *formal* comes down to a question of whether or not it is *substantive.*

The presence or absence of the above three properties constitute the particular meaning of a moral term. Hence, the three properties of *perfection*, *focus* and *substantiveness* constitute a schema against which we can translate moral terms from one language into another.

The English language moral terms, "ethical" or "moral", both have the property of *perfection*, but lack both *focus* and *substantiveness*. Hence, these two terms have the schema: + *perfection*, - *focus*, - *substantiveness*. If a non-English language term is an exact translational match for "ethics" or "morality", it will have the same schema. The meaning of such a term, in plain English, is *A–THING–ABOUT–WHICH–THERE–IS–AN–INCLINATION–TO–GET–ANGRY–IF–IT–IS–VIOLATED–OR–NOT–RESPECTED–IN–SOME–MANNER–IN THE–ABSENCE–OF–MITIGATING– REASONS.*

The English language moral terms "evil" and "immoral" both have the properties of *perfection* and *focus*, but they lack *substantiveness*. Hence, their schema is: + *perfection*, + *focus*, - *substantiveness*. If a foreign language moral term means either "evil" or "immoral", it will have this very schema. The meaning of such a term in English is, *A–THING–ABOUT–WHICH–THERE–IS–AN–INCLINATION–TO–BE–ANGRY–AT–BECAUSE–IT–VIOLATES–OR–FAILS–TO–RESPECT–SOMETHING–OF–IMPORTANCE–IN–THE–ABSENCE–OF–MITIGATING–REASONS.*

In the case of *substantive* moral terms, the particular *substantive content* plays an important role; it can be interpreted as the value that fills in the variable of *substantiveness*. The schema for the moral term "cruel" is: + *perfection*, + *focus*, + *substantiveness* {injuriousness or harm}. A moral term in another language that is an exact match for "cruel" will share the same schema. In plain English, such a term means *INJURIOUSNESS–OR–HARM–THAT–THERE–IS–AN–INCLINATION–TO–BE–ANGRY–AT–BECAUSE–IT–VIOLATES–OR–FAILS–TO–RESPECT–SOMETHING–OF–IMPORTANCE–IN–THE– ABSENCE–OF–MITIGATING–REASONS.*

In the case of *virtually perfect* moral terms, we are often inclined to substitute *virtually perfect* terms for *perfect* terms, as when we interchangeably use "good" and "ethical". We use these terms as synonyms in a way that we do not and cannot use "considerate" as a synonym for "ethical". Hence, I would suggest that *virtually perfect* moral terms are a type of *perfect* moral term. Schematically, though, the virtual nature of a term should be noted for accuracy. Hence, the schema for "good" is: + *perfection* (virtual), - *focus*, - *substantiveness*.

In short, the problem of translating moral terms is a matter of determining which of the three schematic variables are present in a moral term.

2.4.4. Studying Moral Terms

To entertain that a term is moral in nature, we generally have some prior empirical reason for suspecting its moral significance. We may come to be suspicious that a term has an essential moral function by observing that it designates matters that people, including the authors who use the term, are disposed to get angry over.

Coming to suspect that a term designates the *anger inclination* is in part a result of common sense. We know that certain issues are the kinds of things that human beings as a species are disposed to lose their temper over: murder, incest, rape, bribery, dishonesty, violence, theft, betrayal, and so on. Terms that deal with the avoidance or minimization of such matters can be known to be moral terms without *focus*. Those that directly designate such matters are moral terms with *focus*.

The determination of moral terms based on a general knowledge of human nature is indispensable to the acquisition of foreign language moral vocabulary. Knowledge of such moral terms will overlap in large with what the Social Content Theorists and Extentionalists tend to believe is the content of moral terms. The mistake of the Extentionalist is not in noting that much of our moral sentiments have to do with our relationships with others or how we conduct ourselves, but in the attempt to define all moral terms and statements in terms of such matters.

We do not need to always depend upon a knowledge of human nature to determine that a term is moral in nature. Often, we can come to determine that a term is moral by observing that people *frequently* (or, predictably) get angry about the issue that it designates. In this case, the determination that a term is moral in nature is an inference to the best explanation, which connects overt behaviour with a hypothesized *anger inclination*.

Once we have a general conviction regarding the moralness of a term, the next question pertains to its specific meaning, which consists in the presence or absence of the three previously noted properties: *perfection*, *focus* and *substantiveness*.

Judging whether a term is *perfect* or not consists in assessing whether the term has a moral function across a linguistic community. The single critical factor here is how widely the term is circulated. If the term transcends sub-cultural and religious barriers, its *perfection* is clear. How do we come to know that a term is *virtually perfect* or not? Generally, there will be some philosophical reflection in a culture regarding the peculiar status of the term in question. People will as in English make overt gestures to disambiguate the moral or nonmoral meaning of the term: "No, I meant 'good' in the moral sense", "Do you mean 'ought' in a moral sense, or 'ought' in a nonmoral sense?"

Judging whether a term has *substantive content* consists in assessing whether the term is amenable to an *extentional* definition or not. A *formal* moral term will appear to take up and put down *extentions*, left right and centre. Some regularity in the *extentions* of *formal* moral terms is likely to be observed. But on the whole, there will be an air of controversy surrounding the *extentions* of a *formal* moral term. In contrast, *substantive* moral terms will not generally be the subject of controversy.

Whether a moral term has *focus* or not, can be gleaned from whether the matter that the term designates is *the circumstance* or feature that generally elicits the venting of anger. Such terms have *focus*. If the term designates things *whose violation* or minimization elicits anger, then the term lacks *focus*.

Such empirical considerations are pertinent in our initial stages of attempting to differentiate moral terms from nonmoral terms. In no way do such considerations negate, or contradict, the notion that moral meaning is, essentially, an *intentional* matter, with no *extentional* restrictions. For, a moral term may not be used in connection with something that people do get angry about in order for it to be moral. However, we have cause to suspect that a term is moral in nature when it is predictably associated with the expression of anger. Such empirical observations are our foothold in a discourse, with which we can begin to understand the moral dimensions of conversations that do not explicitly display expressions of anger. In any society of sophistication, much moral conversation—particularly in philosophical literature—will be of such a civil variety.

2.4.5. Terms that Designate the Field of Moral Concern

Philosophers are often concerned with two kinds of moral terms: *perfect formal* terms without *focus*, like "ethical" or "moral" and *virtually perfect formal* moral terms, without *focus*, like "good" and "ought". These two kinds of moral terms are philosophically intriguing, in part, because of their *formality*. Moreover, they can be used to organize and define subsidiary moral terms. A moral theory frequently consists in explicating what counts as ethics, morality or the good, or what we ought to do.

In a foreign language it may seem difficult, at first glance, to discern the difference between *virtually perfect, formal* moral terms without *focus*, like "good", and *perfect formal* moral terms without *focus*, like "ethical". For these terms seem interchangeable. However, one important difference as to their functioning is that *virtually perfect formal* moral terms without *focus*, like "good" or "ought", do not function as designators for the whole sphere of moral concern. Yet, "ethics" and "moral" do.

Only *perfect formal* moral terms without *focus* have the peculiar ability to designate the entire field of moral concern, or the subject-matter of ethics. In the preceding sentence, I used the terms "moral" and "ethics" in precisely this way. Such terms can designate the whole field of moral concern because they lack *focus*, they are open to a *nonexpressive* use, they have no *substantive* restrictions on their use and—unlike *virtually perfect* moral terms—they are not morally ambiguous.

The ability of a moral term to designate an entire field of intellectual concern where persons can have differing opinions, thus, is one of the telltale signs of whether a term is an exact translational match for "ethics" or "moral".

2.4.6. Some Criticisms Considered

In criticizing Extentionalist accounts of moral terms, I have presumed that:

1) We can learn something about the nature of moral terms by looking to what they are generally predicated of: they are generally predicated of things that we get angry over or angry at.
2) Some moral terms have *substantive*—i.e. *extentional*—content.

Do these commitments not render the account of moral terms that I have presented here Extentionalist in nature? If my account is a species of Extentionalism, it would seem that it is open to the criticisms that I have directed toward other such accounts.

If the account of moral terms presented here is, at core, Intentionalist, then the following problem arises:

3) How is it possible that moral terms, with no *substantive content*, like "moral" or "ethical", could ever come to have *extentions*, as they are supposed to be without *extentions*, essentially.

Finally, if the Anger Inclination Thesis, and the theory of moral terms based upon it, is not a species of Extentionalism, this is because:

4) The Anger Inclination Thesis appears to be nothing more than Emotivism; for Emotivism holds that moral statements are characterized by a venting of emotions.

If this is true, then it appears that the Anger Inclination Thesis and the theory of moral terms based upon it, implies a Moral Irrealism (one of the principal implications of Emotivism); the view that there is no truth, falsity, or rationality, to moral claims. If this is so, whatever problems the Anger Inclination Thesis promises to solve, it comes at a high price, which many persons concerned with ethics do not want to pay.

Contrary to the criticism, that (1) we can learn something about the nature of moral terms by looking to what they are generally predicated of, fails to imply Extentionalism. This view would imply Extentionalism if it suggested that it is the *extentions* of moral terms that define the nature of moral terms. However, what can be observed from the use of moral concepts is that they are predicated of things that *we have an inclination* to get angry over or at. It is the *anger inclination* that is borne out in the use of moral terms and concepts: this has to do with our dispositions toward things, and not necessarily, things considered in themselves.

Responding to concerns over commitment (2), let us begin by raising the question, "how different is the Anger Inclination Thesis from Frankena's Social Content Thesis, which provides a mixed account of moral terms?" Part of this account is Extentionalist, and another part stresses a "moral point of view" and is Intentionalist. For those who proffer the Social Content Thesis, social *extentions* are part of the moralness of a moral concept. On this view, all moral terms, *qua* moral terms, concern social matters. Moreover, this view holds that moral terms can be predicated only of social matters. Hence, the Social Content Thesis holds that moral terms are defined in terms of having exclusively social *extentions*. This is what makes the Social Content view—even Frankena's (1963; 1973) hybrid—a species of Extentionalism: it defines *all* moral terms and concepts, even in part, in terms of a set of *extentions*.

The Anger Inclination Thesis places no *extentional* restrictions on what all moral terms can be predicated of. It does predict that some moral terms do have *extentional* restrictions on their use that are internal to their meaning. If *extentional* terms are those that can be defined in terms of their *extentions*, it follows that *some* moral terms stand for *extentional–intentional* concepts. However, the category of moral terms on the whole, as well as the category of moral statements, can be defined without respect to *extentional* content: moral terms are terms that refer to the *anger inclination*, while moral statements are those that there is an *anger inclination* about. It follows that the Anger Inclination Thesis is purely Intentionalist, i.e., it does not state that there are *extentional* restrictions on the meaning of all moral terms, statements or concepts. On its account, the essence of the moralness of a term or concept is in its associated *intention* only.

The Definitional Naturalist (spoken of earlier, on p.24) may object that what I have done is led the reader to believe that there are two views: that all moral terms lack content, or that they all have content. On the basis of this dichotomy, I have argued that the latter view is incorrect, and that the former must be correct (via a disjunctive syllogism), only to sneak back into the picture *extentional* restrictions on the application of moral terms. This is misleading.

In reality, I have argued that it is incorrect to define key philosophical terms that delimit a field of philosophical debate in terms of *extentions*. I have argued for a definition of moral statements and terms that allows us to define the key philosophical concept of a *perfect formal* moral term without *focus*, represented by the terms "ethical" and "moral", without specifying *extentional* restrictions on their use. It is true that the Anger Inclination Thesis recognizes that some moral terms have *substantive content*. But recognizing this feature of moral terms does not detract from the Anger Inclination Thesis's ability to define "ethical" and "moral" without specifying *extentional* restrictions. Hence, on its account, there is no limit to what, *extentionally*, a philosopher might think is morally important. Nor in theory is there any moral limit to the variety of moral terms there can be with *substantive content*.

Having argued that the account of moral terms and statements presented here is purely Intentionalist in nature, the problem arises of how (3) moral terms could ever come to have *extentions*. For according to this theory of moral terms, it is not simply *substantive* moral terms that have *extentions*, but *formal* moral terms also pick up *extentions*: contextually. Hence, in the statement "She is moral", she is the *extention* of "moral". So there is a contradiction: *formal* moral terms have *extentions*, and *formal* moral terms, lack *extentions*. How is this contradiction resolved?

For a moral term to be *formal* is for it to lack *substantive* restrictions in its meaning: it is semantically compatible with any *extention*, while *substantive* moral terms can only semantically, or grammatically, be predicated of certain *extentions*. Hence, it is perfectly consistent with the purely *intentional* meaning of a *formal* moral term for it to have *extentions*—the *formality*, and purely *intentional* nature of these concepts are a direct function of the fact that no particular *extention* can be specified in their definition. How do they pick up *extentions*? Just as terms that are primarily *extentional* acquire *intentions* in certain contexts (for examples, see 2.1. Extention and Intention p.13 and p.20) *formal* moral terms acquire *extentions* in certain contexts too. However, in the case of moral terms, their acquired *extentions* are regulated by a moral theory. Hence, we can talk about the *extentions* of the concept of *ETHICAL* according to certain moral theories. The *extentions* of moral terms in the context of a moral theory forms the substance of the moral theory: it is the particular moral theory's account of the *extension* (with an "s") of the concept of a *PERFECT–FORMAL–MORAL–TERM–WITHOUT–FOCUS*, represented by the words "ethical" or "moral".

A critic may object that while I have provided a means of resolving the contradiction in my argument, I have also led my account of moral terms and statements towards a Moral Irrealism, which holds that there is no real subject-matter of morality: that morality is simply what we make of it. For in saying that moral terms pick up *extentions* within the context of a moral theory, I have made it seem as though the question of whether something is in fact good or bad, right or wrong, is a matter of choice.

In one respect, this criticism is correct: the theory I am putting forward leaves us the choice to morally disagree with each other. However, it does not imply that there are no good reasons for thinking that one moral theory is correct, while another is not. Moral theories involve a whole host of considerations that bear upon what we *should* think is right or wrong. For instance, metaphysical considerations tell us what reality is like, and from this, it may follow that there are certain items in the universe, whose violation is wrong, and perhaps, that it is appropriate to express anger over their violation. On the basis of such a metaphysical theory, some moral statements will be true. Epistemological considerations tell us how we can come to know whether something is right or wrong, on the basis of a general theory of knowledge. Some epistemologies tell us that certain convictions are veridical or rational, and that they are the kind that we do, or that we ought to, have the *anger inclination* about. Axiological considerations attempt to justify our adherence to certain moral precepts or convictions on the basis of their fruits in other spheres of value. According to this way of dealing with the veracity or rationality of moral claims, we have reason to accept the truth or rationality of certain moral claims because of their payoff in other spheres of value.

The Anger Inclination Thesis does not attempt to incorporate means of justifying moral claims into a definition of moral statements, any more than it attempts to criticize the possibility of justifying moral claims. It attempts, instead, to capture the skeleton of moral meaning, in reference to which, we can understand diverse moral claims *as* moral claims.

Now we can address the concern that (4) the Anger Inclination Thesis appears to be nothing more than Emotivism, for Emotivism holds that moral statements are characterized by a venting of emotions. In light of the Intentionalist thrust of the Anger Inclination Thesis and the theory of moral terms that is ancillary to it, it might seem as though the Anger Inclination Thesis is simply Emotivism in sheep's clothing. However, in reality, whatever similarities are there between Emotivism and the Anger Inclination Thesis are wholly superficial.

The most important difference between Emotivism and the Anger Inclination Thesis is that Emotivism is generally proffered as an account of the nature of evaluative statements on the whole. The Anger Inclination Thesis concerns only the distinct nature of moral claims. Thus, Emotivism is not an alternative account of the nature of moral statements, like the Overridingness Thesis, or the Anger Inclination Thesis. (This is because Emotivism is a metaethical position, while the Anger Inclination Thesis is a metamoral view.[13])

Second, the Emotivist holds that the evaluative component of a moral statement is simply an emotional response. Hence, the Emotivist will translate the statement "That person is Hitler and he is evil" into "That person is Hitler: Boo!" For Emotivists, there might be a factual component to a moral claim: "That person is Hitler". But that is the extent to which moral claims are rational; the rest is just the expression of emotions. Hence, on the Emotivist's account, a moral statement taken in whole, is neither capable of being true nor false; right nor wrong; rational nor irrational. (On the Emotivist's view, moral statements are *noncognitive* and fail to be *bivalent.*)

In contrast, the Anger Inclination Thesis brings attention to the emotional side of moral claims. But, it does not attempt to understand the evaluative component of a moral statement in terms of a person's emotional response. The Anger Inclination Thesis presupposes that moral statements have an evaluative meaning, which is logically distinct from the *anger inclination*. As the Anger Inclination Thesis does not define the evaluativeness of moral statements in terms of an emotional response, it does not commit itself to Emotivism, or Moral Irrealism.

Likewise, the Anger Inclination Thesis does not stipulate that moral statements are *cognitive* (expressive of a judgement, like "The cat is on the mat") or *noncognitive* (not expressive of a judgement, like "Go!"). This controversy is under-determined by the Anger Inclination Thesis. The Anger Inclination Thesis is thus amenable to the view that moral statements can be true or false; right or wrong; rational or irrational.

Third, Emotivist accounts generally do not attach significance to the character of the emotions attached to moral statements. The Emotivist's point is made simply by the claim that emotions make up the meaning of a moral statement. On the Anger Inclination Thesis, it is not any old emotional response that is associated with a moral statement. The emotional responses associated with moral claims, on the Anger Inclination Thesis, are as a group referred to as "anger".

Fourth, the Emotivist holds that the *expression* of emotions always makes up the meaning of a moral statement. On the Anger Inclination Thesis, it is an *inclination* to express certain emotions that contributes to the moral meaning of moral statements.

2.5. Anger Inclination and Debate

The argument to this point has been geared towards procuring a definition of moral terms, which makes sense of meaningful disagreement. I have argued that many of the current accounts of moral terms and moral statements (such as the Social Content Thesis, the Conduct Thesis, and the Blame Inclination Thesis) render moral terms in such away that we virtually have to be of the same moral persuasion in order to grasp the meaning of moral terms: the Social Content Thesis stipulates that one can only have a moral opinion (i.e. use moral terms and statements meaningfully) if one believes that morality pertains only to (pro) social matters; the Conduct Thesis stipulates (and the Blame Inclination Thesis implies) that one can only make moral statements and terms meaningfully if one is talking about behaviour. In this way, these accounts significantly restrict the scope of meaningful disagreement on moral issues. Some accounts are more inclusive in their account of moral terms and statements, but these stipulate that a person has to be committed to extraneous philosophical views in order to understand and meaningfully use moral terms and statements. The Overridingness Thesis commits us to the philosophical view that moral issues are more important, or obedience worthy, than other value-theoretic issues; the Universalizability Thesis tells us that we have to think that a moral statement is specifiable in universal terms (without loss of content) in order to have a genuinely moral opinion. Given that most people do not know or understand what *universalizability* is, this is a big expectation.

It is fair to point out that any philosophical view about the definition of moral statements and terms will imply that people have to be in agreement on the meaning of moral terms and statements in order to use them meaningfully. If this is so, it follows that any account of the meaning of moral terms and statements will attribute certain views to those who meaningfully use moral terms and statements, but this stipulation is bound to limit debate though, perhaps not viciously.

What, then, are the commitments of the Anger Inclination Thesis? Would these commitments also restrict debate by claiming that all persons who use moral terms and statements meaningfully must be committed to certain philosophical views?

The Anger Inclination Thesis commits people to little, and it seems to me that it commits people who use moral terms and sentences to no significant philosophical theses. If this is so, it does not minimize philosophical debate on moral issues in any significant way.

To recognize what the Anger Inclination Thesis claims that people must understand to use moral terms and statements meaningfully, we might begin by recognizing that the Anger Inclination Thesis has been presented in a seemingly hesitant manner from the start. Instead of laying out what this thesis says about the meaning of moral terms, and statements, all at once, I began by presenting the thesis in the form of a definition of moral statements, and then, I proceeded to explain what its implications are for moral terms. This dry and schematic representation was necessary for a few different reasons. First, it is necessary for us to shake our reliance on an intuitive grasp of the meaning of moral terms in our discussion on moral meaning. The reason that we must shake our reliance on such intuitions is that our emotional, personal, attachment to moral terms ironically conceals the essential role of emotion in moral meaning. So, by discussing the meaning of moral statements first, independently of an account of moral terms, we gain a certain detachment from our attachments to moral terms. Second, moral terms concern many sorts of different matters: some moral terms are *formal*, others are *substantive*; some may be praiseworthy or commendatory while others are critical. In order to gain a grasp of all moral terms, we needed to first define the very essence of moral significance; something that all moral terms bear. Attending to a blanket definition of all moral statements helps us to arrive at a unified concept of morality as such.

The Anger Inclination Thesis says that morality is always related to an inclination to get angry over the violation of the evaluative import of a statement (likely in the absence of, mitigating factors that hold the peace). The Anger Inclination Thesis does not say that one must actually have the *anger inclination* to use the concept of *MORALITY* properly. I need not have the *anger inclination* with respect to the sentence "rocks are good" in order for it to be a moral statement.

The claim that a person must understand that minimally, a moral statement is one that (necessarily) there is some inclination to get angry over, if it is violated, imputes very little to persons using moral terms and statements meaningfully. It does not stipulate that they must formulate their moral claims in any particular way (as the Universalizability Thesis claims) nor does it say that moral claims must be given paramount weight by authors using the moral term or statement. I believe that the Anger Inclination Thesis commits persons using moral statements to no significant philosophical thesis besides the Anger Inclination Thesis itself, and this is not a substantive view on morality.

The Anger Inclination Thesis thus appears to maximize debate in two ways. First, it claims no *substantive* restrictions on what can be a moral issue. It places one formal constraint on moral meaning: moral statements are those evaluative claims where there is an inclination to get angry over. However, unlike other formal accounts of morality (like the Universalizability Thesis or the Overridingness Thesis), the Anger Inclination Thesis places no constraints on how moral claims must be formed in an argumentative context. It thus hardly interferes with what a person can think is moral, or what moral view they wish to defend. Secondly, it implies that a statement that is moral for one person is morally significant for us all. This, in its own way, maximizes debate, for it forces us to recognize that there are genuinely moral alternatives to our own views—alternatives that are radically different or alien to our way of thinking.

The critic is likely to note that, in forming an account of morality that maximizes debate, and permits any issue that a person cares about to be a moral issue, I have also opened the door to all moral statements being vacuously true.

Statements are true, on one account, because a subject belongs, in some way, to a predicate. If moral terms (*ex hypothesi*) are meaningful because they signal that there is an inclination to get angry over the matter at hand if it is violated, then, it would seem that any use of moral language that expresses a moral opinion of someone is thereby vacuously true. Take the statement "cutting grass is (morally) wrong". According to the Anger Inclination Thesis, what this statement entails (strictly) is the statement: "there is an inclination to get angry if grass is cut". If it is the case that there is someone who has such an inclination, then the statement "there is an inclination to get angry if grass is cut" is true. If this is so, it follows that every moral statement ever sincerely believed by someone is a self-fulfilling claim. This, of course, makes a mockery of ethics—it turns ethics into a forum for expressing likes and dislikes. The Anger Inclination Thesis is thus not very different at all from Emotivism.

My response to this predicament is out of step with a trend in philosophy these days. Often, philosophers in the Anglo-American tradition think that the veracity of a philosophical claim can be settled if we understand the meaning of a claim; that the task of determining the meaning of a philosophical claim gives us the truth conditions of a statement. I have avoided this approach precisely because there is a gap between comprehension of meaning in philosophy, and comprehension of truth. In philosophy, we all understand what the statement "minds are real" means. Despite being in full agreement on the meaning of this statement, some persons (Eliminative Materialists) meaningfully disagree with the statement. For this to be possible, there must be some kind of rift between an adequate account of the meaning of a philosophically important statement, and its truth-value.

In short, we need to separate two questions: (1) "what makes a statement a moral statement?" and, (2) "what makes a statement that is moral true or correct?"

The Anger Inclination Thesis attempts an answer to the first question. On its account, the fact that there is an inclination to get angry over the violation of the evaluative import of some statement is what makes it moral. Thus, that someone does have the inclination to get angry if grass is cut simply makes the statement "cutting grass is wrong" into a moral statement. It does not make this statement (or the statement, "cutting grass is evil") true.

Is the Anger Inclination Thesis silent on the matter of what renders a moral statement true or correct? I think that there is an allied account of the truth or propriety of moral statements that can be supplied that is not directly implied by the Anger Inclination Thesis. According to this account, what renders a moral statement true or correct is whether, other things being equal (in the absence of mitigating reasons) it is *appropriate* to get angry over its violation. For the sake of ease of reference, let us call this the "Anger Propriety Thesis". Thus, according to the Anger Propriety Thesis, the statement "cutting grass is evil" is true or correct if and only if, anger is appropriately expressed over the cutting of grass.

To determine whether anger is appropriately expressed over certain concerns, philosophers might bring in several considerations: the nature of the thing in question; a general moral principle that has been justified in some manner; an appeal to some epistemic principle. In principle, the Anger Inclination Thesis places no restrictions on how philosophers might argue that a certain moral claim is true or correct.

Our reason for exploring this question was to determine what, if any, philosophically significant theses regarding morality, the Anger Inclination Thesis imputes to those who meaningfully use moral terms and statements. It may seem that, after this account of what renders a moral statement true or correct, the Anger Inclination Thesis is committed to the view that people who meaningfully use moral statements are also committed to the Anger Propriety Thesis. If this is so, the Anger Inclination Thesis would limit debate objectionably after the fashion of the Overridingness Thesis or the Universalizability Thesis; it would make the bold claim that people who use moral statements meaningfully also believe that the Anger Propriety Thesis is correct.

Properly speaking, the Anger Inclination Thesis does not entail the Anger Propriety Thesis. However, it does entail that, whenever a person uses moral language to express a substantive opinion of their own, they also make it known that they believe that, other things being equal, it is appropriate (at least for themselves) to get angry over the violation of the evaluative import of the statement they are affirming.

This is not a weakness of the theory but its strength; for as a matter of fact, moral issues are precisely those things that we feel justified in being angry about. The exception to this general rule is the case where mitigating reasons weigh in, as in the case of supererogatory statements. Here, but for the strong mitigating reasons that lead us to quell our very real *anger inclination*, we would also feel justified in being angry. All the same, thinking that other things being equal it is appropriate to get angry over the violation of one's moral convictions is not the same as thinking that what makes a moral statement true or correct is whether it is appropriate to get angry over it. The Anger Inclination Thesis, thus, does not entail the Anger Propriety Thesis.

2.6. The Meaning of "Dharma"

For those keeping tabs, it will be apparent that "dharma" of Indian philosophical thought has all the features of a *perfect formal*, moral term without *focus*, including the ability of such terms to designate an entire field of enquiry, within which people can disagree. Before we can discharge the controversy regarding the meaning of "dharma", some qualifications are necessary: history has intervened, making our understanding of the meaning of "dharma" more complicated.

2.6.1. Modern Notion of "Dharma"

In recent times, the term "dharma" in Hindi has been divested of its moral, and *intentional*, significance. According to the *Consolidated Glossary of Technical Terms*, which translates English concepts into the bureaucratically recognized Hindi equivalents (Government of India, Ministry of Education, 1962) "dharma" ("धर्म") is the equivalent for "religion". "Dharma" is also used this way in the *Indian Constitution*, in the description of India's secularity (*dharmanirapekṣa rājya*) (India, 1950).

Is the view that "dharma" means RELIGION correct? As an explanation of what classical Indians meant by "dharma", this view is incorrect.

A religion is a complex of *deontic* and *aretaic* concerns, organized around the goal of soteriology. This is why Marxism is not a religion, though atheistic belief systems like Early Buddhism and Jainism are religions. While the idea of religion refers to belief systems, it is an *extentional* concept. We know this because "religion" can be defined, in full, in terms of what it is applied to ("a complex of *deontic* and *aretaic* concerns, organized around the goal of soteriology"). In contrast, *DHARMA* is an *intentional* concept; the inability of scholars of Indian philosophy to find any regularity or coherency in the unlimited *extentions* of "dharma" is proof of its non*extentional* meaning.

It might seem that there are some *intentional* uses of "religion" as in "give me that old time religion" or "religious experience". In the notion of "religious experience" it is "experience" that is the *intentional* concept; "religious" just classifies the kind of experience it refers to. As for the notion of "that old time religion", we have to come to terms with a person's beliefs in order to understand what "that" refers to. The question of whether "that" is a religion or not is a matter that is decided on the basis of the *extentions* of "religion"—not simply an individual's opinion about what constitutes a religion.

How did "dharma", which is an *intentional* term, ever come to take on the meaning of "religion", which is an *extentional* term? I suspect that "dharma" has taken on the meaning of "religion" because of the problems that we have been concerned with here: Extentionalism.

If Global Extentionalism is consistently used to interpret all of the uses of "dharma" the only possible conclusion is that "dharma" is untranslatable, for no *extentionally* definable concept in any language—including "religion"—corresponds to "dharma"'s complete lack of coherence in *extentions*. Thus, it is no surprise that eminent scholars who have applied this hypothesis to the problem of defining "dharma" have concluded just this. Yet, the effort to define "dharma" on *extentional* grounds suggests that "dharma" means religion, for though there is no consistency in the *extentions* of "dharma", there is tremendous convergence on what counts as "dharma" within India's various religious traditions. The correlation between the divergent lists of *extentions* of "dharma" and religious affiliation is thus the springboard from which some have concluded that "dharma" means religion. Thus, the view that "dharma" means religion is informed by the project of the Extentionalist.[14]

How did Extentionalism ever come to have such influence over official definitions of "dharma" and our common awareness of this concept's significance? Extentionalism is a prominent approach to defining the meaning of terms; the Social Content Thesis, the Conduct Thesis, and Definitional Naturalism all subscribe to Extentionalism. As for Indology, there is good reason to believe that it was committed to the stronger view of Global Extentionalism from the start.

Indology, like so many contemporary social scientific fields, is a child of the nineteenth century. The nineteenth century set a new pace and tone for research in the humanities because of the unprecedented success of the natural sciences. From the nineteenth century on, fledgling academic fields attempted to earn their stripes by aspiring to the model of the natural sciences. This fusion of scientism with matters that were traditionally the province of the humanities results in what Hans-Georg Gadamer (1996) calls the "human sciences"; Indology, with its emphasis on philology, is arguably one such novel human science. Gadamer notes that "the logical self-reflection that accompanied the development of the human sciences in the nineteenth century is wholly governed by the model of the natural sciences" (Gadamer 1996 p.3). The model of the natural sciences at the time is *induction*: the method of arriving at laws and conclusions by generalising empirical observations. The motivation for fusing a scientistic research programme with the humanities is not entirely misinformed. Gadamer elaborates on the rationale behind this fusion:

> Human science too is concerned with establishing similarities, regularities and conformities to law which would make it possible to predict individual phenomena and processes. In the field of natural phenomena this goal cannot always be reached everywhere to the same extent, but the reason for this variation is only that sufficient data on which the similarities are to be established cannot always be obtained. Thus the method of meteorology is just the same as that of physics, but its data is

> incomplete and therefore its predictions are more uncertain. This is true in the field of moral and social phenomena. The use of the inductive method is also free from all metaphysical assumptions and remains perfectly independent of how one conceives of the phenomena that one is observing .... To make deductions from regularities concerning the phenomena to be expected implies no assumption about the *kind of connection whose regularity makes prediction possible*. The involvement of free decisions—if they exist—does not interfere with the regular process, but itself belongs to the universality of regularity which are attained through induction. (Gadamer 1996 p.4, my italics)

In keeping with this research programme, we find Max Müller, a founding father of Indology, arguing, that philology, "the science of language", "has nothing to do with mere theories, whether conceivable or not. It collects facts, and its only object is to account for these facts, as far as possible" (Müller 1861 p.205).

The scientistic research programme of the nineteenth century is not simply characterized by the desire to arrive at conclusions without employing hypotheses. It is also characterized by a strong desire on the part of researchers to be objective by relying solely on empirically observable facts. The facts of Indology, in the main, consist in its texts. If one shuns hypotheses about the connections of words with emotions and mental states of authors (things that are not easily observed) what is left are *extentions* of terms; correlations between a term and the things it is applied to. Global Extentionalism is thus the default option for the scientism of the nineteenth century in areas of semantics: it is the outcome of applying a highly empiricistic inductive methodology to the problem of semantics. Hence, it is also the default option for Indology, as a human science born of the nineteenth century.

The methodological preference of early Indology can not only be identified as the source of our current difficulties in comprehending the meaning of "dharma"—difficulties that are a function of an effort to find the meaning of "dharma" in its *extentions*—but also, we can recognize it as responsible for shifting the meaning of "dharma" to the historically inaccurate rendition: "religion".

2.6.2. Traditional Meaning of "Dharma"

No single account of "dharma" on the bases of its *extentions* can possibly do justice to its meaning—its *extentions* are too diverse. This is because "dharma" betrays all the features of a moral term with the schema of "ethics" or "morality" (+ *perfection*, - *focus*, - *substantiveness*) in the language of Indian philosophy.

"Dharma" transcends religious and sub-cultural barriers of classical India; it functions prominently in the philosophical thought of Buddhists, Jains and Hindus. For instance, authors of all three of India's classical religious traditions refer to those who violate their respective conceptions of dharma as "*nāstikas*" (Nāgārjuna I.43, Vālmīki II.109.33–34, *Sūtrakṛtāṅga* II.I.17).[15] The moral capacity of "dharma" in all of India's classical religious traditions speaks to its *perfection.*

"Dharma" is often used to refer to matters whose violation or minimization leads to the venting of anger. As noted earlier, Indians were apt to cash out the content of "dharma" as consisting in such notions as "compassion, generosity, truth, purity, tenderness and goodness",[16] and "abstention from injuring (creatures), veracity, abstention from unlawfully appropriating (the goods of others)" and "purity" (Manu X.63). The trend continues when we turn to works attributed to philosophers. The great Mahāyāna Buddhist philosopher Nāgārjuna in the *Ratnāvali*[17] explains dharma as consisting in *dāna* (gift giving, charity, liberality, self-sacrifice) *śīla* (praiseworthy precepts) and *kṣamā* (forgiveness or patience) (II.25). Likewise, the Jain Digambara *ācārya* (MASTER), Kundakunda, in his *Pravacanasāra*, commented on by Amritacandra Sūri's *Tattvadīpikā*, explains dharma as *cāritra* (right conduct) *suśīla* (good precepts) and the "veneration of gods, the teacher and ascetics" (I.7, I.69). When authors of Indian philosophy use "dharma" *expressively,* it certainly does not pertain to matters that they are apt to vent anger *at*—though it refers to matters that people are apt to get angry *over*. Hence, "dharma" is a term that lacks the property of *focus*.

Finally, "dharma" appears to pick up and put down *extentions* freely in Indian philosophy. On top of having *deontic* and *aretaic* meanings, "dharma" refers to doctrines (Buddhism, Jainism), constituents of reality (Buddhism), motion (Jainism), cosmic laws (Buddhism), properties, attributes, causes (Buddhism) and the character of a thing (Yoga, Viśiṣṭādvaita).[18] The varied uses of "dharma" with no *extentional* consistency imply that "dharma" lacks substantive content restrictions on its use. Hence, "dharma" is a *formal* term.

On the bases of such considerations, and against the backdrop of the Anger Inclination Thesis, "dharma" is a *perfect formal* moral term, without *focus*. Hence, it is an exact translational match for the terms "ethics" or "moral". As would be expected, "dharma" betrays an additional feature of such terms (2.4.5. Terms that Designate the Field of Moral Concern pp.78–79). It is used to name a field of inquiry in which people can have differing opinions. This is how "dharma" is used in "*dharmaśāstra*" ("treatise on dharma"). The term is also used in this fashion in a classical Jain scripture, when Mahāvīra criticizes philosophers of contrary moral persuasions for proffering a "Dharma of their own" (S II.i.17).

The bare moralness of "dharma" in classical Indian thought is evident from the fact that it stands for things that people are inclined to get angry over. However, Indian classical texts also refer to the connection between the *anger inclination* and "dharma". For instance, in the Pāli Canon, the Buddha criticizes those who master *dhamma* simply for the sake of reproaching others (MN I.133). This presupposes, of course, that *dhamma*, or dharma, is something that one can reproach others over. Part of the contents of "reproach" are abrasive emotions that people do not like to be on the receiving end of. To reproach, thus, is to express the *anger inclination*. This small passage confirms that classical Indians themselves (the Buddha and his followers, at least) affirmed the relationship between "dharma" (in this case, "*dhamma*") and the *anger inclination.*

Vālmīki's *Rāmāyaṇa* bears witness to an explicit venting of anger in connection with "dharma" too. The scene in question takes place in the forest. A party has arrived to convince Rāma, a crown prince deposed from the thrown, to abort a fourteen-year exile in the forest. In the process, one of the royal counsellors, Jābāli, tries to offer a positivistic argument to persuade Rāma that nothing could be profited from remaining in the forest. In the process, Jābāli criticizes many Vedic practises as irrational and foolish.

After listening to Jābāli, Rāma rejects Jābāli's case on orthodox, Brahmanic, grounds, but also by arguing that if he followed Jābāli's advice, he would be acting contrary to his *prima facie* duties as a leader of his people. By the end of Rāma's lengthy response, a surprising change in his humour has occurred: Rāma has gone from being spirited to annoyed, to finally, outright angry. Rāma wraps up his response by stating that:

> I denounce the action mentioned below, of my father, who appointed you as his counsellor-priest, a staunch *nāstika*, who has not only strayed away from the path of dharma but whose mind is set on an un-Vedic path, who is moving about in the world with such an ideology as has been set forth in your foregoing speech. It is a well-known fact that a follower of Buddha deserves to be punished precisely as a thief [because such a heretic robs people of their faith in a Vedically moral universe]; and know a *nāstika* to be on a par with a Buddhist .... (Vālmīki II.108.33–34)

What is truly remarkable about this passage is that it shows Rāma *denouncing* an act of his father.[19] For our purposes, this seeming turncoat behaviour of Rāma is informative for it illustrates the *anger inclination* in connection with "dharma". Not only are Rāma's emotions expressed in the text, but they are also referred to:

> To the high-souled Śrī Rāma—who had never before felt dejected at heart or spoke angrily—the Brahman Jābāli now politely addressed the following wholesome and truthful words, which showed his belief in the authority of the Vedas, the other world and so on .... Perceiving Śrī Rāma to be angry, Vaśiṣtha [the Royal Family's preceptor] too pleaded with Rāma for Jābāli's sake: "Jābāli also recognizes the departure of the human soul from this world and its return to the mortal plane ...." (Vālmīki II.108.37–38)

To summarize the findings of the present section, we may note that "dharma" in classical Indian thought displays the properties of *perfection*, *formality* (or the lack of *substantiveness*) and it lacks *focus*. Schematically, such a term can be represented as having the moral meaning of: + *perfection*, - *focus*, - *substantiveness*. This is the schema of the terms "ethics" and "moral" as well. This schema represents the *intension* of the concept that the terms "ethics" and "moral" stand for. Thus, it appears that "dharma", in classical Indian thought, stands for the same concept as "ethics" and "moral" and it is thus a translational synonym for these terms, when it appears in the language of Indian philosophy. Moreover, we should note that the information that is often adduced for the conclusion that "dharma" has many meanings in classical Indian thought (the *extentions* of "dharma"), in the context of the Anger Inclination Thesis, constitutes evidence towards "dharma"'s *formality*. The objective evidence regarding the uses of "dharma" in classical Indian thought—its endless variety of *extentions* and the fact that the *anger inclination* is understood to be associated with "dharma" by classical Indians themselves—suggests that the varied uses of "dharma" in classical Indian thought are all a function of a unitary, moral meaning.

2.6.3. "Dharma" and the Fact–Value Distinction

A misgiving regarding the meaning of "dharma" expressed by W. Halbfass (1988 pp.311–13) and T.M.P. Mahadevan (1951 p.320) is that "dharma" fails to respect distinctions fundamental to Western thought; specifically the distinction between the ethical order, on the one hand, and the cosmological, physical, or natural order, on the other. Does this speak against the possibility that "dharma" means *ETHICS*?

The response to this misgiving consists in two parts. The first consists in pointing out that the Anger Inclination Thesis, and the theory of moral terms ancillary to it, eschews attempts to fix the meaning of "ethics" in terms of specific *extentions*. It is perfectly consistent with the Anger Inclination Thesis that some persons should think that physical matters are simply factual and not morally important, while others hold that such items are morally important, and that a failure to respect, regard or maximize them is grounds to express anger.

Second, the view that the distinction between the ethical order, on the one hand, and the cosmological, physical, or natural order, on the other, is fundamental to Western thought, is historically mistaken. The distinction that both Mahadevan and Halbfass allude to is commonly known in contemporary philosophical literature as the fact–value distinction, or the view that there is a logical difference between statements of facts and statements of value. While for many the distinction appears to enshrine a logical truism, the distinction comes rather later in the history of Western philosophy, and it is not even a mainstay. Hume in his *Treatise of Human Nature* is generally credited with founding the distinction (cf. Sare-McCord 1995 p.260, Putnam 2002 pp.14-24). It gains currency with the rise of Positivism in the nineteenth century (a movement that often looks on Hume as a precursor) and is taken up in force by the Logical Positivists as well as the social sciences.

The view that morality is built into the fabric of reality, and thus into the cosmos, is as old as the Western tradition itself. For Plato, it is the Good that regulates the nature of the Forms, which, when instantiated, constitute the physical universe. While physical reality constitutes a privation of Goodness, and is judged harshly on that account, it is all the same a moral state of affairs that has the Good as its ultimate formal cause. The relationship between morality and the universe is picked up and stressed in the thought of Neo-Platonists, like Plotinus, who explicitly call matter "Evil" (*Ennead* I.8). This way of looking at moral matters continues to show up in versions of Utilitarianism, which define *utiles* as quantifiable features of the universe. The idea that facts are values too seems to play a role in the thought of some moderns, like Spinoza (in his notion of Substance) and Leibniz (in his Monadology). The view that facts are values too has had many exponents in the Existentialist and Phenomenological tradition, starting, arguably, with Nietzsche. Given the history of Western axiological thought, if there is something more fundamentally Western, it seems that it is not the fact–value distinction but the idea that facts are values too.

2.6.4. When Moral Failings are not Frowned Upon

Another use of "dharma" that might seem at odds with its use as a moral term is the use of "dharma" to name matters of ritual import—particularly the means of bringing about a ritual objective; be it purity, or the benefit of a sacrifice. Those who are familiar with Hindu—and particularly Brahmanic—ritual, will be impressed by the extent to which "dharma" is used to name such matters.

The interpretation of "dharma" as something relevant to ritual purity is not an invention of modern Indology. Traditionally, too, we find that authors were aware that "dharma" often had an overtly ritualistic *extention*, to be distinguished from its ability to designate matters of obligation or virtue. For instance, at one point in his commentary on the *Bhagavad Gītā*, Rāmānuja suggests that "dharma" can be taken to stand not only for rules of obligation, but also, distinctly, for rules pertaining to the ritual expiation of sin. This distinction is important for Rāmānuja because he is trying to interpret *Gītā* 18:66, where Kṛṣṇa exhorts us to "Give up all dharmas"—and the significance of this passage greatly depends upon whether we take him to be designating obligation, or rules pertaining to ritual purity.

Such ritualistic uses of "dharma" appear to contradict the interpretation of the term that I have been proffering. On my account, "dharma" is a *perfect formal*, moral term. Hence, what it indicates in all its various uses, in traditional Indian thought, is the *anger inclination*. It is because "dharma" indicates the *anger inclination* that we can be confident in its moral significance. The apparent problem for my hypothesis is that ritualistic matters appear to be things that people are not inclined to get angry about.

For instance, consider the following passage from Manu'a *Dharmaśāstra*.

> Having killed a cat, an ichneumon, a blue jay, a frog, a dog, an iguana, an owl, or a crow, he [a *Brahmin*] shall perform the penance for the murder of a *Sūdra*; Or he may drink milk during three days, or walk one hundred *yoganas*, or bathe in a river, or mutter the hymn addressed to the Waters. (Manu XI.132–133)

Any of these expiatory measures would be called a "dharma" by the faithful. The question for us is whether any of these dharmas are moral in nature. According to the Anger Inclination Thesis, if these dharmas are the kinds of things that people are *inclined* to get angry over, they are moral matters. The critic will argue that a failure to drink milk for three days, or mutter the hymn to the Waters (even in the case of someone who has killed the relevant animal) is not a trigger for the expression of anger in the classical Indian context.

Ritualistic dharmas are not the only kinds of "dharmas" that classical Indians seemed not to anger over. There are other dharmas—qualified dharmas—that Indians seemed not to anger over. An example of what I intend to designate by "qualified dharma" is the *bhāgavatadharma* spoken about in the *Bhāgavata Purāṇa*.

The *Bhāgavata Purāṇa* sharply distinguishes worldly dharma from a distinct kind of dharma, that it calls the "*bhāgavatadharma*". The normal kind of dharma, according to the *Bhāgavata Purāṇa*, is the type founded upon the strictures of the Vedas, and consists, largely, in duties pertaining to one's caste and station in life. *Bhāgavatadharma*, in contrast, is the norm for the devotee:

> Most men living the life of the householder care only for ... Dharma, Artha and Kāma (duty, wealth and pleasure). (Dharma consists in the performance of Vedic rituals and charitable acts with a view to gaining felicity in the higher worlds; Artha in the acquisition of wealth; and Kāma, in the pursuit of pleasure.) Men pursue these ends time and again without satiation. Being full of self-centred desires, a man is insensitive to the *bhāgavatadharma*—the path of devotion to the Supreme Being. His faith is in the *Devas* [demigods] and *Pitṛs* [manes], and he adores them with the performance of sacrifices dedicated to them .... In contrast to the above are person who follow the *bhāgavatadharma*. They do not look upon or utilize their *Svadharma* [i.e. their own moral obligation] as a means for attaining self-centred objects like power, pleasure and heavenly felicity. Being devoid of desires for worldly pleasures and attainments, they work without attachment, dedicating the fruits of their actions to the Lord. They are calm and pure-minded. They are devoted only to spiritual values, having abandoned all self-centred and egoistic objectives. Through the performance of *Svadharma* with detachment and dedication, they attain to purity of being. (*Bhāgavata Purāṇa* III.32.1–6)

Bhāgavatadharma is reminiscent of the *bhaktiyoga* of the *Bhagavad Gītā*, except that *bhāgavatadharma* is a kind of dharma, and not simply a kind of yoga. Like the case of expiatory dharmas, it is difficult to imagine that classical Indians would have gotten angry if someone failed to inculcate *bhāgavatadharma*.

There are other qualified employments of "dharma" that also seem not to occasion anger if violated. In the *Śāntiparva* section of the *Mahābhārata*, Yudhiṣṭira contemplates whether he ought to renounce *rājadharma* (the moral duty of a king) and pursue *mokṣadharma* (path geared towards procuring liberation). While *rājadharma* is something that might occasion disapproval should someone shirk it, it is difficult to imagine that a failure of someone to pursue *mokṣadharma* will get anyone angry.

To summarize, the criticism under consideration is that there are a good number of things called "dharma" that people in the classical Indian setting do not get angry over, if they are violated. The criticism aims to show that such uses of "dharma" cannot be moral, for, according to the Anger Inclination Thesis, only those matters that people are inclined to get angry over are moral in nature.

The response to the criticism does not take to task the claim that the dharmas in question are the kinds of thing that people do *not* get angry over. The Anger Inclination Thesis does not claim that only those issues that people *do* get angry over are moral in nature. It claims that those issues that people are *inclined* to get angry over are those that are moral, and moreover, that there are mitigating reasons that may counter-balance the inclination to anger, resulting in no expression of anger in many cases. We encountered this phenomenon when reviewing the matter of supererogation (2.3.7.3. Supererogation pp.63–66). Supererogatory matters, such as heroism and saintliness, in contrast to nonmoral matters, are what people are inclined to get angry over if they are violated. Yet, in the case of *strong supererogation*, people have overwhelming mitigating reasons that offset such inclinations to anger. The effect of these mitigating reasons is that people do not get angry at failures to be saintly and heroic, and moreover, they, on consideration, choose never to get angry over such matters.

The cases of dharmas that classical Indians do not get angry over, if they are violated, are similar to the case of supererogation. In fact, a few of the dharmas that have been noted in this section are Indian examples of supererogation. For instance, *bhāgavatadharma* is arguably a supererogatory matter—something that is, strictly speaking, above and beyond the call of duty. For one can fulfil one's duty—or *svadharma*—

without having to resort to *bhāgavatadharma*, and yet, its inculcation is morally praiseworthy. This implies that for the *bhāgavata* who takes the notion of *bhāgavatadharma* seriously, it is a genuine dharma—something that they are inclined to get angry over, if it is violated. Yet, they have strong mitigating reasons that offset their inclination to anger that include the difficulty of inculcating *bhāgavatadharma*; the fact that it is self-denying and contrary to the natural impulses of persons and, moreover, the fact that one can also accomplish one's moral obligations without having to inculcate *bhāgavatadharma*. *Bhāgavatadharma* concerns the inculcation of an aretaic, supererogatory state.

Mokṣadharma is very much like *bhāgavatadharma*, except that it involves giving up worldly pursuits—which in the case of a king, involves the waging of war—and pursuing the life of a recluse. Thus, unlike *bhāgavatadharma*, which largely appears to be an *aretaic* matter, *mokṣadharma* has a *deontic* component to it. Yet it also appears to be a supererogatory matter, for it is something morally praiseworthy, which does not evoke anger if it is not practised. Mitigating reasons that function as a suppressor of anger in the case of failures to practise *mokṣadharma* would include those relevant to *bhāgavatadharma*—e.g. it is a difficult matter that is contrary to natural impulses. As well, there are other considerations. For instance, a person who pursues *mokṣadharma* is likely forsaking some other moral matter, which may not be supererogatory, like *rājadharma*. *Mokṣadharma* thus appears to be an instance of supererogation that Mellema (1996) describes—a matter that is not a means to accomplishing one's normal duties, but is yet morally praiseworthy, and exceeds what is normally expected of people. In the absence of such mitigating reasons, *mokṣadharma* would be something that occasions the expression of anger, if it is violated, for those who countenance it as a genuine dharma.

The case of ritualistic dharmas that are a means to expiation of ritual impurity is challenging, as it does not appear to be a matter of supererogation—there is nothing either saintly or heroic about undertaking a dharma to counteract some *deontic* transgression. Yet, I would argue, it bears a resemblance to matters of supererogation: in the case of ritual dharmas, there are mitigating reasons that offset inclinations to get angry upon failures to respect the relevant dharmas. What could the relevant mitigating reasons be?

In the case of expiatory dharmas, there are two mitigating reasons that I can think of, which seem to offset the faithful's inclination to get angry over a failure to respect the relevant dharma. One mitigating reason consists in the consideration that, a person who fails to undertake an appropriate expiatory dharma will themselves suffer as a result of the consequences of their polluting actions. In other words, those who neglect expiatory dharmas are themselves the losers, and hence, sympathy for the morally polluted person's misfortune mitigates the anger that the onlooker has. Another reason that expiatory dharmas do not elicit anger if they are not adhered to is that expiation itself is, in the Kantian tradition, what is called an "imperfect duty". An imperfect duty is a duty that is not completely specified as to how it is to be accomplished. The hallmark of expiation, in the Brahmanic context, is that there is always more than one way to atone for some sin. Hence, a failure to undertake any particular expiatory dharma is not necessarily a moral failing, though a failure to atone for sin by whatever means is a moral failing.

What we have been concerned with in this section are moral failings that are not frowned upon. Supererogation is a subset of such moral matters, as is the matter of ritual expiation.

2.7. An Argument for the Reform View

This chapter has been devoted to arguing that "dharma" always has the singular meaning of a moral term in classical Indian thought. This thesis is important to establish for, one of the obstacles to interpreting Indian philosophy on the matter of ethics is finding a Sanskritic term that is commensurate with "ethics" or "morality". If "dharma" of classical India is the semantic equivalent of these two terms, we can be justified in interpreting philosophical passages that deal with the topic of dharma, or mention "dharma" itself, as marking off Indian philosophical discourse on ethics.

To establish that "dharma" has a moral meaning in classical Indian thought, it was important to attend to the question of how to define moral statements and terms, independently of the question of the meaning of "dharma". For only having determined the meaning of moral statements and terms, could we, without begging any questions, determine whether "dharma" is a moral term.

As a prelude to the question of the meaning of moral statements, moral terms, and the term "dharma" in particular, the distinction between the intention associated with a term, and its *extention*, was defined. Against the backdrop of this distinction, it is apparent that most commentators on Indian thought have attempted to come up with a definition of "dharma" based on its *extentions*. The outcome of the focus on the *extentions* of "dharma" is the conclusion that "dharma" is a term that eludes all attempts at definition: it is a term that is used in a bewildering variety of ways; a term that stands for several distinct concepts.

Once *intention* is recognized as a genuine element of meaning, and moreover, once it is recognized that some terms can be defined completely with reference to their typical *intention* only, the observation that "dharma" is used to name several different matters is hardly evidence against it having a moral meaning in all such circumstances. Any *extension* we attribute to "dharma" is consistent with an Intentionalist account of the meaning of "dharma". In other words, there is nothing contradictory about the claim that "dharma" is a moral term when it is used as a label for such things as the constituents of reality, or the Principle of Motion, if moral terms have their meaning in their *intention*.

The irony of studying the meaning of "dharma" in contemporary Indology is that more progress would have been made if researchers had reflected on the behaviour of evaluative terms, and less time on philological questions on what "dharma" is applied to. "Good" is an evaluative term that frequently functions as a moral term, and it is a term that has many different *extentions*. If commentators had applied the same methodology to determining the meaning of "good" that they use in the effort to come to terms with "dharma", they would have concluded that "good" is irreducible to anyone definition, for "good" can be meaningfully applied to anything that a speaker wishes to call "good". This of course, is the mark of an *intentional* term: its list of *extentions* is open-ended—not because there is no truth or falsity to *intentional* claims, but because, in some basic way, we can always understand what a person means when they use an *intentional* term like "good", regardless of whether we agree or not.

In conclusion, why ought we to regard "dharma" as always having a moral meaning in classical Indian thought? There are several reasons in support of this view. First, as noted, many terms are definable with respect to their *intention* only (2.1. Extention and Intention pp.13–22). The Orthodox View—the major critic of the possibility of the Reform View—which attempts to convince us that "dharma" has several meanings in classical Indian thought, is without credit. It is based on the unargued assumption that the *extention* of "dharma" always is, or contributes to, its meaning. Second, the Extentionalism that fuels and supports the Orthodox View leads to an inaccurate account of key philosophical terms; an account that is incapable of modelling the kind of meaningful disagreement that we find in philosophy (2.2. Key Philosophical Terms pp.22–31). Third, "dharma" is a term that is ubiquitous in the literature of classical India, and it shows up prominently in philosophical texts (1.2. The Problem of "Dharma" pp.5–9); its *extentions* are particularly divergent in philosophical contexts, suggesting that it is a key philosophical term (one which cannot be defined with respect to *extentions*). Fourth, the uses of "dharma" in classical Indian thought conform to the schema of a special kind of moral term: it bears the schema of *perfection*, *formality*, and a lack of *focus*, which is the same schema that defines "ethical" and "moral", according to the Anger Inclination Thesis (2.6.2. Traditional Meaning of "Dharma" pp.95–98). Fifth, after a review of accounts of moral meaning (2.3. Definitions of Moral Statements p.31–70), only the Anger Inclination Thesis presents itself as the accurate account (2.3.8. Composite Accounts of Moral Statements pp.66–70). In its favour, it is a purely Intentionalist account of moral meaning. Hence, it is capable of modelling the kind of meaningful disagreement we find in philosophy. It attributes no significant philosophical views to those who meaningfully use moral language (and hence, it does not improperly intrude upon substantive philosophical debate) (2.5. Anger Inclination and Debate pp.85–91). Finally, it accurately picks out the defining feature of moral issues: their potential explosiveness (2.3.7. Anger Inclination pp.53–66). As the usual reasons adduced for the equivocality and ambiguity of "dharma" are inconclusive, and consistent with "dharma" being a key philosophical term, which is definable without reference to *extentions*, it follows that there is no good reason to suppose that "dharma" meant anything else but *ETHICS* or *MORAL* in the language of Indian philosophy: the facts about the use of "dharma" (2.6.2. Traditional Meaning of "Dharma" pp.95–98)—its endless list of *extentions*, and the *anger inclination* that Indians themselves seemed to associate with the term—are on the side of the Reform View.

Notes

1 The *Port Royal Logic* is a treatise on logic, authored by Antoine Arnauld, Pierre Nicole, and possibly Pascal, and originally entitled *La logique, ou L'art de penser*—the authors were all connected with a convent at Port-Royal-des-Champs in France (Nadler 1995 p.632). For references to the *Port Royal Logic*, see Arnauld 1964 pt.II ch.17; cf. pt.I. ch.6.

2 The term "phenomenology" has appeared more than once in the history of philosophy, often denoting different endeavours. For instance, the

term appears twice in the thought of Kant, and in the title of Hegel's "Phenomenology of Spirit". Etymologically, the term "phenomenology" stands for a study of "phenomenon". "Phenomenon" often, though not always, stands for observable events. The term "phenomenology" came to stand for a school of philosophy led by Edmund Husserl in the early part of the twentieth century. The school of thought attempted a scientific (systematic) analysis of phenomenon. Early, Husserlian, Phenomenologists were keen to come to grasp phenomenon without the cloud of prejudice or assumptions. Martin Heidegger, a pupil of Husserl, is famous in the history of Phenomenological thought for criticizing this approach to Phenomenology. Heidegger, in contrast, insisted that experience of phenomenon is always already interpreted. Intentionality was particularly important for the early Phenomenologists, as it seemed to be the key mediating factor in the presentation of phenomenon. For a concise introduction to these topics, see Richard Schmitt's article "Husserl, Edmund" (Schmitt 1967 vol.4 p.96–99) and "Phenomenology" (Schmitt 1967 vol.6 pp.135-151).

3 Readers familiar with the recent literature in metaethics and the philosophy of language might be at a loss to see why I have opted for the idiosyncratic distinction between extention and intention, when there is a similar distinction in the literature: the distinction between the referential function of language, and the expressive function. The expressive function of language is what allows us to voice that we regard some item as good or frightening—this function allows us not to simply describe our minds, but to give voice to our perspective. Likewise, what I have called the extention of a concept seems to be nothing more than the referent. The reason that I have not opted for the conventional distinction is that while the idea of intentionality is quite wide, the idea of the expressive function of language is quite narrow. Language functions expressively when we use it to express ourselves. However, language functions intentionally, on my account, when it refers to the mental state of being about something. Thus, while I shall argue that moral concepts are intentional, they need not be used expressively, and hence expressivity is not essential to their nature. (See 2.4.2. Double Role of Some Moral Terms p.74.) This is why I do not regard my account as a version of Expressivism, or the view that moral concepts are essentially expressive devices. Also, on this account, intentionality is as much a referent of a term as what intentions are about, i.e. the extention. Hence, the idea of reference is too wide to cover the more specific issue of extentionality as I present it.

4 Readers familiar with a distinction in the recent ethics literature between thick and thin ethical concepts (cf. Williams 1985) will recognize that my account of pure intentional concepts and those of a mixed intentional-extentional variety provides a way to understand this distinction: pure intentional concepts are thin, while the mixed variety are thick. The following section, 2.2. Key Philosophical Terms (pp.22–31), puts the issue in

the wider context of the type of concepts that philosophy is concerned with. See also 2.4. Definition of Moral Terms (pp.70–85), where the distinction between thick and thin concepts is further cashed-out in terms of what I call formal and substantive moral terms.

5 Definitional Naturalists can be distinguished from Metaphysical Naturalists, like Utilitarians. The latter hold that substantively correct applications of moral terms are predicated of certain *extentions*: particularly, happiness or pleasure. While the former is a metamoral view, the latter is a substantive ethical view about what makes a moral judgement correct. For an explication on this nomenclature, see the discussion in 5.2. On the Pursuits that Answer to "Ethics" (pp.194–201).

6 That we often have good political reasons for compromising our moral convictions seems to be one of the main themes of Rawls's *Political Liberalism* (1996).

7 Other philosophers have held similar views on the relationship between anger and moral judgement. See for instance Allan Gibbard (Darwall, Gibbard, and Railton 1992 p.151) and P.F. Strawson (1962).

8 This attitude of Plato's shows up in the "Divided Line" (*Republic* 507–511e). Plato's tendency to deride things removed from The Good also shows up in his tirade against poetry and the fine arts at the end of the *Republic* (*Republic* 600e–601a).

9 Rawls writes: "... the political conception is a module, an essential constituent part, that fits into and can be supported by various reasonable comprehensive doctrines that endure in the society regulated by it" (Rawls 1996 p.13).

10 Leonard Priestley has voiced the following concern over this line of argument. He writes to me: "As you note ... a child not getting his own way gets angry, and I don't think it works to argue that the child necessarily has a moral conviction that he ought to get his own way (though a child may in time perhaps come to think of it in that way). *He simply wants what he wants, and when he doesnt get what he wants, he becomes frustrated and angry.* Animals similarly get angry when they don't get what they want" (my italics). A key issue it appears to me is whether the child (or animal) in question can be said to have an inclination to get angry. If the anger that a child (or animal) feels when they do not get their way is simply a physiological reaction (to say, being hungry) or is simply a show of emotion, with no underlying belief concerning desert prompting the emotion, then it would be incorrect to attribute a moral belief to the child (or animal) in question. For, in such a circumstance, we would be hard pressed to say that the child in question has an *inclination* to get angry. If the child has an inclination to get angry over certain matters, then it is not so easy for us to dismiss the burst of emotion as unconnected to any ideas that the child

might have regarding desert. For inclinations, as I understand the concept, are internal to a person's belief structure. So, if Prof. Priestley is correct about the nature of the child's tantrum, as unconnected to any underlying inclination, then the Anger Inclination Thesis is behind his conviction that such circumstances do not express moral convictions.

11 Moral terms that do not have *extentional* referents are moral operators, like "ought" and "ought not", or "should" and "should not". All such terms, as a rule, appear to be *virtually perfect* moral terms—at least in the English Language. The concept *VIRTUAL PERFECTION* is explained on p.77.

12 The Extentionalist would disagree. All moral terms for the Extentionalist have *substantive content*. Terms like "ethical" and "moral" on the Extentionalist's account consistently refer to the same *substantive* matters. This, for instance, is the view of the Definitional Naturalist. But the Extentionalist's view has been shown to be unacceptable (2.2. Key Philosophical Terms pp.22–31). Based on arguments presented earlier, the implication here for us is that the Extentionalist (including the Definitional Naturalist) is incorrect in the view that all moral terms are *substantive* in nature.

13 The nomenclature of "metaethical" and "metamoral" jumps ahead of the argument. These are treated later in 5.2. On the Pursuits that Answer to "Ethics" (pp.194–201).

14 I offer this account not as a justification of the view that "dharma" means *RELIGION*, but as an explanation of how it is that the opinion ever got off the ground.

15 The term "*nāstika*" is a term of criticism. Literally, it means "negativist" and ironically it is frequently applied to persons who we would call today "Positivists" (critics will still regard them as negativists though). The *intentional* content of the term is captured, I believe, in the notion of "a good for nothing that rejects and disrupts all decency". The use of the term, it seems to me, expresses anger, and the *anger inclination*.

16 Seventh Aśokan Pillar Edict: Delhi-Topra. Translated by N.K. Wagle and Gibbons of the University of Toronto.

17 Recently, the authenticity of the text has been called into questioned by some who do not believe that Nāgārjuna had anything to do with innovations in the Buddhist tradition like the Mahāyāna movement. (See Franco 1989 and Vetter 1992.) While this is an interesting question in certain limited contexts, this is not one of those contexts. Presently, what is important is not who wrote the text but rather whether it serves as an example of traditional opinions on the content of dharma. Given that the text was widely cited in classical times (and attributed to Nāgārjuna) it serves this purpose well.

18 Such uses are largely reported in Grimes 1996 pp.112–114.

[19] This is the same crown prince who had just spent several cantos defending his father's act of exiling him to the forest against all manner of persuasion—including the argument that his father had no right to promise any such thing to anyone. See Bharata's tirade against his parents at Vālmīki II: 106.

Chapter 3

The *Classical* Meaning of "Dharma"

In the previous chapter I argued that an *intentionally* conceived "dharma" is consistent with its various uses in classical Indian thought, and moreover, that the *intentional* mould that "dharma" and that other *formal* moral terms like "ethics" and "morality" fit is the same; the idea of a *perfect formal*, moral term, without *focus* (2.6.2. Traditional Meaning of "Dharma" pp.95–98). This liberal, purely Intentionalist, conception of moral terms runs counter to commonplace intuitions about moral meaning—intuitions that cherish the notion that morality has to do with persons, pro-social matters or conduct. These intuitions ignore that morality can be about, nonconduct, character-oriented matters. They also fail to gel with the fact that Western thinkers of the stature of Plato have applied moral terms to impersonal matters. If these intuitions took all the facts into account, they too would conclude that the classical Indian uses of "dharma" for varied ontological matters (such as the constituents of reality, or the Principle of Motion) are in keeping with a kind of moral thinking that we find in the West as well; just as Plato thought that the Form of Forms is Good, and Plotinus thought that matter is Evil, Buddhists thought that the constituents of reality are ethical, and Jains thought that Motion is Moral. The ancient Indians, and the Platonistic thinkers, thus, appear to subscribe to the same over-arching school of moral thought; a school that can be called "Moral Impersonalism"—the view that morality, in the first instance, pertains to impersonal matters. The intuition that morality always pertains to social or conduct-oriented matters is, on examination, without historical foundation.

Against the backdrop of the Anger Inclination Thesis, there is a simple argument to be made for why all classical uses of "dharma" are moral. *Ex hypothesi*, it is in the very nature of "dharma", as a *formal*, moral, term, without *focus*, to name diverse matters that various philosophers should choose to apply it to. In other words, given the Anger Inclination Thesis, and its account of moral terms, it is reasonable to expect that "dharma", as a *formal* moral term, retains its essential moral meaning when used for the constituents of reality, or the Principle of Motion: it is in the very nature of "dharma" as a meaningful moral term, without *substantive* content, to be a label for these matters.

Yet, those who are for the idea that "dharma" is equivocal (or ambiguous) have additional reasons for supposing that not all uses of "dharma" in classical Indian thought are moral in nature, which have not yet been raised. Having set out my basic argument for the Reform View (the view that "dharma" has just one, moral meaning in the classical Indian circumstance, which is the meaning of all key philosophical moral terms, like "ethics" and "moral"), I shall attempt to explicate all additional arguments against the Reform View that a defender of Orthodoxy might have in 3.1. Arguments Against the Reform View (pp.116–129). After explicating such criticisms I shall respond to them in 3.2. Defence of the Reform View (pp.129–167).

The case for the Reform View is made not only through responding to criticisms, but also in considering its advantages. In 3.3. Metatheoretical Considerations (pp.157–167), I shall bring explicit attention to metatheoretical considerations that are pertinent to deciding between the Reform, Conservative and Orthodox Views. Before concluding the argument for the Reform View, I shall entertain criticisms of my defence of the Reform View in 3.4. Critics Reprisal (pp.158–167). I shall then summarize the reasons for favouring the Reform View over competing views in 3.5. Four Theories of "Dharma" in Review (pp.167–176).

Because the Anger Inclination Thesis has been argued for as the correct account of moral terms and statements in 2.3. Definitions of Moral Statements (p.31) certain arguments against the Reform View and for the Orthodox View can be dismissed at the outset as having already been dealt with—if, only, implicitly. For instance, one could make the argument on the basis of the Social Content Thesis that "dharma" has more than one meaning, for not all uses of "dharma" concern social matters, and for moral matters are necessarily social in nature. Likewise, one might attempt to argue that on the basis of the Conduct Thesis, it follows that "dharma" has many meanings, for not all uses of "dharma" pertain to conduct, though moral issues necessarily do. These are arguments for the view that "dharma" is equivocal, which are based upon Extentionalist views of moral terms. One could also make the case that "dharma" has more than one meaning on the basis of the Overridingness Thesis, for not all uses of "dharma" concern the "greatest good" or the overriding norm within a particular belief system, though this idea is an essential feature of moral terms. Since these views, apart from the Anger Inclination Thesis, have already been criticized, arguments for the equivocal nature of "dharma" that are based on such views will not be considered. For, the response to all such attempts to argue that "dharma" has more than one meaning would consist in rehearsing the arguments already presented against these views.

It was already noted in the previous chapter that "dharma" in modern times has a meaning that is distinct from its meaning in classical Indian texts. In modern parlance, "dharma" is an *extentional* term meaning *RELIGION*. In classical times, it was argued, "dharma" functioned as an *intentional* term. Hence, the issue at hand is not whether the word "dharma" has more than one meaning—it was argued that there are at least two meanings to the term; a modern meaning and a classical meaning (2.6. The Meaning of "Dharma" pp.91–105). The issue before us is whether, in its classical life, "dharma" has only one meaning.

3.1. Arguments Against the Reform View

3.1.1. Argument from the Principle of Charity

The defender of the Orthodox View may attempt to defend the equivocality of "dharma" by invoking the *principle of charity*. The *principle of charity* is not primarily a principle of ethics: it is a principle purportedly involved in interpretation.

The *principle of charity* often comes up in discussions on *radical translation*—a scenario that bears a resemblance to our problem of interpreting classical Indian uses of "dharma". Radical translation is the circumstance where one person attempts to decipher, or translate, the statements made by another, in a language that they are just coming to learn, without the aid of instructors or translation manuals. The classic example of radical translation is the problem of the anthropologist, or linguist, attempting to understand the language of an isolated culture, about which the outside world knows little or nothing.

W.V.O. Quine, in his discussion of the problem of radical translation in *Word and Object* (1960 p.59), endorses the *principle of charity* and cites N.L. Wilson's formulation of it: "... select as a designatum that individual which will make the largest possible number of ... [some person's] statements true" (Wilson 1959 p.532). In the context of semantics and radical translation, the "designatum" or "individual" is an interpretation of the utterances in question. On this formulation, the *principle of charity* tells us to select that interpretation out of the set of possible interpretations that attributes the most amount of true statements to the speaker.

There are other formulations of the principle. Donald Davidson is famous for writing extensively on the topic, and according to John Upper (1995) Davidson presents three distinct formulations of the principle. Upper notes that Davidson, at many points (Davidson 1980 p.221, p.222, p.238; 1984 p.137, p.152, p.154, p.168, p.197; 1986 p.316), agrees with Wilson and

Quine's formulation of the principle; the *principle of charity*, on this view, compels us to select the interpretation that maximizes the *truth* of the speaker's statements. Thus, if we have two interpretations of a certain passage, and one interpretation has it that the passage in question claims that unicorns (winged horses with horns) exist, and another interpretation depicts the passage in question as talking about horses that have been dressed up with wings and horns, then, according to this account of the *principle of charity*, we should choose the latter interpretation (for, to date, it is not true that unicorns exist).

Upper notes that Davidson provides two other formulations of the *principle of charity.* At many places Davidson (1980 p.239; 1982 p.302; 1984 p.27, p.136, p.137, p.169, pp.196–197, pp.200–201; 1985a p.245) depicts the *principle of charity* as exhorting us to choose the interpretation that maximizes *agreement* between the interpreter and the interpreted. At other junctures, Davidson (1980 p.221, p.222, p.231, p.238; 1982 p.303; 1984 p.27, p.137, p.154, p.159; 1985b p.90; 1987 p.47; 1990a pp.24–25; 1990b pp.319–320, p.325) suggests that the *principle of charity* urges us to select the interpretation that most renders the beliefs or statements of the interpreted *rational.*

Upper is quick to point out that the "truth" and "rationality" formulations of the *principle of charity* are not identical, for what is rational is not necessarily true; *VERACITY* and *RATIONALITY* are distinct concepts (Upper 1995 p.8).

While there is an *extention* of "rational" that is distinct from "veracity", there is also an *extention* of "rational" that is identical with that of "veracity". To be rational, in this latter application of the term, is the same as being reasonable. Reason is concerned with truth. Minimally, reason concerns the preservation of truth. In a larger way, reason (or, perhaps, Reason) is concerned with the maximization of truth. On this view, to be reasonable is to attempt to maximize truth. "Rational", on this view, is code for "truthful" or "truth maximizing", and a set of beliefs that are relatively rational, in this manner, will also be relatively true. I think it is this *extention* of "rational" that Davidson has in mind.

On this latter *extention* of "rational", the view that the *principle of charity* exhorts us to select the most rational interpretation, and the view that the *principle of charity* exhorts us to select the interpretation with the most amount of true statements, both come down to the same thing.

What of the view that the *principle of charity* urges us to select an interpretation that maximizes *agreement*—is this a distinct conception of the *principle of charity*?

When two parties agree, it is because both of them believe the same things to be true. For one party to choose to interpret another party's views with a view to maximizing its truth is to select the interpretation that maximizes agreement between the two parties. Hence, from this perspective, the *agreement* construal of the *principle of charity*, and the *truth* maximizing formulation of the principle, come down to the same thing.

The notions of truth maximization, agreement maximization, and choosing to maximize the rationality of one's interlocutor's messages, are all different ways of formulating one and the same *principle of charity*. Davidson, I believe, is thus justified in formulating the principle in three different ways.

What is the motivation for adhering to the *principle of charity* in any of its forms? According to Quine, "[t]he common sense behind the maxim is that one's interlocutor's silliness, beyond a certain point, is less likely than bad translation, or, in the domestic case, linguistic divergence" (Quine 1960 p.59).

On the basis of the *principle of charity*, so construed, the following objection against the view that "dharma" has only one meaning in classical Indian thought can be made: it is an uncharitable interpretation, which leads us to impute to classical Indians beliefs that we (and arguably they) would not assent to, because they are not true, or because they are irrational. For instance, we today, typically, do not regard the constituents of reality as moral entities; nor do we consider motion, or the

Principle of Motion, to be a moral affair. The view that either of these matters is moral in nature is irrational—or at least, it is silly: no one in their right mind would say such things. If we interpret "dharma" as having more than one meaning in the classical context, we are spared from having to impute such ludicrous beliefs to classical Indians: we can reserve the moral meaning of "dharma" for matters that we think are moral matters, and understand that the ancient Indians were talking about nonmoral matters when it came to matters of ontology and metaphysics.

3.1.2. Evolutionary Perspective on Language

The defender of Orthodoxy might attempt another refutation of the view that "dharma" has only one meaning in classical Indian thought. This other approach starts from the empirical generalisation that language changes and that the meanings of terms are not fixed. On the basis of a sensitivity to the fluid nature of language, it can be argued that it is unlikely that "dharma" had just one meaning for the entire duration of classical Indian thought.

To make the argument even stronger, the defender of orthodoxy might point out that "moral" and "ethics" themselves are terms, in the history of Western thought, whose meanings have changed. "Moral" comes from the Latin word "*mores*" as "ethics" comes form the Greek word "*ethos*". Both "*mores*" and "*ethos*" mean something like "custom". What this suggests is that "moral" and "ethics" are not terms that always had moral meanings—for sure, they did not always have the same meaning. In ancient times, the *extentions* associated with these terms were far fewer than they are today. Moreover, in ancient times, it appears that both "moral" and "ethics" (or their ancient incarnations) were nonevaluative, *extentional* terms.

In more recent times, "moral" seems to have a nonethical meaning as well. In many circles, "moral" or "morality" pertains to the relatively narrow matter of sexual restraint. On this understanding, a person of "loose morals" is a person who is promiscuous—not necessarily someone who is not ethical. If "ethics" and "moral" are terms that have varied meanings over time, it stands to reason that "dharma" too had more than one meaning in ancient times.

3.1.3. Argument from Empiricism

The Intentionalist approach to reading "dharma" in classical Indian thought is being put forward as a panacea for our problems with understanding the place of ethics in classical Indian thought. In truth, it is no more than a placebo; a trick, which overlooks the hard evidence in favour of the view that "dharma" has many meanings in classical Indian thought.

The hard evidence in favour of the equivocal nature of "dharma" is the empirically observable fact that "dharma" is a term that is applied to diverse matters: in other words, "dharma" is a term with many *extentions*. The *intentions* that one speaks about are not really empirically observable facts: the Anger Inclination Thesis is a supposition that cannot be directly verified from linguistic behaviour, for, on the Anger Inclination Theorist's own admission, it is not the expression of anger that renders a matter moral in nature, but an *inclination* to express anger over some matter that renders it moral. Inclinations, like other *intentional* matters, are wholly mysterious entities that cannot either be confirmed or disconfirmed by empirical observation.

If we are to be good scientists, we need to rely solely upon the facts. And the fact of the matter is that "dharma" is a term that has many *extentions*. If meaning is to be a scientifically useful concept, then it must be the *extentions* of a term that is its meaning—for only *extentions* have a chance of being publicly observed.

3.1.4. Argument from Analogy

Leonard Priestley has shared with me the following criticism of the Reform View:

> The use of "dharma" to denote *ATTRIBUTE* does *not* imply that

> what is at stake is a moral issue unless we *assume* that all uses of "dharma" indicate a concern with moral values. But attributes are just attributes. This is like saying that the use of the term "property" to denote *ATTRIBUTE* implies that what is at stake is a legal issue, since ownership is a legal concern.

Let us call this the "Argument from Analogy". This argument attempts to show that the Reform View is misleading, for, if we follow its logic, we would have to conclude that "attribute" is a word for a legal concept. On the face of it, the criticism is cutting, for who would wish to suggest that "attribute" denotes the legal conception of property?

3.1.5. Problem with Translating Formal Moral Terms Consistently

The weakness of the Reform View, with its associated theory, the Anger Inclination Thesis, is apparent when we try to find a practical application for it. *Ex hypothesi*, moral terms are definable according to their schema, as set out in 2.4.3. Meaning of Moral Terms (pp.74–76). According to the argument set out there, "dharma", "ethics" and "moral" are really translational equivalents, or synonyms, for they have the same schema. However, if we were to always translate "dharma" as, say, "ethics" or "ethical", we would end up with statements that don't make much sense, or are misleading.

Consider the famous statement in the *Bhagavad Gītā* at 18:47—*śreyānsvadharma viguṇaḥ paradharmātvanuṣtitāt, svabhavniyatam karma kurvatnāpnoti kilibṣam.* "Dharma" appears twice in this statement and it is conventionally rendered as "duty". A typical translation of the statement runs:

> Better is one's own duty (*svadharma*), though ill-done, than the duty of another (*paradharma*), though well performed. When one does the duty ordained by his own nature, he incurs no stain.

Imagine that we should follow the advice given in 2.4.3. Meaning of Moral Terms (p.74). We would have to translate the statement as:

> Better is one's own morality, though ill-done, than the morality of another, though well performed. When one does the morality ordained by his own nature, he incurs no stain.

This translation is confusing and misleading, for in English, "one's morality" is a phrase that typically designates one's own ethical theory or ethical views. The same misleading consequence would occur if "dharma" were translated as "ethics". It would certainly make no sense if "dharma" were to be translated as "ethical" or "moral" ("Better one's own ethical ...").

The fact that "duty" for "dharma" appears to be the more appropriate translation in the case of *Gītā* at 18:47 suggests that the Orthodox View is right: the translation of "dharma" is best facilitated by stating the *extention* of "dharma" as its contextual synonym. In other words, it is untenable to hold that "dharma" has one, unitary, meaning. Rather, its meaning varies according to its *extention*.

3.1.6. The Character of Indian Philosophy

The Anger Inclination Thesis cannot be the right account of moral meaning, for if it were, it would imply that there is no ethics in Indian philosophy. Indian philosophy, above all else, promotes the values of renunciation, and in keeping with its ascetic tendencies, it particularly eschews anger. Indian philosophy is unanimously geared towards a dispassionate contemplation of ultimate principles. The Anger Inclination Thesis is out of character with Indian philosophy. And since Indian philosophy has some ethics in it, it follows that the Anger Inclination Thesis cannot be the correct account of moral meaning.

3.1.7. Grammatical Argument for Equivocality

There is a very simple justification for the Orthodox View, which has not been adumbrated yet. This justification pertains to the grammar of "dharma".

The defender of the Reform View wants to draw an analogy between Plato's use of the term "Good" for the Form of Forms, Plotinus's claim that matter is Evil, and the Indian uses of "dharma". For the Reform View, Indian uses of "dharma" that pertain to metaphysical matters are moral claims, after the fashion of Platonic claims. There are two problems with this view.

First, Plato's use of the term that is translated as "Good" in English does not pertain to any *particular* thing, but an abstract entity, which other things can partake of. Plotinus does apply "Evil" to something particular (matter) but here "Evil" is in an attributive construction. In the Western setting, thus, when we have moral terms applied to things of a nonpersonal, ontological nature, the moral term always stands for an abstract thing, a property or form that other concrete things can partake of. In the Indian setting, in contrast, "dharma" is not always used in this fashion.

When moral language appears in a cognitive construction (not noncognitive or imperative, like, "you ought to do x") that states some fact, almost as a rule, the moral term appears in an attributive construction—and when it is not in an attributive construction, it functions as a noun for the moral attribute itself. Textbook examples of such statements are "*x* is ethical", "that is not fair". In other words, in the Western setting, moral terms never appear as nouns (proper nouns) for *particular* things.

In the disputed uses of "dharma", as when it is used in Buddhist texts for the constituents of reality, or when it is used in Jain texts for the Principle of Motion, "dharma" stands neither for an abstract property, nor is it used as a predicate. Rather, "dharma" is a noun, designating a particular thing.

Eminent scholars who have endorsed the Orthodox View do so on sound grammatical ground. If "dharma" appeared as either (a) the name for an abstract entity like Plato's Good, or (b) as the predicate in a statement, they too would have entertained the notion that "dharma" is used in a moral sense in Indian thought, when it is applied to nonpersonal matters. However, they have not observed this, and thus, on the basis of the grammar of the statements containing "dharma", they have soundly concluded that "dharma" functions not as a moral term, but as a proper noun of sorts, which contextually designates the *extention* in question.

3.1.8. Appeal to Authority

The defender of Orthodoxy might make the following argument against the Reform View.

If we survey the learned opinion of those who have written on the meaning of "dharma", we find that the *virtually* unanimous view is that "dharma" is a term with many meanings; particularly in the classical setting. Thus, most all scholars of Buddhism do not hold that "dharma" has a moral meaning when it stands for constituents of reality. Likewise, scholars of Jainism do not assert that "dharma" has a moral meaning when it designates the Principle of Motion. Most scholars of Yoga do not hold that the Yoga use of the term "dharma" to stand for properties or attributes is moral in nature. Most scholars of traditional Hindu law do not regard the dharma of the law books as primarily moral in nature. If there is one thing we can thus deduce from learned opinion it is that "dharma" is not always a moral term.

The defender of Orthodoxy may say that the author of the present work voices a radical opinion that is not supported by other scholars or the literature. Prudence dictates that we put aside his recommendations and side with the authorities on Indian thought, eminent Sanskritists and historians of Indian philosophy. After all, they are the authorities on the matter.

3.1.9. Qualified Criticism

Joseph O'Connell has shared with me the following criticism of the Reform View—a criticism that I call the "Qualified Criticism".

According to this criticism, the Reform View is not

without its merits, but its validity is limited to an explanation of certain uses of "dharma":

> You may be right about a general tendency to approach dharma *extentionally*. But that may be justified to some extent by virtue of "dharma" itself being chock-full of *extentional* content—along with the (underlying? more fundamental? essential?) *intentional* component of its semantic range ... If you stick to a more nuanced argument—that the "fundamental" meaning of "dharma" is moral in nature—then who could object? It may indeed allow one to say that "dharma" as *intentional* means ETHICS when applied to human behaviour in social relations, but may mean something else when applied to nonhuman situations (or to human aspirations toward *mokṣa*).

There are two components to this criticism. One presumes the validity of some versions or hybrid of the Social-Content or Conduct Theses. I have argued against these views at an earlier point.

There is a second component to this qualified criticism that I have not dealt with in any explicit fashion: this is the suggestion that the fact that "dharma" is used to stand for different things implies that "dharma" actually has *extentional* layers or components to its meaning. If this is so, it seems that different uses of "dharma" with different *extentional* components constitute wholly different meanings.

3.1.10. Charge of Equivocation

A criticism that can be brought against the Reform View is that it is guilty of *equivocation*.

Equivocation is the use of an expression in two or more different senses in a single context (Wilson 1995 p.238). To equivocate, thus, is to rely upon the ambiguity of a word to gain argumentative ground. Technically, for a term to be ambiguous is for it to have more than one possible meaning, whose actual meaning is determined contextually.

According to this criticism, the Reform View improperly

reasons that simply because something is called "dharma" it must thereby be a moral matter. This inference about the moral significance of "dharma" is made not on the basis of the appropriate, contextually relevant, semantic content of "dharma", but via the coincidence of "dharma" standing for a moral notion in other contexts.

This criticism is similar to the 3.1.4. Argument from Analogy (pp.120–121), except that there, the criticism was that the Reform View *assumes* improperly that the actual word "dharma" has just one meaning (i.e. without argument) whereas here, the criticism is that the Reform View fails to take note of the linguistic fact that words with a certain phonemic identity may stand for distinct concepts with distinct (and often, unrelated) meanings.[1]

3.1.11. Argument from Family Resemblance Theory

The argument presented in favour of the Reform View has presumed that moral terms have a common, essential, meaning. If no moral term has a common, essential, meaning, but on the other hand if they have a range of meanings, there is then no reason to believe that "dharma" will always bear an essential moral meaning, though it may have a moral meaning sometime.

A hard-line position has been consistently adopted in the argument for the Reform View; that there is such a thing as an essential meaning to all moral terms. This approach to meaning is not terribly fashionable these days. Since Wittgenstein's *Philosophical Investigations*, a popular approach to meaning holds that concepts are defined by a range of meanings; that uses of any given concept bears a certain *family resemblance* with other uses of the same concept but that there is no one, common, meaning present in all its applications. A concept having this range of meanings is also known as a "*cluster concept*".

Even W.D. Falk, who is sympathetic to the view that we must understand moral terms in a *formal* light, argues that our current concept of morality vacillates between two distinct traditions of morality; the Christian and the Greek traditions (Falk 1963 p.28). The notion of morality grounded in the Christian tradition holds that the moral is that which is selfless and is motivated by a concern for others; in short, the Christian Tradition embodies the Social Content Thesis. The Greeks emphasized the defining role of principled decisions and actions in morality; the Universalizability Thesis is arguably our modern-day answer to this conception of morality.

Even though Falk criticizes the Social Content Thesis for being too narrow and failing to capture the full range of what we mean by "morality" these days, he nonetheless recognizes that sometimes "morality" must be understood just as the Social Content Thesis describes it. On Falk's account, thus, "moral" or "ethics" are terms that have a range of meanings, and the full range is not always present in every use of moral terms.

Falk's approach is reasonable, and not dogmatic, for it defers to the facts of the matter: it does not prescribe to us how we must conceive of moral terms, as the Reform View does.

If we follow the route that Falk takes, we must admit that terms do not have essential meanings, but rather, that they embody a family of meanings. If this is so, it follows that "dharma" itself would have its own distinct family of meanings, which only partially overlaps with the family of meanings associated with the word "moral". If we adopt this ordinary language approach to our investigation, it is clear that "dharma" in the classical Indian circumstance has more than one meaning, and not all of its meanings are moral in nature.

3.1.12. Falsifying Evidence: Morally Reprehensible Dharmas

The Reform View might seem to be immune to falsifying evidence because of its interpretive nature. Genuine historical or scientific proposals make a claim about the observability of data. If the data are observed, the proposal remains justified for the day: if the data are not observed, and if, in their place, contrary data are observed, the proposal is falsified. The Reform View, in contrast, does not make a claim about the observability of data, but rather, it is a proposal on *how* such data is to be interpreted. As such, it appears that there are no data in the annals of Indian literature that speak against it—this is how the proponent of the Reform View would like us to regard it. However, there is a falsifying datum to be found that shows definitively that (a), the Reform View is an empirical hypothesis about the use of "dharma" in classical Indian philosophy, and that (b), it is falsified by the data contained within the history of Indian thought.

The falsifying datum in question consists in the occurrence of the concept *MORALLY–REPREHENSIBLE–DHARMAS* in classical Indian thought. "Dharma" could not be a moral term, for if it were, the concept *MORALLY–REPREHENSIBLE–DHARMAS* would constitute an outright contradiction. To adhere to the view that "dharma" always functions as a moral term would thus commit us to the view that very reasonable Indian thinkers were patently irrational and self-contradictory when they spoke of morally reprehensible dharmas.

An example of the occurrence of the concept *MORALLY–REPREHENSIBLE–DHARMAS* is that of the *DHARMA–OF–THE–PROSTITUTE*—this is a concept that occurs in Kautilya's *Arthaśāstra*.

Another example of *MORALLY–REPREHENSIBLE–DHARMAS* is to be found in Buddhist literature. In Buddhism, "dharma" is a term that stands for many entities, though, frequently, it stands for constituents of reality. Included in this list are *intentional* objects—thoughts and their contents, ideas, etc. Given the wide range of application of the term "dharma" to *virtually* everything in Buddhist cosmology and metaphysics, it follows that not all uses of "dharma" are moral in nature: as some regions of the universe are morally reprehensible, it follows that some dharmas will also, thereby, be morally reprehensible. Hence, in Buddhist literature, there is often a distinction drawn between good dharmas, bad dharmas, and evaluatively neutral dharmas. A good dharma is a dharma that aids a person in their efforts to better themselves; one which promotes a moral outlook and moral action. An example of a good dharma might be the thought of, or impulse towards, philanthropy. A bad dharma is something that debases one; which detracts from efforts to better one's self. The thought of theft, or the desire to injure someone, would constitute a bad dharma. A morally neutral dharma would be an entity that neither hinders nor promotes one's betterment. An example of a morally neutral dharma, in Buddhism, might be an atom; thoughts of facts of the matter, or facts of the matter themselves.

3.2. Defence of the Reform View

The issue at hand is whether "dharma" in classical Indian thought is univocal or equivocal. The Orthodox position is that "dharma" in this context is equivocal, and the Intentionalist view that I have been putting forward urges us to regard "dharma" as univocal in classical Indian thought. The preceding section voiced objections to my approach to "dharma". I will now respond to the preceding criticisms, in the order that they were presented.

3.2.1. Debate Maximization

In response to the objection voiced in 3.1.1. Argument from the Principle of Charity (pp.116–119), I would put forth a contrary principle of interpretation, which I think is a fundamental philosophical value. I call this principle "*debate maximization*".

What I designate by the term "*debate maximization*" is the effort, in our practise and teaching of philosophy, to pursue differences of opinion, and not to settle for easy argumentative victories. That *debate maximization* is a fundamental value in the practise of philosophy is apparent from the fact that it is no philosophical victory to silence one's opponent by political pressure or brute force. We might, sometimes, pressure people to desist from expressing a certain view—because the views are morally objectionable, as a racist or sexist view might be—but we do not fool ourselves into thinking that the silence of our opponents is proof that we are philosophically correct.

Debate maximization is a difficult value to come to terms with because it exhorts us to challenge all of our views—at times, it seems that it will rob us of the few beliefs we require to stand on. Nevertheless, it is a value that we do respect in our practise of philosophy.

As further proof of the role of *debate maximization* in our practise of philosophy, consider the manner in which the history of philosophy is presented. In standard presentations, several different historical views are given, and an effort is made to compare and contrast these. At times, commentators have suggested that the entire history of philosophy (and usually, they are only thinking about the history of Western philosophy) unanimously subscribes to a certain philosophical package. But here too, commentators draw attention to hegemony with the purpose of bringing to light an alternative philosophical perspective.

The insight behind the value of *debate maximization* is that one cannot do philosophy—i.e. love wisdom—if one simply revels in the affirmation of those who agree with us: to love wisdom is to embrace disagreement as a positive thing.

The *principle of charity* exhorts us to maximize agreement between ourselves and our interlocutors. The *principle of debate maximization*, in contrast, tells us to maximize disagreement. Which of these values should we adhere to in the context of philosophy?

It is significant that the *principle of charity* is often discussed in the context of radical translation; a context where we are trying to understand the medium of communication of another culture. In this circumstance our goal is not to come to terms with our subject's beliefs but to come to terms with the medium through which our subject expresses their beliefs—a medium that could be used to express contrary opinions. Whether the *principle of charity* is an appropriate maxim to adhere to in such circumstances is a debate for another time. One thing is for certain: our problem is not that of radical translation: we (those of us reading this in English) are not anthropologists in the cities of ancient India trying to communicate for the first time with natives who only speak Sanskrit. Even if we were such anthropologists, we would likely have help from translators—for example, a Persian who understands both a Western language and Sanskrit.

Whatever the applicability of the *principle of charity* in the context of radical translation, it is not an appropriate maxim to adhere to in the context of philosophy. In philosophy, frequently, our interlocutors have radically different opinions from us. In philosophy, there is no rational reason for us to, *a priori*, select the interpretation that maximizes agreement.

We are often taught that when we are assessing an argument in philosophy, we should do so charitably—that is, we should not attribute a ludicrous position to our opponent, and then criticize them on that basis. While this is well-meaning advice, it is misinformed: in philosophy, the last thing we want to do is attribute to someone an opinion that they do not hold. However, others may hold opinions that we personally find crazy or ludicrous—particularly in the context of philosophy: to attempt to select the "charitable" interpretation would be to deny that others see the world very differently from us.

Those who are taken with the *principle of charity* are often impressed by the view that there would be something morally wrong with attributing an opinion that is ridiculous to others, when we can interpret others as holding an opinion that we do not find ridiculous. This way of thinking misses some important points: first, we ought to be challenging our preconceptions about what is sensible and what is ridiculous. To fail to embrace challenges to our own opinions is to revel in prejudice. Secondly, and perhaps more importantly, to morally respect others, we ought not to pretend that there are no major differences between us—rather, we must respect others by recognizing our very real differences.

The principle of *debate maximization* leads us to respect others by placing our own opinions in context. It removes us from the security of provincial life and forces us to recognize the contingencies of our opinions. Importantly, it cautions us against concluding hastily that any view is silly; *debate maximization*, thus, does better by those who are different from us, for it does not presume that the radically different is silly or ludicrous—as the *principle of charity* implies.

Does the principle of *debate maximization* impel us to accept such views that we disagree with? Of course not; that would minimize debate.

The view that "dharma" has only one meaning in classical Indian thought actually maximizes debate. For, on this account, it turns out that classical Indians had many divergent and contrary views on what is morally important. In contrast, the *principle of charity* robs our picture of Indian thought of debate: it, along with Extentionalist accounts of "dharma", renders contrary views on what "dharma" is into nondebates, for, according to its lights, classical Indians were not talking about one and the same thing when they used the term "dharma"; the meaning of "dharma" changed according to what was being talked about.

The *principle of charity*, thus, is a filter, through which we view classical Indian thought so as to not upset our preconceptions of what is reasonable and what is unreasonable. The view that "dharma" has many meanings, based on the application of the *principle of charity*, is thus the epitome of an unphilosophical disposition towards Indian philosophy.

3.2.2. Constancy in Language

Another argument against the view that "dharma" has only one meaning in classical Indian thought is informed by the view that language is fluid, and that the meanings of terms constantly change over time. If this is so, it is bound to be the case that "dharma" meant more than one thing during the whole history of Indian philosophy. This is the argument set out in 3.1.2. Evolutionary Perspective on Language (p.119).

The view that language is fluid and that the meanings of words are prone to change, is actually an exaggeration of an empirical observation. It is true that the meanings of some terms change over time. However, it is quite unreasonable to presume that change is the norm.

A condition of a term's meaningfulness is its ability to consistently have a meaning; whether it be *extentional* or *intentional.* If terms lose this constancy, they cease to be meaningful. There is thus a strong pragmatic pressure to conserve the meaning of terms—it is only by conserving meaning that we are able to use language as a means of intercourse between persons. Thus, when we teach our children language, we do not invent new meanings for terms; rather, we conserve the meanings of terms.

The norm, thus, is for language to resist change in meaning. Despite this pressure, it so happens that terms have a shift in meaning over time. However, here too, claims of change in sense are exaggerated. For instance, it is often claimed that "ethics" and "moral" did not always have moral meanings; that their ancient counterparts, "*ethos*" and "*mores*", meant something more like *CUSTOM*. Knowing what we know about moral terms in the light of earlier discussions (2.4. Definition of Moral Terms pp.70–85) it is obvious that "*mores*" and "*ethos*" were *perfect substantive* moral terms: they designated things that people had the *anger inclination* about. Over time, these terms lost their *substantive* meaning, but retained their *intentional* meaning, and thus, became *formal* in nature.

The case of "moral" as a designation for sexual restraint is often presented as evidence that even "moral" does not always have an ethical meaning. Here too, however, the claim is exaggerated. "Moral" in reference to sexual matters still functions as a moral term: those people who use "moral" to designate sexual restraint have the *anger inclination* in connection to it; they tend to scorn people of "loose morals". Arguably, what we have here is not a shift of "moral" from being a *formal* term to a *substantive* term, but an instance in which the *extention* of "moral" is so phenomenologically large (though not semantically large) that it almost eclipses its *intention*; this is just like the Indian case of "dharma" being used to stand for the constituents of reality or the Principle of Motion.

As flux in language is not the dominant pressure governing the meaning of terms, it follows that there is no reason to suppose that the meaning of "dharma" was bound to change over time.

3.2.3. Inference to the Best Explanation

A certain kind of empiricism challenged the Intentionalist account of "dharma" in 3.1.3. Argument from Empiricism (p.120). The argument presented there suffers from being excessively simplistic in its conception of science.

The account of "dharma" that I have provided is allegedly without empirical foundation, because *intentions* are not things that can be directly observed by others. On the basis of this truism, a defender of Orthodoxy might think that the traditional view in Indology regarding the equivocal nature of "dharma" must be correct, for it bases its account on the objectively observable *extentions* of "dharma".

It is true that *intentions* are not the kinds of things that others can observe. However, they are things that we can introduce in our efforts to explain empirically observable data.

Things that cannot be directly observed are constantly brought into scientific explanations. They function in hypotheses that scientists propose to explain observable data. Frequently, the hypothesis can itself be tested. Many times, however, the hypothesis cannot be tested—particularly historical hypotheses concerning past times that are gone for good. For instance, the hypothesis that life evolved on earth via the process of natural selection cannot be tested, for we cannot turn back the clock; nor can the hypothesis that the universe began with a big bang be tested. The justification for holding on to these hypotheses comes down to their ability to explain the empirically observable phenomenon, in a law-like manner. We hold on to these hypotheses because they are *inferences to the best explanation*.

The view that there is an *intentional* core to the various uses of dharma in classical Indian thought is supported by an inference to the best explanation. The datum that requires explaining is that "dharma" is associated with a bewildering assortment of *extentions* in classical Indian thought. The question, thus, is why is one and the same term used to designate so many different *extentions*? By hypothesizing that there is an *intentional* commonality to the various uses of "dharma" in classical Indian thought, the purely Intentionalist approach provides an explanation for why classical Indians used one and the same term for so many different things: the proposed *intentional* meaning is the explanation. In the case of the Reform View, the explanation that it provides is that "dharma" is another way of representing the concept *ETHICAL* or *MORAL*; key philosophical concepts that are central to the articulation of distinct philosophical views. Classical Indians used one and the same term, "dharma" (or "*dhamma*") for various matters in order to articulate their distinct views on morality.

Any view of "dharma"'s uses in classical Indian thought which attempts to differentiate meanings of "dharma" in terms of *extentions* would be a very bad explanation of the data. For, it would be unable to explain why classical Indians chose to use one and the same term—"dharma"—for so many different things, for on this Extentionalist approach, distinct applications of the term (to distinct *extentions*) warrant distinct *explanations*.

It is also important to note that while *intentions* cannot be directly observed, we can sometimes come, objectively, to know that an *intention* is associated with a term or concept, when the connection is explicitly affirmed by our subjects. In the case of the classical Indian use of the concept *DHARMA* one such explicit affirmation was noted: the case in point is where the Buddha criticizes those who have mastered *dhamma* simply for the sake of reproaching others. This instance ties the *anger inclination* to "*dhamma*" (MN I.133).

3.2.4. Response to Argument from Analogy

3.1.4. Argument from Analogy (p.120) attempts a *reductio ad absurdum* argument against the view that "dharma" denotes a moral value, when it is used as a designator for things like attributes. This argument suggests that if we take the view seriously that "dharma" always denotes a moral value because it has a moral meaning (at times) we could reason, in an analogous fashion, that "attribute" denotes a legal concept for "property" is a word that can be used to denote an attribute, and "property" also denotes the legal concept of something to which one claims ownership.

The argument would be a successful criticism if the two cases were appropriately analogous. However, there is an important difference between the case of "dharma" standing for an attribute and "property" standing for an attribute. "Property", it seems, is an *extentional* term, for it changes its meaning according to its *extentions*. "Dharma", I argued, is an *intentional* term in classical Indian thought. The hallmark of an *intentional* term is that it can retain its meaning, regardless of its *extention*. Hence, analytically, it is consistent that "dharma" should stand for an attribute, or even the idea of attributes, and still retain its overall moral meaning. Prof. Priestley's argument from analogy thus misses a crucial contention: that "dharma" in classical Indian thought is a kind of word that is very different from words like "property".[2]

The chief drawback of the Argument from Analogy is that it is voiced as though an argument was never presented on the basis of which terms like "dharma" are distinguished from terms like "property". The Argument from Analogy holds that the Reform View erroneously *assumes* that all uses of "dharma" are moral in nature in the classical Indian circumstance (p.120). The view that key philosophical terms, like "moral" or "real" are semantically different from terms like "attribute" or "property", and the view that "dharma" is such a key philosophical term was the subject of extensive argumentation in Part II Chapter 2. The Argument from Analogy is thus misinformed.

3.2.5. Translation and Paraphrase

The criticism considered in 3.1.5. Problem with Translating

Formal Moral Terms Consistently (pp.121–122) is that the view that "dharma" has one moral meaning in classical Indian thought leads to the practical consequence of misleading translations: if "dharma" means "ethics" or "moral", we could not translate it as "duty", which is a *substantive* moral term. Yet, at most junctures, it seems appropriate to translate "dharma" as almost any term except "ethics" and "moral".

In contrast to the view presented by the critic, I would argue that the only justification there could be for translating "dharma" as "duty" and not, say, "ethic" or "morality", is that *perfect formal* moral terms are not as refined in their ability to uniquely pick out their *extentions*, as, say, *perfect substantive* moral terms are. Consider the passage from *Bhagavad Gītā* at 18:47:

> Better is one's own dharma, though ill-done, than the dharma of another, though well performed. When one does the dharma ordained by his own nature, he incurs no stain.

Here, the *extention* of "dharma" is clearly a *deontic* matter, for the passage is concerned with *doing* dharma. Thus, "duty" is an appropriate substitute for "dharma" as "moral obligation would have been, for these terms have the quality of *perfection*; they lack *focus* just as "dharma" does, but they have the *substantive* content of *ACTION* or *CONDUCT*. These substitutions would not be translations but paraphrases.

Contrary to the criticism presented in 3.1.5. Problem with Translating Formal Moral Terms Consistently (p.121), I would suggest that there would have been nothing wrong if translators had chosen to translate "dharma" with a *perfect formal*, moral term, without *focus*, from English: in fact, this approach to rendering the passage would have been semantically more accurate. Thus, the translator could have written:

> Better is one's own ethics (*svadharma*), though ill-done, than the ethics of another (*paradharma*), though well-performed. When one does the ethics ordained by his own nature, he

incurs no stain.

According to the Orthodox View, this rendering is productive of misunderstanding, for "ethic" can be taken, in this sense, to stand for one's own moral theory, just as, depicting the passage as talking about "one's own morality" would have produced the same misunderstanding. This is a kind of practical misunderstanding, which is not a function of any putative ambiguity of "ethics", though. Such a misunderstanding would rest on the presumption (on the part of the reader) that the author of the passage was necessarily talking about a moral theory under the guise of "ethics". But, in English, we talk about people's "ethics", and thereby denote moral obligations: we might ask, for instance, of a certain professional, what ethics they are supposed to follow. By this, we would wish to find out what professional standards or guidelines they must conform to. An "ethics committee", most of the time, would be responsible for laying out the ethics of people within a certain organization; their *svadharma*. It may be less common for us to use "ethics" in such a fashion, but it is within our very idea of the term "ethics" for it to be able to function in this way.

Thus, on the Reform View's account, there is nothing inappropriate about translating "dharma" as a *perfect formal* moral term. Moreover, according to the Reform View, there is something misleading about presenting paraphrases of moral terms as their translations—particularly when the paraphrases divest the representation of an original text of its moral significance.

Translators of Indological texts have often failed us when it comes to paraphrasing the moral gist of passages in Indian philosophy. This is what occurs when "dharma" is frequently paraphrased as "attribute", when "character trait" or "virtue" would be more revealing as to the *intentions* of the original authors. Likewise, "dharmas" as a designation for the constituents of reality could have been rendered "ethicals"—the information that this use of "ethical" aims at conveying would have taken some training to appreciate, but no more training than the view that "dharma" stands for the constituents of reality takes.

By failing to note that *extentional* renditions of "dharma" are paraphrases, and not translations, our translators have, in many circumstances, filtered and removed all traces of moral thought from our Indological texts. This practise is at the root of the poor estimation of the place of ethics in Indian philosophy.

3.2.6. Indian Philosophy is not a Dispassionate Endeavour

If the Anger Inclination Thesis accurately captured moral significance, then, according to the argument presented in 3.1.6. The Character of Indian Philosophy (p.122), we would have to conclude that Indian philosophy is bereft of ethical speculation, for the entire character of Indian philosophy runs contrary to the *anger inclination.* The only conclusion that can be drawn, hence, is that the Reform View (as it is presented here), which depends upon the Anger Inclination Thesis, cannot be correct. This criticism must be rejected.

The view that Indian philosophy is an emotionless discourse concerned solely with a dispassionate end is a myth. An examination of the annals of Indian philosophy reveals that Indian philosophers were very passionate about their arguments and objectives, and that they did not look lightly upon those who contradicted their moral doctrines. We need only look to the prolific use of "*nāstika*" by *virtually* all schools of Indian thought as confirmation that Indian philosophers felt, and expressed, anger and scorn against the very possibility that their strictures might be violated (Nāgārjuna I.43, Vālmīki II.109.33–34, *Sūtrakṛtāṅga* II.I.17).

Those who would stress the emotionless (perhaps, otherworldly) aspect of Indian philosophy myopically seize upon one value in Indian philosophy, and promote it to the level of sole concern of Indian philosophers. The value that such persons seize upon is *mokṣa*—the value of soteriological, or spiritual, liberation. Abandonment of strong emotional responses is generally depicted as antecedent to the realisation of *mokṣa*. However, *mokṣa* is not the only value that Indian philosophers were concerned with. They frequently operated against the background of what they called the "*puruṣārthas*", which is a list of four values: dharma (*ETHICS*), *artha* (*ECONOMIC PROSPERITY*), *kāma* (*PLEASURE*) and *mokṣa* (*SPIRITUAL LIBERATION*). This collection of four—*caturvarga* (*Amarakoṣa* v.1467)—is testimony to the broad axiological concern that gripped Indian thinkers. Amongst the *puruṣārthas*, dharma gets top billing, second, perhaps, to *mokṣa*.

The Anger Inclination Thesis is thus consonant with portions of Indian philosophical thought; those that pertain to moral matters, or "dharma". As well, the Anger Inclination Thesis is consistent with the over all passion that drives Indian philosophy; a passion that leads authors to engage in very worldly and heated debates.[3]

3.2.7. Response to Grammatical Argument for Equivocality

It was suggested in 3.1.7. Grammatical Argument for Equivocality (pp.122–124), that genuine moral terms are used in one of two ways: either as parts of attributive constructions in a sentence (as part of a predicate) or as a proper noun for the abstractly conceived moral property that other things participate in. Moral terms are never used as proper nouns for concrete things, according to this argument. In contrast, in the Indian context, "dharma" is used as a proper noun for concrete particulars. It follows that such uses of the term "dharma" cannot be moral in nature. Hence, the use of "dharma" for the constituents of reality or the Principle of Motion cannot be moral.

Let us not dispute that "dharma" is used as a proper noun for concrete things in the Indian setting. This is patently true. Instead, let us ask: how much can we glean from the Western practice of employing moral terms as predicates, or designators of attributes, only? Is this an essential feature of moral language as such, or is it simply an artefact of a Western way of talking about ethics?

To answer this question, let us consider another question: would anyone fail to understand that the statement "evil is coming to dinner" is a moral statement? Surely, it is not standard to use moral terms as nouns for nonabstract particulars in English. We would say, instead, "the evil person is coming to dinner" or, "the person coming to dinner is evil". While it is our practise in English to avoid using moral terms as nouns for nonabstract particulars, we still understand that the oddly constructed sentence is moral in nature, for "evil" is a moral term.

Why is it that we who use the English language are inclined to avoid using moral terms as nouns for nonabstract particulars? Our custom stems, I believe, from the pervasive influence of Platonic thought on Western culture.

It is a matter of some irony that modern-day commentators forget that Plato morally evaluated nonsocial, and impersonal matters, for his way of thinking about moral issues has had an enduring effect on Western thought. For Plato, something is good not owing to anything particular to it, but because of its participation in "The Good". On the Platonic way of thinking, it would be incorrect to use "Good" as a proper noun for a particular, for that would obfuscate that the particular in question owes its goodness to something else: Goodness as such. The Western aversion to using moral terms as proper nouns for particulars is simply an artefact of a pervasive Platonism: it is not indicative of the nature of moral language as such.

What appears as a grammatical argument against the Reform View, I would suggest, is really a token of a Western custom. Thus, nothing regarding the moral status of "dharma" can be gleaned from whether it is used as a proper noun for particulars, or not.

3.2.8. Response to the Appeal to Authority

In 3.1.8. Appeal to Authority (p.124), I noted a line of argument against the Reform View that appeals to the consensus of Indological scholars (an argument that has been put to me by more than one person, on more than one occasion). The argument accurately points out that I am advocating a view not endorsed by most eminent authorities on Indian thought. Should we not, thus, disregard the Reform View?

In response to the criticism presented in 3.1.8. Appeal to Authority (p.124) one might attempt to argue that appeals to authority are inappropriate in academia. For sure, once it was thought that appealing to authority constituted an informal, logical, fallacy. These days we tend to have a different opinion on the matter. We rightfully defer to authorities on matters in which they are expert; why else train and support experts? Experts have detailed knowledge in things that most do not, and in acquiring their expertise, they benefit us all by sharing their informed opinion.

If the eminent Indologists who disagree with me are the authorities on the meaning of "dharma," then it seems to me that it would be rational to defer to their opinion. However, while such authors may be authorities on Indian thought and language, they are not experts on the definition of moral terms and moral statements.

In order to determine whether "dharma" is or is not (always) a moral term, we need to be conversant with the essential features of moral terms. This is a philosophical issue, regretfully, to which few attend. Even amongst scholars of Western philosophy, this is a much-neglected matter. Nevertheless, here, an effort has been made to recognize and evaluate the prominent options in the literature. Our investigation has exceeded what is normally granted to the question of the definition of moral terms and statements.

Our eminent authorities on Sanskrit and the history of Indian philosophy are thus not necessarily the authorities on the question of the meaning of "dharma". It is incumbent upon us to delve into the literature on the nature of moral terms, and evaluate the evidence for "dharma" qualifying as a moral term. Thus, the view voiced in 3.1.8. Appeal to Authority (p.124) does not refute the credibility of the Reform View.

In response, a proponent of the argument from authority might suggest that I have misconstrued the argument, or presented it in an unfavourable light. The proponent of the argument might suggest that what is at issue is not the credentials of the present author, but the fact that so many credible scholars on Indian thought are of a contrary opinion. That the dominant view in Indology is the Orthodox View (with the Conservative View ranking as the second most popular account) and that scholars have not given voice to the Reform View suggests that the Reform View is without foundation and that the Orthodox View is credible.

This argument brushes over a key aspect of the received tradition that is very dissatisfactory. Scholars who have written on the meaning of "dharma" have not, as a rule, given their reasons for deciding the meaning of "dharma". They, by and large, simply assert that "dharma" means different things in different circumstances; they by and large simply assert that "dharma" has a moral meaning in some circumstance, and that in other circumstances it does not.

Hence, the apparent lack of the support for the Reform View amongst scholars correlates with a widespread tendency to not justify the Orthodox or Conservative Views. When sparse reasons are provided, we find no extended inquiry into contrary views, their justifications and relative merits.

As things stand, hence, the scholarly consensus on the meanings of "dharma" is not to be taken too seriously.

3.2.9. Response to a Qualified Criticism

In 3.1.9. Qualified Criticism (p.124), I addressed a criticism that alleged that the Reform View is valid only in certain circumstances. As noted, there are two aspects to this criticism. A portion of the Qualified Criticism depends upon the Social Content or Conduct Thesis (or some variant of it). This is the portion of the criticism that suggests that the Reform View is valid only with respect to pro-social or conduct issues. No further response to the Social Content or Conduct Theses is necessary, as

I have already presented arguments against these views (2.3.1. Social Content and Conduct pp.35–38). The Social Content and Conduct Theses are some of the prominent philosophical prejudices of our times; prejudices that do not do justice to the history of Western moral thinking, let alone Indian thinking.

The second portion of the criticism seizes on the fact that there are *extentional* dimensions to the use of "dharma". On the basis of such observations, it seems reasonable to conclude that there are, indeed, different meanings of "dharma" corresponding to its various *extentional* contents.

The key point that this argument relies upon is that external reference, or *extention*, is always something that is (necessarily) part of the meaning of a word; if a term refers to some object, that object must be part of its meaning. Common parlance supports this line of reasoning. In the English language, it is not uncommon for us to ask the question "what do you mean" when we wish to clarify the reference of a person's words. Thus, for instance, if someone were to say, "it is ugly", and if we are not sure what "it" refers to, we might ask, "what did you mean by that?" or "what do you mean by 'it'?"

While external reference does in some circumstances contribute to the meaning of a word, we need to temper the inclination to always include it within our idea of the meaning of a term.

As an example, take the word "it". "It" refers to many different things, depending upon who is using the term, and what it is being applied to: i.e., it has many *extentions*. "It" might stand for a book in one circumstance; an idea in another. Despite the ability of "it" to take on diverse *extentions*, one would never dream of attempting to define the meaning of "it" by its *extentions*. If one was attempting to explain the meaning of "it" to a person new to the English language, it would be misleading to say that "it" is a word with several different meanings, depending upon what it is referring to. If one tried to account for the meaning of "it" by specifying its *extentions*, one would have to do one of two things. Either one would have to try to present a thorough inventory of the various *extentions* of "it". If one did this, the student would be at a loss when they came upon an *extention* of "it" that one did not specify. Or, one would have to instruct the student to take "it" to stand for a distinct concept, with a distinct meaning, every time it is applied to a distinct object. On this latter view, "it" has countless different meanings. No single introduction to the meaning of "it" could suffice, for there are, in theory, an infinite number of concepts corresponding to "it" on this view.

Such are the absurd results of taking too seriously the notion that the *extentions* of all terms are part of their meaning. Our colloquial manner of talking about the "meaning" of someone's utterance, when we really want to understand what they are referring to, misleads us at this point.

The Qualified Criticism suggested that "dharma" must have more than one meaning in the classical context because it has such significant and diverse *extentions*. My suggestion is that this approach to defining "dharma" is as misguided as attempting to define "it" as meaning "book", when one uses it to stand for a book, or as "imaginary pink elephants", when one uses "it" to refer to this idea.

The problem may very well be that our ordinary language way of talking about reference frequently involves using the term "mean" or "meaning". If one is gripped by this usage, it might seem that I am denying the very important differences between Buddhist, Jain and Hindu uses of the term "dharma". By no means do I wish to deny that such uses of "dharma" are distinct with respect to their external referents (*extentions*). If we are going to use the term "mean" as a stand-in for "refer", then I could not possibly deny that the Jains meant something different from Hindus when they used the term to refer to the Principle of Motion. If we go down this route, every distinct use of "dharma" is a different meaning. This is a mistake.

The account of the meaning of "dharma" that the Reform View urges is an account of the meaning of "dharma" apart from any particular use of the term. In no way does the Reform View downplay the differences in the *contexts* in which "dharma" is employed. The Reform View does wish to stress, however, that for "dharma" to be a meaningful term within the context of all of Indian philosophy—a commodity that Indian philosophers trade in—Indian philosophers must have had a way to grasp the meaning of "dharma" apart from any particular application of the term. The Anger Inclination Thesis applied to "dharma" is one account of what it is that Indian philosophers commonly grasped when "dharma" was used in odd circumstances.

Why has this point been largely lost on Indology? I suspect this is because Indology is driven largely by an interest in history—that is, what has past. If we attempt to understand Indian philosophy as something that is over, and not alive in some eternal way, then we are not concerned with novel uses of "dharma" that we are not privy too: we are simply concerned with just those uses of "dharma" that occurred in the past. This is a definite set, and it seems that in theory we could catalogue all such uses. For the philosopher, however, philosophy is always alive and present, and the very possibility of novel and contrary philosophical claims is always immanent to such a person.

The philosopher approaches Indian philosophy as a potential participant in its debates. To this end, such a person asks the question: how do I distinguish the unique, philosophical contributions of a particular individual, perspective or school, from the common fund of concepts and terms over which there is debate?—for I potentially wish to enter into this debate, and will thus have to avail myself of such common resources.

"Dharma" is just such a common resource in Indian philosophy. Virtually every philosophical school attempts to use it to articulate its unique philosophical perspective. The error of the Orthodox View is in failing to distinguish between the particular philosophical opinions of the various schools of Indian philosophy and the meaning of "dharma" itself.

3.2.10. Response to the Charge of Equivocation

According to the argument presented in 3.1.10. Charge of Equivocation (pp.125–126), the Reform View fails to give due attention to the fact that terms with a phonemic identity can stand for diverse concepts with diverse meanings.

With respect to the term "dharma" itself, the Reform View recognizes that it is a term with more than one meaning. The argument for the Reform View is that there is no good reason, to date, presented in the literature, to suggest that "dharma" had anything more than one moral meaning in classical India. Accordingly, all classical uses of "dharma" can be understood as conforming to the definition of a *perfect formal*, moral term, without *focus*. In the modern context, the bureaucratic notion of "dharma" cannot be subsumed under the classical definition, for the modern context stipulates that the meaning of "dharma" is *RELIGION*—an *extentional* term.

The Reform View is thus not guilty of equivocation. It recognizes that "dharma" does not always have the same meaning. It simply disagrees with Orthodoxy on the view that "dharma" had more than one meaning in the classical Indian circumstance.

3.2.11. Response to the Family Resemblance Argument

In 3.1.11. Argument from Family Resemblance Theory (pp.126–127), it was made out that moral terms, and "dharma" itself, are not characterized by any invariable, essential meaning, but by a range or family of meanings. According to this argument, it is unreasonable to expect that, (a) "dharma" had just one meaning in the classical Indian circumstance, and that (b) it always functioned as a moral term.

From one perspective, the view that the meaning of a term is characterized by a family of meanings, as opposed to one, unitary meaning, does not detract from the plausibility of "dharma" always functioning as a moral term. In fact, on the view that a moral term is not characterized by one, essential, meaning, but by a range of meanings, there is even less reason to criticize all uses of "dharma" as counting as moral, for, on the cluster, Family Resemblance approach, there is no essential moral meaning against which to judge whether a particular use of "dharma" is moral or not. In other words, if we defined moral terms as standing for cluster concepts, then the various uses of "dharma" would simply constitute an exotic end of the semantic range of moral terms; seemingly technical uses of "dharma" in Indian philosophy as a designation for ontological matters would constitute a side of the moral family not frequently heard from.

The proponent of the Argument from Family Resemblance might object that this rebuttal misses the point. If terms have their meaning in a semantic range, and not in some semantic essence, it follows that "dharma" is a designation for a unique concept, defined by its own semantic range, which is distinct from the concept and semantic range of "ethics" or "moral". If this is so, it follows that "dharma" is not a moral term, by definition, for only "ethics" and "moral" are such terms. While the semantic range of "dharma" overlaps, partially, with that of "ethics" and "moral", technically, "dharma" is not a moral term: it is a *dharmic* term. It follows from this that when "dharma" is a name for the constituents of reality or for the Principle of Motion, it is not a moral term, for "moral" and "ethics" are never used as names for such things.

The key premise that this criticism rests upon is the plausibility of the Family Resemblance conception of meaning. Why is this thought to be plausible?

The proponents of the Family Resemblance theory fancy that their account is scientific, and hence, plausible, in an important respect: it is based on the reality of the way language is used and functions, and not on the basis of an *a priori*, prescriptive, theory, which is out of step with reality.

What are the grounds for concluding that the Family Resemblance account is more plausible than the alternative, traditional view? Let us first distinguish the two views. The

Traditional View holds that there is a tight, one-to-one, relationship between a concept and its meaning. On the Traditional View concepts, themselves, are not ambiguous, though terms might be ambiguous insofar as they stand for more than one concept. According to the Family Resemblance view, concepts are themselves ambiguous: every concept is associated with a plethora of meanings, none of which, singly, sums up the import of a concept.

Historically, the Family Resemblance account was thought to be plausible only after it seemed that the Traditional View was unworkable. In other words, philosophers have favoured the Traditional View, over the Family Resemblance account. Why is the Traditional View preferable? It is simpler: it defines a concept with respect to one meaning; the Family Resemblance account attributes an underdetermined number of meanings to a single concept. The simplicity of the Traditional View is an asset because it renders concepts computationally less cumbersome, and clearly definable. On the Family Resemblance account, one must grasp a plethora of meanings associated with a term in order to have a proper command over the associated concept—on the traditional account, one need only master one meaning for every concept. As well, the Traditional View supports the expectation that simple, clear, and unambiguous definitions of concepts are possible. The Family Resemblance Theory implies that no such definitions are possible.

The classic argument for the Family Resemblance account of concepts is provided by the latter Wittgenstein—in fact, it is Wittgenstein who gives us the semantic notion of *FAMILY RESEMBLANCE* (*Philosophical Investigations* §67).

Early in his career, Wittgenstein, in the *Tractatus*, puts forward a picture theory of meaning, which holds that, (a) *thoughts* are pictures of *facts* (states of affairs) (*Tractatus* 3), (b) *propositions* sensually express our thoughts (*Tractatus* 3.1), (c) the simple components of propositions represent objects (*Tractatus* 3.202), and (d) the logic of a proposition represents the relationship between the objects that form them into facts. On this account, words have clearly definable meanings: the objects that they represent. It is a word's ability to stand for an object, on this account, that accounts for its meaningfulness.

In sharp contrast, Wittgenstein begins the *Philosophical Investigations* by singling out his old theory of meaning for criticism. However, instead of quoting his own prior adumbration of the theory, he quotes St. Augustine who, in the *Confessions* (I.8), describes a child's acquisition of language as a matter of learning the objects that words stand for. Wittgenstein describes Augustine's account thus:

> ... the individual words in language name objects—sentences are a combination of such names.—In this picture of language we find the roots of the following idea: Every word has a meaning. This meaning is correlated with the word. It is the object for which the word stands. (*Philosophical Investigations* §1)

Wittgenstein spends a good deal of the first portion of the *Philosophical Investigations* arguing against this conception of language. Particularly, he attacks the associated view that meaning is a picture in our head of the object that a word designates—a view expressed in the *Tractatus*. The matter of private, mental processes, is the subject of a persistent criticism by Wittgenstein. The exact purport of Wittgenstein's criticism of private states, and his so called "*private language argument*" that he delivers in this criticism, is a matter of scholarly debate, and subject to different interpretations. However, we need not be terribly worried by Wittgenstein's criticisms in this direction, for it seems that private experiences are essential to the definition of some concepts—a possibility that Wittgenstein overlooks early in his dialectic. If we cannot dispense with private experiences in our account of the meaning of some terms, Wittgenstein's criticism of the Traditional View of meaning cannot be affirmed.

Wittgenstein passes over the key role of private, *intentional*, phenomenon, in the definition of certain concepts, when he is setting forth his theory of Family Resemblances.

At an earlier point in the *Philosophical Investigations*, Wittgenstein stipulates that concrete, everyday uses of language, for various purposes, constitute a kind of game—a *language game* (*Philosophical Investigation* §§7–24). Later, he raises the question of whether the concept of a game can be unambiguously defined. He argues that it cannot be (the implication being that *LANGUAGE*, itself, cannot be summed up in a univocal definition). He writes:

> Consider for example the proceedings that we call "games". I mean board-games, card-games, ball-games, Olympic games, and so on. What is common to them all? — Don't say: "There must be something common, or they would not be called *GAMES*" — but look and see whether there is anything common to them all?—For if you look at them you will not see something that is common to all, but similarities, relationships, and a whole series of them at that .... Look for example at board-games, with their multifarious relationships. Now pass to card-games; here you find many correspondences with the first group, but many common features drop out, and others appear. When we pass next to ball-games, much that is common is retained, but much is lost.—Are they all "amusing"? Compare chess with noughts and crosses. Or is there always winning and losing, or competition between players? Think of patience. In ball games there is winning and losing; but when a child throws his ball at the wall and catches it again, this feature has disappeared. Look at the parts played by skill and luck; and at the difference between skill in chess and skill in tennis. Think now of games like ring-a-ring-a-roses; here is the element of amusement, but how many other characteristic features have disappeared! ... And the result of this examination is: we see a complicated network of similarities overlapping and criss-crossing .... I can think of no better expression to characterize these similarities than "family resemblances" .... (*Philosophical Investigations* §§66–67)

Wittgenstein raises the possibility that "games" can be

defined by an *intentional* criterion, when he suggests that, perhaps, games are all amusing—but he does not pursue this line of inquiry. Instead, he investigates games *qua extentions* of the term "game" (he tells us to "look and see" games themselves—not the *intention* associated with the notion of a *GAME*). His conclusion is that there is nothing, *extentionally*, to be found invariably in games. This apparently is the case. However, he is not entitled to the conclusion that "game" is an ambiguous term that supports a family of meanings, and no, unique, common, unitary meaning. Games are defined according to *intentional* criteria I submit. The word "game" stands for the concept *ACTIVITIES–THAT–PRESENT–BOTH–A–CHALLENGE–AND–ENTERTAINMENT–TO–THOSE–WHO–UNDERTAKE–THEM* (*CHALLENGE* and *ENTERTAINMENT* are both *intentional* concepts). *GAME* is thus an unambiguous, *intentional* concept.

Wittgenstein squandered *intentions* in his early account of meaning on a redundancy. In his early thought, he held that the meaning is always something *intentional*; and that the *intention* of a term is a mentalistic copy of the *extention* of the term. Wittgenstein ends up rejecting the role of *intentions* in meaning, but he really should have rejected the notion that all meaning is *intentional* in nature, and moreover, that *intention* necessarily mirrors the *extention* of a term. It is because the *extention* and *intention* of a term are not necessarily symmetrical, or mirror images that it is possible for there to be constancy in *intention* while a term displays a disjunction of *extentions*. Moreover, it is because *intention* does not always mirror *extention* that words need not all name objects to be meaningful.

The Family Resemblance account, hence, is a result of a dialectic process that attempts to exclude the possibility of there being unambiguous definitions for every concept. Wittgenstein in his dialectic passes over a possibility that would save the traditional intuition that there is a one-to-one correlation between a concept and its meaning. In so doing, he arrives at a conclusion regarding the ambiguity of concepts that is premature.

The biggest sign that the Family Resemblance account is

false, is the enormous computational capacity it demands of a person to be proficient with the use of a single concept. On Wittgenstein's account, to understand a concept, we need to be aware of a whole set of related meanings that have no common element. On this account, no simple definition of a concept is possible; every concept requires its own essay as an introduction. We need to look no further than our current investigation into the meaning of "dharma" to know that this approach is impractical. On the view that "dharma" is a term with many meanings, scholars end up "bewildered" at the complexity of the use of the term—how were ordinary people ever supposed to learn the meaning of *DHARMA* if it were so ambiguous.

Concepts are our tools. Hence, they have to be simple enough for us to grasp and make use of them. The only way that concepts can be sufficiently simple is if there is a one-to-one correlation between a concept and its meaning. The Family Resemblance account cannot be right.

There are other reasons why we, in our quest to do the history of philosophy, should distance ourselves from the approach to language propagated by the latter Wittgenstein. On the Family Resemblance account, concepts are themselves ambiguous. Hence, it follows, on this account, that disagreements in philosophy are really a function of a failure to appreciate the full semantic range of any given concept. When philosophers realize, owing to the breadth of the family of meanings associated with a concept, that any given concept can *uncontroversially* be used to affirm radically contrary positions, the philosophical problem is dissolved. It follows from this that, (a) philosophy is an activity that only arises when we are confused about the way language works. Wittgenstein himself recognizes and supports this perspective on philosophy. He writes:

> It is not our aim to refine or complete the system of rules for the use of our words in unheard-of ways. For the clarity that we are aiming at is indeed complete clarity. But this simply means that the philosophical problems should completely disappear.

> The real discovery is the one that makes me capable of stopping doing philosophy when I want to.—The one that gives philosophy peace, so that it is no longer tormented by questions which bring itself in question .... There is not a philosophical method, though there are indeed methods, like different therapies. (*Philosophical Investigations* §133)

A corollary to the Family Resemblance account of language is that, (b) there are no genuine philosophical disagreements; at best, there are only different *language games*. This outcome follows directly from the view that concepts have many distinct meanings associated with them that are a function of their various uses. What seems like a disagreement is really, on the Family Resemblance account, distinct uses of concepts, which are, nevertheless, analytically sanctioned by the diversity of meanings associated with a concept.

From the fact that the Family Resemblance account implies (a) and (b) we can only conclude that the Family Resemblance account is allied with a metaphilosophical view that is unsympathetic to philosophy. For one who loves all of philosophy, and the history of philosophy in particular, it makes little sense to subscribe to the Family Resemblance account, for it commits one to the view that there are no genuine philosophical disagreements, and that philosophy is only symptomatic of a confusion.

Plato, in the *Republic,* argues that justice is something valuable both in war and in peace time; I would urge that philosophy is something of value both when we are confused, and when we are not confused. What we require is a theory of meaning that affirms this reality.

Both the Orthodox View, which is allied to the Traditional View of meaning, and the Family Resemblance account, are to be rejected by one who is sympathetic to the cause of philosophy. Both of these views build ambiguity into key philosophical resources—*the Orthodox View builds in unlimited ambiguity into the term "dharma" and the Family Resemblance account builds unlimited ambiguity into the concept DHARMA.* In so doing, both accounts make disagreement in philosophy disappear. In contrast, the Reform View eschews ambiguity in its definition of moral terms, and hence, it accommodates genuine philosophical disagreements. In other words, the Reform View, on comparison, maximizes debate.

3.2.12. *EVIL ETHIC*

In 3.1.12. Falsifying Evidence: Morally Reprehensible Dharmas (pp.127–129), the claim was made that the Reform View is falsified by the fact that Indian authors countenanced the concept of *MORALLY–REPREHENSIBLE–DHARMAS*. The argument was made that "dharma" could not always function as a moral term, for if it did, the concept *MORALLY–REPREHENSIBLE–DHARMAS* would constitute an outright contradiction. Since we ought not to attribute self-contradictory views to historical thinkers if we can countenance an alternate interpretation, we ought to drop the view that "dharma" always functions as a moral term.

The specific examples of morally reprehensible dharmas that were cited were the case of the *PROSTITUTE'S–DHARMA* (found in the *Arthaśāstra*) and that of *BAD–DHARMAS* in Buddhist thought.

The concept *PROSTITUTE'S–DHARMA* refers to the code of conduct that a prostitute must follow: how they are to conduct business; what their professional obligations consist in; how much of their earnings they must surrender to taxation, etc. To some, this constitutes an inherently morally reprehensible matter. I would urge that the view that the code of conduct of a prostitute cannot possibly be moral is due to a lack of philosophical imagination. It is the case that most moralities that predominate in any given society eschew prostitution; however, within the realm of possibilities, there are moral theories that do not adopt this stand towards prostitution. We can even imagine a moral theory that regards prostitution as a morally good thing. This would be a strange morality, for us, but it would still be a morality. This thought experiment ought to illustrate that there is nothing, *analytically*, self-contradictory about the notion of a prostitute's ethic. The view that prostitution is necessarily a morally criticisable affair is an overstatement: from the perspective of some moral theories, prostitution is a bad thing. On the same count, from the perspective of some moral theories, prostitution is a good thing.

One might object to my defence of the notion of a prostitute's ethic in the following manner: the point that 3.1.12. Falsifying Evidence: Morally Reprehensible Dharmas tried to make is not that it is possible, for someone, to think that prostitution is a good thing, but that, for the authors who spoke of it, it was a bad thing. Hence, they could not possibly have meant "dharma" in a moral sense in such a circumstance.

This criticism fails to take into account that we use moral terms for things that we do not necessarily endorse. For instance, I, and many others, find Fascism morally repugnant. Yet, we can recognize that the Nazis had an ethic: the Nazi Ethic. To use "ethic" in this circumstance in no way implies that I am endorsing the views that it denotes: the Nazi Ethic, which is comprised of beliefs of racial superiority, and the belief in the right of groups of people to wipe out other peoples in order to preserve their culture and propagate their phenotype. This is wrong: ethically wrong. I could even call the Nazi Ethic an "Evil Ethic". However, by no means is such a turn of phrase self-contradictory.

The apparent contradiction involved in the moral sense of "dharma" in the context of Buddhist talk of good, bad, and neutral, dharmas is resolved in the same manner. "Dharma", as a *perfect formal*, moral term, without *focus*, does not always express the approval of the author—sometimes, it simply implies that the thing it names is morally significant—i.e., that it can be evaluated, in a moral manner, as either good, bad, or neither. The case of a bad dharma is like that of an Evil Ethic; it is something that the author criticizes, on moral grounds.

The critic might argue that I am trying to have things both ways. On the one hand, I criticize contrary accounts of concepts for multiplying their meanings, and yet, here, I am suggesting that moral terms have two distinct meanings: one that is evaluative, and one that categorizes a matter as morally significant. It is only on the basis of distinguishing two distinct meanings of "dharma" and moral terms, that one could argue that there is nothing contradictory about the notion of an *EVIL ETHIC* or a *BAD–DHARMA*.

This criticism misses what I think is a strength of the Reform View, and the Anger Inclination Thesis: it can account for how *perfect, formal* moral terms, without *focus*, sometimes function to communicate an evaluative judgement of an author, and sometimes communicate the bare moral significance of some matter, without attributing more than one meaning to such terms. This was adumbrated earlier in 2.4.2. Double Role of Some Moral Terms (p.74).

3.3. Metatheoretical Considerations

The question whether "dharma" had just one or many meanings in classical Indian thought is an empirical and scientific question of sorts, for the question aims at procuring a satisfactory explanation of the data—the various uses of "dharma" in classical Indian thought. Like all scientific issues, the data are not the only adjudicating factors. When comparing scientific theories there are metatheoretical criteria that can help us decide between theories.

One metatheoretical consideration that has been discussed at length, already, is the *principle of debate maximization*: when choosing between interpretations of philosophical terms, this principle, as I have argued, is relevant to deciding between competing theories (3.2.1. Debate Maximization pp.129–132).

Another important metatheoretical criterion in assessing the strength of a scientific theory is that of *parsimony*.

"Parsimony" is a term that refers to theoretical economy or simplicity. Generally, the simplicity or theoretical economy that "parsimony" designates concerns the number of theoretical postulates in a theory. There a few formulations of the principle:

- *Pluralitas non est ponenda sine neccesitate*—Plurality is not to be assumed without necessity.

- *Frustra fit per plura quod potest fieri per pauciora*—What can be done with fewer [assumptions] is done in vain with more.

- *Entia non sunt multiplicanda praeter necessitatem*—Entities are not to be multiplied without necessity.

The *principle of parsimony* is often also called "Ockham's Razor" after the mediaeval philosopher William of Ockham (though Ockham seems to have not ever used the last formulation of the principle, according to Ernest A. Moody, 1967 p.307).

The principle of parsimony is a widely applicable metatheoretical constraint, which has a certain *a priori* appeal. Generally, the principle is taken to imply that when we are choosing between theories that explain the same data, we ought to favour those that countenance fewer theoretical postulates. If we compare the Intentionalist account of "dharma" in classical Indian thought, such as the Conservative or Reform View, with an Extentionalist account, like the Orthodox View or a Family Resemblance account, which holds that "dharma" has several meanings in classical Indian thought, it turns out that the Intentionalist approaches are far more parsimonious. Both the Reform and the Conservative View attribute only one meaning to "dharma" in the classical Indian circumstance, whereas the Orthodox View and the Family Resemblance account multiply the meanings of "dharma". If bare theoretical economy is a critical criterion, then, Extentionalist accounts lose in the competition to the Reform and Conservative Views.

3.4. Critics Reprisal

Criticism 1. Much weight has been placed upon debate

maximization. It is partially on the weight of this putative principle that you argue that we are justified in holding that all classical uses of "dharma" are moral in nature.

The argument can be made that the preceding presentation of the Reform View breaks its own rules about debate maximization when it draws a distinction between a modern and classical meaning of "dharma".

Response 1. The principle of debate maximization is not asserted as the only consideration when interpreting philosophically relevant terms. Rather, it is asserted as one consideration amongst others. Hence, *other things being equal*, we ought to choose the interpretation of key philosophical terms that maximizes debate.

The Reform View draws a distinction between a modern sense of "dharma", grounded in the Indian Constitution, and a classical use of the term. It is the Reform View's contention that these contexts are not equal.

The context of the Indian Constitution is wholly novel in the Indian scene. It is a definitive statement of the foundations of Indian law. Some scholars incorrectly refer to the *dharmaśāstras* as the "law books". This is incorrect, for in them, the question of what is in fact "dharma" is in debate; every author presents their own account of "dharma". At best, they are interpretations of Hindu ethical rules; this renders them legalistic in nature, but not, in any way, a strict digest of law. The Indian Constitution is very different: it is not presented as simply one opinion in a dialogue, but rather, it is the final statement on certain basic legal issues for the Republic of India. This is what renders it a constitution, and not a political pamphlet or manifesto.

The Indian Constitution is thus a context that is conspicuously not part of a *wider* debate; rather, it delimits all subsequent debates on the correct interpretation of the laws of India. In it, "dharma" is used as a synonym for "religion". In this context, the term "dharma" is granted a purely *extentional* interpretation.

As the modern meaning of "dharma" is granted to it by a

context that is explicitly not concerned with situating itself within a wider debate, it would be incorrect to attempt to include this use of "dharma" amongst other uses of "dharma", and to, furthermore, attempt to find one common meaning, on the basis of the principle of debate maximization.

In the context of classical uses of "dharma", strange uses of the term appear precisely in philosophical and disputational texts. Hence, it is appropriate to conclude that all such varied uses are part of a wider debate of what is, in fact, dharma.

Given these considerations, it would be inappropriate to attempt to construe both the modern and classical uses of "dharma" as part of one debate. The principle of debate maximization, then, cannot be used as evidence that the same notion of "dharma" is operative in both contexts.

Moreover, in the modern context, we have incontrovertible evidence that "dharma" does not mean *ETHICS* (the modern definition of "dharma" as *RELIGION*). No such incontrovertible evidence regarding the nonmoral nature of "dharma" is to be found in classical Indian thought. On this count, the two contexts are incommensurate, and it would thus be inappropriate to apply the principle of debate maximization to both contexts to produce one account of the meaning of "dharma".

Criticism 2. Much weight has been placed on debate maximization, and the fact that Plato and the Platonists morally evaluated ontological, impersonal things. What makes you so sure that they meant "moral" the way we do? What we mean by "moral," these days, is typically a matter that is bound to conduct, or social matters. Hence, it is simply a historical accident that Plato called "The Good" what he did, for, today we mean something very different from Plato.

Response 2. The critic would have us look upon Plato's comments on The Good, and modern debates on goodness, as positions taken in distinct debates. Why? Because the Moral Impersonalism of Plato is so radically different from common opinions of today.

There is a strong impulse in philosophy of today to distinguish issues and compartmentalize arguments. There is a practical motive behind this move. By limiting the number of contending positions in a philosophical debate, it gives us hope that we can definitively resolve the debate. This problem-solving impulse may be of short-term benefit in philosophy, but it is not the way that philosophy actually works. Philosophers of historical significance are precisely those who push the envelope, widen our perspective, and lead us to consider possibilities that we could not fathom on our own: they are not, necessarily, philosophers who definitively resolve a debate, and hence, persons whom we agree with. If philosophy were a subject that thrived on compartmentalization and restriction of debate, it would not have the timeless quality that it has. Philosophy written two thousand years ago is still relevant for us today because it makes contributions to debates that we are still involved in. In other words, the only reason that Plato is relevant for us today is because he participates in the debate on ethics—amongst other things—with us. His distinct opinion on the nature of moral matters is his contribution to our debate; the view that morality is necessarily bound up with social matters is a modern contribution to this debate.

It may seem dogmatic to assert that any reasonable definition of moral terms must maximize debate. However, I submit that it is a dogma that propels philosophy forward, and gives it its longevity. It is a foundational law of philosophical discourse; a law that we need to respect in our attempts to capture the meaning of key philosophical terms.

Criticism 3. the principle of debate maximization that you place so much weight upon is open to the criticism that it is self-contradictory. If we are to take it seriously, we would have to do two things: (a) we could not settle upon anything in philosophy, for we would have to continually subject it to debate; therefore, we could not even accept the Anger Inclination Thesis as the correct account of moral meaning. Secondly, we would have to subject the principle of debate maximization itself to debate. In other words, the principle of debate maximization renders itself not fit as a foundational principle of philosophy because it must itself be the subject of controversy.

Response 3. I would like to note that the principle of debate maximization does not exhort us not to believe in the validity or truth of any particular view. It tells us, rather, that all things in philosophy must be subject to debate (that they must, in principle, be open to criticism) and it further informs us that in our speculations about the nature of a philosophical field, we must leave room within all such fields for divergent opinions, for it is of the nature of philosophy to accommodate debate. Hence, it does not follow from the principle of debate maximization that we cannot make a case for the validity or veracity of some thesis; be it the Anger Inclination Thesis, or the principle of debate maximization itself. Nor is it an implication of the principle of debate maximization that we must reject its validity or veracity. It is an implication of the principle of debate maximization that it must itself be open to philosophical criticism. There is nothing contradictory about this implication, given that subjecting something to debate is not the same as rejecting its veracity. Debate, after all, can occur between parties who are mutually convinced of the veracity of their own views.

Criticism 4. It is a contention of the Reform View's argument that "dharma" is an *intentional* term. However, according to its own lights, "dharma" also has an *extentional* meaning (in modern times). Hence, it appears that "dharma" is also an *extentional* term. If this is so, then the whole edifice of the argument for the Reform View is lacking, for "dharma" appears to be like any other term; a term with different meanings in different contexts. It cannot thus be claimed that "dharma" belongs to some unique class of terms, for which *extentions* do not matter in their definition.

Response 4. The argument for the Reform View rests not on the contention that "dharma" is always an *intentional* term, but that, in classical Indian thought, "dharma" is an *intentional* term.

Criticism 5. If "dharma" were a key philosophical term,

we would expect that Indian philosophers would *occasionally* take exception to contrary uses of the term "dharma". Hence, we would expect that the Hindu philosopher objects to the Buddhist view of "dharma" as constituents of reality. Similarly, we might expect the Buddhist to object to the Jain use of "dharma" for the Principle of Motion. However, what we see is something very different. Indian philosophers typically approach such differences as merely terminological divergence. Hence, a Hindu thinker is likely to say that "the Jain uses 'dharma' to stand for the Principle of Motion". Likewise, we find that a Buddhist thinker typically would say that "Pūrvamīmāṃsā uses 'dharma' to denote Vedically prescribed rituals". Indian philosophers thus, themselves, do not make the proper use of "dharma" the subject of philosophical controversy. They are happy to regard divergent uses of "dharma" as simply terminological differences. This not only speaks against the view that "dharma" is a key philosophical term but also speaks to the fact that Indians themselves defined "dharma" *extentionally.*

Response 5. The deferential approach to uses of "dharma" on the part of Indian philosophers is a sign of their philosophical sophistication and nothing more. To make this argument clear, let us consider an analogous case of the debate between Idealists and Eliminative Materialists.

For the savvy student of philosophy, Idealist, Materialist, or Pluralist, one thing is clear: there is a metaphysical debate at stake between these positions on the question of what is *real.* "Real" or "reality" is the key philosophical term of this debate. For the Idealist of many stripes, matter, as something mind-independent, is not real: if anything is real for such thinkers, it is minds or mental objects. For the Eliminative Materialist, minds are not real but are rather the result of misleading linguistic fictions; artefacts of folk psychology. The savvy student of philosophy, whether they be Materialist or Idealist, will be quite willing to affirm their opponent's use of "real" while disagreeing with its veracity. Thus, such a savvy philosophical Idealist will be seen saying "for the Eliminative

Materialist, *REAL* denotes matter only". Likewise, the Materialist would be seen saying "the Idealist holds that minds are real", or alternatively "for the Idealist, *REAL* is applicable to minds". Moreover, the savvy philosopher is likely not to make an explicit issue of their opponent's use of the term "real", even though they fundamentally disagree with the veracity of their opponents claims. Hence, the savvy Idealist is likely not to be seen saying "materialists should not use 'real' to denote matter". Why would the savvy Idealist not be seen saying such a thing? Because the savvy philosopher is already cognizant of the fact that they differ radically on the *appropriate* use of the term "real": this central aspect of the debate is old news for them. Hence, the savvy Materialist is likely to be seen saying, "the Idealist calls minds 'real', but they are wrong".

This is exactly what we find in the Indian circumstance. Traditional Indian philosophers may affirm that their opponents have divergent philosophical views from them. Because they are imminently cognizant about the fact that they radically disagree with their opponents on the question of *what is in fact dharma*, they do not make a big deal out of their different uses of "dharma". What they do say, however, is that their opponents are wrong—globally wrong.

An Indian philosophical view, or *darśana*, is ultimately a list of philosophical principles and propositions. Some of these propositions concern epistemology and metaphysics. Many of these propositions concern morality. The principles regarding morality are of the nature, "dharma is ...". By rejecting an opponent's *darśana*, Indian philosophers are thereby rejecting their opponent's claims about *what is in fact dharma*.

Criticism 6. Even if one were to grant the argument made earlier, that key philosophical terms must be defined without inclusion of *extentions*, and even if we are to grant that "dharma" is a key philosophical term, there is no reason for us to conclude that "dharma" is always such a key philosophical term, in classical Indian thought.

Response 6. There are reasons for us to not seriously

consider mixed accounts of the meaning of "dharma" in classical Indian thought. First, all such accounts would be less parsimonious than either the Reform or Conservative Views, for they would imply that "dharma" in classical Indian thought had more than one meaning. As well, all such accounts would minimize debate, by rendering "dharma" into a term that stands for many distinct concepts, defined in terms of mixed criteria. I would also argue that there are no good reasons to countenance "dharma" as a mixed *intentional–extentional* term in classical Indian thought, for "dharma", conceived as a key philosophical term, is consistent with any number of distinct *extentions*. And, I would urge, there is no good reason to hypothesize that "dharma" had more than one *intentional* meaning in classical Indian thought.

Moreover, the argument can be made that the possibility that "dharma" has many meanings in the context of Indian philosophy is at odds with its function as a key philosophical term, for the function of a key philosophical term is to provide a pervasive meaning to a single term, which functions as the common ground for disagreements on what the appropriate *extentions* of the term is. If "dharma" is such a key philosophical term, as I have argued (2.7. An Argument for the Reform View pp.105–107), it is implausible that "dharma" had anything more than one meaning in the context of classical Indian philosophy.

Criticism 7. The assumption all along has been that if someone wished to argue that "dharma" had more than one meaning in classical Indian thought, they would pin their case on an appeal to diverse *extentions* of "dharma". The possibility has not been taken seriously that one might proffer an Intentionalist argument, for the equivocality of "dharma". According to such an argument, "dharma" has more than one meaning, based not on what it is applied to, but with respect to varying, accompanying *intentions*. A plausible version of such an account would differentiate the meanings of "dharma" on the basis of religious affiliation; thus, "dharma" in the Buddhist thought stands for a Buddhist concept defined by a certain Buddhist *intention*, while "dharma" in Hinduism is defined by a Hindu *intention*.

Response 7. Such an Intentionalist, Equivocal stance on "dharma" would be as unacceptable as the Orthodox View for similar reasons: such a view multiplies the meanings of "dharma", and hence, fails to be parsimonious. And, by multiplying the meanings of "dharma", such a view minimizes debate.

The view that the meaning of "dharma" shifts across religious traditions is not sustainable, given that "dharma" is used in a clearly (uncontroversially) moral sense in all of India's three major religious traditions. Hence, the evidence suggests that the same *intentional* meaning is associated with "dharma" across religious traditions.

The issue is not so much if there are extra *intentions* associated with "dharma" in classical Indian thought—for even if the Reform View were true, it would still be possible for individuals to have extra *intentional* states associated with "dharma". For one person, what is called "dharma" is a source of happiness, for another, what is called "dharma" is associated with drudgery. The semantic question at hand is not, is there more than one *intention* associated with "dharma" in classical Indian thought, but, is there a single *intention* that is the meaning of "dharma" in classical Indian thought; a single *intention* that all would have understood "dharma" in association with.

It is not true that the possibility that "dharma" has more than one *intentional* meaning in classical Indian thought has been altogether ignored. Examples of terms with more than one *intentional* meaning are *virtually perfect* moral terms, like "good" and "ought". It was argued that "dharma" does not have the sign of a *virtually perfect* moral term, because, it can stand for the whole domain of moral discourse (2.4.5. Terms that Designate the Field of Moral Concern p.78, 2.6.2. Traditional Meaning of "Dharma" p.95–98). The fact that it can designate the entire field of moral discourse implies that it is not a *virtually perfect* moral term, but that it has only one, unambiguous moral meaning, without *substantive content* or *focus* (2.4.5. Terms that Designate the Field of Moral Concern p.78). As argued, in response to the previous objection, if "dharma" is a key philosophical term, it is implausible that it had anything more than one meaning in the context of classical Indian philosophy.

3.5. Four Theories of "Dharma" in Review

I explicitly named three accounts of the meaning of "dharma". Two of the theories are familiar fixtures in modern secondary literature on Indian philosophy. These theories are what I respectively call the "Orthodox View" and the "Conservative View" on the meaning of "dharma". In addition, another account of the meaning of "dharma" has been recognized, if only implicitly: this is the Family Resemblance account of "dharma". In contrast to these theories, I have made a case for what I have called the "Reform View". This view is reformative because it asks us to reconsider our contemporary practises of interpreting the meaning of "dharma".

I call the first theory the "Orthodox View" because of its adherence to a strict criterion of meaning. The Orthodox View holds that the only evidence that determines the meaning of a term is what it is applied to. On the basis of this positivistic, Extentionalism, the Orthodox View concludes that:

1) "dharma" cannot be consistently translated into one term in other languages, and
2) "dharma" of classical Indian thought is a term with a variety of distinct concepts, with distinct meanings, attached to it.

In contrast, there is the view that the underlying unity of "dharma" is to be found in an account of its etymology. I call this the "Conservative View" because of its attempted appeal to the history of the meaning of "dharma" and because it has a long history in Indological literature. The most prominent version of the Conservative View holds that "dharma" is derived from the root "*dhṛ*", which means *TO–UPHOLD* or *TO–SUPPORT*.

While the Orthodox View is a purely Extentionalist account, the Conservative View (at least in its plausible form) is an Intentionalist account. An Extentionalist version of the Conservative View holds that the meaning of "dharma" is to be found in its ability to stand for the property of *upholding*, or support. If this account were correct, the term "dharma" would have been used as a synonym for "bridge" or "crutch"—this is not the case. The Intentionalist version of the Conservative View has it that:

1) "dharma" stands for one concept, *DHARMA*,
2) whose meaning is the belief that the thing called "dharma" has the property of buttressing or supporting.

In contrast to the Conservative View, and like the Orthodox View, the Family Resemblance View holds that meaning consists in *extentions*. Unlike the other accounts of the meaning of "dharma" considered here, the Family Resemblance View holds that terms stand for concepts that are, themselves, ambiguous, while the other accounts regard terms, and not concepts, as the *loci* of ambiguity. According to the Family Resemblance View:

1) "dharma" stands for the concept *DHARMA*, which in turn is defined by an underdetermined number of related meanings,
2) the various meanings of *DHARMA* are the *extentions* of the term "dharma", and
3) all of the underdetermined number of meanings attached to *DHARMA* are essential to its definition.

In contrast, the Reform View holds that:

1) the meaning of "dharma" of classical Indian thought is not to be found in what it is applied to, but in its

reference to a certain *intention*,

2) "dharma" is a term that stands for one concept, with one meaning, in classical Indian thought (though, it stands for a distinct concept in modern times), and
3) the *intentional* state that the classical use of "dharma" signals—the meaning of the concept that "dharma" stands for in classical Indian thought—is the essential meaning of all moral terms, which is the common ground of meaningful, philosophical, disagreement on moral matters.

The Reform View, as I have presented it, also urges the following:

4) the essential *intention* of all moral terms is the *anger inclination*. On this account, the meaning of "dharma", or "ethical" and "moral" is *A–THING–ABOUT–WHICH–THERE–IS–AN–INCLINATION–TO–GET–ANGRY–(SHOULD–IT–BE–VIOLATED–OR–NOT–RESPECTED–IN–SOME–MANNER)–IN–THE–ABSENCE–OF– MITIGATING– REASONS.*

In theory, it is possible to present a version of the Reform View that does not depend upon the Anger Inclination Thesis for its account of moral meaning. However, I have argued in Part II Chapter 2 that the Anger Inclination Thesis is our best account of moral meaning.

I have bestowed a lot of attention on the Orthodox View, mostly because of its influence on Indological thought. The motivation behind this approach is admirable: those who endorse the Orthodox View wish to be objective about their research, and above all else, they wish to avoid projecting their presuppositions on to their subject-matter. Hence, the Orthodox View attempts to determine the meaning of "dharma" solely on the basis of the data: it presumes that the observable data regarding the meaning of "dharma", and its associated concepts, are its meanings. This approach is naive however: it fails to recognize that it too is not simply an empirical hypothesis about the meaning of "dharma", but an interpretive theory, based on a dubious premise: that the meaning of a term like "dharma" lies invariably in its *extentions*.

Once *intentionality* is recognized as an element in the meaning of a term, the Orthodox View ceases to have the incontrovertible support of the data. Upon comparison with alternate accounts, which do recognize *intention* as an element in the meaning of "dharma", the Orthodox View becomes patently implausible for more than one reason.

It was argued that key philosophical terms by their very nature are items that can only be defined by their accompanying *intention*. To deny this is to assert that *extention* plays a part in the definition of key philosophical terms (like "ethical", "real", "knowledge"). If *extentions* determined the definition of key philosophical terms, it would follow that every philosophical school was talking about a distinct concept when they used key philosophical terms like "ethical". If this is so, it follows that there has never been a philosophically meaningful disagreement. For those who take philosophy seriously, this cannot be so. Thus, it must be the case that key philosophical terms are definable by reference to their *intentions* only. If ever there were a candidate for a key philosophical term it is "dharma". It appears everywhere in Indian philosophy. If "dharma" is a key philosophical term, it follows that it too must be definable solely by reference to its accompanying *intention* (2.2. Key Philosophical Terms pp.22–31). If this is so, the Orthodox View cannot be correct.

There are other good reasons to abandon the Orthodox View. If it is granted that terms can have their meaning in their *intention*, it follows that the Orthodox View is widely implausible. For, if we are to take the Orthodox View seriously, we must interpret "dharma" to mean something new every time a distinct Indian philosophical school uses it, and every time, within an Indian philosophical school, different items are called "dharma". If this is so, we must believe that all Indian philosophers used a common term and granted idiosyncratic meanings to it—by fiat, and without limit. What is the motivation to use "dharma" to mean something different every time one applies it to a novel or idiosyncratic concern? There is no rational reason for such linguistic behaviour. There is, however, a rational reason to use one and the same term for novel items if it retains its original meaning: to express a philosophical view. In short, the Orthodox View is criticisable because it renders Indians' usage of "dharma" bewildering, without order and arbitrary. In contrast, an Intentionalist account of "dharma" affirms that the diverse applications of "dharma" are orderly and pragmatically meaningful. In comparison, thus, the Extentionalist, Orthodox View is implausible.

The same line of criticism was logged against the Family Resemblance account at an earlier point (3.2.11. Response to the Family Resemblance Argument pp.147–155), for it dissolves philosophical disagreement by construing every distinct use of the term "dharma" as constituting a unique meaning. Just as the Orthodox View fails to account for why one term, "dharma", is used to stand for so many things in Indian thought, the Family Resemblance account fails to explain why one concept, *DHARMA*, is used for so many matters. Both Extentionalist Views suffer from a common problem: in failing to explain the common, semantic element in all uses of the term "dharma", they leave the linguistic behaviour of classical Indians unexplained, and unexplainable.

The Family Resemblance account also falls to a different criticism: it renders concepts, themselves, computationally cumbersome, and impractical to employ (3.2.11. Response to the Family Resemblance Argument pp.147–155).

I have said very little about the Conservative View. It is generally rejected by those who have given extended attention to the question of the meaning of "dharma", but for the wrong reasons. Generally, those who are gripped by the question of the meaning of "dharma" gravitate, as a result of their seemingly scrupulous, empirical, methodology, to the Orthodox View, and for this reason reject the Conservative View.

The Conservative View, in its Intentionalist incarnation,

is to be applauded, for, in pinning its hopes on one, common meaning to all uses of "dharma", it provides an attempted explanation for the linguistic behaviour of classical Indians. On consideration, however, it must be rejected as well.

The Conservative View, as an Intentionalist theory, has certain advantages over the Orthodox View. For instance, it is far more theoretically economical: it only recognizes one meaning of "dharma" whereas the Orthodox View recognizes a seemingly endless list of meanings of "dharma". Because the Conservative View recognizes only one meaning of "dharma", it maximizes debate; on its account, the various schools of Indian thought were all contributing to a unified debate on the question of what is dharma.

In comparison, the Reform View fares similarly to the Conservative View, from the perspective of metatheoretical considerations. It recognizes only one meaning of "dharma" in classical Indian thought; as an explanation of historical Indian thinking, it is as economical as the Conservative View: both only countenance one classical meaning of "dharma". The Reform View surpasses the Conservative View in maximizing debate however. For the Conservative View, "dharma" has a peculiarly Indian meaning. The debate on "dharma" on its account extends only to those forums where the actual term "dharma" is used. For all practical purposes, this renders the debate on "dharma" a peculiarly South Asian, or Asian, matter. The Reform View holds that "dharma" is a synonym for any *perfect formal*, moral term, without *focus*, like "ethics", "ethical", or "moral". Hence, on its account, a debate on "dharma" is part of the wider, global debate on morality. The superiority of the Reform View in maximizing debate implies that the Reform View is more economical than the Conservative View. The Conservative View asks us to countenance one meaning for "dharma" and a distinct meaning for what it regards as moral terms. The Reform View, in contrast, recognizes one meaning for "dharma" and other *perfect formal*, moral terms without *focus*.

One could make the argument that, from another angle,

the Reform View fails to adequately maximize debate: by recognizing a modern and a distinct classical meaning of "dharma", it implies that modern, legal, references to "dharma" constitute a distinct discourse from the classical question of "dharma". If this is indeed a critical mark against the Reform View, the same criticism can be directed towards the Conservative View. The Conservative View would have to recognize a distinct meaning for "dharma" in modern times for the same reason that prompts the Reform View in this direction: the modern notion of "dharma" is an *extentional* term, whereas both the Reform and Conservative Views hold that the classical meaning of "dharma" is purely *intentional* in nature.

It is true that the Reform View urges us to accept a distinct meaning of "dharma" in modern times, but it can be no other way. The modern conception of "dharma" is a direct consequence of the Western political and cultural intervention in India in modern times, which resulted in an imperfect epistemic circumstance. It was an epistemic circumstance defined by unequal power relations, geared towards maintaining the political and cultural superiority of the West. It would have been much easier for Western academics of early Indology to recognize that "dharma" means *ETHICS* in the classical texts. But this would entail recognizing that there is a genuine debate to be entered into on the topic of morals; this would entail that the West could not simply win the moral argument by default, and moreover, that it must recognize the East as an equal partner in a contemporary moral debate. To have recognized that India has things to say on the topic of ethics would have compromised Western efforts to present itself as the only moral option in the East.

We might press for a justification for countenancing debate maximization as *the* reason to choose between the Reform interpretation of "dharma" and the Conservative interpretation. What if "dharma" is a peculiarly Asian concern? Why should we shy away from the Conservative View because it recognizes one meaning for classical "dharma", and another meaning for moral terms?

One reason for preferring the Reform View over the Conservative View is that moral concerns constitute a philosophical natural kind. Morality or ethics is not an artefact of Western philosophical perspectives that is particularly indicative of a Western cultural preoccupation, but, rather, "ethics" or "morality" are words that designate something that, in the world of ideas, constitutes a fundamental division of philosophy, just as epistemology, metaphysics, and logic constitute fundamental divisions of philosophy. If ethics is a philosophical natural kind of a fundamental order, it stands to reason that Indian philosophers would have addressed moral issues, just as they ventured into the realms of metaphysics, epistemology and logic. The Reform View provides us a means to understand how Indian philosophers ventured into the realm of ethics; by interpreting "dharma" as a key philosophical moral term, on its advice, we then see that Indian philosophers have been talking about ethical issues, in plain view, all this time; just as we would expect if ethics is a fundamental, philosophical, kind. The Conservative View, in contrast, cannot help us discern Indian philosophy's contribution to ethics.

Proof of the Conservative View's inability to enlighten us on moral endeavours of Indian philosophers is that *UPHOLDINGNESS* or *SUPPORTIVENESS* are not essential moral ideas. Frequently, Indian philosophers apply the term "dharma" to matters that they regard as having this feature—for that matter, frequently Western philosophers too apply "good" or "moral" to things that they regard as having the qualities of upholdingness or supportiveness; Plato's "Good", for instance, supports the world in a way, by giving it life and what little reality it has. However, supportiveness or upholdingness are not things that we necessarily always desire in something that we regard as moral. Sometimes we desire radical change, and moreover, we regard such change, which undoes order, as a good thing, for order as such is not necessarily a morally positive matter (order can be oppressive, tyrannical, and immoral). Thus, it is not surprising that in the history of Indian philosophy, views that are asserted by those who have no particular interest in upholdingness or supportingness have been called "dharma". In an account of Indian Materialist thought, the pure Hedonism ascribed to this school by one secondary, classical, Indian author, has been called their "dharma" (Guṇarantna 1990 p.276). Likewise, "dharma" is frequently used as a term, in Hinduism, for expiatory rites; these are things that are revolutionary; things that have the power to change our moral status. It is difficult to see how those who would have regarded such things as genuine dharmas would have thought that they, particularly, have the property of supportiveness, or upholdingness. In light of the fact that they reverse our moral failures, it is clear how such dharmas are morally relevant (2.6.4. When Moral Failings are not Frowned Upon pp.100–105). But their function appears to be precisely the opposite of upholding or supporting; they are cleansing; they take down and remove our moral pollution.

What is the character of this distinct, natural, philosophical kind that is ethics? The domain of philosophical interest that we pick out with the terms "ethics" and "moral", I would argue, is delimited by the *anger inclination*. This makes ethics, arguably, a very humanistic endeavour, for inclinations to get angry seem to be our forte. However, I think that this conforms to the humanistic implications of ethics that we are often so sensitive to.

In the end, I think that we should accept the Reform View (with the Anger Inclination Thesis) because it is the best explanation, not only of the phenomenon of "dharma", but also of moral matters on the whole. Indicators that it is the best explanation of the matters at hand is that it is theoretically economical, and that it maximizes debate. Through the lens of the Reform View, we can understand Indian philosophers to be involved in the same debate that Plato and other Western moralists have been involved in. This is what we ought to expect. Indians have contributed their share to the debate of metaphysics, epistemology, semantics and logic. It stands to reason that such an accomplished philosophical tradition would also have significant things to say on ethics. It further stands to reason that it is the term "dharma" that they used to express their opinions on morals.

Could "dharma" have a nonmoral meaning in the classical circumstance, despite all that has been said to date? I suspect that some would wish that I leave this possibility open. However, to do so would be irrational. The only motivation that I can see for retaining an equivocal account of classical "dharma", once the Orthodox View has been rejected, is to save our received interpretations of "dharma". This is not a good reason to hold on to view that "dharma" had more than one meaning in the classical Indian setting.

Notes

1 For those who are sympathetic to the Reform View, many of these criticisms will appear to be redundant and, moreover, question begging. As someone who is sympathetic to the Reform View, I feel that an argument has been delivered in Part II Chapter 2 that pre-empts many of these criticisms by criticizing their foundation; i.e., Extentionalism applied to key philosophical terms. Yet, for those who are not sympathetic to the Reform View, these various objections appear to be new and distinct ideas, and thus, they deserve to be addressed, individually.

2 Professor Priestley's argument from analogy is not the only version of an analogical argument for the equivocality of "dharma". One might attempt to cite terms like "Christian" in an analogical argument for the equivocality of "dharma". This argument rightly points out that "Christian" is a term that, at times, functions as a moral term. So, we hear people saying of practises "that is very Christian" or "that is not very Christian of you"—in these circumstances, "Christian" is used as a term of moral approval. In other circumstances, "Christian" is simply a label designating a certain belief structure. By analogy, one might argue that "dharma" too at times functions as a moral term (in classical times) and at other times it is simply a label for things (be they the constituents of reality or properties). This attempt at the argument from analogy fails for the same reason that the previous argument fails—it does not give proper attention to the distinction between purely *intentional* and *extentional* terms. It fails to note that "Christian" is primarily an *extentional* term, with a secondary, parasitic, *intentional* meaning, and it presumes that "dharma" is a

similar term, when, according to the argument of the Reform View, "dharma" is a very different kind of term, with no *extentional* restrictions on its use.

3 A strong argument can be made that the view that Indian philosophy is dominated by other worldly concerns, and that it shuns ethics, is symptomatic of a colonial discourse, dominated by Orientalist caricatures of Indian thought and civilisation. The chief feature of Orientalist constructs is the depiction of the oriental as being devoid of normal human qualities; concern for the practical things of life, dispositions to get angry, etc. For more on colonial discourse, and the issue of Orientalist representations of the East, see E.W. Said (1994) and Ronald B.Inden (1990).

Part III: Implications of the Moral Meaning of "Dharma"

Chapter 4

Indian Axiology

The account of moral terms proffered in the argument for the Reform View has certain implications for our study of Indian thought. At least two commonplace accounts of Indian moral thought are mistaken if the Anger Inclination Thesis is correct.

4.1. The *Puruṣārtha* Explanation of Indian Ethics

In the exposition of Indian moral thought, one will frequently find reference to the *puruṣārthas.*[1] "*Puruṣārtha*" is a compound term that is usually translated as the "ends of man". The word breaks down into the terms "*puruṣa*" and "*artha*". "*Puruṣa*" generally means *PERSON*, though in Sanskrit, being a genderred language (and patriarchy being what it is) the term is male genderred. The term "*artha*" is an interesting word from the standpoint of axiological concerns because it has several distinct value-theoretic applications. It can be used to stand for (i) material possession or wealth, (ii) a goal, (iii) the meaning of an expression or word, or even (iv) a thing, but it also stands for (v) value.[2] A better translation, thus, of the term "*puruṣārtha*" is "values of persons" because what it stands for are four distinct value-theoretic spheres. These are (1) dharma, (2) *artha* (taken in this context, generally, to name material prosperity) (3) *kāma*, or pleasure, and (4) *mokṣa*, or soteriological liberation.[3]

According to a common account of Indian ethics, which we might call the "*Puruṣārtha* Explanation of Indian Ethics", Indian ethics—all Indian ethics—consists of the view that there are four ends to a person's life, and that pursuing, or maximizing, these ends constitutes one's moral obligations or objectives—the ends being dharma, *artha*, *kāma* and *mokṣa*.

There is no gainsaying that this four-fold scheme has dominated Indian axiological awareness, and moreover, that most major philosophical movements of India have countenanced these distinct values—if only conceptually. In fact, the history of Indian philosophy can be understood as a debate, amongst various Indian philosophers and schools, regarding how these four spheres of value are related to each other, and what—if anything—constitutes their *extensions.* While these values no doubt form the axiological backdrop against which Indian philosophy is done, it is a mistake to construe them as constituting Indian moral thinking.

The first reason for rejecting the *Puruṣārtha* explanation of Indian ethics is that not all schools of Indian thought recognize these values: early Pūrvamīmāṃsā thinkers, for instance, and the Indian Materialist school—Cārvāka—did not recognize *mokṣa.*

Another point of disagreement between the various schools of Indian thought is the relationship that obtains between these goals. Even amongst those philosophies that recognize all four values, there is a great difference amongst them as to how another field (say, the field of economic success) is related to the field of dharma.

Importantly, from the perspective of the Anger Inclination Thesis, there is a criticism to be dealt to notion that pursuing all the four *puruṣārthas* constitutes Indian moral theory. The criticism begins with the understanding that "dharma" is India's *perfect formal* moral term, without *focus*, and with the view that neither "*artha*", nor "*kāma*", nor "*mokṣa*" has the tell-tale signs of moral terms: the *anger inclination* is not *perfectly* associated with these ideas. The use of the terms "*artha*", "*kāma*" and "*mokṣa*", I believe, do not (*intentionally*) communicate to interlocutors the *anger inclination.* If this is so, it follows that the concepts of *ARTHA*, *KĀMA* and *MOKṢA* are not, intrinsically, moral in nature.

When I say that *ARTHA, KĀMA* and *MOKṢA* are not moral in nature, I do not wish to communicate the view that they are immoral: only that the *intension* (the meaning) of these *concepts* are nonmoral in nature. Not all value concepts are moral concepts, and frequently in the study of Indian ethics, the distinction between moral concepts and nonmoral concepts is collapsed, leading to the view that the pursuit of the *puruṣārthas* is, analytically, an objective of morality.

Examples of Western terms that stand for value-theoretic concepts that are not moral in nature are "beauty", "success", "true"—the referents of these words are arguably all good things to maximize; but their maximization is not, as a matter of semantics, a moral pursuit.

How are we to view the *puruṣārthas*? I believe that they are simply a list of value-theoretic concepts that Indian thinkers recognized. In fact, another name for the *puruṣārthas*, as specified in the traditional Sanskrit dictionary, the *Amarakoṣa*, is "*caturvarga*", which literally means *A–COLLECTION–OR–GROUP–OF–FOUR* (the "*trivarga*" is defined as the same list, minus "*mokṣa*") (*Amarakoṣa* vs.1467).

If we properly apply the Anger Inclination Thesis to the *puruṣārthas*, *MORALITY*, or *ETHICS*, is really a subset of the values listed in the *puruṣārthas*—the *puruṣārthas* do not comprise the notion of *DHARMA*. Yet, the Anger Inclination Thesis also tells us that the *extentions* of the concepts specified as *puruṣārthas* may take on moral dimensions in certain contexts, in relation to certain moral theories. For instance, the pursuit of *artha* is the dharma of the head of a householder in the context of the ethics of the Pūrvamīmāṃsā—not because *ARTHA* is a moral concept, but because *artha* constitutes an *extention* of "dharma" in this philosophy; sometimes. In the context of Jain thought, in contrast, the pursuit of *artha* is contrary to dharma, for *artha* involves harm to others, whereas dharma, on the Jain view, consists in the abstention from injuring others. Likewise, it could be argued that for some persons—spiritual leaders of certain religious communities of India—the pursuit of *mokṣa* is their dharma, for they are morally bound to pursue this objective in return for the patronage that they receive from others. If a spiritual master lives off the patronage of others, while making no effort to genuinely pursue *mokṣa,* we could imagine that others (their disciples, and the public at large) would regard such a person as morally despicable—and the failure to strive for *mokṣa* a moral failure. To recognize, however, that such objectives in certain contexts are moral in nature is a distinct position from the view that the various *puruṣārthas,* apart from dharma, are always moral, or part of (all) Indian moral theory; if "*mokṣa*", "*artha*", or "*kāma*" are moral terms, they are *imperfect* moral terms. Hence, it is not the case that (all) Indian philosophy countenances the values designated by these terms as moral ends.

4.2. The *Summum Bonum* and Indian Ethics

Another account of Indian moral thought claims that Indian ethics is concerned with the "*summum bonum*" of human life; a Latin phrase meaning the GREATEST–GOOD.[4] The Indian equivalent of this term is "*niḥśreyasa*"—a term which is usually used to name *mokṣa*. The *summum bonum* view of Indian ethics is thus the view that the "highest goal of Indian ethics is the attainment of *mokṣa*" (Sharma 1965 p.62). We may call this the "*Summum Bonum* Explanation of Indian Ethics".

On the basis of the Anger Inclination Thesis, this approach to explicating Indian ethics meets with two objections.

The view that Indian ethics concerns the greatest good presents *mokṣa* as the subject of Indian ethics. "*Mokṣa*", however lacks the signs of being a *perfect* moral term, of classical Indian thought: its use does not communicate the *anger inclination*. In short, there is nothing essentially moral about MOKṢA in Indian philosophy.

In response, one might argue that ethics always concerns itself with the greatest good, and since *mokṣa* is the typical denotation of "*niḥśreyasa*" in Indian philosophical thought, it follows that Indian ethics is typically concerned with *mokṣa*. This way of saving the *Summum Bonum* Explanation of Indian Ethics presumes a version of the Overridingness Thesis.

The greatest good in any axiological scheme is one whose maximization, or value-theoretic appeal, is greater than all other values. Evaluative statements about the greatest good would be statements that trump other evaluative statements, either in fact, or normatively. The only way that the greatest good on any axiological scheme could be considered to be identical with a moral goal is if statements about them are by definition always moral statements. The view that statements about the greatest good on any axiological scheme are, by definition, moral statements is a version of the Overridingness Thesis. This thesis was considered at length at an earlier point (2.3.3 Importance and Overridingness pp.43–47). As noted, the chief problem for this view is that moral values are not, invariably, those that we either give the most weight to, or those that we regard as the most important. What makes a value moral in nature is its essential connection to the *anger inclination*. What makes a value the greatest good is whether we are willing to sacrifice all other goods for its sake.

Thus, the *Summum Bonum* account of Indian Ethics mistakes a nonmoral concept as the essential subject of Indian ethics. As with the *Puruṣārtha* Explanation of Indian Ethics, we can restate the same disclaimer: what is being argued is not the view that *mokṣa* cannot be the object of an Indian moral theory. What is being argued is that there is nothing definitionally moral in nature about *THE GREATEST GOOD* or the concept *MOKṢA*.

Notes

1 See Puruṣottama Bilimoria (1991 p.45), M. Christopher Byrski (1976), Austin B. Creel's chapter entitled "The Context of Values in Hindu Ethics" (1977 pp.48–72), Sanat Kumar Sen (1967 p.64) and I.C. Sharma (1965 p.61).

2 I came upon the rendering of "*artha*" as "value" in Svāmī Ādidevānanda's translation of *Gītā* 18:32.—*Adharmaṁ dharmam iti yā manyate tamasa avṛtā / sarva arthān viparītām ca buddhiḥ sā pārtha tāmasī.*—"That Buddhi, O Arjuna, which, enveloped in darkness, regards adharma as dharma and which reverses every value [*artha*], is *tāmasika*". For the translation, see Rāmānuja (1991).

3 Karl Potter (1963 pp.6–8) has suggested that these various *arthas* should be understood as attitudes that Indians thought we ought to adopt. I find the intended clarification perplexing. The view that values come down to attitudes of persons is often known as "Expressivism." As it is an Intentionalist account of values, I think that it is on the right track. However, Potter does not proffer this account for all values, but simply *arthas*. This leaves me with the impression that Potter regards the *arthas* as their own philosophical kind, distinct from values. I know of no reason to regard *arthas* as distinct philosophical kinds, apart from values on the whole. On a separate note, Donald R. Davis Jr. has argued in a recent article (2004) that *puruṣārthas* are not values or axiological at all. The references of these concepts are not the ends of actions, according to Davis, but the activities themselves. And thus these concepts are "classificatory categories." There are several virtues to this article, most importantly it sets out the importance of the *puruṣārthas* scheme in various Indian philosophical traditions beyond the pail of Hinduism. However, Davis's argument relies upon the spurious conceptual distinction between facts and values. If facts can be values too, then activities that these concepts refer to can be values as well. Moreover, there is no incongruity between the *puruṣārthas* being axiological in nature and serving categorizational functions. In fact, this is one of the principle functions of perfect, formal value terms without focus.

4 For examples, see Keith E. Yandell (1984 p.64), Frederick C. Copleston, S.J. (1977 p.78), I.C. Sharma (1965 p.29, p.32), and S. Cromewell Crawford (1974 p.xiv).

Part IV: Moral Philosophy

Chapter 5

Ethics in Philosophy

Our goal is to recognize Indian ethics, or Indian moral philosophy, for what it is: an important part of the history of Indian philosophy. To this end, it was argued that "dharma" is the *perfect formal* moral term, without *focus*, *par excellence*, of Indian philosophical literature (2.6. The Meaning of "Dharma" pp.91–105, 2.7. An Argument for the Reform View pp.105–107; Chapter 3, The Classical Meaning of "Dharma" pp.113–176). What this implies is that we are justified in believing that passages that mention "dharma" or discuss dharma in classical Indian philosophy are of ethical significance.

One of the criticisms levelled against Indian philosophy is that it simply did not do ethics—the argument to the effect that "dharma" is a moral term in classical Indian thought goes a long way to proving this criticism wrong, for philosophical discussions that involve "dharma" constitute concrete proof of Indian philosophers' attention to moral matters. There is another, more subtle criticism though: this criticism suggests that, while Indian philosophers may have occasionally addressed matters of ethical importance, their involvement in ethics is insignificant; that ethics is not an important part of the history of Indian philosophy (1.1. Problem of Ethics in Indian Philosophy pp.3–5).

In order to settle such doubts, we must ask the question, what is ethics? Without an account of the subject-matter of ethics, or the discipline of ethics, we are hardly in a position to comment on whether Indian philosophers did or did not do ethics, or to what extent they contributed to this field.

5.1. What is Ethics?

The astute reader will note that the question "what is 'ethics'", and even "what is *ETHICS*", is a matter that we have been addressing, all along, in our effort to come to terms with the meaning of "dharma". Several arguments have been advanced to prove that "ethics" is a term—and that *ETHICS* is a concept—that must be understood not in terms of what it is applied to, but in terms of the *intentional* state that is invariably associated with it.

The first argument that was made for this Reform View is that (a) "ethics", like "real" or "knowledge", is a key philosophical term, which functions centrally in the articulation of a philosophical perspective, and (b) that such terms cannot be defined (or, rather, are not definable) with respect to their *extentions* (the things they are applied to) for such terms retain a unitary meaning across philosophical theories in spite of the fact that they are used as labels for diverse matters. Any attempt to define such terms with respect to what they are applied to would render them philosophically useless, and not amenable to functioning as focal points of philosophical debate (2.2. Key Philosophical Terms pp.22–31).

The second argument that was presented in favour of the Reform View (the view that "ethics" cannot be defined in terms of what it is applied to, but with respect to its accompanying *intention*) is the argument for the Anger Inclination Thesis. The Anger Inclination Thesis is the view that the essence of moral significance is a direct relationship with the *anger inclination*. According to this view, what makes something morally significant—what makes it moral or ethical—is simply the connection with the *anger inclination*. This perspective on moral significance criticizes all efforts to pin down the nature of the things that we call "moral" or "ethics" to the exclusion of other things, for such efforts (i) fail to respect the diversity of moral concerns that people have, and (ii) fail to take into account the very real relevance of radical philosophical debate and disagreement to moral issues (2.3.7. Anger Inclination pp.53–66, and 2.3.8. Composite Accounts of Moral Statements pp.66–70).

It has been argued that the Orthodox approach to the meaning of "ethics" is Extentionalist in nature (1.2. The Problem of "Dharma" pp.5–9; 2.2. Key Philosophical Terms pp.22–31). This view holds that there are certain things that "we call ethics", and moreover, that what we call ethics is its meaning. This Extentionalism is not only present in criticisms of the meaning of "dharma" but also in the few accounts of the subject-matter of ethics that we gain from Indological scholars.

Schweitzer, for instance, tells us that ethics has to do with "world and life" (Schweitzer 1936 p.2). On the basis of a putative positive disposition towards this matter in the West, and a putative negative disposition towards this matter on the Indian side, Schweitzer argues that Indian philosophy is bereft of ethics. Likewise, Deutsch gives us a specific account of what he takes ethics to consist of. According to Deutsch, ethics is a "... rigorous, independent inquiry into problems of, and questions concerning, the meaning of value, the justification of judgements, and the analysis of moral concepts and concrete existential modes of behaviour ..." (Deutsch 1969 p.99). On the basis of this account of "ethics", Deutsch suggests that the assessment that Indian philosophy turns its back on moral issues is fair.

We may give both Schweitzer and Deutsch credit for attempting a definition of "ethics". However, such Extentionalist approaches to defining "ethics" open themselves to various problems. Schweitzer's account of the *meaning* of *ETHICS* has the problem of failing to embrace Neo-Platonic views, which conceive matter as Evil, and The Good as an otherworldly matter. What Deutsch identifies as "ethics" is in reality a composite of many distinct philosophical concerns—some of which do not typically go under the heading of "ethics". If we were to separate these matters, we would land with the following list:

1) ethics is a rigorous and "independent" inquiry,
2) ethics concerns an inquiry into the meaning of value,
3) ethics concerns the justification of [moral] judgements,

4) ethics concerns the analysis of moral concepts, and
5) ethics concerns the analysis of "concrete existential modes of behaviour".

The question of (2) the meaning of value is what axiology, or value theory, is. Axiology, on many accounts, is a distinct field from ethics. Arguably, the open-ended question of the nature of value as such, without regard to the question of what moral values are specifically like, is not a moral question, but, rather, an axiological question.

The question of (3) the justification of moral judgements is most definitely a matter that falls into the province of ethics. However, there are many activities that fall into the domain of ethics, and not all of them are concerned with justifying moral judgements. The pursuits treated under the heading of "metaethics" are moral in nature—like the question of whether moral statements are *cognitive* or *noncognitive*. Yet, such a pursuit is not primarily concerned with justifying moral judgements: the thesis that moral statements are *cognitive*, or *noncognitive*, does not constitute a *justification* of moral judgements; it is merely a *classification* of moral judgements.

The (4) analysis of moral concepts no doubt falls within the province of ethics, but, once again, I would argue that it is not the case that all activities that count as ethics involve the analysis of moral concepts. For instance, the question of whether a certain concrete scenario presents a moral dilemma is a question for ethics but it is unlikely that answering this question will hinge upon the analyses of moral concepts. Rather, the possible courses of action, agents and their choices are likely to be the subject of analysis. Likewise, not all philosophical activities that count as ethics concern themselves with (5) an analysis of "concrete existential modes of behaviour". For instance, the elaboration of a theory of virtue ethics could eschew questions of behaviour (2.3.1. Social Content and Conduct pp.35, 37–38).

I would argue that few philosophical texts within the history of Western philosophy itself would qualify as bearing ethics according to Deutsch's account. The most problematic aspect of Deutsch's definition is the notion that (1) ethics must in some way be "independent" from other philosophical concerns, or that it must be discussed to the exclusion of other philosophical matters. Philosophy, by its very nature, does not lend itself to independent investigations. I would argue that it is unfair to expect that for a philosopher to do ethics that they must refrain from addressing other philosophical issues.

Plato's *Republic*, for instance, is a text of moral significance, and a classic text of the history of moral philosophy, and yet, it attends to matters of diverse philosophical importance: politics, metaphysics, and epistemology are all touched upon in this work. Moreover, the epistemological and metaphysical issues that are broached contribute to a moral thesis (an account of the nature of The Good). If we were to accurately apply Deutsch's criteria of ethics to the *Republic*, it would turn out that the *Republic* is not a text on (or of) ethics, for it does not constitute an independent inquiry into the questions of ethics.

Arguably, there are some tokens of philosophy that appear to treat moral matters independently of other philosophical issues; philosophical texts that compare and contrast moral theories (such as deontology, and utilitarianism) bear the title "ethics". It has certainly become increasingly the norm in philosophy, since Mill's *On Liberty*, to deal with ethics by itself, or, in conjunction with political questions only. But my sense is that we would be hard pressed to find many texts from the history of philosophy, prior to this, which dealt with moral issues to the exclusion of other philosophical matters.

Extentionalist accounts of the meaning of "ethics" or what "we mean by 'ethics'" are doomed to failure, I would argue, because what we *mean* by the term "ethics" and the concept *ETHICS* cannot be captured in a list of items that we apply the term "ethics" to (2.2. Key Philosophical Terms pp.22–31, 2.3.1. Social Content and Conduct pp.35–38, 2.3.6. Punishment pp.52–53).

To make this point even clearer, we might take the opportunity to recognize the variety of activities and concerns in the history of Western thought that lay claim to the title "ethics".

5.2. On the Pursuits that Answer to "Ethics"

Philosophical treatments of ethics over the past hundred years have been enormously influenced by the criticisms of Logical Positivism. The self-conscious refinement and differentiation between different disciplines of ethics is in part a consequence of the critical stance of Logical Positivism towards moral issues.

Logical Positivism is one of the most significant *darśanas* (PHILOSOPHICAL–VIEWS) of the twentieth century, with one of the simplest *pramāṇas* (MEANS–OF–KNOWLEDGE). The *darśana* Positivism holds that the empirical sciences, and only the empirical sciences, constitute *pramāṇa*. Logical Positivism is a related *darśana*, which holds that the empirical sciences, and logic (which includes mathematics on its reckoning) and only these two, constitute *pramāṇa*.

The glamour and sensation of Logical Positivism was in part a function of its determination to eradicate many traditional provinces of philosophy: metaphysics, on its account, is mere poetry, since there is putatively nothing in the province of metaphysics that could be put to the test; epistemology is a matter to be phased out, and archived in psychology, for we already know that only science and logic constitute *pramāṇa*. Moral questions, on the account of Logical Positivism, are the paradigm of unscientific issues, for, according to Logical Positivism, they have nothing to do with what can be tested, but with the likes and dislikes of people. As well, moral issues have nothing to do with the relationships between our ideas, says the Logical Positivist, and hence, logic cannot have anything to do with moral issues.[1] What is left for the subject of philosophy to study? At best, philosophy can only be conceptual clarification, for Logical Positivism.

While there is no real sense to moral questions, in Logical Positivism's view, the philosopher as clear thinker *par excellence* does have something to contribute to moral conflict. The philosopher can elucidate why it is that there is no truth or falsity to moral claims, and she can lend her services by clarifying whatever peripheral issues there are that bear upon moral conflicts. Thus while the philosopher, *qua* rational critic, cannot contribute to moral debate (for the notion that there is something to debate about in morality is a confusion, according to Logical Positivism) the philosopher can referee moral conflict. This project has been called "ethics", in the past.[2]

Logical Positivism, with its sceptical stance towards moral debate, engenders a noninterventionist spirit in philosophy regarding the possibility of substantive ethics as a topic for philosophical investigation. In addition to the referee approach to ethics, the general noninterventionist spirit defines two additionally distinct philosophical activities that attempt to treat moral concerns without treading upon substantive moral questions. These versions of ethics are often called "metaethics" and "metamorality".

Metaethics concerns universal features of moral claims that are not exclusive to them. The classic debate in metaethics centres around whether moral statements are *cognitive* or *noncognitive*. Within the fold of metaethics also fall questions of whether there is any truth to evaluative claims, whether evaluative terms and statements are *intentional* or *extentional* in meaning, whether moral argumentation is a species of rational argumentation, and whether moral belief as a species of value belief is intrinsically motivating. Philosophers who deal simply with metaethical issues frequently regard their subject-matter as a speciality within ethics.

A close relative to metaethics is something that we might call "moral metaphysics". Issues that fall into this category are those of a metaphysical nature that are yet morally relevant. Examples are the question of the nature of moral patients, the question of the compatibility of freedom and determinism, and the question of the nature of moral properties as such. Moral metaphysics is like metaethics, in that it is not primarily concerned with substantive questions of what is right or wrong. Unlike metaethics, moral metaphysics's heyday predates the rise of Logical Positivism. Philosophers who treat of just these issue say in good conscience that their philosophical speciality is ethics.

Metamorality is the philosophical pursuit of delimiting the sphere of the moral, or ethical, from the nonmoral or nonethical. This field does treat only those universal features of moral statements and issues that are peculiar to moral subject-matter. The views regarding the definition of moral statements and subject-matter discussed in 2.3. Definitions of Moral Statements (pp.31–70) constitute the better part of metamoral debate. insofar as this activity concerns moral issues, it has been known by the title of "ethics" as well.

Logical Positivism did not stay forever at the top. Criticisms from within, particularly from the latter Wittgenstein (1958) and W.V.O. Quine (1960), threatened the distinction between empirical observation and logical consequence that was essential to the older generation. As a consequence of the writings of Wittgenstein, the social sciences—particularly linguistics—gains a new legitimacy as the archetype of scientific research and experience; not the natural sciences—as the older generation held.

If Logical Positivism is defined wholly in terms of *pramāṇa*, it is still arguably a major force in philosophy to this day. However, it lost its thunder by the 1960s. By the 1970s, the philosophical activity of directly taking sides in moral debate experienced a renaissance. The work that decisively brings in a revised optimism towards dealing with substantive moral issues is John Rawls's *A Theory of Justice* (1970).

Prior to Logical Positivism, there tended not to be distinctions drawn between philosophical treatments of ethics that take sides in substantive moral debate. After Logical Positivism, the substantive conception of ethics becomes consciously divided into two different endeavours by many philosophers: (i) applied ethics, and (ii) nonapplied ethics.

Applied ethics is the version of ethics that promises to give answers to concrete, everyday, moral conundrums, on the authority of a general theory of morality. Applied ethics thus reasons from first principles; its main concern is to apply moral theories to real-life circumstances.

Philosophers do not usually self-consciously breakdown the remaining, substantive, notion of ethics, distinct from applied ethics, nor do they give it a title, aside from the general label of "ethics". However, we could divide this subject into two distinct treatments of moral subject-matter.

"Dialectical ethics" is an apt term for just one of these disciplines. Dialectical ethics is the project of attempting to arrive at moral doctrine by philosophical means. This project answers to Aristotle's description of ethics, in the *Nicomachean Ethics* (1095a30), as a discipline that reasons not *from* first principles but *to* first principles. A classic example of dialectical ethics is Plato's *Meno*, where Socrates and his interlocutor, Meno, attempt (and fail) to arrive at a substantive account of the nature of virtue. Dialectical ethics is thus a version of "ethics" that is characteristic of Greek thought on the subject: it is a discoverative endeavour. It is also very much alive today in the writings of those moral philosophers who believe that moral theory attempts to capture and systematize pre-reflective moral intuitions.

There is an activity that attempts to take sides in moral controversy, though it neither attempts to reason to first principles (like dialectical ethics) nor from first principles (like applied ethics). The goal of this activity is to *justify* a moral outlook, captured in moral principles. This version of ethics is closer to dialectical ethics than to applied ethics, as it is concerned with attempting to prove something with respect to first principles. However, while in the case of dialectical ethics, first principles are something to be procured, this latter conception of ethics starts off with putative ethical principles, and proceeds to a philosophical justification of these principles. To distinguish this activity from dialectical ethics, we could call it "justificative ethics".

The idea of justificative ethics shows up in Kant's thought. Paton, in his introduction to his translation of Kant's *Groundwork of the Metaphysics of Morals*, explains Kant's view as:

> ... if there are moral principles in accordance with which men ought to act, knowledge of these principles must be *a priori* knowledge: it cannot be based on sensuous experience. The *a priori* part of ethics is concerned with the formulation and justification of moral principles .... This *a priori* part of ethics may be called a *metaphysics of morals* .... For detailed knowledge of particular human duties we require experience of human nature (and indeed of many other things). This belongs to the empirical part of ethics and is called by Kant "*practical anthropology*", though his use of the term is not altogether clear. (Paton 1956 p.14)

The distinction in question is made in Kant's preface to his *Groundwork of the Metaphysics of Morals* (1956 p.56).

Kant's "*metaphysics of morals*", on Paton's account, is roughly what I have identified as "justificative ethics".[3]

What of Kant's "practical anthropology?" Contrary to Paton, I think that it is rather clear what Kant intends to designate by this term. It is a thorough elaboration of the content of a moral theory; the kind of thing that would show up in an ethnography. A practical anthropology concerns an inventory of items that form the *extension* of a particular account of the concept of morality. This conception complements Kant's thoroughly argumentative notion of the *metaphysics of morals*, for it is a particular conception of practical anthropology, enshrined in a set of moral principles, that one justifies in a philosophical setting. While Kant's conception of practical anthropology is ancillary to his conception of a philosophical version of ethics that justifies it, it constitutes another version of "ethics", for it concerns moral matters.

Up to this point, eight logically distinct activities that go by the name of "ethics" have been noted. These are:

1) the refereeing of moral conflict ("referee function of ethics")
2) the philosophical clarification of universal features of moral claims that are not exclusive to them ("metaethics")
3) the investigation of metaphysical questions that are morally significant ("moral metaphysics")
4) the philosophical delineation of moral concerns from nonmoral concerns ("metamorality")
5) the deduction of practical counsel from moral first principles ("applied ethics")
6) the philosophical process of arriving at or developing moral doctrine ("dialectical ethics")
7) the philosophical justification of moral first principles ("justificative ethics")
8) the inventory of the *extension* of an account of the concept *MORALITY*, from the perspective of a particular substantive view ("practical anthropology")

There are other schemes that are employed in distinguishing activities that qualify as ethics. A standard schematic account these days divides ethics into "metaethics" and "normative ethics". As G.H. Green notes, "[d]istinguishing between metaethics and normative ethics has come to be standard procedure, as encyclopedia articles, textbooks, and introductory lectures amply testify" (Green 1982 p.131). This two-tier division leans heavily on an etymological understanding of "metaethics". According to one version of the etymological understanding, "metaethics" takes the whole field of ethics as its object: this is why it is *meta*-ethics. Normative ethics would thus be the remainder of ethics; that which is the object of metaethical inquiry. On another understanding, "metaethics" concerns second-order ethical questions, just as "metalanguage" concerns a second-order discourse on language (Gewirth 1968 p.214). Normative ethics, in contrast, would be the first-order, moral inquiry.

This standard division of ethics into just two fields hints

of a latent Extentionalism with respect to the field of ethics on the whole. This suspicion is arguably confirmed by the fact that the division causes problems for the doing of ethics.

The metaethics–normative ethics division is associated with a problematization of philosophy's role in substantive issues. On most versions of the two-tier account, normative ethics is the side of ethics concerned with substantive matters. Metaethics, in contrast, is construed as the first stop for philosophy in matters of ethics. Voicing this view, Gary Foulk argues that "answers to the questions asked by metaethics must not only be obtained prior to the answers to the questions asked by normative ethics, but the former answers place clear limitations on the latter" (Foulk 1973 p.172). Similarly, Michael Smith writes:

> Subjects in normative ethics ... [have] names like "Practical Ethics", "Applied Ethics", "Contemporary Moral Issues", "Crime and Punishment", "Ethics and the Environment", "The Good Things of Life" and so on ... Despite their interest in normative ethics, however, philosophers have not tended to think that these sorts of questions are of the first importance in moral philosophy [i.e. ethics] .... Rather they have thought that we should do normative ethics only after we have given satisfactory answers to certain questions in metaethics. (Smith 1994 pp.1–2)

As per this two-tier scheme, metaethics is, by definition, the part of ethics that is not concerned with substantive issues. As metaethics is the aspect of ethics that is philosophically more pressing, on this account, it follows that philosophy has nothing primarily to do in substantive matters. By defining ethics thus, this two-fold scheme invents a philosophical crisis for substantive ethics: it renders this aspect of ethics philosophically less ripe and less amenable to independent philosophical inquiry.

Secondly, the two-fold scheme of metaethics and normative ethics also gives rise to the controversy of whether metaethical questions can be substantively neutral or not. The traditional view is that metaethics is concerned with matters that do not have any clear substantive implications. However, many authors have argued against this view, sighting the logical relationship between metaethical issues and substantive issues (Gewirth 1960 p.205, Solomon 1970 p.97, Green 1982 p.137, D. Zimmerman 1980).

The enumeration of activities that answer to the notion of "ethics" has not been put forward as the conclusive account of what "ethics" consists in; quite the contrary. I have enumerated various activities that have been called "ethics" to make the point that there is no single or common intellectual activity that answers to this title. We could, for whatever motive, distinguish between distinct activities that answer to the label "ethics"—but here, we would err if we thought that we were doing little more than giving labels to gestalts that we have picked out. When we start to take such labels and distinctions between activities that count as "ethics" too seriously, we land with artificial controversies, like the question of whether metaethics is substantively neutral or not. Moreover, we overlook that philosophers, in their attempt to deal with ethics, involve themselves in many different activities that are defined in relation to *their* interests.

5.3. "Moral Philosophy"?

The main problem with the question of what ethics is is that "ethics" is a *perfect formal* moral term, without *focus*. Such a term has no substantive restrictions built into its meaning, and so we cannot attempt to define what ethics is by looking to what we call ethics.

How do we settle, then, the question of whether Indian philosophers did or did not do ethics? To settle this question, let us rephrase it. Instead of asking whether Indian philosophers did "ethics", let us ask if Indian philosophers did "moral philosophy". If they produced works on moral philosophy and contributed to this field of philosophy, we could say, with confidence, that ethics was a matter that they wrote on; that ethics constitutes a part of the history of Indian philosophy; that Indian philosophers *did* ethics.

How does rephrasing the question help us? For "moral" too is a *perfect formal*, moral term, without *focus*, just like "ethics". "Moral" thus has no substantive restrictions on its applications built into its meaning. Are we not back to the same problem? Moreover, is it not the case that "philosophy" is itself an *intentional* term, that functions as a key philosophical term? If "philosophy" is itself an *intentional* term, it appears that we will arrive at the same difficulties in specifying what philosophy is that we have encountered in relationship to *ETHICS*.

My belief is that our question is made easier to determine by shifting the focus from *ETHICS* to *MORAL–PHILOSOPHY*. For, while "moral" is an *intentional* term, and while "philosophy" is also an *intentional* term, in combination, they lead to a compound term, and a composite concept, that has a narrower meaning.

5.3.1. What Does "Philosophy" Mean?

As a prelude to the question whether Indian philosophers contributed to moral philosophy, let us arrive at a definition of *PHILOSOPHY*.

The question of what philosophy is often appears daunting for philosophers. Deleuze and Gauttari argue:

> The question *what is philosophy?* can perhaps be posed only late in life, with the arrival of old age and the time for speaking concretely. In fact, the bibliography on the nature of philosophy is very limited. It is a question posed in a moment of quite restlessness, at midnight, when there is no longer anything to ask. It was asked before; it was always being asked, but too indirectly or obliquely; the question was too artificial, to abstract. Instead of being seized by it, those who asked the question set it out and controlled it in passing. They were not sober enough. There was too much desire to *do* philosophy to wonder what it was, except as a stylistic exercise. (Deleuze and Gauttari 1994 p.1)

Deleuze and Gauttari attempt to answer the question of what philosophy is by an account of its etymology.

While I find their full account of the *extension* of *PHILOSOPHY* fantastical, I do think they are patently correct with respect to one matter: that the meaning of "philosophy" can be read off of an account of its etymology.

Philosophy divides into "*philo*" and "*sophy*". "*Philo*" comes down to us from Middle English; from Old French; from Latin; from the Greek "*philo*", which means *DEAR, FRIENDLY.* "*Sophy*" comes down to us in the same manner; from the Greek "*sophia*", which means *WISDOM. PHILOSOPHY* is thus that which is friendly or dear to wisdom; *PHILOSOPHY* pertains to that which is amenable to wisdom.

We call something "friendly" when it is supportive and favourably disposed to something; we call something *DEAR* when we regard it favourably and affectionately. Thus, *PHILO* captures both the notion of loving, or valuing, and being loved, or valued. What do we mean by *WISDOM*? *WISDOM* is itself an *intentional* concept, that we have intractable disagreements over; what is wise in one person's eyes is not wise to another's. Yet, by wisdom we generally mean to name something that *we regard* as being *epistemically revealing*. If this is the correct *intentional* account of *WISDOM*, we could define "philosophy" as *THAT–WHICH–IS–REGARDED–AS–FRIENDLY–OR–DEAR–TO– WHAT–IS– REGARDED–AS– EPISTEMIC–REVELATION.*

This may seem like an odd definition of philosophy, in light of the fact that philosophy is a narrowly conceived profession these days, and by the fact that there are several fields of learning that promote and are valued by wisdom outside of "philosophy". But here it is instructive to remember that we call accomplished scholars in various fields "Doctors in the philosophy of ..." when they earn their Ph.D degree. The significance of philosophy is thus quite wide.

There are two ways that we could proffer the etymological definition of "philosophy": we could formulate it *extentionally*, in which case "philosophy" would simply be a name for certain things. Or, "philosophy" could be defined *intentionally*, in which case it is a term that is definable with respect to an inclination to view things called "philosophy" as being friendly or dear to wisdom.

"Philosophy", I would suggest, is an *intentional* concept. If *PHILOSOPHY* is an *intentional* concept, we can define its meaning as *THAT–WHICH–IS–REGARDED–AS–FRIENDLY–OR–DEAR–TO–WHAT–IS–REGARDED–AS–EPISTEMIC–REVELATION*.

There are a few signs that speak to the fact that "philosophy" is an *intentional* term.

In common parlance, "philosophy" is often applied to things that people think are profound, even though those who call themselves "philosophers" (like myself) would never think that such matters are philosophical. For instance, discourses on practical or folk psychology are often regarded by nonprofessional philosophers as "philosophical". (An older person at a party once lectured me on how I should read more fiction, for that would aid my study of philosophy.) When people put their losses in to the context of a bigger picture, to console themselves, they often say they are "trying to be philosophical about the matter". Businesses often have what they call "a philosophy" about how they think they should tackle their particular area of commerce—something that those who are called "philosophers" would not spend much time thinking about. People often have what they call personal "philosophies" on how they think they should live their life; views on how to respond to adversity; to deal with people, and so on.

In common parlance, "philosophy" bears the trait of a key philosophical term: it is able to function as a term of commendation. Just as saying of something that "it is real" or "that one knows" or that something "is moral" has a commendatory function, so does calling something "philosophical" communicate, often, a kind of approval on the part of the speaker.

Those of us who think of ourselves as philosophers trained in a modern university with academic roots in the West often have a different view of philosophy. Here, a conscious effort is made not to communicate a commendation when something is called "philosophy" or "philosophical". Rather, those who call themselves "philosophers" would typically have us think that "philosophy" is a proper noun for a certain kind of activity, which can be done properly or improperly.

Yet again, philosophers disagree about what philosophy is. Analytic philosophers, for instance, believe that "philosophy" is a term that ought only to be applied to the activity of conceptual analysis. According to some self-proclaimed Analytic philosophers, texts authored in Continental Europe, by Phenomenologists and Existentialists, do not constitute philosophy. Post Modernists often believe that "philosophy" is a name for a peculiarly Western intellectual tradition, which, ironically, is the antithesis to wisdom; the wise thing to do, on the Post Modernist account, is to put an end to doing philosophy. A similar view that I have heard expressed is that "philosophy" is really a name for a tradition of texts that have their roots in Greece; it stands for nothing more than a particular Western, Eurocentric, discourse, which, in its antiquity, went under the name "philosophy". Others regard philosophy as concerned primarily with the scientific treatment of questions of value. While the other disciplines, such as chemistry or physics, may be able to tell one how things are, only the philosopher, *ex hypothesi*, could give us scientific (systematic) reasons for endorsing particular sets of values.

The most telling facts in favour of the view that *PHILOSOPHY* is an *intentional* term is that its component concepts—*PHILO* or friend/dear and *SOPHIA* or wisdom—are *intentional* notions as well, whose meaningfulness is defined by *intentional* criteria.

Facts like these, regarding the use of *PHILOSOPHY*, and the etymological meaning of *PHILOSOPHY*, point to the fact that it is an *intentional* concept; a kind of concept whose application is a matter of debate and disagreement, which, in theory, is not resolvable to everyone's satisfaction. On this view, there is an analogy to be drawn between the meaning of moral concepts, and how people have differences of opinion on what they should be applied to, and the meaning and uses of *PHILOSOPHY.* If we do not bear in mind a certain distinction, we are likely to get confused between two kinds of views regarding what philosophy is. The distinction we need to keep in mind is the distinction between (i) an account of the meaning of key philosophical concepts, and (ii) a substantive theory on what we ought to regard as the appropriate *extentions* of key philosophical concepts.

The view that *PHILOSOPHY* means *THAT–WHICH–IS–REGARDED–AS–FRIENDLY–OR–DEAR–TO–WHAT–IS–REGARDED–AS–EPISTEMIC–REVELATION* is an account of the meaning of *PHILOSOPHY qua* key philosophical concept—a concept that is central to the articulation of a particular philosophical view, which constitutes one view within a larger debate. This is not a substantive account of what we ought to call "philosophy".

5.3.2. Substantive Accounts of Philosophy

There are various substantive theories on what "philosophy" should be applied to. Such substantive views, as a matter of convention, are called "metaphilosophical" views.

As noted, there is the Analytic notion that the only real philosophy there is concerns the analysis of concepts: this constitutes one metaphilosophical view. Another such view that Jocelyne Couture and Kai Nielsen (1993 pp.2–5) identify is what they call the "anti-philosophy philosophy"—the view that there is a thing that we call philosophy but that the wise thing would be to put an end to this activity. On such a view there is in reality nothing that genuinely answers to the label of "philosophy", though traditionally people have regarded a certain tradition of texts as "philosophy". Another substantive metaphilosophical view that comes down to us from antiquity is summarized in Plato's account of dialectic: a process of reasoning that takes us from particulars toward universals (*Republic* 533b). If *dialectic* is what philosophy is, when it is properly done (as Plato seems to believe), then *PHILOSOPHY* is that which proceeds from considerations of a particular kind to those of a universal and general nature.

As for a metaphilosophical account of what "philosophy" should be applied to, I think that Plato is on the right track.

My suggestion is that "philosophy" is a term that should only be applied to discourses that have something of a universal and general nature to tell us—even if such information is implicitly stated. Let us call this the Universal and General account of the *extension* of *PHILOSOPHY*. What do I mean by "universal" and "general"? *UNIVERSAL* is the logical notion of not specifying individuals or particulars (things that, minimally, have the dimensions of space and time, as criteria of identity, are particulars). Accounts of matters that are universal in nature, thus, leave out mention of particularity. (Thus, a universal account of the human experience would be an account which does not speak about particular human beings' experiences, but the experience that is essential to things that fall under the concept of *HUMAN*.) A universal account of some matter may be applicable to many particulars, or a few particulars. When something falls under the notion of being *GENERAL*, it applies to a wide range of particulars. By having something of both a universal and general nature to tell us, philosophy, on this account, is always something that communicates to us matters of a high order of abstraction.

What is my justification for this view? I have a mob mentality, practical, justification for this view: as a matter of fact, academically trained philosophers tend to understand their discipline in this manner. In our contemporary practise of philosophy, we tend to identify texts and discourses as philosophical on the basis of whether they have something of a universal or general nature to teach us.

There are many philosophers who would have us restrict the application of the term "philosophy" to discourses that explicitly display argumentation. While philosophers are typically fond of arguments, I would suggest that there is nothing essentially philosophical about an argument: lawyers make arguments, and so do scientists, but their arguments are not really philosophical. If a philosopher's proper subject is that which is of universal or general import, it follows that argument is their only real aid in providing any rigour to their efforts to justify their particular philosophical views. All the same, it is not the argument that makes a view philosophical.

There is also the view amongst many historians of philosophy that certain philosophers, from the history of philosophy (like, say, Hegel and Nietzsche) do not really make arguments, but rather, try to get us to see things from a particular perspective. It is not only philosophers who stress the paradoxical who appear to not, explicitly at least, make any arguments (in the formal way, of drawing conclusions deductively from premises). Many philosophers who we have reason to believe were inclined to defend their views via argument appear to have left records of their views to us that are bereft of argumentation.

This is particularly true of ancient philosophers of the Indian tradition. In antiquity, Indian philosophy was an oral tradition: writing apparently did not come to Indian philosophy till after many of the foundational philosophical views were expounded. In these early times, our authors had to condense their philosophical texts for the sake of mnemonic ease and economy. Thus, *sūtras* like the *Vedānta Sūtra*, or the *Sāṅkhya Kārika*, considered in themselves, without commentaries, present little argumentation. Yet, we look upon such works as expressing a philosophy.

Then there are the works of cryptic philosophers, like Wittgenstein, who do not ever appear to make clear arguments—if an argument is understood in the formal way; as a conclusion drawn deductively from a set of premises. Wittgensteinians are apt to think that Wittgenstein made many arguments, but I would suggest that this view is not accurate: Wittgensteinians in their effort to make clear and justify Wittgenstein's genuinely philosophical thought provide arguments that are based upon his views, but strictly speaking, I think that the objective observer would be hard pressed to find many arguments in the writings of Wittgenstein (indeed, his earlier work, the *Tractatus*, appears very much like the *sūtra* texts of ancient India, and his later work, the *Philosophical Investigations*, appears to be a collection of thought experiments). Yet, Wittgenstein's works constitute philosophy because they have things of a universal and general character to tell us.

There is a justification for the metaphilosophical view that I am forwarding that does not appeal to a mob mentality. The view that philosophy has to do with the universal and general is a function, I believe, of the *formality* of key philosophical terms; terms whose meaning abstract from particulars (*extentions*). Primarily the abstraction of key philosophical concepts is a function of their ability to be employed as the focal point of substantive disagreement. This contributes to their universality.[4] The fact that they are, factually, applied to so many different items implies their generality. These pragmatic features of key philosophical terms lead to the inevitability that a philosophical view can be summed up in terms of what it implies about matters of universal and general importance. Universal and General import, thus, is a universal feature of philosophical views; views that are expressible with key philosophical terms.

Another justification for the Universal and General metaphilosophical view is that wisdom constitutes an understanding of the universal and general. The wise person is one who approaches omniscience, and prescience; one for whom there are no real surprises. Wisdom situates our concerns within a larger picture: if wisdom continues on this path, it leads to matters of a universal and general nature. That which communicates something to us of a universal and general nature would thus be friendly or dear to wisdom; it would be philosophical.

Does the view that I am proffering rule out views like Existentialism from counting as a philosophical theory, for after all, Existentialism insists that particularity is something that we must always retain and try to respect in philosophy. The view that "philosophy" ought to be applied to things that have something of a universal and general nature to communicate to us does not forbid such discourses as also having things of a particular nature to tell us about; but particularity is inessential to what renders a view philosophical. If an Existentialist view has nothing of a universal and general nature to tell us about, then, such a view could not be philosophical. However, despite the emphasis on particularity, such views typically do have something of a universal and general nature to tell us about: they often attempt to enlighten us as to what experience (without remainder) is; what Being (without remainder) is, and what beings are like.

It is important for us to be clear on an issue: the Universal and General view of philosophy is not an account of what we mean by the concept *PHILOSOPHY*. Rather, it is an account of what we should endeavour to regard as being dear or friendly to wisdom. As I have argued, the meaning of *PHILOSOPHY* is *intentional*, and it is the inclination to regard an *extention* as friendly or dear to wisdom. The Universal and General account is a view about what makes something genuinely (or, appropriately regarded as) philosophical. Perspectives of a universal and general nature are just such views that deserve to be called "philosophical".

5.3.3. Extensions of *MORAL PHILOSOPHY*

Ultimately, we want to be able to judge whether the works of Indian philosophers figure amongst the items that constitute the *extension* of *MORAL–PHILOSOPHY*. Before we get to the matter of the *extension* of *MORAL–PHILOSOPHY*, let us be clear on its *intension*.

If we combine the meanings of *MORAL* and *PHILOSOPHY* we get the combined, meaning of *MORAL–PHILOSOPHY*. "Moral" means, *A–THING–ABOUT–WHICH–THERE–IS–AN–INCLINATION–TO–GET–ANGRY–(SHOULD–IT–BE–VIOLATED–OR–NOT–RESPECTED IN–SOME–MANNER)–IN–THE–ABSENCE OF MITIGATING–REASONS* (2.4.3. Meaning of Moral Terms p.75). "Philosophy" means, *THAT–WHICH–IS–REGARDED–AS–FRIENDLY–OR–DEAR–TO–WHAT–IS–REGARDED–AS–EPISTEMIC–REVELATION* (5.3.1. What Does "Philosophy" Mean? pp.202–206). We could combine the two ideas thus: "moral philosophy" means *A–THING–ABOUT–WHICH–THERE–IS–AN–INCLINATION–TO–GET–ANGRY–(SHOULD–IT–BE–VIOLATED–OR–NOT–RESPECTED–IN–SOME–MANNER)–IN–THE–ABSENCE–OF–MITIGATING–REASONS,* and *THAT–WHICH–IS–REGARDED–AS–BEING–DEAR–OR–FRIENDLY–TO–WISDOM.* This is quite a vague notion, which does not really integrate the two components of the concept.

If we were to arrive at a more integrated account of the meaning of "moral philosophy" I believe we would define it as *THAT–WHICH–IS–REGARDED–AS–DEAR–OR– FRIENDLY–TO– WHAT–IS–REGARDED–AS–EPISTEMIC–REVELATION–ABOUT–A–THING–THAT–THERE–IS–AN–INCLINATION–TO–GET–ANGRY–ABOUT–(SHOULD–IT–BE–VIOLATED–OR–NOT–RESPECTED–IN–SOME–MANNER)–IN–THE–ABSENCE–OF–MITIGATING–REASONS. MORAL–PHILOSOPHY* is not simply the numerical addition of the concerns of wisdom and morality, but rather, it is philosophy about moral matters—it is one variety of philosophy.

What then counts as part of the *extension* of *MORAL–PHILOSOPHY*? For some discourse to fall within the *extension* of *MORAL–PHILOSOPHY* it must satisfy two conditions: it must be (a) something that there is an inclination to regard as dear or friendly to wisdom, and (b) the putative wisdom in question must in some way be *about* things that there is also an inclination to get angry over, should they be violated, or not respected in some manner, in the absence of mitigating reasons. There are a few ways that we could apply such criteria to arrive at an account of the *extension* of *MORAL–PHILOSOPHY.*

On one manner of usage, the concept *MORAL–PHILOSOPHY* would communicate our personal views regarding the matters designated by its term. For instance, I think that the Jain texts not only shed light, substantively, on the nature of what is morally good and morally bad, but, I also believe that these texts are philosophical, because I regard them as being friendly to wisdom—particularly about moral matters. Here, my use of "moral philosophy" would imply a substantive, moral, and philosophical, estimation of mine. I could thus define the *extension* of *MORAL–PHILOSOPHY* by counting only my *intentions* regarding these matters. The *extension* of moral philosophy, on this approach, would be relatively small and selective. We could call this kind of account of *MORAL–PHILOSOPHY* a *substantive account of the extension of an intentional concept.*

Another way to apply the criteria of the *extention* of *MORAL–PHILOSOPHY* is to make no distinctions between historically distinct *intentions*. The *extension* of *MORAL–PHILOSOPHY* would be quite large on this account. Such an account would not specify any particular person's views on what is philosophical or moral, but it would give us an account of all the things that people have regarded as morally philosophical *in the past*. We could call this kind of account a *historical account of the extension of an intentional concept.*

Finally, we could, if we wished, count not only historical *intentions* as relevant, but also hypothetical *intentions* as relevant. We could call this a *logical account of the extension of an intentional concept*. Or, we could countenance only factual (past and future) *intentions* as relevant in our estimation of the *extension* of an *intentional* concept. We could call this, thus, the *atemporal, factual account of the extension of an intentional concept*.

Not all of these ways of applying the criteria of the *extension* of *MORAL–PHILOSOPHY* are appropriate for us in our efforts to come to terms with the history of philosophy.

The most inappropriate application of the criteria to determine the *extension* of *MORAL–PHILOSOPHY* for a historian of philosophy is the substantive account. A historian of philosophy does this when they argue that only "world and life" is relevant to the moral, for here, they confuse a substantive opinion on morality with an account of the meaning of *ETHICS*. A historian of philosophy also makes this mistake when they look in Indian philosophy for what "*we* call moral philosophy". The issue is not what any particular philosopher or cultural group regards as being moral and philosophical in nature; this is not the criteria that a historian of philosophy ought to employ in their efforts to discern whether Indian philosophers wrote on moral philosophy. Why is this inappropriate?

The historian is a kind of empirical scientist, whose primary task is not to tell the story of their life; but that of other people. The historian of philosophy's, or the historian of ideas's, primary task is thus not to recount their own opinions, but other people's opinions. The historian of philosophy fails in this task when they attempt to emphasise views that echo their own sentiments, or the sentiments of their cohort. The historian of philosophy is also a philosopher, and is thus more than entitled to have an opinion on what, substantively, we should regard as moral or philosophical: but this is the individual historian's opinion: not the opinion of the entire history of humanity.

In short, the historian of philosophy and moral thought has no right to discriminate against *whose intentions* they are going to count as defining moral subject-matter. To the extent that the historical, logical, and atemporal factual approaches to the *extension* of an *intentional* concept do not discriminate against those *intentions* from the past, they appear to uphold the objectivity that we require from historical research. The problem with the historical approach to defining the *extension* of an *intentional* concept is that it quickly becomes dated and discriminatory: for the account that it yields is not an account of the *extension* of *MORAL–PHILOSOPHY* pure and simple; with every new moral opinion, the account becomes falsified.

This leaves the logical, and the atemporal, factual approaches. I suspect that, in reality, it is the latter approach that is fitting to the historian's purpose, for the historian, as an empirical scientist, is interested in facts, not mere possibilities. However, the logical account would be fitting for historical purposes as well, for it would never become falsified.

5.4. Indian Moral Philosophy?

Our goal is not really to enumerate, extensively, the items that constitute the *extension* of *MORAL–PHILOSOPHY.* We wish to know whether the works of classical Indian thought (particularly those that we already regard as being philosophical) constitute moral philosophy. If we abandon the criticisable practise of discriminating against whose *intentions* we count in our account of the *extension* of *MORAL–PHILOSOPHY*, we are quite easily led to the conclusion that Indian philosophers forwarded philosophies and texts that constitute moral philosophy.

An important issue that we need to come to terms with is whether Indian philosophers, themselves, thought that they were authoring texts that are friendly or dear to wisdom about moral matters. They clearly wrote on moral matters. We know this because virtually every Indian philosophical school and major philosopher had something to say about *DHARMA*. Sometimes, they simply used the term "dharma". Other times they give us an insight into what they take, substantively, to be the *extension* of this concept—particularly by comparing and contrasting it to their substantive account of the *extension* of other value-theoretic concepts (like *MOKṢA*).

The key issue for us to determine, thus, is whether Indian philosophers, themselves, thought that they were authoring something that was friendly or dear to wisdom, or epistemic revelations *about*, *DHARMA*. I think that all of Indian philosophy is proffered, in part, in the hopes that we, the readers, will become enlightened as to the nature of morality.

We could argue that Indian philosophers' use of *DHARMA* in their works shows that they thought that they were doing moral philosophy; this fact speaks to the presence of moral philosophy in Indian philosophical thought. However, as noted earlier, moral philosophy is not simply the analysis of moral concepts. Thus, moral philosophy need not, itself, employ moral concepts in its discourse.

I would suggest that Indian philosophers themselves thought that they were doing what *we mean* by the concept (though, not necessarily what we designate under) *MORAL–PHILOSOPHY.* As proof of this fact, we might reflect on the fact that Indian philosophical views can be reduced to a systematic view on the relationship between various values.

The people that we identify as "Indian philosophers"—the professional philosophers of classical India—defended *darśanas*, or whole philosophical views. Typically, in our understanding of what Indian *darśanas* consist in, we focus on their epistemological and metaphysical arguments. But *darśanas* also have things to say about the nature of, and the relationship between, various spheres of values—of which, dharma is one such value. *Darśana* texts frequently enlighten us on what they take to constitute the *extension* of *DHARMA*. They also, frequently, provide accounts of how they hold their particular account of *DHARMA* is justified.

These various facts about the history of Indian philosophy speak to the fact that Indian philosophers themselves thought that they were being friendly or dear to wisdom about morality; that they were themselves being congenial to the inculcation of wisdom regarding moral matters in others and themselves. Thus, I would not only urge the conclusion that ethics, or moral philosophy, is an important part of the history of Indian philosophy, but also, that it pervades almost all Indian philosophy: even when Indian philosophers were not explicitly talking about *DHARMA*, they were nonetheless contributing to a systematic view of things, which included morality. In light of this moral import of Indian philosophy, the view that Indian philosophy gave little notice or attention to ethics is untenable. From the fact that virtually all the major schools of Indian philosophy had something to say about dharma, we can conclude, I believe, that moral philosophy constitutes an important part of the history of Indian philosophy.

Notes

1 For a full adumbration of the Logical Positivist's programme, see Ayer's *Language Truth and Logic* (1946).

2 This conception of ethics finds its fullest expression in the philosophy of C.L. Stevenson. See his *Ethics and Language* (1944).

3 I say that the metaphysics of morals roughly corresponds to the idea of justificative ethics because on Paton's reading, the former also includes efforts to formulate moral principles. What I have identified as justificative ethics does not necessarily involve the task of formulating moral principles. The reason that I do not explicitly include the formulation of moral principles as part of justificative ethics's task is that the formulation of moral principles is simply ancillary to most philosophical treatments of ethics. The distinctiveness of Kant's conception of the metaphysics of morals is in the stress on the role of justification; this clearly demarcates this endeavour from applied ethics, dialectical ethics or other activities answering to the notion of "ethics". "Justificative ethics" is proffered as a term to capture this unique approach to ethics.

4 It is important to distinguish between the universality that philosophical concepts are capable of, and the demand that moral claims be *universalizable*. The former is an account of the logical character of certain philosophical concepts, while the latter is a claim about the logical status of moral statements. Moral concepts may be universal in the logical sense, though they may be used in claims that resist abstraction from particulars so long as the particularity of the subject under discussion is regarded as unreducible by the statement, e.g., "*this* action of mine, and no other, is ethical". While this statement may maintain its un-*universalizability*, it does so at the expense of being unphilosophical. In other words, moral statements need not be universalizable, but they need to be if they are to be philosophical.

Part V:
Explication of Indian Ethics

Chapter 6

Introduction to Indian Ethics

No account of the history of Indian moral philosophy would be complete without some account of what Indian moral philosophers themselves thought about ethics. In the following chapters, I shall attempt to summarize Indian philosophers' stand on moral issues.

Moral philosophy is philosophy about moral matters; it is that which is regarded as friendly and dear to wisdom about morality (5.3. "Moral Philosophy"? p.201–213). On the basis of this understanding, there is more than one way to define the contributions of Indian philosophers to moral philosophy.

On one approach, we would note what Indian philosophers, themselves, considered to be their own philosophical views on morality. Another approach to discerning Indian philosophers' contribution to moral philosophy is to take note of what I, or we, personally find morally salutary in their writings; here the criterion of what counts as moral in the writings of Indian authors is not necessarily theirs, but ours.

This latter *substantive* approach to discerning a philosopher's stand on what is moral is inappropriate for us to employ in a study of the history of philosophy, for it overlooks that what is considered the *extention* (and *extension*) of concepts like *MORAL* and *ETHICAL* is the subject of philosophical debate. If we wish to understand what Indian philosophers thought on moral matters, we have to attempt to discern what they thought was morally relevant.

Previous accounts of Indian ethics have often failed us, I believe, in mislocating moral concerns in Indian thought in matters such as *mokṣa* or the *puruṣārthas*. Such accounts fail Indian philosophy itself, for "dharma" is the term that Indian philosophers primarily used to communicate what they take to be moral matters; not "*mokṣa*" or "*puruṣārtha*". In other words, Indian philosophers might have regarded *mokṣa* or the *puruṣārthas* as morally relevant, but they could not have made this opinion of theirs known by simply using the terms "*mokṣa*" or "*puruṣārtha*" for these, as argued, are not moral terms (4.1. The Puruṣārtha Explanation of Indian Ethics pp.181–184, 4.2. The Summum Bonum and Indian Ethics pp.184–185).

Like all people, Indian philosophers used moral terms to make clear their views on moral matters—their answer to our terms "ethics" and "moral" was "dharma" or "*dhamma*" (Chapter 2, "Dharma" as a Moral Term pp.13–107, and Chapter 3, The Classical Meaning of "Dharma" pp.113–176). Like all people, they did not always explicitly identify matters that they regarded as morally significant by flagging it with a moral term. However, within the context of their moral theories, we can come to know what it is that they regarded as morally relevant by attending to what they regarded as relevant to the concept *DHARMA*. The following explication of Indian ethics shall thus stick closely to what Indian philosophers regarded as relating to *DHARMA*.

While *PHILOSOPHY* means, simply, *THAT–WHICH–IS–REGARDED–AS–FRIENDLY–OR–DEAR–TO–THAT–WHICH–IS–REGARDED–AS–EPISTEMICALLY–REVEALING* (5.3.1. What Does "Philosophy" Mean? pp.202–206) there are substantive views on what being amenable to wisdom consists in. I argued earlier that my favoured view—that philosophy has to do with the universal and general—is a function of the *formality* of key philosophical terms; terms whose meaning abstract from particulars (*extentions*) (5.3.2. Substantive Accounts of Philosophy pp.206–210). Primarily the abstraction of key philosophical terms is a function of their ability to be employed as the focal point of substantive disagreement. This contributes to their universality (nonparticularity). The fact that they are, factually, applied to many different items constitutes their generality. These pragmatic features of key philosophical terms lead to the general inevitability (though not necessarily) that a philosophical view, expressed with key philosophical terms, can be summed up in terms of its universal and general implications.[1]

Our concern is to discern what Indian philosophers believed was their contribution to being friendly or dear to wisdom about moral matters. Hence, it might seem that any personal substantive views about what philosophy consists in is irrelevant to an explication of Indian moral philosophy. However, the emphasis on the universal and general in an account of a thinker's philosophy serves a heuristic purpose: by approaching Indian philosophers' statements on morality with a view to uncovering the universal and general import of their views, we gain the advantage of being able to summarize their views on a full gamut of particular moral issues.

Indian philosophers themselves, it might be argued, rarely spend time drawing out the universal and general import of their positions. Yet, by employing key philosophical terms, which are, by nature, abstract, they frequently make their views on matters of universal and general import clear—even when they speak about something particular. If, thus, we feel that Indian philosophers have not given us their views on matters of universal and general import, the fault is ours, for not being attentive enough to their use of philosophically ripe language.

The philosophical schools that I have chosen to concentrate on are those that are standardly presented as comprising the canon of Indian philosophy. This canon is comprised of: three anti-Vedic schools of Buddhism (Early and Mahāyāna) (Chapter 7), Jainism (Chapter 8) and Cārvāka (Chapter 13); and the six pro-Vedic or Hindu schools of Sāṅkhya, Yoga (Chapter 9), Nyāya, Vaiśeṣika (Chapter 10), Pūrvamīmāṃsā (Chapter 11), and Vedānta (Advaita Viśiṣṭādvaita and Dvaita) (Chapter 12). The order in which I have explicated these schools is in no way intended to represent their chronology.

The order of explication was chosen for explicatory reasons. Many of the schools of Indian philosophy touched upon here are comparatively ancient. Moreover, most of these schools continued to maintain an important presence throughout the history of Indian philosophy; making many of them contemporaneous.

The schools of Sāṅkhya and Yoga appear to be amongst the earliest philosophical schools of India; existing in some form prior to the rise to prominence of Jainism. On Jainism's own historical reckoning, its codifier, Mahāvīra, is really the twenty-fourth in a series of Jain Path Makers; suggesting an ancient beginning for this school. Mahāvīra was a senior contemporary of the Buddha, whose date is often placed a few centuries before the beginning of the Common Era. The latter Mahāyāna Buddhist movement is often placed a few centuries into the Common Era. The Cārvāka school is something of a mystery, for most of our information about this school is second-hand. While the schools of Pūrvamīmāṃsā and Vedānta are rooted in the Vedas—which constitute some of India's oldest texts—they appear to be formalised at a later date. The Vedāntin Rāmānuja is frequently placed in the 11th Century CE; Madhva at the 13th Century CE and (Ādi) Śaṅkara at around the 9th Century CE. Nyāya and Vaiśeṣika, presumably, have a relatively ancient history, arising sometime after the inception of Buddhism.

Indian philosophers themselves did not make distinctions with respect to different kinds of ethics—metaethics, applied ethics, and so on. They simply did moral philosophy whenever they thought they were being friendly or dear to wisdom about moral matters. The custom of distinguishing kinds of ethical issues is a recent phenomenon. Nonetheless we can, in our effort to look back at Indian moral philosophy, notice that Indian philosophers commented on matters that correspond to distinct notions of ethics these days.

All the canonical schools of Indian philosophy, but the Cārvāka system, have expressed clear theses of justificative ethics. In the case of the Cārvāka school, the problem is not that they did not venture into the field of justificative ethics, but that our information about this school is largely second-hand and fragmentary. While, across the board, justificative ethics appears to be the version of ethics most frequently ventured into by Indian philosophers, many schools of Indian philosophy have contributed to their own practical anthropology. Buddhism, Jainism, Vaiśeṣika and Pūrvamīmāṃsā concern themselves unceasingly with specifying what they take to be the *extension* of *DHARMA*. To this end, these philosophies constitute an extended analysis of *DHARMA*. Other philosophical schools, such as Yoga, have a lot to tell us about the nature of morality itself; what the *extension* of morality consists in.

After justificative ethics, it appears that moral metaphysics is the philosophical version of ethics that Indian philosophers attended to most. Buddhism at many turns is an extended account of the nature of moral things, or dharmas. While many schools of thought affirm a substantial conception of Morality, later Buddhism criticizes such efforts, and suggests that Morality as such is something less than substantial; that it is Empty. Jainism too ventures into this realm of moral metaphysics. On its account, Motion is what Morality is, considered substantially; it is an objective ingredient in the Universe. The schools of Yoga and Sāṅkhya also contribute to moral metaphysics by elaborating an ontology that supports moral properties; epiphenomenally. The ontology that they specify is found in the *triguṇa* theory of *sattva*, *rajas* and *tamas*.

A moral metaphysical issue that many Indian philosophers broached is the relationship between freedom and determinism. The way that this matter appears in the context of Indian philosophy is in the question of the nature of persons. A prominent view in the history of Indian philosophy is that persons are devoid of agency and choice-making capacity; that agency is really a function of something external to persons, such as nature; biology. This view is known as the "Akriyāvāda", or *NONACTION THEORY*. The most prominent proponent of this view is Sāṅkhya.

Critics of this view, such as the Jains, note that it has implications for moral culpability. Specifically, if the Akriyāvād view is correct, it follows that persons are not morally culpable for their actions. In contrast, a prominent view advanced in the history of Indian philosophy is called the Kriyāvāda, or *ACTION THEORY*, which holds that agency, or moral culpability for choices, is a genuine feature of persons. The most vocal proponents of this view appear to be the Jains, though it is a position endorsed by most schools of Indian philosophy, including Buddhism, Yoga, Vedānta, and arguably, Nyāya, Vaiśeṣika and Pūrvamīmāṃsā schools.

Some philosophers in the history of Indian philosophy have also ventured into the field of metaethics. Pūrvamīmāṃsā appears to argue for Prescriptivism. (Ādi) Śaṅkara's Advaita Vedānta is itself an Error Theory, which defends the view of Moral Irrealism.

Applied ethics is also something that we find in the writings of Indian philosophers. However I have not made any special effort to look for applied ethics in the writings of Indian philosophers, as the focus of applied ethics is away from the universal and general, and on the particular; it is not a version of ethics that can be summarized easily in a secondary account of the history of philosophy. Yet, the Vedānta response to the question of the moral propriety of ritualistic violence is noted because it cuts to the heart of Vedānta justificative ethics and practical anthropology.

It has been charged that Indian philosophy does not devote any time to analysing the nature of value (1.1. Problem of Ethics in Indian Philosophy pp.3–5). The charge fails to appreciate the complexity of Indian axiology. Indian philosophy persistently concerns itself not just with value, but with values. The traditional view in the secondary literature on Indian philosophy is that Indian philosophy is primarily concerned with the value of *mokṣa*. This is certainly not true. All Indian philosophical schools have had something to say about the nature of dharma. The failure to recognize that Indian philosophy devotes substantial energy to the question of moral goodness is a direct function of a failure to appreciate that "dharma" is a *perfect formal*, moral term, without *focus*.

Notes

1 I argued at an earlier point that moral views are not those that are necessarily *universalizable* (2.3.2. Categoricality and Universalizability pp.38–43). Now it seems that I am contradicting this view by arguing that views expressed using key philosophical terms are always *universalizable*. The view I am presenting here pertains to how we are to interpret key philosophical terms—like "dharma", "real", and "knowledge"—defined at 2.2. Key Philosophical Terms (pp.22–31). Views presented using these terms, it seems to me, are, in general, though not necessarily, *universalizable*. It is also worth noting that it is possible to have a moral view without expressing it with the aid of key philosophical terms like "dharma" or "ethical", though. One could use virtually perfect moral terms (like "ought" or "good", which, technically, are not key philosophical terms owing to their ambiguity) or substantive moral terms (like "cruel" or "compassionate" which are not key philosophical terms, owing to their lack of formality) to express a moral conviction. These words have a more tenuous connection to *universalizability*.

Chapter 7

A Buddhist Debate in Ethics

7.1. Buddhism and the History of Indian Philosophy

A seemingly chronic problem in the exposition of the history of Indian philosophy is a tendency in the literature to marginalize Buddhism's place in it. If Buddhism were consistently affirmed as an integral part of the history of Indian philosophy, which is just as Indian as Hindu philosophical thought, then the thesis that ethics plays little or no part in Indian philosophy would be patently implausible.

Buddhism, in the context of the history of Indian philosophy and religion, is quite unique in that its ultimate statement of doctrine is not to be found in a text but in a person. For Hindu philosophers, it is either the foundational texts of a particular *darśana* (like the *Nyāya Sūtra*) or the Vedas that are looked upon as definitively expressing doctrine. While Mahāvīra is an important figure in the history of Jainism, he is not the founder of Jainism, but merely the systematizer. Hence, Jain *sūtras* function as the Vedas do for the Hindu: as doctrine itself. For the Buddhist, however, Buddhist scripture is a historical record of the views of the Buddha, and it is his views that constitute doctrine for the Buddhist. According to Buddhist tradition itself, what is recorded for posterity and what was actually meant by the Buddha are two different things.

In the Pāli Canon, the Buddha likens the grasping of Buddhist thought on *dhamma* to a person attempting to grasp a water snake: if the person grasps the snake by the neck, then the person has prevented harm; if one grasps it by the tail, one will certainly suffer the harm of a snakebite (MN 1.133–134). Prior to relating this parable, the Buddha argues:

> [Some] having mastered *dhamma* do not test the meaning of these things by intuitive wisdom; and these things whose meaning is untested by intuitive wisdom do not become clear; they master this *dhamma* simply for the advantage of reproaching others and for the advantage of gossiping, and they do not arrive at the goal for the sake of which they mastered *dhamma*". (MN 1.133)

As things turned out in the history of Indian philosophy, many Buddhists had different ideas about what "intuitive wisdom" amounts to. Hence, we find in Buddhism's early phase no less than eighteen schools of Buddhism arising in South Asia.

Despite various disagreements internal to the history of Buddhism, Indian Buddhist thought on axiological and ethical matters divides itself into two phases. The earlier phase finds its expression in discourses of the Buddha in the Pāli Canon. The later phase in Indian Buddhist axiological thought, commonly known as "Mahāyāna Buddhism", is expressed in the later Mahāyāna *sūtras* and the writings of latter Buddhist philosophers. Despite these differences, there is a level of core moral doctrine common to both movements.

7.2. Dependent Origination and Dharma

Core Buddhist doctrine on dharma, common to both phases of Indian Buddhism, can be summed up, I believe, by (a) the Four Noble Truths, (b) the Eight-Fold Path, and (c) the Principle of Dependent Origination (*Paticcasamuppāda*, *Pratītyasamutpāda*) which is the view that "all *dhammas*/dharmas (constituents of

Reality) occur by way of causes". This last principle has been taken, in early times, to imply the doctrine of the momentariness of the constituents of reality (all constituents come into existence on the backs of other such entities, and exist just long enough for the next generation to be born). Throughout Buddhist thought, though, this principle has been taken to imply that all constituents of reality are part of a nexus of mediation; the idea of being an intermediate, and the function of mediation, is thus central to the Buddhist notion of a constituent of reality (i.e. a dharma) and the Principle of Dependent Origination.

It is quite clear, thus, that the term "dharma" is used in Buddhist thought not only to designate doctrinal, moral theoretical, issues, but to refer to specific kinds of things called "dharmas". As Edward Conze notes in his essay "Dharma and Dharmas" (Conze 1967 pp.92–106) the ontological *extentions* of "dharma" in Buddhism include (i) "a transcendental reality which is real in absolute truth and in the ultimate sense", (ii) "order and law of the universe", (iii) "a truly real event", (iv) *intentional* objects, and (v) characteristics, attributes or properties (Conze 1967 pp.92–93). Conze argues that these various "*dharmas*" have a few properties in common. Most importantly, *dharmas*:

> ... "carry" ... persons and things, because they are "ultimates", simple and elementary constituents of emancipating cognition, and all persons and things can be understood as combinations of elemental dharmas. They come very much nearer to what is really there than the units of everyday experience, because they are shorn of all the greed, aggressiveness and delusion that struggling and deceptive selves carry into the presentation of that experience. They are truly there, unfalsified by greed, etc. They are "carried" by conditions and, though separate (*pṛthak*) in their existence, they nevertheless co-operate (*saṃsarga*). It is not easy for us to realize that at this point dharmas ... are very closely related to DHARMA in the sense ... [of] MORAL LAW ... because the causality is essentially a moral one. In this Order of the Dharma the rational and the ethical elements are fused into one. (Conze 1967 p.97)

In short, the reason that dharmas are designated by "dharma" is that they are supportive of others, on Conze's account. Supporting others thus appears to be a fundamental moral principle of Buddhist thought. It is also an idea that is captured by the Principle of *Pratītyasamutpāda*, or Dependent Origination, in its description of dharmas as essentially mediating entities.

There is onc problem with this line of interpreting the meaning of "dharma". The usual reasons that are adduced against construing Buddhist "dharmas" as moral in nature (Chapter 1 Problem of Ethics in Indian Philosophy pp.3–13) have been addressed in advance: they are based upon the Orthodox View; an Extentionalist interpretation of both moral terms and the meaning of "dharma" in classical Indian thought (2.2. Key Philosophical Terms pp.22–31), which, more often than not, is wedded to a Social Content or Conduct view of moral matters (2.3.1. Social Content and Conduct pp.35–38). These positions have been compared and criticized (3.5. Four Theories of "Dharma" in Review p.167–176). With such issues out of the way, we can conclude that there is no *analytic* implausibility in Conze's view that "dharma" always has a moral meaning in Buddhist thought—even when it is used as a name for the constituents of reality. Such uses of the term "dharma" are analogous to modern uses of the term "good" to refer to individual things, or "goods". The tension for us to come to terms with is that not all dharmas appear to be morally good (3.1.12. Falsifying Evidence: Morally Reprehensible Dharmas pp.127–129).

Conze suggests that the Principle of Dependent Origination is itself a foundational moral principle of Buddhist thought—here, the term "moral" functions to communicate the knowledge that, from Buddhism's perspective, things that conform to the Principle of Dependent Origination are morally good or approvable. This is a very plausible reading, particularly because Buddhism calls itself "Dharma", and because, on the Buddha's own account, the Principle of Dependent Origination is central to Buddhist thought. According to the Buddha, it "is through not understanding this doctrine, through not penetrating it, that this generation [i.e. the live person] ... become[s] a tangled skein ... unable to overpass ... the Woeful Way, the Downfall, the Constant Round" (D 2.56). Reflecting on the importance of the Principle of Dependent Origination, the Buddha touches upon the Four Noble Truths, which is something like an expansion on the philosophical importance and implications of the Principle of Dependent Origination. And within the Four Noble Truths, the Eight-Fold Path constitutes an elaboration of the Fourth Noble Truth. Hence, the Principle of Dependent Origination is the highest, theoretical, principle of Buddhist thought; this principle constitutes Buddhist "Dharma". As "dharmas" instantiate "Dharma", by being dependently originated, mediating and supporting other dharmas, they conform their behaviour to this principle, and thus, they take the name of the principle (this is like calling a particular thing "a good" or "good" when it instantiates "The Good"). As "dharma" is Indian philosophy's *perfect formal*, moral term, without *focus*, *par excellence* (2.6.2. Traditional Meaning of "Dharma" pp.95–98 and Chapter 3 The Classical Meaning of "Dharma" pp.113–243) we can translate "dharmas" as "ethicals" (3.2.5. Translation and Paraphrase pp.136–139).

The problem, as noted before, is that not all dharmas are morally praiseworthy (3.1.12. Falsifying Evidence: Morally Reprehensible Dharmas pp.127–129); the desire to injure others is, on many Buddhist accounts, a "dharma", and moreover, it is morally criticisable.

The way to resolving this tension is to remind ourselves about the communicative versatility of *perfect formal*, moral terms, without *focus*, of which "dharma" is just one example. Such terms can either express the opinion of an author that (a) the thing being designated by the term is morally commendable, and deserving of our respect, or, such terms can communicate the information that (b) the thing designated is morally significant, though not necessarily approved of by the author; this is what "moral" tells us in the phrase "morally significant" (2.4.2. Double Role of Some Moral Terms p.74 and 3.2.12. EVIL ETHIC pp.155–157). Buddhism's use of "dharma" makes good use of its dual utility.

Conze's suggestion is correct in this respect, I believe: the Principle of Dependent Origination constitutes the highest order of moral principle in Buddhism: it tells us what moral goodness consists in. Moral goodness, in Buddhist thought, consists in being a mediator and in being supportive of others. All dharmas, thus, are morally good to the extent that they conform to the Principle of Dependent Origination. In addition, some dharmas are also injurious to the spiritual and moral betterment of persons; these dharmas function dharmically with respect to some dharmas, but not with respect to persons (which, on most Buddhist accounts, are not dharmas, but aggregates or functions of dharmas). Such dharmas, thus, both instantiate the behaviour enshrined in the Principle of Dependent Origination, and they also exemplify behaviour that is contrary to this law. Thus, such "dharmas" are both (a) morally good, in one respect, and (b) morally significant, to the extent that they are morally bad (dharmically bad). Hence, the use of "dharma" to be a name for such entities is consistent with both (a) and (b) and it communicates both (a) and (b).

Buddhist ethics thus appears to affirm the fundamental goodness of all dharmas, and yet, it finds that some such fundamentally ethical things are yet ethically criticisable, with respect to a certain mode of their behaviour and nature, and that some good dharmas, which aid people in their dharmically praiseworthy endeavours, are exceptionally dharmic, or good; while some dharmas are not bad, but are also not particularly helpful toward people (these are "neutral" dharmas).

A few objections can be raised against this account of things. First, it might be argued that dharmas are not necessarily involved in the process of mediation and being of support to other things, on the Buddhist account. If this is so, the moral interpretation of the Principle of Dependent Origination and the notion of "dharmas" cannot be sustained, as argued.

Not all dharmas are supportive. For instance, on some

Buddhist accounts, *nirvāṇa* is a dharma. Conze himself notes that "*Nirvāṇa* is the dharma which is the object of supreme knowledge, or supreme dharma, and it is in *Nirvāṇa* that one takes refuge when he takes refuge in the Dharma" (Conze 1967 pp.92–3). *Nirvāṇa* is the Buddhist word for the state of liberation (meaning, VOID). On most Buddhist accounts, *nirvāṇa* is the end of the process of transmigration of persons, and hence, nothing comes after *nirvāṇa*. If nothing comes after *nirvāṇa*, it cannot be supportive to others.

In response to this argument, it is important to note that *nirvāṇa* is only the end of the line for a particular person. Hence there is no reason to suppose that *nirvāṇa*, *qua* dharma, does not play a continuing role in mediating between other dharmas, after any given person has attained *nirvāṇa*. In fact, it would seem that *nirvāṇa* would play just such a role; in order to facilitate the liberation of other persons.

Another argument can be made against the interpretation of dharmas being presented here. This argument does not take exception to the notion that dharmas are in some essential way supportive; however, it takes to task the explanatory role of supportiveness in this moral interpretation of Buddhist thought. At an earlier point, the Conservative View, which holds that "dharma" is a term that has to do with things that are (regarded as being) supportive, was criticized (3.5. Four Theories of "Dharma" in Review p.167, p.171). Yet, now, it seems that the Conservative account of the meaning of "dharma" is being endorsed. Is this not a blatant contradiction?

In order to resolve this concern, we need to draw a distinction between a view regarding the veracity of claims about "dharma", and a view regarding the meaning of "dharma". Consider an analogous instance: Utilitarians believe that the Good (moral goodness) consists in utility. Thus, on Utilitarianism's account, "good" is correctly applied to those things that it regards as having the property of utility. This is Utilitarianism's account of what makes claims about goodness true (true claims about the good on this account, are those that apply the term "good" to things that have utility). It would be a mistake for us to interpret this theory as an account of the *meaning* of "good", for then, it would be apparent that Utilitarianism is not offering a contrary moral theory to that of Deontology, which holds that "good" (on most accounts) is appropriately applied to things that are dutiful. Clearly, Utilitarianism and Deontology are locked in a *meaningful* debate on what is in fact good: the common ground of the debate is a mutual, practical, understanding of the meaning of "good" as accounted for by the Anger Inclination Thesis (2.3.7. Anger Inclination pp.53–66, 2.4. Definition of Moral Terms pp.70–85); their individual contributions to ethics consist in accounts of what the *extension* of good (*qua virtually perfect formal*, moral term, 2.4.1. Subsidiary Features of Moral Terms pp.72–74) is.

In reality, the Conservative View's account of the meaning of "dharma" is not being endorsed here. What is being suggested by Conze is that Buddhism's particular moral theory regards the property of being supportive (or being a mediator) as the single determinant of whether something is appropriately called "dharma". The feature of supportiveness thus determines not the *meaning* of "dharma", for Buddhism, but the *veracity* of claims regarding "dharma". False claims about "dharma", on Buddhism's account, would be those applications of "dharma" to things that fail, in its eyes, to have the property of being supportive or being a mediator. True claims about "dharma" would be those that apply the term to things that do function as being supportive or as mediators, on its account.[1]

The Conservative View thus comes close to the truth about "dharma". It notes, appropriately, that in many cases, Indian philosophers have used the term "dharma" for things that they regard as having the property of being supportive. But the Conservative View is wrong, fundamentally, for it mistakes an observation regarding the substance of some Indian moral theories for an account of the meaning of "dharma". Not all Indian philosophers apply "dharma" to things that are supportive or that have the property of mediation—yet they all participate in one philosophical tradition, with a unified debate on the nature of morality (3.5. Four Theories of "Dharma" in Review p.167, p.175) or dharma.[2]

7.3. Noble Truths and the Path

As both the Four Noble Truths and the Eight-Fold path are regarded as major implications of Buddhist Dharma, they are worth noting.

The First Noble Truth of Buddhism is that life (unrealized life) is difficult (*duḥkha*). The Second Noble Truth is the view that the difficulty of life is a function of attachments to sensual pleasures, and the cravings either for continued existence, or annihilation. Why should cravings give rise to difficulty? According to Buddhist thinking, acquisitive dispositions on our part run contrary to the real ebb and flow of life, which is Dependent Origination. Thus, according to the Third Noble Truth, the abandonment of all attachments leads to the emancipation of one from difficulty. According to the Fourth Noble truth, in order to actualize one's emancipation from difficulty, one must embrace the moral life (i.e. Dharma, or Dependent Origination) that leads to the cessation of suffering. In the *Discourse on the Analysis of the Truths* (*Saccavibhaṅgasutta*) the content of the Fourth Noble Truth is given as the Eight-Fold Path (MN 3.248-252).

A glance at the Eight-Fold Path reveals that it is no small matter. The *Saccavibhaṅgasutta* sets out the Eight-Fold Path as: right view, right aspiration, right speech, right action, right mode of livelihood, right endeavour, right mindfulness and right concentration.

(1) The content of Right View has been reviewed: the Four Noble Truths and the Principle of Dependent Origination. (2) Right Aspiration consists in a view towards renunciation, nonmalevolence and harmlessness. (3) Right Speech consists in virtuous speech (avoidance of slander and verbal abuse, truthfulness, refraining from gossip). (4) Right Action consists in

"refraining from onslaught on creatures, refraining from taking what has not been given, refraining from going wrongly among the sense-pleasures". (5) Right Livelihood is under-explained in the *Saccavibhaṅgasutta.* The text informs us that it involves getting rid of wrong modes of livelihood, but little else.[3] (6) Right Endeavour consists in efforts to eradicate and prevent morally criticisable *aretaic* states. (7) Right Mindfulness consists in "contemplating the body in the body ... the feelings in the feelings ... the mind in the mind ... the mental states in the mental states, ardent, clearly conscious (of them) mindful (of them) so as to control the covetousness and dejection in the world". Finally, (8) Right Concentration consists in "being aloof from pleasures of the senses, aloof from unskilled states of mind ... [and] allaying initial thought and discursive thought" (MN 3.251–252).

7.4. Early Buddhist Justificative Ethics

There are two noteworthy aspects of the Early Buddhist moral doctrine. First, like Aristotelian Ethics, Early Buddhist ethics stresses moderation, or the Middle Path between extremes. Secondly, according to Early Buddhist axiological thought, morality's rational basis consists in being a means to liberation; upon liberation, morality becomes redundant.[4]

The moderation of Buddhist ethics is primarily borne out in its view that the severity of a moral transgression is a function not only of a violation of *deontic* expectations, but a failure to cultivate the proper *aretaic* states.

> A certain person who has not properly cultivated his body, behaviour, thought and intelligence, is inferior and insignificant and his life is short and miserable; of such a person ... even a trifling evil action done leads him to hell. In the case of a person who has proper culture of the body, behaviour, thought and intelligence, who is superior and not insignificant, and who is endowed with long life, the

> consequences of a similar evil action are to be experienced in this very life, and sometimes may not appear at all. (An 1.219)

On this Early Buddhist account, the sincere claim "I didn't mean to do it" is a valid moral excuse. As in the case of Aristotelian ethics, virtue plays an important role in Buddhist ethics in both the cultivation of a moral life, and in the minimization of evil and pragmatically undesirable states of affairs (like suffering). David Kalupahana characterizes Early Buddhist thought as constituting a version of Moral Pragmatism (Kalupahana 1995 p.16). On reflection, this is quite fitting.

Many of the arguments that Kalupahana presents for construing Early Buddhist ethics as a form of Pragmatism rest on wider considerations concerning the pragmatic nature of the Buddha's concept of truth. He notes that for the Buddha, any "conception of truth not relevant to making human life wholesome and good would simply be metaphysical and therefore unedifying" (Kalupahana 1995 p.35). For us, however, there are textual reasons for considering Early Buddhist axiology as comprising a theory of Moral Pragmatism. The textual consideration is the Buddha's likening of *Dhamma* to a raft.

After relating the Parable of the Water Snake, the Buddha proceeds to liken *Dhamma* to a raft that he has, with effort, put together to cross over *saṁsāra* (*THE–WHORL–OF–BIRTH–AND–REBIRTH*). Once a person has used the raft of *Dhamma* to cross over *saṁsāra*, the Buddha asks: should one place the raft on one's head and proceed to walk on dry land, or should one discard the raft? The Buddha states:

> In this case, monks, it might occur to that man who has crossed over, gone beyond: "Now, this raft has been very useful to me. Depending on this raft and striving with my hands and feet, I have crossed over safely to the beyond. Suppose now that I, having beached this raft on dry ground or having submerged it under the water, should proceed as I desire?" In doing this, monks, that man would be doing what should be done with the raft. Even so, monks, is the Parable of the Raft *Dhamma* taught

> by me for crossing over, not retaining. You, monks, by understanding the parable of the Raft, should get rid even of (right) mental objects, all the more wrong ones. (MN 1.134-135)

Early Buddhist justificative ethics thus holds that morality's ultimate justification consists in its instrumentality in bringing about liberation.

7.5. Mahāyāna Ethics

There is an ambiguity in the Parable of the Raft: what exactly does "*Dhamma*" refer to in the story: *Dhamma* (Buddhist doctrine, or Morality) or *dhammas*, which are the constituents of reality? The Parable of the Raft proceeds the Buddha's likening of his teachings—*Dhamma*—to a water snake, which one must grasp correctly to avoid harm. In this context, it is quite reasonable to conclude that what the Buddha continues to talk about is all of his teachings, and not simply the constituents of reality. On this reading, the Parable of the Raft, in the Pāli Canon, makes *Dhamma* out to be the Raft, which one ought to discard.

Edward Conze notes that while Early Buddhism seems to have regarded Dharma (the entire moral teaching of Buddhism) as the subject of the Parable of the Raft, the Mahāyāna tradition takes it that only dharmas—the constituents of reality—are what are named in the simile of the raft (Conze 1967 p.94).[5] The cause for Conze's observation is a passage from the Mahāyāna *Diamond Sūtra.* It states:

> If, Subhuti, these Bodhisattvas should have a perception of either a dharma, or a no-dharma, they would thereby seize on a self, on a being, on a soul, on a person. And why? Because a Bodhisattva should not seize on either a dharma or a no dharma. Therefore this saying has been taught by the Tathāgata [Buddha] with a hidden meaning: By those who know the discourse on dharma as like unto a raft, dharmas should be forsaken, still more so no-dharmas. (*Diamond Sūtra*

p.34)

On the latter Mahāyāna view, Dharma is not to be abandoned after one has achieved liberation; this is, accordingly, a secret teaching of the Buddha. Rather, it is merely individual dharmas, and no[n]-dharmas, that one should abandon.

What is responsible for this shift in thinking? On this point, Conze is once again quite helpful (see Conze 1967 pp.130–131). He points out that a rather extreme view developed in the early school: that persons do not exist at all. This view is extreme because Early Buddhist scripture itself criticizes such a view:

> To say, "The living entity persists", is to fall short of the truth; to say, "it is annihilated", is to outrun the truth. Therefore has the Blessed One said:—"There are two heresies, O priests, which possess both gods and men, by which some fall short of the truth, and some outrun the truth; but the intelligent know the truth". (*Visuddhi magga* p.235)

The extreme view regarding the nonexistence of persons gave many Buddhists occasion to reconsider the importance of persons. As a correction to this earlier excess, the Mahāyāna was born. In this latter movement, the welfare of all persons takes centre-stage. Corresponding to this shift in attitude toward persons is the privileging of dharma over *mokṣa*. Dharma becomes the *niḥiśreyasa* (HIGHEST GOOD) of Mahāyāna Buddhist axiology. Thus we find a Perfection of Wisdom Sūtra stating "Ah the Dharma, ah the Dharma, ah the dharmahood of Dharma!" (*Aṣṭasāhasrikā Prajñāpāramitā* II.48). In the Mahāyāna, liberation, or *mokṣa*, becomes a function of the pursuit of the moral life: not its fulfilment. So, we find Nāgārjuna's *Ratnāvali* concluding:

> Whenever there is perfection in the Dharma the supreme happiness of salvation will also appear later on, because those who have reached the perfect life will gradually attain to

> salvation. Indeed, the perfect life is considered to be happiness and salvation to be final emancipation from contingent life. (*Ratnāvali* I.3–4)

On the latter Mahāyāna account, Morality is intrinsically important and rewarding, and its importance is not simply instrumental, as Early Buddhism seems to have held. On this view, the moral life is the perfect life.

Leonard Priestley has shared with me the following criticism of this interpretation of Buddhist thought:

> Conze ... [in] *Buddhist Thought in India* is talking about "dharma" and "adharma", not about the Dharma. He's saying that the Sthaviras [Early Buddhists] understood these terms in this *sūtra* to mean "good and bad", whereas the Mahāyānaists understood them to mean "thing and nonthing". He's not saying that the Mahāyānaists thought that the Dharma should not be abandoned. In fact the Mahāyānaists were very clear that the Dharma too, considered as a thing (*bhāva*), should be abandoned. But it is only through nonattachment to the Dharma that the Dharma can be realized in one's life. The Mahāyāna *sūtras* are full of warnings not to be attached to the Dharma as if it were ultimately real, but also not to misunderstand the ultimate emptiness of everything as the nonexistence of morality and karma at the conventional level.

This comment has two components to it. First, there is the claim that, Conze is not claiming that the Early Buddhists thought that one should give up Dharma; they simply thought that one should give up "good" and "bad". This criticism presupposes that "Dharma" does not mean, simply, MORALITY. If Dharma is morality, then talk of giving up good and bad ("going beyond good and evil") is just talk of giving up Dharma, or morality. Conze does seem to read "Dharma" as meaning morality, insofar as individual dharmas are ethicals because they conform to Dharma, or Morality, on his account (7.2. Dependent Origination and Dharma pp.228–235). Thus, I do not believe that I have read Conze incorrectly on this point. Moreover, the issue is not so much what Conze thinks, but what the Early Buddhists thought. If Early Buddhists did believe that one ought to eventually give up good and bad, then we have no choice but to conclude that they believed that morality itself is something to be given up, upon liberation. The reading of Early Buddhist ethics, presented here (7.4. Early Buddhist Justificative Ethics pp.236–238), thus, appears to be correct.

The second component of the criticism brings up the fact (which cannot be controverted) that the Mahāyāna *sūtras* are full of warnings not to be attached to Dharma (and The Dharma), as if it were ultimately real; that one ought not to regard Dharma as a *bhāva* (thing) for all things, ultimately, are empty, though, on a conventional level, we must affirm the existence of things, including dharmas, and the nonexistence or absence of other things (no-dharmas). If I understand Prof. Priestley's point, the Mahāyāna appears to affirm the opinion that I (by interpreting Conze) am attributing to the Early Buddhists; that Dharma is to be given up upon liberation.

The issue of the Ultimate Emptiness of all things, according to much Mahāyāna philosophy is a direct result of the Principle of Dependent Origination, plus an additional metaphysical thesis; that things that are dependant, or mediatory, are not genuine things. The idea behind this critique is that, for something to be a thing, it must be self-sufficient. The Principle of Dependent Origination tells us that no thing is self-sufficient; that all dharmas depend upon other things. Hence, if dependence means nonsubstantiality, and if substantiality is essential for thinghood, it follows that all things are empty (*śūṇya*).[6] "Emptiness", thus, is simply code for Dharma, as determined by the Principle of Dependent Origination. Not to be attached to Dharma as though it were a thing, on this account, is to understand the true nature of Dharma—Prof. Priestley himself recognizes this when he says "it is only through nonattachment to the Dharma that the Dharma can be realized in one's life". This is not, however, the same thing as giving up Dharma, for Emptiness, as such, cannot be given up: it is itself Empty, and bereft of things and a very thinghood to give up. Thus, it follows, that it is consistent with the Mahāyāna view that Dharma, even upon Liberation, is not to be given up; to think that Dharma is a thing is to misunderstand both Dharma, and the nature of Liberation, on this account. If one gives up anything, it is the notion of thinghood and the idea of absence of thinghood: not Dharma (its antithesis, on the Mahāyāna account). We should thus conclude that the Mahāyāna is against the very idea of giving up Dharma. As conformation of this view, we might note that Nāgārjuna, in the *Ratnāvali*, argues that "Truth in reality [i.e., Ultimate Truth] is not that which is devoid of falsehood, nor that which develops in a pure mind; truth is the absolute good done to others; its contrary is falsehood on account of its being harmful to others" (*Ratnāvali* II 35).

Often, in the exposition of the distinction between Mahāyāna and Early Buddhist thought, one is told that in Early Buddhism, the soteriological ideal is that of the Arhat, who seeks individual liberation, while in the latter school, it is the Bodhisattva; a person who is concerned with gaining liberation for all. While this is certainly an aspect of the axiological shift in Buddhism—and a distinction that is important to Mahāyāna self-understanding—there is a more profound difference between the two phases of Indian Buddhism. This difference concerns the shift from Moral Pragmatism, to a kind of Moral Absolutism, which *justifies* the importance of morality, independently of its efficacy in bringing about liberation. The main difference between Early and Mahāyāna Buddhism, thus, is not a result of a different soteriological view, but a result of a difference on justificative ethics.

7.6. Buddhism and Indian Ethics

The exposition of Buddhism has focused upon the core principles of Buddhist ethics, and the philosophical ethical theory of Buddhism—its view of why its account of "dharma" is justified or worth taking seriously. In summary, there are two different justificative ethics in the history of Indian Buddhism: Early Buddhist justificative ethics, and Mahāyāna justificative ethics.

The exposition of Buddhist ethics is relatively short. From the length of this chapter no conclusions about Buddhism's contribution to Indian ethics should be drawn. In reality, Buddhism is almost entirely ethics, or dharma. Virtually every philosophical work in Buddhism constitutes a contribution to Indian ethics.

Buddhist thought on justificative ethics is daunting if we do not take seriously the notion that what is called "dharma" or "*dhamma*" in the context of Buddhism is ethical. However, with the Intentionalist account of moral terms in hand, we are led quickly to a handful of core moral principles: (1) the Principle Of Dependent Origination, (2) the Four Noble Truths and (3) the Eight-Fold Path. The main internal difference that we find in Indian Buddhist ethics is the account of the justification of "dharma". What is at stake here is the debate over whether "dharma" is pragmatically justified or intrinsically important and fulfilling. The positions of Early Buddhism and Mahāyāna Buddhism can be defined over the sides they take on this debate.

Notes

1 While I think that Conze is correct, I wonder if Conze's stress on the supportiveness of dharma, as opposed to is essential role as mediating, is a result of Conze's own personal moral views. As things that are mediators also have the function of supporting, Conze, I believe, is entitled to cash out the Buddhist notion of dharma in terms of support; but a more accurate, and inclusive, account would stress the centrality of mediation to the Buddhist notion of morality.

2 It is unfortunate that repeatedly in the study of the history of Indian philosophy, insufficient care has been given to distinguish between accounts of the meaning of "dharma" and substantive, philosophical views on the nature of "dharma". The failure to distinguish between these two issues leads to the Conservative View, the Orthodox View, and to the chimerical disappearance of ethics from the forum of classical Indian philosophy.

3 According to the Buddha, the acquisition of wealth is not only acceptable, but something that a lay person can take satisfaction in if it does not violate other aspects of the Path (An 2.69-70).

4 The question has been put to me, by J. O'Connell, as to whether the belief in moderation, or the Middle Path, being referred to here, really falls under the province of Buddhist *sādhana*, or soteriological practise, and not Buddhist ethics. I would not wish to deny that there are soteriological implications of the Middle Path. However, to the extent that what is understood as the Middle Path in Buddhism falls under the heading of "Buddhist Dharma", it is a moral matter, and hence, part of Buddhist ethics. The distinction between soteriology and morality is a conceptual distinction, pertaining to the *intension* of soteriological and moral concepts; not to their putative *extensions*, or *extentions*. Hence, one and the same item can be both morally and soteriologically significant, though the concepts of morality and soteriology are distinct.

5 He writes, "When the Buddha said 'those who know the discourse on Dharma as like unto a raft should forsake dharmas, still more so no-dharmas', the Sthaviras take the word "dharmas" in its moral [sense], the Mahāyānists in its ontological sense" (Conze 1967 p.94).

6 A corollary of this dialectic is that no thing, or no-dharma, is ever really absent, or a nonexistent, for all things—including a nothing, like the concept of Emptiness—is always mediated by other dharmas; the notion that any given thing doesn't exist is, on this understanding, part of the same heresy that leads to the view that some things exist.

Chapter 8

Jainism

8.1. Sectarian Differences

Jainism is one of India's oldest religious and philosophical systems. Jainism has the distinction of being the one non-Vedic religious and philosophical system from ancient times that has persisted in India up to the present. Like other religious movements, Jainism has its internal sectarian (and scriptural) differences.

There are two sects of Jainism: the Śvetāmbaras, and the Digambaras. There are two important differences between these two schools: both concern soteriological matters. First, there is a difference between the two schools as to whether ascetics are to wear clothes or not. Śvetāmbara ascetics wear clothes, whereas Digambara monks are ideally nude, or wear very little. (This difference holds despite the fact that the Śvetāmbara canon notes that Mahāvīra, the systematizer of Jainism, instituted the law of nakedness for monks and nuns. U xxiii.13) Secondly, there is a controversy between the two schools as to whether women are eligible for enlightenment. Paul Dundas, author of *The Jains*, points out that the second doctrinal controversy is in part a function of the first controversy. For Jains (as for Buddhists) one must be an ascetic in order to be in a position to attain enlightenment. The Śvetāmbaras hold that women can be ascetics. According to at least one Digambara author, Prabachandra, there is a practical obstacle to women being ascetics. In order to be a Digambara ascetic, one must eschew clothing. Given social realities—the argument goes—a woman cannot move about in society naked, without suffering the deleterious affects of sexual harassment (Prabachandra 1941 pp.865–870 and Dundas 1992 p.50).

On most other doctrinal matters, particularly those pertaining to Jain justificative ethics, both sects appear to be in full agreement.[1] Despite sectarian differences on what composes the canonical literature of Jainism, if we avoid the two main doctrinal differences between the schools, we can paint an accurate picture of Jain justificative ethics, with *virtually* any Jain philosophical work.

8.2. Historical Background of Jainism

Mahāvīra, also known as "Nātaputta" or as "Vardhamāna", was a senior contemporary of the Buddha. According to Jain tradition, he is the twenty-fourth Path Maker, or *Tīrthaṅkara*, in the history of Jainism. Like Buddhism, Jain literature refers to its own doctrine as "Dharma". The usual translation of "Dharma" in this context is "Law" or "Doctrine" (sometimes, even "Religion"). However, these renditions are fuelled by the Orthodox View (Chapter 1 Introduction pp.3–13), which is an Extentionalist approach to the meaning of "dharma" and moral terms. This approach has been criticized for failing to model the functioning of philosophically salient terms (2.2. Key Philosophical Terms pp.22–31) and for failing to provide an acceptable account of "dharma" in classical Indian thought in particular (3.5. Four Theories of "Dharma" in Review pp.167–176). In the place of the Orthodox View, the argument has been forwarded that the moral meaning of "dharma" in classical Indian thought is central to its classical semantics; that "dharma" in classical Indian thought has the meaning of a *perfect formal*, moral term, without *focus*; regardless of what the term "dharma" is applied to (Chapter 2, "Dharma" as a Moral Term, 2.6.2. Traditional Meaning of "Dharma" pp.95–98 and Chapter 3, The Classical Meaning of

"Dharma" p.113). Other terms that have this meaning are the English language terms "moral" and "ethics" (2.4.3. Meaning of Moral Terms pp.74–75). Hence, the phrase "Jain Dharma" is properly translated as "Jain Ethics", or "Jain Morality". I would suggest that to translate "Dharma" as "Law" or "Religion" in this context is a paraphrase: not a translation (3.2.5. Translation and Paraphrase pp.136–139). From the fact that "Jain Dharma" is most accurately translated as "Jain Morality" or "Jain Ethics", it follows that all of Jain philosophy is a moral theory; on Jainism's philosophical self-understanding.

Like Buddhism, Mahāvīra's philosophy is a *śramaṇa* or ascetic movement, to be distinguished from the *brāhmaṇa* or Vedic movement, which stresses the importance of the householder's life within society. Together, the Buddha's thought and Mahāvīra's Jainism stand out sharply from the *śramaṇa* milieu of their day; particularly in the affirmative stance they take on moral matters.

The Buddhist Pāli Canon bears witness to a wave of *śramaṇa* philosophers who advocated Materialism and some form of Axiological Nihilism.[2] Specifically, the text refers to four such philosophers:

1) Ajita Kesakambali,
2) Pūraṇa Kassapa,
3) Pakudha Kaccāyana, and
4) Makkhali Gosāla.

According to the account in the Buddhist canonical text *Sāmaññaphala Suttanta* (*The Fruits of the Life of the Ascetic*) Ajita Kesakambali held a form of Materialism conjoined with Soteriological Nihilism (DN 1.55). Pūraṇa Kassapa, in contrast, put forth the thesis of Moral Nihilism. He is recorded as stating:

> If with a discus with an edge sharp as a razor ... [one] should make all the living creatures on the earth one heap, one mass of flesh ... [if one were] to go along the south bank of the Ganges striking and slaying, mutilating and having men mutilated,

> oppressing and having men oppressed, there would be no guilt thence resulting: no increase of guilt would ensue. (DN 1.52)

Pakudha Kaccāyana held some form of Materialism and an Anti-Realism about persons. He stated, "[w]hen one with a sharp sword cleaves a head in twain, no one thereby deprives anyone of life: a sword has only penetrated into the interval between seven elementary substances" (DN 1.56). Finally, there was Makkhali Gosāla, the leader of a now extinct ascetic order called the "Ājīvakas". Philosophically, he is the most intriguing of the A-Moralists, because he thought that there is such a thing as liberation and that there is such a thing as right and wrong. However, he held the position of Hard Determinism, or Incompatibilism: the view that, (a) events are causally determined (in advance), and (b) this determination is incompatible with moral freedom. On Makkhali Gosāla's account, we are all simply victims of fate with no freedom to alter or change our lives (DN 1.54).

All of these views found their most vehement critic in Mahāvīra.

While Mahāvīra sharply disassociated himself from the A-Moralist philosophers of his day, he was in agreement with them in one respect. He too saw the universe as being composed of physical elements. So strong is the Physicalist outlook in Jainism that it conceives karma as a material substance that clings to a soul (U xxviii.14 and U xxix.73). Individual souls, which are immortal, on this account, are not material in any normal way, but, apparently, have the physical properties of spatiotemporal coordinates and are capable of being dragged down and weighted by karma.

Jainism (on the one hand) and the ancient materialist-ascetic movements of India (on the other) part ways on moral matters. Mahāvīra has nothing but scorn for the moral outlook of his ascetic contemporaries. He is recorded as stating:

> [The] murderer says: "Kill, dig, slay, burn, cook, cut or break

to pieces, destroy! Life ends here; there is no world beyond". These (Nāstikas) cannot inform you on the following points: whether an action is good or bad, meritorious or not, well done or not well done, whether one reaches perfection or not, whether one goes to hell or not. Thus undertaking various works they engage in various pleasures and amusements for their own enjoyment. Thus some shameless men becoming monks propagate a Law (Dharma) of their own. And others believe it, put their faith in it, adopt it, (saying:) "Well, you speak the truth, O Brāhmana, (or) O Śramaṇa! We shall present you with food, drink, spices, and sweetmeats, with a robe, a bowl, or a broom ...." (S II.i.17)

8.3. The Kriyāvāda–Akriyāvāda Debate

According to the classical Jain texts, Mahāvīra had understood and mastered all the philosophical doctrines of his day, which include:

1) Vainayakivāda (the view that liberation is possible through idolatry),
2) Agñanavāda (agnosticism) (S I.vi.27),
3) Vinayavāda (the view that liberation is possible through discipline),
4) Akriyāvāda, and
5) Kriyāvāda (S I.xii.1).

Mahāvīra dismisses the views that liberation can be achieved by discipline, or through religious worship. He also rejects the position of Agnosticism. The records of his criticisms of these schools are brief: in general, he views these philosophies as confused. In contrast, the same texts have much more to say about the Akriyāvāda position.

According to Mahāvīra, the Akriyāvāda denies the existence of karma and the notion that decisions and actions of the soul bring forth results in future moments (S I.xii.4). The classical texts also describe the position thus: "When a man acts or causes another to act, it is not his soul (*ātman*) which acts or causes to act; Thus they (viz. the adherents of the Sāṅkhya philosophy) boldly proclaim" (S I.i.1.13).[3] Akriyāvāda, if nothing else, is the view that persons are not actors or agents.

The Kriyāvāda holds the opposite: (i) that actions (*kriyā*) have effects, (ii) that persons can and do act, and (iii) that these actions are morally significant. While these theses constitute the bare essentials of the Kriyāvāda view according to Jain scripture, Mahāvīra is inclined to describe the Kriyāvāda, and its implications, in a more expansive manner. According to Mahāvīra:

> The (Kriyāvādins) Śramaṇas and Brāhmaṇas understanding the world (according to their lights) speak thus: misery is produced by one's own works, not by those of somebody else (viz. fate, creator, &c.). But right knowledge and conduct lead to liberation .... The (*Tīrthaṅkaras*) being (as it were) the eyes of the world and its leaders, teach the path which is salutary to men; they have declared that the world is eternal inasmuch as creatures are (forever) living in it .... Averse to injury of living beings, they do not act, nor cause others to act. Always restraining themselves, those pious men practise control, and some become heroes through their knowledge. He regards small beings and large beings, the whole world, as equal to himself; he comprehends the immense world, and being awakened he controls himself among the careless. Those who have learned (the truth) by themselves or from others are able (to save) themselves and others. One should always honour a man who is like a light and makes manifest the Law (Dharma) after having well considered it. He who knows himself and the world; who knows where (the creatures) go, and whence they will not return, who knows what is eternal, and what is transient, birth and death, and the future existences of men: He who knows the tortures of beings below (i.e. in hell); who knows the influx of sin and its stoppage: who knows misery and its annihilation, he is entitled to expound the Kriyāvāda. (S I.xii.11-21)

For Mahāvīra, the Kriyāvāda is only consistent with the Jain view; that the universe is teaming with beings,[4] and that to understand one's capacity for moral action is to take care to not interfere with the welfare of any being.

8.4. Motion and *Mokṣa*

The Jains, like the Buddhists, conceive of their doctrine simply as Dharma (S I.ix). Like Buddhism, Jainism also employs "dharma" in a *seemingly* technical sense, in connection with ontological matters. Specifically, the unusual Jain *extention* of "dharma" is motion (U xxviii.7–9) or the Principle of Motion.

Motion is important in Jain thinking because to be unliberated is to be nonmotile. The state of lacking *mokṣa* in Jain thought is characterized by being weighted down and bound by karma and other physical substances. By living a life according to dharma, one ends the reign of immotility, and becomes, though slowly at first, motile. Thus, Dharma (in essence) is Motion. Motion, on the Jain account, is a kind of substance that permeates the universe.

With the cultivation of dharma in one's self, the "soul takes the form of a straight line, goes in one moment, without touching anything and taking up no space, (upward to the highest *Ākāsa* [space]), and there develops into its natural form, [and] obtains perfection" (U xxix.73). Dharma does not stop in a state of liberation. As the state of liberation consists in motility, a liberated soul is morally perfect:

> Earth-lives are individual beings, so are water-lives, fire-lives, and wind-lives; grass, trees, corn; ... A wise man should study them with all means of philosophical research. All beings hate pain; therefore one should not kill them.; This is the quintessence of wisdom: not to kill anything. Know this to be the legitimate conclusion from the principle of the reciprocity with regard to nonkilling. He should cease to injure living beings whether they move or not, on high, below, and on earth. For this has been called the "*Nirvāṇa*"; which consists in

peace. (S I.xi.7–10)

In the history of Indian philosophy, dharma is generally regarded as something that can be practised well and upheld, without simultaneously achieving liberation. The Jain view, in contrast, is that the only way to do the morally right thing is to achieve liberation. Hence, on the Jain view, the reality that corresponds to the notion of *mokṣa* is also a moral value.

A critic might argue that this interpretation of Jain thought is absurd: *MOTION* is not a moral concern for anyone (the critic might say). What we have to do is look to the particular context in which a term is used, and determine its meaning on that basis; in this context, "dharma" stands for motion, or for the Principle of Motion. Thus, that is what "dharma" means in this context.

In response, I would challenge this contextual Extentionalism: why should the context be our clue to the meaning of "dharma"? Why should we not, instead, set ourselves a different task—to figure out why Jain thinkers have used a term of clear moral importance for the Principle of Motion? The critic thinks that this approach is ridiculous, for the very idea that motion could be of moral importance is ridiculous. Here, we must ask, whether our concerns about what is ridiculous should be a factor in our attempt to understand the philosophical thought of others. Obviously—I would argue—the ancient Jains did not think that it was ridiculous to morally evaluate motion, for that is exactly what they did: they applied a moral term to motion, and in so doing, at the very least, communicated the view to us that the Principle of Motion is morally significant.

In the context of Jainism's Physicalist thinking, it stands to reason that Morality itself would end up having a physical correlate. We are more comfortable with thinking of Morality, or The Good, as an Idea, or the Form of Forms—this is a result of our (those of us reading this in English) Platonic heritage. However, the view that The Good is an ideal thing is an artefact of an idealist perspective on things. For one who has a

Materialist, or Physicalist, view, the Platonic view of Moral Goodness is not entirely intuitive. Certainly, a view on the existence of ideal objects is not in keeping with the Jain Cosmology. A view on the existence of physical objects, elements, dimensions and relations, is in keeping with a Jain Cosmology.

Motion is thus Jainism's analogue to Plato's Form of Forms, I would argue. It is morality, given objectivity, or at least, thinghood. By making it clear that Dharma is Motion, Jainism is making a strong, realist statement on the nature of morality: (a) that it is not an invention of one's subjective whims or fancies; (b) that it is a very real feature of a real, physicalistic, universe; and (c) that it is a genuine, and literally, liberating force.

8.5. Important Moral Terms in Jain Literature

While Jain literature specifies many moral directives as constituting dharma, five moral concerns are singled out by Jain tradition as constituting the Great Vows, or *mahāvratas* (Ac II.15.i.1–v.1). In Sanskrit, the five vows are designated as "*satya*" (truth-telling) "*asteya*" (nonstealing) "*ahiṁsā*" (noninjury) "*aparigraha*" (nongreediness/nonacquisitiveness) and "*brahmacarya*" (sexual restraint or celibacy). According to Jain tradition, the early *Tīrtaṅkara* (Path Maker) Pārśva only recognized four of these vows. Mahāvīra is said to have added sexual restraint to the list (U XXIII.12).[5]

The terms designating the five vows are moral terms that are not unique to Jain literature. As will be noted later, this five-fold list is to be found in one other Indian philosophical school: the Yoga system (p.269). The terms comprising the *mahāvratas* are also found individually in circulation throughout Indian literature, as terms designating matters that authors have the *anger inclination* about. The terms comprising the *mahāvratas* are, themselves, *perfect* moral terms, without *focus*, but with *substantive content*. It is their collection under the heading of "*mahāvratas*" that is significant for a study of Jain ethics.

Another moral term of note, with respect to Jain thought, is "*cāritra*". It was noted earlier (2.6.2. Traditional Meaning of "Dharma" p.95) that *cāritra* is put forward as comprising dharma, according to one Jain author (Kundakunda I.7, I.69). "*Cāritra*" is a *perfect* moral term without *focus*, with the *substantive content* of "conduct". In the context of Jain thought, it refers to conduct that is uniquely approved of by Jain tradition. Thus, "*cāritra*" is often used in the Jain context to denote particular *deontic* matters that are unique to Jain culture and forms of life.

8.6. Jain Criticism of Early Buddhist Ethics

Of interest in an exposition of Indian ethics is that the ancient Jain literature has a particular criticism to pass on Early Buddhist ethics. The *Sūtrakṛtāṅga* draws attention to a particular aspect of the Early Buddhist thought: the role that *aretaic* states play in assessing the severity of *deontic* transgressions. The text depicts a Buddhist as stating:

> If a savage thrusts a spit through the side of a granary, mistaking it for a man; or through a gourd, mistaking it for a baby, and roasts it, he will be guilty of murder according to our views. If a savage puts a man on a spit and roasts him, mistaking him for a fragment of the granary; or a baby, mistaking him for a gourd, he will not be guilty of murder according to our views. If anybody thrusts a spit through a man or a baby, mistaking him for a fragment of the granary, puts on the fire and roasts him, that will be a meal fit for Buddhas to break fast upon. (S II.6.26–28)

In response to this view, presented as the Buddhist's, the Jain named Ādraka states:

> Well controlled men cannot accept your denial of guilt incurred

> by unintentionally doing harm to living beings. It will cause error and no good to both who teach such doctrines and who believe them .... Do not use such speech by means of which you do evil; for such speech is incompatible with virtues. No ordained monk should speak empty words. (S II.6.30–31)

The closest record of such a view in the Buddhist Pāli Canon is found in the *Aṅguttara Nikāya*:

> A certain person who has not properly cultivated his body, behaviour, thought and intelligence, is inferior and insignificant and his life is short and miserable; of such a person ... even a trifling evil action done leads him to hell. In the case of a person who has proper culture of the body, behaviour, thought and intelligence, who is superior and not insignificant, and who is endowed with long life, the consequences of a similar evil action are to be experienced in this very life, and sometimes may not appear at all. (An 1.219)

I am not sure if the Jain characterization of the Buddhist view is entirely accurate. The passage paraphrasing Early Buddhist ethics imputes to it the view that only intentions count; that it makes no difference whether one actually does the right thing or not. This may be the logical consequence of Early Buddhist ethics, but it certainly is not a position explicitly affirmed in the classical texts.

There is something positive for us to glean, however, from the Jain criticism of Early Buddhist ethics. Jainism does not countenance the possibility of virtuous mental states mitigating the guilt that accrues to *deontic* wrong-doings. On the Jain view, it seems, there are no excuses for doing the wrong thing.

8.7. Jainism and Negative Utilitarianism?

Kalupahana in his account of Pre-Buddhist moral theories argues that "Deontology and Utilitarianism belonged to two different cultures". According to him, Deontology was the hallmark of Brahmanic ethics, while Utilitarianism belonged to the *Śramaṇa*, or ascetic philosophical culture (Kalupahana 1995 p.10). It seems quite reasonable to interpret Brahmanic ethics as largely Deontological, since many Brahmanic ethical systems concern themselves with the fulfilment of obligations; specifically, those specified by the Vedas. Is it true that the *Śramaṇa* tradition was highly Utilitarian in its outlook? I do not think so, but let us address the question of whether Jain Dharma constitutes a form of Utilitarianism. If Jainism is not a form of Utilitarianism, the general hypothesis that *Śramaṇa* ethics is Utilitarian cannot be right.

Utilitarianism comes in two forms: Positive Utilitarianism, and Negative Utilitarianism. Positive Utilitarianism is usually just called "Utilitarianism", and its view is that happiness, or pleasure, is what is to be maximized and that failing to do so is a moral failure. Negative Utilitarianism holds that unhappiness, or pain, should be minimized, and that a failure to do this is a moral failure. Does Jainism hold either of these views?

Jainism's concern for not causing other beings pain and its insight that all beings desire happiness (S I.vii.2) might lead us to conclude that Jainism is a form of Utilitarianism; however, this conclusion is premature. When we examine Jain thought more closely, we find that it is not happiness or pain that Jain ethics wishes to maximize or avoid. Rather, it is the concern not to violate persons or interfere with their well-being that Jainism says is everyone's responsibility. Thus a Jain passage argues:

> Those who praise the gift are accessory to the killing of beings; those who forbid it, deprive others of the means of sustenance. Those, however, who give neither answer, viz., that it is meritorious, or is not so, do not expose themselves to guilt, and will reach Beatitude. (S I.ii.20–21)

Consequentialists are apt to define Deontology as the view that morality is concerned not with the consequences of actions, but with following rules. According to this definition, Jainism appears to be a version of Deontology. There is another way to make the distinction, which Deontologists (particularly of the Kantian variety) themselves are inclined to proffer. On this second view, Deontology is not concerned with consequences of actions, but with persons, which are entities that demand our respect, and which we are obligated not to violate. On this understanding of Deontology, Jainism is the very archetype of a Deontological moral theory.

Is there any room for construing Jainism as a form of Utilitarianism? I do not see how. If Jainism were a form of Utilitarianism, it would advocate either the maximization of happiness, or the minimization of pain. However, Jain philosophical texts advocate neither.

Kamal Chand Sogani argues that we ought to conceive of the Jain moral theory as "Ahiṁsā Utilitarianism". Sogani argues:

> This Ahiṁsā Utilitarianism is to be distinguished from Hedonistic Utilitarianism of Mill, but it has some resemblance with the Ideal Utilitarianism of Moore and Rashdall. The point to be noted here is that Moore distinguishes between good as a means and good as an end (good in itself). When we say that an action or a thing is good as a means, we say that it is liable to produce something which is good in itself (Intrinsically Good). The Jaina recognizes that Ahiṁsā can be both good as a means and good as an end. This means that both means and ends are to be tested by the criterion of Ahiṁsā. (Sogani 1975 p.178)

Given that the Jain texts advocate neither the maximization of well-being, or happiness, nor the minimization of harm or sadness, there are no grounds for construing Jain moral thought as a form of Utilitarianism. However, we can salvage Sogani's suggestion thus: perhaps Jain moral thought is a form of Consequentialism, *because* it recognizes moral principles like *ahiṁsā* as means to other goods, such as liberation.

This revised suggestion is untenable for two reasons. If Jain moral thought were a form of Consequentialism, it would urge that we judge the rightness or wrongness of an action on the basis of its consequences. If this were so, such a view would be enshrined as a fundamental principle of Jain moral thought. In contrast, the Jain view is that we ought to avoid action altogether, for that is the only way that we can avoid interfering with others' well-being. Secondly, it does not seem as though *ahiṁsā*, on the Jain view, is a means to liberation. The Jain view seems to be that the only way to practise *ahiṁsā* is to be liberated.

What does this say about the concept of *ahiṁsā* as it figures in Jain ethics? Normally the term has a highly *deontic* significance, designating the idea of noninjury. In Jainism, I believe, the concept of *ahiṁsā* takes on important *aretaic* significance: it has to do with our attitudes toward other persons. In Jainism, to adhere to *ahiṁsā* is to *regard* others as Ends. Jain ethics criticizes those who would attempt to act in such a way as to alter the world. The world, as it stands, is already maximally valuable from a moral perspective, on the Jain's account. Arguably, from the Jain perspective, the world is literally a Kingdom of Ends. Our obligation, thus, is to not disrupt the Kingdom of Ends. Thus, to act in accordance with *ahiṁsā*, for Jainism, is ironically to not act. Hence, the normal *deontic* reading of *ahiṁsā* is re-understood in the context of Jainism. It is not a positive duty, but a duty to avoid doing the wrong thing.

8.8. Implications of Jain Ethics

Jainism leaves us with two intriguing hypotheses:

1) the world is the way it is because of the choices that people make, and
2) everyone would be better off if they were left alone.

The paradox of Jainism is that, while it is Indian philosophy's most vocal proponent of the Kriyāvāda doctrine, it advises us that if we want to do the morally right thing, we would consistently do nothing at all.[6]

Here, *doing* nothing has a double implication. One implication of this advice is that we, by doing nothing, would stop acting; however, "karma" means (literally) "action". Thus, not to do anything, or to avoid action, is also to avoid accumulating karma, on the Jain view. By defining karma as a weighty substance that drags originally free, omniscient, and blissful souls into a state of bondage, the very notion of "karma" is given an ironic spin in Jain thought. "Karma" may seem like movement, or motility, but, on the Jain view, it is not: it is stagnation; a dirt that accrues to us. Genuine freedom, is Motion, or Dharma; to practise, Dharma, thus, is to dissociate oneself from a false kind of freedom, which is karma. By leaving off an unhealthy, illusory freedom in action, we gain a genuine kind of freedom in ethics, on the Jain account.

This critical view of karma is also, no doubt, intended as an implicit criticism of Vedic Ethics, propagated by the Pūrvamīmāṃsā and Vedānta schools. For these schools, dharma consists in karma; actions. Moreover, in these systems, "karma" often refers to that which is prescribed by the Vedas. In casting karma as something that is polluting, and contrary to Dharma, Jain ethics makes it clear that, on its lights, what is considered as dharma by Vedicists is in fact immoral and polluting.

Jain ethics also has an important criticism to deliver to activistic types like Schweitzer: for them, the ethical thing is to go out into the world and to try and help people. Jainism puts such aspirations into a sober perspective: how is such a project possible? Any time we attempt to do something for others, or even for ourselves, we are complicit in the death and destruction of living things: housing and feeding the homeless, charity, and so on—all of these activities involve killing some entities (plants and animals) and redistributing their corpses to others. Jainism cuts to the heart of the matter: activity in the world is a sordid affair, generally involved in wrong-doing. Thus, if we are to really do the right thing, we ought, on Jainism's view, to civilly abstain from the wrong-doing. If we carry out this programme far enough, we will eventually stop doing things altogether. While

Mahātma Gāndhi did not take this programme to this extreme, his programme of civil disobedience seems to have obvious affinities to Jain ethics.

Notes

1 This is a point made more than once in Dundas's discussion of Jain sectarian differences. See Dundas 1992 pp.40–52.

2 Someone who wishes to defend the importance of ethics to the Indian philosophical tradition would be sharp to point out that none of the A-Moralist schools fashionable at the time had any staying power: out of the ancient *śramaṇa* milieu, only Jainism and Buddhism survived as philosophical movements to be reckoned with.

3 The diagnosis that the Sāṅkhya philosophy is a form of the Akriyāvāda is perceptive; a credit to classical Jain philosophers, and Mahāvīra himself. In fact, the only reasonable way to distinguish between the Yoga school and the Sāṅkhya philosophy is on the issue of the Kriyāvāda–Akriyāvāda debate. This matter is taken up in 9.4. Akriyāvāda and Kriyāvāda (pp.267–273).

4 Water, air, fire and wood are all said to have living entities in them. See S I.xii.7.

5 Hermann Jacobi (1987 Part I p.121 fn.3) suggests that sexual restraint was implicitly understood as contained within the fourth vow of *aparigraha*, in the earlier list.

6 The resolve of doing nothing at all, in Jainism, is termed "*sallekhana*" or in the recent parlance of the Therāpanti Śvetāmbara order, "*santhārā*". It consists of a fast unto death. This resolve is distinguished from suicide which is done out of desperation, or euthanasia, which concerns itself with minimizing pain and suffering. While suicide involves action, *sallekhana* does not.

Chapter 9

Sāṅkhya and Yoga

9.1. Background of Sāṅkhya and Yoga

For a historical understanding of Hindu philosophical thought, an acquaintance with the schools of Sāṅkhya and Yoga is indispensable. Yet, it is not easy to gain an introduction into the topic of the two schools that does not leave one wondering in what way these two schools are alike, or in what way they are different. Part of the problem is that both philosophical schools have a vast literature with many internal differences: to find the common mark within each school might be daunting, if one embarks on a vast survey of technical differences between exponents of the respective schools. Secondly, there is much in common with the two schools. So much so that while it is noted in the *Encyclopedia of Indian Philosophies* that the series will have a separate volume on Yoga (Larson 1987 p.15), in its volume on the Sāṅkhya philosophy, works by authors within the Yoga tradition, like Patañjali, are listed in the chronology of works on Sāṅkhya. Moreover, the philosophy of Patañjali—the codifier of the Yoga system—is presented as a form of Sāṅkhya: "Patañjala Sāṅkhya".[1]

The common history between the two schools of Indian philosophy also contributes to the impression that they are really isomers of the same philosophy. Traces of both systems can be found in Vedic literature. The *Kaṭha Upaniṣad*, for instance, sets out many of the categories of Sāṅkhya, including that of *puruṣa*, or person (I.3.10–11), plus a definition of "*yoga*" that prefigures the one that later authors in the Yoga tradition provide (II.3.11).[2] In ancient times, prior to the formalisation of two separate traditions there seems to have been little attention paid to differentiating between the two schools of thought. Ian Whicher notes:

> Yoga was very closely allied with Sāṅkhya. This fact is reflected in the *Mahābhārata,* which utilizes the compound *sāṅkhya–yoga* (chapter II of the *Bhagavadgītā* is entitled "Sāṅkhya–Yoga") and also asserts that Sāṅkhya and Yoga can be looked upon as being identical (*Mahābhārata* XII.293.30 and *Bhagavadgītā* V.5) .... The epic schools of Sāṅkhya and Yoga gave rise in part to the Sāṅkhya–Yoga syncretism. However, both traditions were likewise asserted as being already distinct and independent developments at the time of the final composition of the *Mahābhārata*. (Whicher 1998 p.51)

Whicher provides us with another reason for the abiding syncretism of Sāṅkhya and Yoga:

> Whatever may be the case with Sāṅkhya, Yoga is a living tradition and gurus to this day continue to teach the *Yoga Sūtra* in the *aśramas*, homes, and monasteries in an unbroken lineage .... As many of the categories of the Sāṅkhya philosophy are so closely allied to the Yoga system, the Sāṅkhya tradition has survived as a supportive school in association with Yoga. The Yoga school of philosophy is often referred to as Sāṅkhya–Yoga. (Whicher 1998 p.49)

How are we to make sense of the distinction between Sāṅkhya and Yoga in the face of an unbroken tradition of syncretism between the two schools? It might be useful to note that "*sāṅkhya*" etymologically means *ENUMERATION* and it seems to be the ancient label for our contemporary activity of analysis (breaking down an issue into its components) while *yoga* (whatever its etymology) has always been associated with practises and disciplines of both mental and physical varieties; however, on examination, it seems that the Yoga philosophy too engages in an analysis or enumeration of things akin to Sāṅkhya. True, the *Yoga Sūtra* in comparison to the *Sāṅkhya Kārikā* goes to great lengths to specify practises that one must engage in. But against all the other commonalities, one might be inclined to think that the difference is merely one of emphasis.

In truth, there is an extremely important difference between the two schools of thought. This difference is not to be found in an acquaintance with the largely identical ontology and cosmology of both schools, but in their moral thought. While both schools share a common ontological framework, the Sāṅkhya philosophy falls into the Akriyāvāda camp (so heavily criticized by the ancient Jain literature) while the Yoga philosophy is a Kriyāvāda philosophy (8.3. The Kriyāvāda–Akriyāvāda Debate pp.249–273). In order for this to become apparent, we need to be familiar with the common cosmological framework of both schools.

9.2. Common Framework

Both Sāṅkhya and Yoga recognize two important metaphysical categories: *Prakṛti* (*NATURE*) and *Puruṣa* (*PERSON*). Both schools recognize a plurality of persons. This is explicitly stated at SK 18, and implicit in YS I.24 where God—or the Lord (*Īśvara*)—is recognized as a special kind of person (*puruṣaviśeṣa*). *Prakṛti* does a great deal of work in both systems. It comprises not only matter, but mentality—called "*citta*" in Yoga (YS I.2), and "*Mahat*" or the *GREAT–ONE* in Sāṅkhya (SK 22). Both systems believe that the two categories of *Puruṣa* and *Prakṛti* make contact so that persons can come to have knowledge of their nature and achieve liberation (SK 21, YS II.18). However, as we shall see, Yoga regards persons as actors while Sāṅkhya regards them as passive spectators.

In both systems, Nature is comprised of three "*guṇas*" or properties. The commonly held properties are *sattva*, *rajas* and *tamas*.

On the nature of these three *guṇas*, the *Sāṅkhya Kārikā* states:

> The constituents [of *Prakṛti*] are of the nature of pleasure [*prīti*], pain [*aprīti*] and indifference [*viṣāda*]; they serve to illumine [*prakāśa*], to actuate [*pravṛtti*] and to restrain [*niyamārtha*]; each of these functions through suppression, co-operation, transformation and intimate intercourse with and by the rest. *Sattva* (alone) is considered to be buoyant and illuminating; *Rajas* (alone) to be stimulating and mobile; *Tamas* alone is heavy and enveloping; their functioning for the goal [of the *puruṣa*] ... is like (the action of) a lamp. (SK 12–13)

Similarly, the *Yoga Sūtra* states:

> The object of experience is composed of the three *guṇas*—the principles of illumination (*prakāśa*), activity (*kriyā*), and inertia (*stithi*). From these the whole universe has evolved together with the instruments of knowledge—such as the mind, senses, etc.—and the objects perceived—such as the physical elements. The universe exists in order that the experiencer may become liberated". (YS II.18)

It is important that the authors of the *Sāṅkhya Kārikā* and the *Yoga Sūtra* presume a familiarity with the terms "*sattva*", "*rajas*", and "*tamas*". They do not formally define these terms. Rather, they presume that the reader will understand that it is *sattva* that is spoken of as pleasure (*prīti*) or illumination (*prakāśa*); that it is *rajas* that is referred to as the principle of pain (*aprīti*) or actuation (*pravṛtti*) and action (*kriyā*); that it is *tamas* that is referred to as indifference (*viṣāda*), restraint (*niyamārtha*) and stillness (*stithi*). The authors of both the works are falling back on a common understanding of these categories. For us to appreciate the importance of the *guṇas* in Sāṅkhya and Yoga, we must understand these concepts not as technical categories of these schools but as concepts that were very much common coin in the philosophical environment of Sāṅkhya and Yoga.

9.3. Moral Significance of the *Guṇas*

Philosophical Sāṅkhya and Yoga appear to have been codified by Īśvarakṛṣṇa and Patañjali, respectively, at the close of the epic period of Indian literature (Whicher 1998 p.51, Larson 1987 pp.4–10). Accounts of the three *guṇas* in the *Mahābhārata*, specifically in the *Bhagavad Gītā*, constitute a kind of record of the history of these common terms, prior to the codification of the two philosophies.

The nature of the three *guṇas* is a topic discussed at length in the *Bhagavad Gītā*. In it we find the common cosmology of Sāṅkhya and Yoga declared: "*sattva*, *rajas* and *tamas* are the *guṇas* that arise from *Prakṛti*. They bind the immutable self in the body. Of these, *sattva*, being without impurity, is luminous and free from morbidity ..." (*Gītā* XIV.5–6). The categories of *sattva*, *rajas* and *tamas* play a part in India's traditional system of medicine (*Ayurveda*) and so the *Gītā* too discusses the dietary implications of the *guṇa* theory. It tells us that foods liked by persons whose nature is predominantly *sattvic* are healthy and agreeable; foods liked by those of a *rajasic* nature are pungent and burning, while the *tamasic* person likes rancid food (*Gītā* XVII.8–10). What is important for our concerns is the great moral importance that the *Gītā* gives to the *guṇas*. In several passages, the following doctrine is put forth. Actions that issue from a strong Deontological consciousness—a consciousness which motivates a person to perform their dharma without regard to personal benefit or the consequences but because it ought to be done—issue from the preponderance of the *sattva guṇa* (*Gītā* XVII.11,17,20). Obligations performed for the sake of their consequences, or for ostentation, or those done grudgingly, issue from the *rajas guṇa* (*Gītā* XVII.12,18,21). Actions that are not sanctioned by moral authority, those done for the sake of injuring oneself or another, or performances of obligations incorrectly, issue from the *tamas guṇa* (*Gītā*

XVII.13,19,22). In short, what is presented in the *Gītā* is a theory of the *guṇas* that defines them according to the kind of moral criticism that is appropriate to choices issuing from each of the respective *guṇas*. Choices that issue from the *sattva guṇa* are neither to be *deontically* blamed nor *aretaically* faulted. Choices issuing from the *rajas guṇa* are not to be *deontically* blamed, but to be *aretaically* faulted. Choices issuing from the *tamas guṇa* are to be *deontically* blamed and *aretaically* faulted.

In another vein, the *Gītā* fleshes out the nature of the *guṇas* in terms of the kind of knowledge that issues from them. Once again, the elaboration is morally significant. Knowledge that arises from *sattva* is of the nature of gnosis, or *jñāna*; that arising from *rajas* is superficially accurate, but fundamentally mistaken, and that which arises from *tamas* is unreasonable, false and distorted (*Gītā* XVIII.20–22); *sattva* results in the correct understanding of dharma and adharma, where as *rajas* results in an incorrect account of dharma and adharma, while the intellect dominated by *tamas* "regards adharma as dharma and ... reverses every value" (*Gītā* XVIII.30–32).

The lesson for our study, issuing from a glance at the *Bhagavad Gītā*, is that the *guṇas* are not valueless aspects of reality. Rather, they are inherently evaluative. Whicher makes the similar point: "Descriptions of the *guṇas* ... point to an interpretation that would stress that their psychological and even moral components are both indispensable for the definition and existence of individual entities or persons within the world" (Whicher 1998 p.63).

An undischarged question concerning the nature of the *guṇas* is whether they are themselves moral properties, or whether they take on a definite moral value in combination and in relative preponderance and relation to other *guṇas*. On the first option *tamas* is simply evil no matter what. On the latter view, *tamas* is not synonymous with evil; rather, a preponderance of *tamas* in a person's nature constitutes evil. Arguably, this latter view is suggested by the *Sāṅkhya Kārikā* when it states that "their functioning", i.e. the *guṇas*, "for the goal [of the *Puruṣa*] ... is like (the action of) a lamp" (SK 12–13). The implication here seems to be that all the *guṇas* are necessary to bring about a good. Likewise we have a similar view presented in the *Yoga Sūtra*, where the *guṇas* are depicted as being evolved by *Prakṛti* so that *Puruṣas* can come to know themselves (YS II.18). The implication seems to be that all the *guṇas* can function towards an axiologically desirable state of affairs. Thus, if any *guṇa* should give rise to undesirable states of affairs, the problem is one of preponderance and domination; not its simple presence in an object.

It seems as though there is a certain tension in the *guṇa* theory. On the one hand, *guṇas* appear to be inherently evaluative, and on the other hand it appears that their real evaluative significance is determined by their chemical relations with other *guṇas*. The tension is modulated, to a certain extent, if we assume that their inherent evaluative significance is moral in nature and fixed. It seems that on the Sāṅkhya and Yoga account the *guṇas* are evaluatively significant in themselves (i.e., having evaluative implications is inherent to their nature) but their moral significance is only determinable within the context of their relationship to other *guṇas*. Moral values, thus, appear to supervene on the *guṇas*. Moreover, on the *guṇa* theory, moral values are in some sense reducible to the relational structure of *guṇas* in objects.

9.4. Akriyāvāda and Kriyāvāda

We need to bring back into our discussion the distinctions between Kriyāvādin doctrines and Akriyāvādin doctrines—a distinction that Jain justificative ethics places a great stress on. As noted earlier, the essence of the Akriyāvāda view is that persons are not agents or actors, whereas, the Kriyāvāda affirms the agency of persons (8.3. The Kriyāvāda–Akriyāvāda Debate pp.249–251). While the Yoga philosophy is a strong version of Kriyāvāda, the Sāṅkhya philosophy is virtually the archetype of Akriyāvādin thought.

The Sāṅkhya tradition recognizes both the values of dharma and *mokṣa*. Kumārila, the Pūrvamīmāṃsā author, singles out the Sāṅkhya tradition for emphasizing dharma as a mode of the intellect; in other words, a virtue (SV II.195–96). According to the *Sāṅkhya Kārikā*, the three worlds (the heavens, earth, and the nether-worlds) are respectively characterised by the preponderance of *sattva*, *rajas* and *tamas* (SK 54). The cultivation of dharma leads one to the higher worlds (and presumably increases the preponderance of *sattva* in one's body and mind) whereas adharma leads to the lower worlds (and presumably increases *tamas* in one's constitution). However, it is only nonattachment that yields final liberation (SK 64–65).

While the Sāṅkhya tradition recognizes morality and final liberation as real values, it holds that persons play no part in maximizing value. "Of a certainty, therefore, not any is bound, or liberated, nor (does any) migrate; it is Primal Nature (*Prakṛti*) abiding in manifold forms, that is bound, is liberated, and migrates" (SK 62). Persons, on the Sāṅkhya account, are completely extraneous to events in life. What role does the person have to play? "[From] the contrast with that (which is composed of the three constituents etc.) there follows for *Puruṣa* the character of being a witness, freedom (from misery), neutrality, percipience and nonagency" (SK 19). The only thing that *Puruṣa* contributes to life is the light of consciousness. Aside from that, persons, on the Sāṅkhya account, are essentially nonagents: they do nothing. The moral praiseworthiness of one person, and the vile nature of another, are a function of the natural qualities that comprise a person's body and mind; qualities that are both distinct from a person, and which a person has no power to alter.

In contrast, the Yoga system, while sharing much of the ontology of Sāṅkhya, places great emphasis on the power of persons to change their lives. The *kriyāvāda* doctrine is negatively borne out in Yoga by the conspicuous absence of bold statements, of the kind found in Sāṅkhya literature, which attribute nonagency to the self. Positively, the *kriyāvāda* doctrine appears to be affirmed in Yoga's view that the *puruṣa* is the *lord of the mind* (*cittavṛttayastatprabhoḥ*) (YS IV.18)—i.e. the one in control. Indeed, at the outset of the *Yoga Sūtra*, we are told that the objective of Yoga is to control modifications in the mind (YS I.2), which results in a person abiding in their real nature (YS I.3). Accomplishing the control of mental modifications culminates in liberation. Yoga requires constant practise (*YS* I.12-13). Thus, success in yoga comes to one who has energy (*vīrya*) (YS I.20). Such a programme appears to affirm an optimistic view of a person's ability to gain control of the nature that constitutes their body and mind.

An integral part of the practise of the Yoga philosophy, according to Patañjali, is the "eight-limbs" of yoga (*aṣṭānga yoga*) (YS II.29). Limbs two to eight of the *aṣṭānga yoga* are:

- *niyamas* – various observances, which include the cultivation of purity (*sauca*), contentment (*santoṣ*) and austerities (*tapas*)
- *āsana* – posture
- *prāṇāyāma* – control of breath
- *pratyāhāra* – withdrawal of the mind from sense objects
- *dhāranā* – concentration
- *dhyāna* – meditation
- *samādhi* – absorption in the self

Importantly for our study, the first limb of the *aṣṭānga yoga* is that of "*yama*", which is a group of concerns that are individually designated by terms that have all the marks of *perfect substantive* moral terms: "*Yama* is abstention from harming others (*ahiṁsā*), [abstention from] telling false hoods (*satya*), [abstention from] acquisitiveness (*asteya*) ... and [abstention from] greed/envy (*aparigraha*)". It seems that the *yamas* are constituted by conspicuously moral *deontic* and *aretaic* concerns. Included in the list is the virtue of sexual restraint (*brahmacarya*) (YS II.32).

The *yama* rules "are basic rules .... They must be practised without any reservations as to time, place, purpose, or caste rules" (YS II.31). The failure to live a morally pure life constitutes a major obstacle to the practise of Yoga (YS II.34). On the plus side, by living the morally pure life, all of one's needs and desires are fulfilled:

> When [one] becomes steadfast in ... abstention from harming others, then all living creatures will cease to feel enmity in [one's] presence. When [one] becomes steadfast in ... abstention from falsehood, [one] gets the power of obtaining for [oneself] and others the fruits of good deeds, without [others] having to perform the deeds themselves. When [one] becomes steadfast in ... abstention from theft, all wealth comes .... Moreover, one achieves purification of the heart, cheerfulness of mind, the power of concentration, control of the passions and fitness for vision of the *Ātma* [self]. (YS II.35–41)

It is important to note that the virtues and obligations that constitute the *yamas* are the kinds of things that if violated, many persons have an inclination to express anger about. They are precisely the kinds of things listed in the Hindu *dharmaśāstras*. Importantly, the list of *yamas* are also identical with the list of *mahāvratas*, or *GREAT VOWS*, of Jainism (8.5. Important Moral Terms in Jain Literature p.253). On the basis of a sound account of moral terms (2.4. Definition of Moral Terms p.70–85) that respects the *intentional* basis of moral meaning, the fact that these terms are part of classical Indian literature at large, and the sociological facts surrounding people's dispositions towards the matters that they designate, we can conclude that the *yama* terms are *perfect substantive* moral terms. Yet, at least one author argues that the *yamas* and "*ahiṁsā*" are not moral at all.

V.K. Bharadwaja states, "Doing an action for the good of everybody is doing it from the moral point of view; and it is such actions alone which are the subject of moral judgement" (Bharadwaja 1984 p.171). He further claims that *ahiṁsā* along with the *yamas* are not undertaken for the sake of others, but for the sake of the yogi's own soteriological pursuits:

> The ethical notions of *GOOD* and *BAD*, *RIGHT* and *WRONG*, *OUGHT* and ought not thus have no relevance to the *yogāṅgānuṣṭhāna* which is only a complex of causal factors .... Besides, moral judgement necessarily presupposes moral responsibility. In the case of the *yogin*, the notion of responsibility plays no place in his scheme of things. He is concerned with himself for himself in order to land himself in an isolated island of *kaivalya* consciousness. (Bharadwaja 1984 pp.173–174)

Bharadwaja's objection to construing *ahiṁsā* in the *Yoga Sūtra* as a moral concept rests on several confusions. True, the liberated state in Yoga is described as a kind of aloneness (*kaivalya*) (YS IV.34). However, nowhere in the *Yoga Sūtra* does it say that one ought to disregard the welfare of others, or that the *yamas* are simply for one's own benefit and no one else's. In fact, the *sūtra* seems to state the opposite: "When [one] becomes steadfast in ... abstention from falsehood, [one] gets the power of obtaining for [oneself] and others the fruits of good deeds, without [others] having to perform the deeds themselves" (YS II.36). Clearly, everyone benefits from the yogi's uncommon restraint.

As for the view that the yogi can have no association with responsibility, this is pure conjecture, which has nothing to do with the *Yoga Sūtra*. The *Yoga Sūtra*'s view that a person is the "lord of the mind" (YS IV.17/18), and its stress on the role that a person can play in their own betterment, places the Yoga philosophy in the Kriyāvāda group of Indian philosophical views—a group of philosophical views that countenance persons' moral responsibility.

It is apparent from Bharadwaja's remarks that his argument rests on the Social Content Thesis; "*Ahiṁsā* is not even a social concept on the *yogin*'s view. If it were a moral concept, it would necessarily be a social concept too" (Bharadwaja 1984 p.175). The Social Content Thesis was considered at an earlier point (2.3.1. Social Content and Conduct pp.35–37). Arguments were presented against this approach to defining moral statements and moral subject-matter (2.2. Key Philosophical Terms pp.22–31).

One might argue that the *yamas* are not moral in nature, because, having the *anger inclination* seems contrary to the thrust of the Yoga philosophy. Or, we might be impressed with the notion that "*ahiṁsā*" and the *yamas* are matters that persons generally have the *anger inclination* toward in Indian philosophical literature, but that this inclination is absent in the head-space of the yogi. I think that neither of these views has any foundation in the *Yoga Sūtra*. The telling evidence that speaks against viewing the *yamas* as a-moral in character is that the terms that constitute the *yamas* appear as *perfect* moral terms throughout Indian philosophical literature. The fact that the author of the *Yoga Sūtra* chose the terms that he did to describe the *yamas* is no coincidence.

To make our point clear, let us consider an analogous circumstance where an English speaking ascetic enumerates virtues dictated by his philosophical outlook. Amongst these virtues, he lists, "considerateness", "kindness", "truthfulness", and "gentleness". Could anyone reasonably argue that the author in question was *not* enumerating moral virtues? To make such an argument, one would have to disregard the patently moral significance of these terms—their *perfection*; one would have to disregard what our Anglophone ascetic obviously meant, and instead, hypothesise and speculate as to what he might of idiosyncratically meant.

As a member of the South Asian, Sanskritic, linguistic community, Patañjali would have understood the moral *perfection* of the terms he uses for his *yamas*. If he wished not to have communicated that he thinks that the matters under discussion are moral in nature, he could have chosen terms or elaborate phrases that are bereft of moral significance. He did not take this route. What we must draw from his choice of words is that he meant what everyone else would have meant by their use of these terms and that the things under discussion are morally significant.

9.5. *Dharmamegha Samādhi*

Moral discipline not only forms the back-drop for yogic enlightenment, but moral perfection seems to be involved in the finalisation of the yogi's enlightenment. In YS IV.29, we find that the final state of liberation is closely prefigured by the *samādhi* (*ABSORPTION*) of (or in the) *dharmamegha* (*CLOUD OF MORALITY*).[3] Ian Whicher, drawing on the input of the commentarial tradition, expands on the state of *dharmamegha samādhi*:

> A permanent identity shift—from the perspective of the human personality to *puruṣa*—takes place. Now free from ... the world of misidentification (*saṃyoga*), the *yogin* yet retains the purified *guṇic* powers of virtue including illuminating "knowledge of all" (due to purified *sattva*), non–afflicted activity (due to purified *rajas*), and a healthy, stable body form (due to purified *tamas*). Fully awakened to the self-effulgent nature of *puruṣa*, the *yogin* witnesses, observes, perceives *prakṛti*, yet ceases to be ensnared and consumed by the drama or play of the *guṇas*. (Whicher 1998 p.283)

The *Yoga Sūtra* depicts the state of *dharmamegha samādhi* as a pivotal event in the career of the yogi. From *dharmamegha samādhi kleśas* (*AFFLICTIONS*) and *karmas* (either actions themselves or past karmas) are removed (YS IV.30). Or, alternatively, *afflicted action* is said to end (Whicher 1998 p.284). The sequence of mutations of the *guṇas* also come to an end (YS IV.32). The *guṇas* no longer serve any purpose for the person, and the yogi achieves final liberation, or *kaivalya* (*ALONENESS, ISOLATION*) (YS IV.34). All of these events appear to be a direct consequence of *dharmamegha samādhi.*

The *Yoga Sūtra* distinguishes *dharmamegha samādhi* from final liberation or *kaivalya* (YS IV.34). While *DHARMAMEGHA SAMĀDHI* is a moral concept, denoting what the Yoga tradition takes to be the state of moral perfection, it is also a kind of soteriological or liberated state, logically distinct from final liberation. We know this not only because *dharmamegha samādhi* frees persons of afflictions, but because the term "*samādhi*" (absorption) has strong soteriological connotations, and is used to designate states of liberation that occur in body (e.g. trances).

What then is the relationship between *dharmamegha samādhi* and final liberation? Are they two states or one? They are two closely related states. *Dharmamegha samādhi* is the new element in the life of the yogi that causes her isolation. The *Yoga Sūtra* thus uses the metaphors of a cloud and isolation for the ideas of dharma and *mokṣa*.

The interpretation that the notion of *KAIVALYA* typically garners holds that the goal of the yogi is an a-moral objective. We have cause, thus, to wonder why this is so. If *kaivalya* were promoted in another context, then perhaps such an interpretation would be justified, for there may be no linguistic or orthographic cues to tell us that the process that *kaivalya* is the end state of is a moral endeavour. However, there are several indications in the *Yoga Sūtra* that the yogi's process is one of moral betterment. To begin with, there are the *yamas*, which consist of *deontic* and *aretaic* affairs that are designated by *perfect* moral terms. Then, prior to the announcement of *kaivalya,* there is mention of "*dharmamegha samādhi*". Even if one views "dharma" through the lens of Extentionalism, it is difficult to explain away the moral significance of this phrase. Given that *kaivalya* follows directly after *dharmamegha samādhi*, there is no textual justification for viewing *kaivalya* as an a-moral goal. In fact, all indications point in the opposite direction. The aloneness that the yogi finds herself in is one where there are no peers. This lack of equal association is a direct result of the yogi's efforts at moral betterment.

9.6. Yoga's Technical use of "Dharma"

On conventional readings, there is a nonmoral use of "dharma" in the *Yoga Sūtra.* Specifically, the *Yoga Sūtra* states "*ethena bhuthendriyeṣu dharma–lakṣaṇa–avasthā parīṇāmā vyakhyātāh:· // śāntodītāvyapadeśyadharmānupāto dharmi*" (YS III.13–14). The two lines describe the understanding of a person who has reached one-pointed concentration, free from distractions (cf. YS III.11–12). The following is a translation of the lines just quoted:

> In this state, it [the yogi's understanding] passes beyond the three kinds of changes which take place in subtle or gross matter, and in the organs: change of form (dharma), change of time (*lakṣaṇa*), and change of condition (*avasthā*). A compound object has attributes and is subject to change, either past, present, or yet to be manifested. (YS III.13–14)

Whicher, in his explication of this passage, concurs with the view that "dharma" is the form of a thing, as opposed to the substance (*dharmin*) which is *prakṛti*. "*Prakṛti* is the permanent *SUBSTANCE* (*dharmin*) and its series of manifestations are the forms (*dharma*)" (Whicher 1998 p.61). Whicher, like most, is of the opinion that the use of "dharma" here is technical and nonstandard. Is it really?

While the *guṇas* themselves might not be moral properties, as argued earlier, the *tri-guṇa* theory associated with the Sāṅkhya and Yoga schools holds that the combination of the *guṇas*, into natural objects, constitutes morally evaluatable states of affairs (9.3. Moral Significance of the Guṇas pp.265–267). While *lakṣaṇa* designates the relational properties of an object with respect to other objects, and *avasthā* concerns the health of an object, "dharma" refers, in the passage above, to the combination and preponderance of the *guṇas* in an object. Hence, to call this aspect of an object its "dharma" is to draw attention to the *aretaic* character of the object; its *moralness*; a quality of an object that is a function of the combination and preponderances of the three *guṇas*. This use of "dharma" is thus neither neological nor technical.

9.7. Contrast

Comparing the views of Sāṅkhya and Yoga illustrates that no philosophical difference is too small to sharply separate two philosophical perspectives.

The cosmology of the two schools is very much alike: both view *Prakṛti* as an impersonal but yet morally significant principle that functions to bring about the greatest good of individuals. Both schools are of the opinion that selves, or *puruṣas*, are conscious beings that give light to *Prakṛti*. Both schools hold that *Prakṛti* is comprised of three properties, which in combination give rise to morally evaluatable states of affairs. The main difference between the two schools pertains to where moral responsibility lies.

For Sāṅkhya, *Prakṛti* is what is active: it is ultimately responsible for one's state of affairs. *Puruṣas*, thus, by implication, have no moral responsibility, because they are not agents. For Yoga, *Prakṛti* is simply grist to a person's experience: it is ultimately *puruṣas* who are in control and who determine their states of being. Thus, on Yoga's view, each *puruṣa* not only has the ability to alter their future but must also share in responsibility for their present plight.

The two schools also differ on the role of dharma. For Sāṅkhya, dharma is something that leads one to higher worlds, and at the same time increases the predominance of *sattva* in a mind and body. In contrast, the maximization of dharma, on Yoga's account, constitutes a unique, liberated state: *dharmamegha samādhi*.

It also strikes me that the Yoga and Sāṅkhya traditions take a different view on liberation. While Sāṅkhya regards liberation as resulting from discriminative knowledge, the Yoga view is that final liberation results from moral perfection. The aloneness and isolation (*kaivalya*) of final liberation, on the Yoga view, is arguably a direct function of being absorbed in the cloud of morality (*dharmamegha samādhi*). On the Yoga philosophy's account, moral perfection sets the yogi apart from others, like a vast mist or abyss.

Notes

1 See Larson 1987 p.23. While Larson's treatment of the tradition of Sāṅkhya philosophy in the *Encyclopedia of Indian Philosophies* is to be commended for its breadth, there are a few problems with it. First he seems to cast his net too wide in including schools of thought like Patañjali's as constituting a strand of the Sāṅkhya tradition. There is a very important difference between the Yoga philosophy as adumbrated by Patañjali, and the Sāṅkhya of an author like Īśvarakṛṣṇa, as we shall see. Secondly, Larson fails to draw the distinction between soteriological pursuits and moral ones. For example, he states that the "ethic" of Īśvarakṛṣṇa's *Kārikā* is "a rational renunciation of ordinary experience based upon a psychological hedonism that generates an awareness that the entire pleasure-pain continuum must finally be overcome" (Larson 1987 p.26). This may be Īśvarakṛṣṇa's stand on what leads to *mokṣa*, but it is not his view on what leads to dharma, or his view on what dharma consists in.

2 Ian Whicher's account of the history of these two schools, in the first two chapters of his *Integrity of the Yoga Darśana,* is very informative. See Whicher, 1998 pp.1–88.

3 Klaus Klostermaier (1986) has written an article on the topic: "*Dharmamegha samādhi*: Comments on *Yogasūtra* IV.29". The article presents a rather extensive survey of opinions relevant to making sense of the term as it appears in the *Yoga Sūtra*. The article also makes the interesting point that the term "*dharmamega*" occurs in *Mahāyāna* Buddhist literature. However, I find the discussion disappointing because Klostermaier deflates the term of its moral significance. Moreover, he injects into his reading of the term a dose of illusionism and *two-truths* that is frankly absent from the *Yoga Sūtra*: "The insight into the nature of everything as 'dharmic' is irrevocable: the *puruṣa* will never be able to mistake any particular object as real after the unreality (in ultimate terms) of everything has been intuited" (Klostermaier 1986 p.261). The Yoga *darśana* is neither Advaita Vedānta, nor is it Mahāyāna Buddhism.

Chapter 10

Nyāya and Vaiśeṣika

On traditional doxographical reckoning, six "schools" or *darśanas* constitute the philosophical options within Hinduism. They are, Nyāya, Vaiśeṣika, Sāṅkhya, Yoga, Pūrvamīmāṃsa and Vedānta. Moreover, there is a tradition of grouping these six schools into three groups of two. Pūrvamīmāṃsā and Vedānta are grouped together because of their seemingly complementary emphasis on the different portions of the Vedas; the concern of Pūrvamīmāṃsā is mainly with the early part of the Vedas, while "Vedānta" literally translates "End of the Vedas" and concerns itself primarily with the Upaniṣads. Sāṅkhya and Yoga are grouped together because of their common cosmology. Nyāya and Vaiśeṣika are also paired together. And while the pairing of the other four schools distorts their uniqueness, the grouping in the case of Nyāya and Vaiśeṣika may be justified: the two schools appear to have developed a genuine bond of syncretism in later times and the outlooks of the two schools are remarkably similar—despite differences in technical vocabulary.

Karl Potter in his introduction to the two systems speaks about them in unison. He writes:

> Nyāya–Vaiśeṣika offers one of the most vigorous efforts at the construction of a substantialist, realist ontology that the world has ever seen. It provides an extended critique of event–ontologies and idealist metaphysics. It starts from a unique basis for ontology that incorporates several of the most recent Western insights into the question of how to defend realism most successfully. This ontology is "Platonistic" (it admits repeatable properties as Plato's did), realistic (it builds the

world from "timeless" individuals as well as spatio-temporal points or events), but neither exclusively physicalistic or phenomenalistic. (Potter 1978 p.1)

On top of a shared realism with regard to the existence of universals, both systems propound some form of atomism (VS VII.1.8, NS IV.2.4.16). Both schools of thought are pro-Vedic. Lastly, both schools of thought do not ever affirm the Akriyāvā da view: that persons are not agents. The *Nyāya Sūtra*'s prolonged focus on the practical problems of argumentation, and the *Vaiśeṣika Sūtra*'s recognition of action as a metaphysical category distinct from other predicables (VS I.1.4), suggests a Kriyāvāda tendency in both schools.

10.1. Nyāya

The major indication of what kind of things the Nyāya system considers morally important consists in the weight that it puts behind the Vedas. The Vedas, on the Nyāya account, are valid, and hence, its moral concerns ought to be looked upon by all as their moral concerns. According to the *Nyāya Sūtra*, the Vedas are valid owing to the reliability of its authors (NS II.1.68). Aside from this mention, the Vedas get little attention in the *Nyā ya Sūtra*.

On comparison, the topic of morality gets less mention in the *Nyāya Sūtra*, than the *Vaiśeṣika Sūtra*. According to the index provided by Chandra Vidyābhaṣana in his edition and translation of Gautama's (1930) *Nyāya Sūtra*, "dharma" appears only once in the text. Moreover, the term appears *nonexpressively*. Instead of denoting a moral concern of the author, "dharma" is used to designate the idea of moral prescriptiveness. The Sanskrit verse runs: "*dharmavikalpanirdeśe arthasaḍbhāvapratiṣedha upacā racchalam*" (NS I.2.14). The sentence breaks down into the following ideas[1].

- *dharma* = moral
- *vikalpa* = mental construction
- *nirdeśa* = definition
- *artha* = importance, meaning
- *saḍbhāva* = which thing
- *pratiṣedha* = denial, negation
- *upacāra* = approach
- *cchalam* = quibble

Translated, the statement means: "The *approach* quibble raises an objection to a proposition, based on the denial of the possibility of the sense of a morally, prescriptively defined concept". The "approach" quibble is a subset of quibbles, which are "opposition[s] offered to a proposition by the assumption of an alternative meaning" (NS I.2.11). What kind of concept is morally-prescriptively defined? A neologism. The "approach quibble" thus is an argumentative objection that does not take aim at the substance of what is asserted—i.e. the *extention* of the "*dharmavikalpa*"—but the manner in which a neologism comes to have currency. By using "dharma" to describe the kind of concept at hand, the author of the *Nyāya Sūtra* makes it clear that the *dharmavikalpa* being employed has an emotional importance to the person employing it; that person has the *anger inclination* regarding its employment.

10.2. Vaiśeṣika

There are some intriguing points of concordance between the Vaiśeṣika system, on the one hand, and Jainism, on the other. One similarity is the physicalistic outlook that both systems take—while both the Nyāya and Vaiśeṣika systems propound a form of atomism, the view is most pronounced in the latter. Moreover, unlike the Nyāya system, and like Jainism, the Vaiśeṣika system places the concept of *DHARMA* at the centre of its concerns.[2]

The opening line of the *Vaiśeṣika Sūtra* (VS I.1.1) states:

> Now, therefore, we shall explain Dharma.

The second line (VS I.1.2) states:

> Dharma (is) that from which (results) the accomplishment of Exaltation (*abhyudaya*) and of the Supreme Good (*niḥśreyasa*).

"*Niḥśreyasa*" is commonly taken to denote *mokṣa*. It is of note that the latter day commentator, Śaṅkara Misra, defines "*abhyudaya*" as "knowledge of the essences" (Śaṅkara Misra 1923 p.5). However, the term has a wider axiological meaning. As John Grimes notes, the term literally means: "prosperity; festival; rise of any heavenly body; the purpose of life as related to material prosperity and individual and social welfare. It is enjoined by the ritual section of the Vedas (*karma–kāṇḍa*) and is the empirical objective of everyone" (Grimes 1996 p.8). Given the antiquity of the text, I am inclined to presume that the author of the *sūtra* meant "*artha*" (as in one of the four *puruṣārthas*) by "*abhyudaya*". Thus, according to the second line, dharma results not only in *mokṣa* (*niḥśreyasa*) but also in *artha* (*abhyudaya*).

The third *sūtra* (VS I.1.3) is very ambiguous ("*tadvacanādāmnāyasya prāmāṇyam*"). The commentator Śaṅkara Misra notes that it can be read in two ways:

> The authoritativeness (*prāmāṇyam*) of the Vedas (*Āmnāyasya*) derives from it being God's Word (*tadvacanāt*)

or, it can be read as stating

> The authoritativeness (*prāmāṇyam*) of the Vedas (*Āmnāyasya*) derives from it being an exposition (*vacanāt*) of dharma (*tad*)"

At issue is what "*tadvacanāt*" means. For two reasons, the latter interpretation strikes me as a more coherent rendition of the *sūtra*. First, "*tad*" is a pronoun meaning THAT, and *sūtra* authors frequently employ pronouns to refer to *explicitly* identified topics that are proximate to the use of the pronoun. In this case, God has not been explicitly named, though dharma has. Secondly, the author of the *sūtra* has already told us that he intends to discuss dharma. It would be odd for him to change the topic and move on to God so quickly. These considerations speak towards the second interpretation of the *sūtra*.

Having stated my preference for the latter interpretation, it is important to note that the passage was likely meant to be ambiguous. God plays an important part in the Vaiśeṣika system (according to Śaṅkara Misra) in being the author of the Vedas and in being a "great and good person" (Śaṅkara Misra 1923 p.7). The former interpretation brings to prominence God's justifying role in relationship to the contents of the Vedas, which is dharma. Here, Śaṅkara Misra echoes the Nyāya sentiment, that the contents of the Vedas are justified because of the reliability of its authors. The *Vaiśeṣika Sūtra* goes beyond the *Nyāya Sūtra*, on Śaṅkara Misra's reading, by specifying God as its author.[3]

The fourth *sūtra* is quite dense. It states:

> The Supreme Good (*niḥśreya*) results from the knowledge, produced by a particular dharma, of the Predicables, [which are] Substance, Attribute, Action, Genus, Species, and Combination by means of their resemblances and differences. (VS I.1.4)

In this passage we get, in a nutshell, a summary of the Vaiśeṣika system. The Vaiśeṣika philosophy is a system of atomic realism. According to the Vaiśeṣika system, the list defined here as "the predicables" are an exhaustive list of ontological categories. Notably, genus and species, which are logical categories, are distinguished from attributes and their substrata. Also of importance, action is recognized as a distinct category, to be distinguished from material things, their attributes, and the logical categories. "Combinations by means of their resemblances and differences", I suspect, is a cryptic way of referring to Vaiśeṣika's atomism.

"Knowledge of the predicables" which results in the Supreme good (i.e. *mokṣa*)—as defined by the Vaiśeṣika system—constitutes the Vaiśeṣika system. Hence, the passage states that knowledge of the Vaiśeṣika system results in liberation. The passage also states that the Supreme Good, or liberation, results from a particular virtue, or dharma.

The second *sūtra* states that liberation issues from dharma. The implication of the first few *sūtras* seems to be that the Vaiśeṣika system itself constitutes a particular virtue or moral doctrine: this is consonant with it being an exposition of dharma (VS I.1.1).

The question that remains is how the Vaiśeṣika system could constitute a *particular dharma*, and not simply dharma? Śaṅkara Misra suggests that dharma understood as a particular virtue is a kind of sagely forbearance or withdrawal from the world (Śaṅkara Misra 1923 p.12). In a similar vein, another commentator, Chandrakānta, states:

> Dharma presents two aspects, that is under the characteristic of *Pravṛitti* or worldly activity, and the characteristic of *Nivṛitti* or withdrawal from worldly activity. Of these, Dharma characterised by *Nivṛitti*, brings forth *tattva–jñāna* or knowledge of truths, by means of removal of sins and other blemishes. (Chandrakānta 1923 p.15).

Thus, the view of the commentators appears to be that the Vaiśeṣika system, which yields a "knowledge of truths" (*tattva–jñāna*) (Chandrakānta 1923 p.15) "knowledge of the predicables" (VS I.1.4) or "knowledge of the essences" (Śaṅkara Misra's reading of "*abhyudaya*", 1923 p.5) is a moral virtue of the person who is initiated into the system—i.e. a "particular dharma" of that person.

While "dharma" is always understood as a *perfect formal* moral term in the Indian philosophical tradition, it has different *extentions* that vary according to moral theory. In the Vaiśeṣika system, "dharma" is used to name: (a) that which results in *abhyudaya* and *niḥśreyasa*, (b) the teachings of the Vedas, and (c) the Vaiśeṣika system itself. According to this conception of "dharma", the Vaiśeṣika system itself embodies the teachings of the Vedas, which results in *abhyudaya* and *niḥśreyasa*. By providing an explication of the Vaiśeṣika system, the *Vaiśeṣika*

Sūtra fulfils its promise of providing an account of dharma. In short, by expounding the Vaiśeṣika system's various categories, summarized as the "Predicables, [which are] Substance, Attribute, Action, Genus, Species, and Combination by means of their resemblances and differences", (VS I.1.4) the *Vaiśeṣika Sūtra* provides an analysis of what constitutes dharma: knowledge of the various categories of the Vaiśeṣika system. Such knowledge constitutes a moral virtue, and results not only in worldly success, but in liberation on the Vaiśeṣika account.

Notes

1 This breakdown of the statement restates Chandra Vidyābhaṣana's analysis of the statement (Gautama 1930) except in the rendering of "*dharmavikalpa*", which Vidyābhaṣana depicts as "metaphor".

2 Jacobi (1987 Part I xxxvii) notes that some historical Jain authors have claimed that the Vaiśeṣika are really schismatical teachers of theirs, with whom originated the sixth schism of the Jains in about 18 C.E.

3 I am inclined to believe that this interpretation of Śaṅkara Misra's is really a foreign Nyāya gloss on the *Vaiśeṣika Sūtra*.

Chapter 11

Pūrvamīmāṃsā

11.1. Vedic Foundationalism

The Pūrvamīmāṃsā system finds its scholastic roots in a work by Jaimini called the "*Mīmāṃsā Sūtra*". Whereas the *Brahma Sūtra* that is the foundation of the Vedānta group of systems is concerned with summarizing the purport of the latter part of the Vedas (the *Upaniṣads*), the *Mīmāṃsā Sūtra* is concerned with summarizing the former part of the Vedas, known as the "*karma–kāṇḍa*", or *action–oriented section* of the Vedas, which largely concerns itself with sacrifices to deities. Like other *darśanas* we have examined so far, Pūrvamīmāṃsā concerns itself primarily with dharma. Like the *Vaiśeṣika Sūtra*, the *Mīmāṃsā Sūtra* begins:

> Next, therefore, comes the enquiry into dharma. (MS I.i.1)
>
> Dharma is that which is indicated by means of the Veda as conducive to the highest good. (MS I.i.2)[1]

Like the Vaiśeṣika system, the Pūrvamīmāṃsā system attempts to give a reasoned account of how and why the Vedas are a source of dharma. Unlike the Vaiśeṣika system, or most other Indian philosophical schools for that matter, the Pūrvamīmāṃsā system does not concern itself very much with matters of soteriology: *mokṣa*, on its account, is not presented as having any special relationship with dharma.

The Pūrvamīmāṃsā system is further distinguished from

other Hindu philosophical schools—except for the Vedānta systems—in its Vedic Foundationalism. Foundationalism is the view that certain knowledge claims are independently valid (which means that no further justificative reasons are either possible or necessary to justify these claims), and moreover, that these independently valid knowledge claims are able to serve as justifications for beliefs that are based upon them. Such independently valid knowledge claims are thought to be justificative *foundations* of a system of beliefs. While all Hindu philosophical schools recognize the validity of the Vedas, only the Pūrvamīmāṃsā and Vedānta systems explicitly regard the Vedas as *justificatively foundational*, and being in no need of further justification: "... instruction [in the Vedas] is the means of knowing it (dharma)—infallible regarding all that is imperceptible; it is a valid means of knowledge, as it is independent ..."(MS I.i.5).

If the Vedas are the ultimate authority on Dharma, the question arises whether there can be any other nominal sources of dharma. The disputant to the Pūrvamīmāṃsā view argues, "in as much as dharma is based upon the Veda, what is not Veda should be disregarded" (MS I.iii.1). According to the Pūrvamīmāṃsā system, while the Vedas or *śruti*, which is the revealed or *heard* word, is the ultimate authority on dharma, the *remembered* word, or *smṛti*—being the sacred tradition based on revelation—is also to be regarded as authoritative on matters of dharma *because* it is based on the Vedas (MS I.iii.2). The Vedas, hence, function as the foundational justification for *smṛti*. In cases where there is a conflict between *smṛti* and *śruti*, the former is to be disregarded in favour of the latter. When there is no such conflict, the *Mīmāṃsā Sūtra* tells us, we are entitled to presume that the Vedas stand behind the *smṛti* text in question (MS I.iii.3).

11.2. Dharma and *Artha*

The *sūtra* dealing with the definition of dharma, quoted above, is liable to several interpretations and translations.

The translation of MS I.i.2 listed above is Ganganatha Jha's translation of the *sūtra*, which is based on the classic commentary of Śabara on the *Mīmāṃsā Sūtra*, called "*Śabara Bhāṣya*", a commentary which forms the foundation for much of the Pūrvamīmāṃsā tradition. Jha's translation of the *sūtra* runs: "Dharma is that which is indicated by means of the Veda as conducive to the highest good". In Sanskrit, MS I.i.2 states: "*codanālakṣaṇārtho dharmah*".[2] The proposition breaks down into the following components:

- *codanā* = injunction; command
- *lakṣaṇa* = definition; characteristic; attribute; sign; mark; indicator
- *artha* = welfare, material prosperity, wealth, worldly success, value, goal
- *dharma* = morality

Conspicuously absent from the statement is any explicit reference to the Vedas, or liberation. Commenting on MS I.i.2, Śabara explains his understanding of these terms thus:

> The term "*codanā*" they use in the sense of the injunctive text: men are found saying "I am doing this act on being enjoined (*codanā*) by the Teacher",—*Lakṣaṇa* is that by which something is indicated (pointed out): for instance, when fire is indicated by smoke, they say that smoke is the *lakṣaṇa* (indicator) of fire.—That which is indicated by the said Injunctive Text is "*artha*", "something conducive to the highest good"; that is, it brings man into contact with his highest good;—this is what we assert. (Śabara on MS I.i.2 p.4)

There are other translations. John Grimes translates the *sūtra* as "The mark of reality is Vedic commands" (Grimes 1996 p.107). Mohan Lal Sandal translates the *sūtra* as "Duty is an object distinguished by a command" (see Jaimini 1923 p.1). I am inclined to stress the notion of *command* and *artha* in a rendering of the *sūtra*: "Dharma is a command that has the distinction of bringing about *artha*". For sure, the relevant commands are those of the Vedas, which in large concern sacrificial acts.

Śabara's reference to a *highest good* in his gloss is curious, for it makes it seem as though dharma is something that leads to *artha*, which in turn leads to another highest good external to the definition of dharma. This reference to the *highest good* appears to be Śabara's enthusiastic way of talking about *artha* itself, for later on in his commentary, he stops talking about *artha* as something that brings about the highest good, and describes it simply as our good:

> As a matter of fact, the Veda indicates both what is moral and what is immoral.—"What is moral?"—That which is conducive to good, such as the *Jyotiṣtoma* and other acts—"What is immoral?"—That which leads to evil (sin), such as the *Syena*, the *Varja*, the *Iṣu* and other (malevolent) acts.—Thus the *Sūtra* has used the term "*artha*", "what is conducive to good", in order to preclude the possibility of the Immoral act being included under the term "dharma". (Śabara on MS I.i.2 p.6)

The acts named in this passage and called "immoral" are those that are intended to produce harm against other human beings; they involve the "inflicting of injury, and the inflicting of injury has been forbidden" (Śabara on MS I.i.2 p.7). To inflict injury is to fail to maximize *artha*. Thus, on Śabara's reading of the *Mīmāṃsā Sūtra*, dharma is identical with that which promotes the well-being of people in general: *artha*. This is in keeping with MS I.i.2, which defines dharma as that which brings about *artha*.

Having noted that acts that are harmful to others are mentioned in the Vedas, Śabara recognizes that there is a problem: why are such sacrifices laid out at all in the Vedas? Is not the Vedas the ultimate source of dharma, and as such, should it not simply be concerned with prescribing morally praiseworthy acts? In response, he argues that such acts are not prescribed by the Vedas, but simply described (Śabara on MS I.i.2 p.7).

There is another problem for Śabara, which he does not address in any detail: how is violence done to animals in the course of Vedic sacrifices to be accounted for? Doesn't this run contrary to *artha*, conceived broadly as *WELFARE*? The only author in the tradition who comes close to addressing this question is Kumārila.

Kumārila's view is that of the fundamentalist: "He who would attribute sinfulness even to the enjoined ... on the ground of its being a 'Slaughter', like any ordinary slaughter (outside a sacrifice), would be courting a contradiction of the Scriptures" (SV II.273–274). In keeping with the Pūrvamīmāṃsā line, Kumārila asserts that "for the comprehension of Dharma and Adharma, there is no other means save the fact of their being enjoined and prohibited (respectively) [by the Vedas]" (SV II.242–43). According to Kumārila, the Vedas do not assert "any sinfulness ... in connection with such slaughter ... nor is such (sinful character) to be assumed (in the case of such slaughter) through other prohibitions ..." (SV II.261–62). He concludes from these observations that "sinfulness belongs to only that slaughter which does not form part of a sacrifice" (SV II.265). In the case of slaughter not enjoined by scripture, "the disgust that we feel is only based upon the prohibitive scriptural texts" (SV II.234). In other words, our critical stance towards violence, outside of the sacrificial circumstance, is only justified by (and perhaps even derived from) the Vedas itself, according to Kumārila.

11.3. Who is Eligible to Practise Dharma?

The anthropocentricism of the Pūrvamīmāṃsā view does not stop at assenting to the harming of animals in ordained sacrifices.

The *pūrvapakṣa*, or dissenting view, holds that "in as much as an act is performed for the purpose of obtaining results, all beings should be entitled to perform the acts prescribed in the scriptures" (MS IV.i.4). The Pūrvamīmāṃsā system holds that "in reality, the injunctions of an act should be taken to apply to only such an agent as may be able to carry out the entire details of the act; because such is the sense of the Vedic texts" (MS IV.i.5).

The Pūrvamīmāṃsā view, arguably, is that *ought implies can*. Elaborating on this response, Śabara writes:

> It is not correct to hold that animals are also entitled to perform sacrifices.—"Who then is entitled?"—Only one who is able to carry out the whole act. As a matter of fact, animals and others are not able to carry out the details of the sacrifice in their entirety;—hence for these beings the sacrifice cannot be a means of securing happiness; how can an act that one cannot do be a means of happiness to him?—The *deities* also are not entitled to perform sacrifices, because from themselves there are no other deities (to whom they could offer the sacrifice) and there can be no offering to one's own self .... Then again animals are never found to desire results expected to appear in the remote future; they desire only what is immediately present before them [hence, they are not fit to perform sacrifices].—"But we have already pointed out that animals are actually found to desire results in the future when, for instance, dogs fast on the fourteenth, and kites on the eighth, day of the month".—The answer to this is that these animals do not fast with a view to any result to accrue to them in their next life.—"How do you know that?"—We deduce it from the fact that they have not studied the Veda ... nor the *Smṛti* scriptures; nor can they learn it from teachers. Hence it follows that they are not cognizant of what dharma, DUTY, is. Being ignorant of dharma, how could they perform any dharma? (Śabara on MS IV.i.5 pp.973–974).

Śabara's argument at this point seems to lose its focus. He moves from the point that animals are incapable of performing dharma to the point that animals are never seen to perform dharma, and finally to the point that animals are not informed on what dharma is. One thing is clear from Śabara's gloss: that dharma is something that is peculiarly human, and other beings, such as the gods, or animals, are not eligible to lead the moral life.

The Pūrvamīmāṃsā focus on human beings is surprisingly thoroughgoing in some respects. For, according to MS IV.i.8, women are as entitled to perform sacrifices as men.

Commenting on this *sūtra*, Śabara writes: "It is not true that *man* alone is entitled to perform sacrifices; in fact, Bādarāyaṇa [quoted in the *Mīmāṃsā Sūtra* as an authority on the tradition] has held that 'the whole genus' is entitled .... From all this it follows that women also should be regarded as entitled to perform sacrifices because the genus [of eligibility to perform sacrifices] is equally present in all" (Śabara on MS IV.i.8 pp.977–978). Yet, within the genus of human beings, there are exceptions to who can perform sacrifices, according to the *Mīmāṃsā Sūtra* and Śabara. Out of the four Vedic castes—Brahmans (priests), *Kṣatriyas* (marshal class), *Vaiśyas* (merchants) and *Sūdras* (labourers)—the *Sūdra* caste is not eligible to perform sacrifices (MS, IV.i.26). As well, according to Śabara, Sages, who are the head of Brahmanic lineages (*gotras*), are not eligible to perform sacrifices, for they themselves lack a lineage (Śabara on MS IV.i.5 p.973), a prerequisite for sacrificial performances.

11.4. Motive and Consequences

MS IV.i.2 makes a distinction between two kinds of injunctions: *puruṣārtha* injunctions and *kratvartha* injunctions. Here the term "*puruṣārtha*" does not designate the four-fold axiological scheme of dharma, *artha*, *kāma* and *mokṣa*, but stands for, literally, *SERVING–THE–PURPOSE–OF–A–PERSON*. In contrast to *puruṣārtha acts*, there are actions enjoined by scripture that do not directly fulfil the needs of a person, but subserve the purpose of an act. These are *kratvartha injunctions*.

How are we to distinguish between the two kinds of acts? Śabara's gloss has it that the *sūtra* in question defines a *puruṣārtha* act as "that upon which follows the happiness of a man". All other enjoined acts are *kratvartha* injunctions. On Śabara's account, a *puruṣārtha* act has the distinct nature of being *instrumental* to the needs and happiness of a person (Śabara on MS IV.i.2 pp.709–710).

Another author in the Pūrvamīmāṃsā tradition takes

exception to this interpretation of the *Mīmāṃsā Sūtra.* Sālikanātha in his *Ṛjuvimalā* (which is a commentary on Prabhākara's[3] commentary on Śabara's commentary on the *Mīmāṃsā Sūtra*) argues that *puruṣārtha* acts should not be defined as those which bring about happiness, since this would not apply to compulsory duties, which people are often not naturally inclined to perform. Rather, it should be conceived of as an act that subserves the Principal Sacrifice *and also* the purposes of the agent, by itself, and not through being employed in another act (Sālikanāthamiśra's *Ṛjuvimalā* on MS IV.i.2).[4]

The distinction between *puruṣārtha* and *kratvartha* acts concerns the degree to which an act is instrumental in the accomplishment of an injunction. A *puruṣārtha* act is one that directly accomplishes a prescribed act. Whereas, *kratvartha* acts are those that are removed from the accomplishment of a principal injunction by some degree. As well, the distinction between the two kinds of actions pertains to the motive that prompts one to perform them. In the case of the *puruṣārtha* act, the practical motive consists, at least in part, in a desire to procure some beneficial result associated with a sacrifice. In the case of the *kratvartha* act, the motive is to accomplish an act that is ancillary to another enjoined act.

The distinction between *puruṣārtha* and *kratvartha* acts resembles the distinction between hypothetical and *categorical* oughts that we find in the West, particularly if we interpret *kratvartha* as *FOR–THE–PURPOSE–OF–THE–ACT*—which has a strong Deontological ring to it. However, it would be a mistake to equate *puruṣārtha* acts with hypothetical imperatives, and *kratvartha* acts with *categorical* imperatives, for the distinction pertains to acts that are prescribed by scripture. Moreover, *puruṣārtha* acts include compulsory acts, which are acts that relevant persons, by virtue of their membership in a particular category, are obliged to perform. Thus, *puruṣārtha* acts are *categorical* imperatives too.

How then are we to conceive of the Pūrvamīmāṃsā ethic? Is it Deontological, or Consequentialist? One might make the argument that since dharma by definition yields *artha*, one can always understand morality, on the Pūrvamīmāṃsā view, as being defined by its beneficial consequences. This would make the Pūrvamīmāṃsā ethic a version of Consequentialism: right? My sense is that one cannot view it as a form of Consequentialism. Usually, the distinction between Deontology and Consequentialism is cashed out in terms of *how* one determines whether something is right or wrong. The Pūrvamīmāṃsā view is not that one should assess the consequences of an action in order to determine whether it is right or wrong. Hence, it cannot be a version of Consequentialism. The Pūrvamīmāṃsā view is that one must look to scripture to tell us what is right or wrong. It so happens, in the Pūrvamīmāṃsā view, that what scripture prescribes coincides with our interests: but this cannot be known in advance of studying the Vedas. Reason by itself is unable to determine moral truths on the Pūrvamīmāṃsā view.

Kumārila makes these points himself, in a slightly facetious manner:

> For the comprehension of Dharma and Adharma, there is no other means save the fact of their being enjoined and prohibited (respectively). Hence the introduction of an inferential argument in this connection is not proper. For those who declare Dharma to be due to helping others to happiness, and Adharma to be due to causing pain to others ... though with qualms of conscience, if he has intercourse with his preceptor's wife, he would be incurring a great Dharma, because thereby he would be conferring a great benefit of happiness to the woman .... And further, he who would ascertain (the character of) Adharma independently of Scriptural prohibitions, would land himself on "Mutual Dependency"—in as much as he would be attributing sinfulness to pain, and pain again to sinfulness. (SV II.242–47)

Kumārila does not take aim at all versions of Consequentialism, but he does take aim at a kind of Utilitarianism, which appears to him (though perhaps not to us) to lead to absurd consequences. More importantly, Kumārila suggests that Utilitarianism lands itself in trouble by defining moral error in terms of pain; Kumārila's argument here anticipates G.E. Moore's criticisms of Naturalisms (Moore 1903 ch.1).

Is the Pūrvamīmāṃsā view, by default, a version of Deontology? A Consequentialist who views Deontological ethics as moral theories concerned with rule following[5] would likely say so. Even Deontologists who understand Deontological ethics as primarily concerned about our obligations to others could understand the Pūrvamīmāṃsā view as a form of Deontology, given that the sacrifices that form the practical anthropology of the Pūrvamīmāṃsā ethics are all geared towards fulfilling the requirements of deities. Our duty to deities as specified by the Vedas is dharma; the benefits that dutiful conduct yields are *artha*.

11.5. Eternality, Meaning and the Vedas

How can the Vedas have their own validity, independently of any other means of knowledge? According to the Pūrvamīmāṃsā way of thinking, the sovereign validity of the Vedas could come into question if it had an author, for, then, the Vedas would not be an eternally valid scripture: "... if the Veda be eternal, its denotation cannot but be eternal; and if it be noneternal (caused), then it can have no validity ..." (SV XXVII–XXXII). If the Vedas were eternally valid, then the question of authorial validity is dispensed with, and the Vedas can be conceived as being its own, Platonically existing, scripture. How is it possible for a text to have no author? It is possible only if the meaning of the words contained there-in are eternal, and independent of people's activities. This is the tact taken by Pūrvamīmāṃsā authors in general, and the *Mīmāṃsā Sūtra* in particular: "... the relation of the word with its denotation is inborn ..."(MS I.i.5).

In response to this seemingly Platonistic view of the

nature of meaning, the *Sūtra* notes a *pūrvapakṣa* view, characteristic of the Nyāya school of thought (NS II.ii.13):

> Word is a product (noneternal) because it is seen to follow (after effort) ... because it does not persist ... because there is simultaneity (of the perception of the word) in diverse places ... because there are original forms and modifications ... [and because] there is an augmentation for the word (sound) due to the multiplicity of its producers (speakers). (MS I.i.6–11)

The *Mīmāṃsā Sūtra*'s responses to the objections are cryptic as usual. Śabara's comments are helpful here:

> ... the word is *manifested* (not *produced*) by human effort; that is to say, if, before being pronounced, the word was not manifest, it becomes manifested by the effort (or pronouncing). Thus it is found that the fact of words being "seen after effort" is equally compatible with both views .... The Word must be eternal;—why?—because its utterance is for the purpose of another .... If the word ceased to exist as soon as uttered then no one could speak of any thing to others .... Whenever the word "*go*" (cow) is uttered, there is a notion of all cows simultaneously. From this it follows that the word denotes the Class. And it is not possible to create the relation of the Word to a Class; because in creating the relation, the creator would have to lay down the relation by pointing to the Class; and without actually using the word "*go*" (which he could not use before he has laid down its relation to its denotation) in what manner could he point to the distinct class denoted by the word "*go*".... (Śabara on MS I.i.12-19 pp.33–38)

As for the view that words are seen (heard?) to be augmented, the *Mīmāṃsā Sūtra* responds: "the 'augmentation' spoken of is the augmentation of the noise (not of the word)" (MS I.i.17).

Kumārila thinks that this Platonistic conception of language provides the model for understanding how the Vedas are independently valid:

> Vedic assertions are not false—because in regard to their own

> signification, they are independent of the speaker—like the notions of the word and its denotation. Or, Ideas originating in the Vedas are true—because they arise from sentences that are eternal—like the signification of a sentence. (SV V.xi.1)

11.6. Noncognitivism

The notion of command in the definition of dharma signals a commitment on the part of Pūrvamīmāṃsā to Prescriptivism. Prescriptivism is a form of Noncognitivism. Noncognitivism is the view that moral or evaluative statements are not declarative (i.e. that they do not state facts). Prescriptivism holds that the mark of a moral statement is that it is an imperative, something that commands.

There are other marks in the *Mīmāṃsā Sūtra* that betray a strong Noncognitivist leaning. Modern Noncognitivists are often inclined to point out the variance between matters of science, and matters of morality. Similarly, we find the *Mīmāṃsā Sūtra* stating:

> The cognition by a person which appears when there is contact with the sense-organs is "sense-perception", and it is not a means of knowing dharma, as it apprehends only things existing at the present time. (MS I.i.4)

Commenting on this passage, Śabara explains:

> ... Dharma, however, is something that is yet to come, and it does not exist at the time that it is to be known; while sense perception is the apprehending of an object that is actually present and not non–existent at the time (of cognition);—hence sense-perception cannot be the means (of knowing) dharma". (Śabara on MS I.i.4 p.8)

While Noncognitivism is typically a view propounded with reference to moral or evaluative statements, the *Mīmāṃsā Sūtra* may actually hold a bolder view: that all meaning is essentially *noncognitive*. The evidence for this view consists in

MS I.i.25: "[in the sentence] there is only a predication (or mention) of words with definite denotations along with a word denoting an action; as the meaning (of the sentence) is based upon that" (translation can be found in Śabara 1933 p.44). The translator, Ganganatha Jha, has had to fill in what the statement refers to. Jha takes it that the "rules of interpretation involved in the *Mīmāṃsā Sūtra* are of universal application, useful wherever texts have to be interpreted" (Jha 1942 p.359). On such a wide view of the relevance of the *Mīmāṃsā Sūtra*, it is not simply Vedic Injunctions that are act-oriented, but all language. If this is so, the Pūrvamīmāṃsā view is that the essential role of a statement is not declarative (saying that things are so) but imperative (saying what ought to be done).

11.7. The Greatest Good

The *Mīmāṃsā Sūtra* makes no reference to *mokṣa*. The matter of its importance for the Pūrvamīmāṃsā system is underdetermined by the foundational text.

The definition of dharma provided by the *Mīmāṃsā Sūtra* focuses not on liberation, but welfare and benefit: *artha.* Dharma is a value, which, when maximized, results in *artha.* Hence, *artha* is arguably the *niḥśreyasa* of early Pūrvamīmāṃsā thought.

It is only in the later stages of this school that *mokṣa* is explicitly recognized. The first major exponent of the tradition to recognize *mokṣa* was Kumārila. According to Kumārila:

> For those who have understood the real nature of the Soul, all their past karma having become exhausted through experience, and there being no further Karmic residue left to wipe off, there comes no further body; as it is only for the experiencing of the reactions of past karma that the Soul is burdened with the Body; therefore the seeker for Liberation should not do any such act as has been forbidden or even what has been enjoined for certain purposes; (as both these would bring about Karmic reaction which would have to be expiated by experience); but

> *he should continue to perform the compulsory acts,* as the omission of these would involve sin, which would have to be expiated by painful experience through a physical body. (SV V.xvi.108–110, translation from Jha 1942 p.37)

11.8. Is Pūrvamīmāṃsā a Unique Ethic?

On the standard view, the Pūrvamīmāṃsā system is not by any means its own philosophical system, but rather, it is *the* ethics of Hindu philosophical thinking. Karl Potter makes this point in his comments on the moral thought of the Nyāya and Vaiśeṣika systems:

> The Nyāya–Vaiśeṣika system provides no startling new ideas [about ethics] over and beyond what is generally acceptable to Hindus .... It does not discuss questions of "ethical theory" as we understand that term in contemporary philosophy, since that was the business of others (Mīmāṃsākas) in the peculiar division of labour adopted by the ancient Indian thinkers. (Potter 1978 p.2)

The division of labour that Potter refers to is a phenomenon in the history of Hindu philosophical schools, whereby, if a thinker of a particular school wished to make a contribution to logic, even if they were a proponent of a school contrary to the Nyāya fold, they would study the Nyāya system, and write a tract on it (for example, the Vedāntin Madhva is reputed to have done this). Thus, in this respect, the Nyāya system has been regarded by Hindu thinkers as the school of Hindu thought specialised in logic. Likewise, a case can be made that the Pūrvamīmāṃsā system is to ethics what Nyāya is to logic: a specialised Hindu philosophical school concerned with ethics; a speciality that relieves thinkers in other Hindu schools from having to address issues of morality themselves, for the work has been done by the Mīmāṃsāka.

The view that the Pūrvamīmāṃsā system is simply the

ethics of all Hindu philosophical schools is untenable. As noted earlier, there is a distinction to be made between justificative ethics and a practical anthropology. The latter concerns itself with adumbrating substantive obligations or moral values that we ought to maximize. The former concerns a justification of moral theory, which specifies the *extentions* of morality. Given the distinction, it is possible for two thinkers to share the same practical anthropology but differ on justificative approaches on how to defend their shared substantive views. These differences constitute different justificative ethics, or simply, different ethics.

The Nyāya and Pūrvamīmāṃsā systems cannot thus be regarded as complementary or modular philosophies, because from the perspective of ethics, they constitute two different justificative approaches. One difference between the two schools, pertaining to justificative ethics, concerns how the Vedas—which both consider to be sources of dharma—are valid. The Nyāya view is that the Vedas are valid owing to the reliability of its authors (NS II:i.68). The Pūrvamīmāṃsā view is that the Vedas are independently valid; the question of authorship does not come into the picture. As well, there is a dispute between the two schools regarding the eternality of words. The issue bears upon ethics because, on the Pūrvamīmāṃsā view, the eternality of words and their meanings are a transcendental condition of the Vedas' independent validity: the Vedas need no author because the meanings of statements in them have an eternal significance. The Nyāya view is presented in the *Mīmāṃsā Sūtra* as the *pūrvapakṣa* (alternative) to the Pūrvamīmāṃsā view; that words are not eternal (MS I.i.6–11 and NS II.ii.13).

Even if the Nyāya and Pūrvamīmāṃsā systems constitute different philosophical approaches to ethics, is it the case that the Pūrvamīmāṃsā system functions as a moral module for other Hindu philosophical systems? Arguably, the Pūrvamīmāṃsā system serves this function for Vedānta systems. Ganganatha Jha makes a similar point strongly—that it is incorrect to regard these two schools as distinct philosophical systems:

> [A]s regards the Mīmāṃsā and the Vedānta, there has never been any justification for regarding them as two distinct Systems of Philosophy. They have always been, and continue to be, known as "Pūrva" (PRELIMINARY) and "Uttara" (FINAL) "Mīmāṃsā". Pūrva Mīmāṃsā—i.e. Mīmāṃsā proper—has never claimed to be a Darśana; a system of Philosophy. In fact, so far as the *Sūtra* is concerned, it does not take cognizance of any philosophical topic except that of *Pramāna*; and these also are brought in only negatively, to show that Dharma is not within the purview of the ordinary *Pramānas*, perception and the rest ... We are alive to the fact that later on differences cropped up between the two "Mīmāṃsās"; but they always appertained to minor details; on the main issues, there has not arisen any serious controversy. (Jha 1942 p.4–5)

I think that Jha's point is overstated: seemingly small differences are grounds for distinguishing philosophical views (he also incorrectly leaves out dharma as counting as a philosophical topic). As we shall see, Vedānta authors, while sharing the Vedic Foundationalism of Pūrvamīmāṃsā authors, have unique contributions of their own to make to the subject of ethics.

Notes

1 Usually, translations quoted are those found in the edition and translation cited in the bibliography. In this case, the translations of the *Mīmāṃsā Sūtra* are found in Jha's translation of Śabara's commentary on the *Mīmāṃsā Sūtra*, listed in the bibliography.

2 There appears to be a typographical error in the edition of the *Mīmāṃsā Sūtra* cited in the bibliography (Jaimini 1923: *Mīmāṃsā Sūtra*. Ed. and Trans. Mohan Lal Sandal). It lists MS I.i.2 as stating "*codanālakśano'rtho dharmaḥ*". According to it, MS I.i.2 relies not on the idea of LAKṢAṆA, which means DEFINITION, CHARACTERISTIC, ATTRIBUTE, SIGN, MARK OR INDICATOR, but LAKṢAṆĀ, which means SECONDARY or IMPLIED MEANING (Grimes 1996 p.173). No one, including the editor of the suspect edition, translates the statement as though it relies upon the notion of an implied or secondary meaning. Rather, the opinion even of Śabara is that the text relies upon the term "*lakṣaṇa*". So, I have

quoted Grime's presentation of this *sūtra* in his definition of "*codanā* "(Grimes 1996 p.107). If "*codanālakśano'rtho dharmaḥ*" is the actual text, it makes little sense.

3 While Prabhākara is an important author in the tradition of Pūrvamīmāṃsā, I have left out mention of his views because he seems not to swerve from the thought of Śabara, who is by far the more significant in the history of Pūrvamīmāṃsā. This impression is echoed by Jha, who writes: "Prabhākara's commentary on the *Śabara Bhāṣya*—known as '*Bṛhatī*'—is a commentary in a strict sense of the term; he does not criticize the *Bhāṣya* on any point, he simply puts forward the *Bhāṣyakāra*'s view as understood by himself. In fact, he does not criticize other views either, except in very few places" (Jha 1942 p.17). Prabhākara, unlike Kumārila, appears to be a thorough explicator of Śabara's thought, not so much an original exponent of the Pūrvamīmāṃsā tradition.

4 Quoted in Jha, 1942 p.292. He cites a manuscript; MS. Vol. II, p.369.

5 For instance, see Singer 1993 p.3.

Chapter 12

Vedānta

12.1. Versions

Often, there is the impression surrounding the use of the term "Vedānta" that it designates one particular philosophical view. The term literally means THE–END–OF–THE–VEDAS and as such, it is a term that designates the principal teachings of the *Upaniṣads,* which constitute the end portions of the Vedas. This is the etymological meaning of the term "Vedānta". In reality, the term designates a constellation of distinct philosophical views. Their common intersection is an effort to articulate a coherent philosophical interpretation of the teachings of the *Upaniṣads*.

Any philosophical view that is formally (or narrowly) to count as a version of Vedānta must be primarily articulated as a commentary on Bādarāyaṇa's *Brahma Sūtra,* also known as the *Vedānta Sūtra*, which is taken by its commentators to be an authoritative summary of the philosophy of the *Upaniṣads*. There are many authors in the history of Indian philosophy who have done just this. According to B.N.K. Sharma, there are no less than twenty-one commentators on the *Brahma Sūtra* prior to Madhva (the thirteenth century Dvaita commentator) (Sharma 1986 vol.1 p.15). Madhva is by no means the last commentator on the *Brahma Sūtra* either. Important names in the history of Indian theology are amongst the latter-day commentators: Nimbārka, Vallabha, Śrīkaṇṭha and Baladeva. Yet, in most introductory accounts of the history of Indian philosophy, three and only three authors in the history of Vedānta get mentioned. The authors are,

(Ādi) Śaṅkara,[1] Rāmānuja, and Madhva, the respective exponents of the Advaita, Viśiṣṭādvaita and Dvaita schools of Vedānta. As Sharma notes, the commentaries written prior to Madhva, with the exception of the commentaries by Bhāskara, (Ādi) Śaṅkara and Rāmānuja are lost to history, "either because they were eclipsed by the more brilliant ones in the field or had died a natural death for want of sufficient following" (Sharma 1986 vol.1 p.15).

(Ādi) Śaṅkara, Rāmānuja, and Madhva stand out in the history of Vedānta, and the history of Indian philosophy, for that matter, for a few reasons. First, each of the respective authors adumbrates a distinct philosophical view based on the *Brahma Sūtras*. The principal issue that they disagree upon is the relationship between individuals (some times known as *"ātmas"*, and at other times *"jīvas"*) and things, on the one hand, and Brahman on the other. (Brahman is the highest entity on the Vedānta view, whose attainment on the part of the individual constitutes *mokṣa*.) Each of the three systems is a distinct response to the question, which collectively run the gamut of logically coherent alternatives. The Advaita view is that any apparent difference between individual persons, things and Brahman is a function of cognitive error. The Viśiṣṭādvaita view is that persons and things constitute Brahman's body, and moreover that Brahman is a personal God, in a monotheistic manner (Brahman is omnipotent, omniscient, and morally perfect). The Dvaita view is that individuals and things are distinct from Brahman, which is the highest, monotheistic Deity; all other persons and things are eternally distinguished from Brahman, though they are dependent upon it.

The philosophical view dominant amongst Vedānta authors after Madhva is known as "Bhedābheda": *DIFFERENCE–AND–NONDIFFERENCE*. This is also the view of Bhāskara, one of the few pre–Rāmānuja commentators whose work has survived. According to this view, things apart from Brahman are both identical with and different from Brahman. While this view makes for interesting theology, it makes for unclear philosophy, for it leaves the logical quandaries of the Vedas untouched. I suspect that this is why the writings of Bhedābheda thinkers are overpassed in most accounts of the history of Indian philosophy.

Given the synoptic nature of the present work, the explication of Vedānta philosophies will be restricted to the thought of the three Vedāntins, commonly dealt with in introductory accounts of the history of Indian philosophy.

12.2. Basic Vedānta Doctrine

While the substance and interpretation of the *Brahma Sūtra* is under dispute between the three schools of Vedānta, some aspects of the text are relatively uncontroversial, from a hermeneutic perspective. What follows is an account of points of convergence between the three schools of Vedānta, on Vedānta doctrine.

The *Brahma Sūtra* begins by stating that an inquiry into "Brahman" is to be taken up (*athatho brahmajijñāsā*) (ŚaṅB, ŚrīB and MB I.i.1). All three schools agree that from Brahman proceeds the origin of the universe and things in general (ŚaṅB, ŚrīB and MB I.i.2). The three major schools are also in agreement that the Vedas constitute an independently valid means of knowledge, which is the source of our knowledge of Brahman (ŚaṅB, ŚrīB and MB I.i.3). The three major schools of Vedānta betray an affinity with the Pūrvamīmāṃsā system in rejecting the need for external evidence for the validity of the Vedas. Like Pūrvamīmāṃsā authors, the Vedas have the ability to confer justification on practises and beliefs based upon it for Vedānta authors. This latter view is a function of the view that the Vedas are an independently valid source of knowledge (ŚaṅB, ŚrīB and MB I.i.3). This is the view of Vedic Foundationalism, defined in 11.1. Vedic Foundationalism (pp.287–307). The relatively clearer expression of the thesis of Vedic Foundationalism in the *Mīmāṃsā Sūtra* (MS I.i.5) is attributed to the authority of Bādarāyaṇa, who, on the basis of doctrine, appears to be the same Bādarāyaṇa as the author of the *Brahma Sūtra*.

The common perspective of Pūrvamīmāṃsā and the three

schools of Vedānta on the nature of the Vedas does not stop at Vedic Foundationalism. On all accounts, the view of the *Brahma Sūtra*, like the *Mīmāṃsā Sūtra*, is that the Vedas are eternal and not authored. However, the *Brahma Sūtra* differs from the view expressed in the *Mīmāṃsā Sūtra* in holding that the Vedas are conserved by, and issue forth from, Brahman (ŚaṅB and ŚrīB I.iii.28; MB I.iii. 28–30).

Where basic Vedānta thought significantly diverges from Pūrvamīmāṃsā thought is on the issue of liberation. While this value is not part of the foundations of Pūrvamīmāṃsā thought, it is the central focus of the Vedānta constellation of philosophies. Beyond a doubt, for Vedānta thinkers, *mokṣa*, and not *artha* (as early Pūrvamīmāṃsā holds) is the greatest good. All three Vedānta schools agree that *mokṣa* is a value that is actualised by attaining, in some manner, to the nature of Brahman. How close one can come to be like Brahman is a matter of dispute. The Advaita school holds that *mokṣa* consists in total identity with Brahman, and the complete annihilation of any individual identity (ŚaṅB IV.iv.4). The Viśiṣṭādvaita school holds that *mokṣa* consists in virtually attaining to the identity of Brahman, by realising its intelligence, and being free from evil and defects, without also realising Brahman's creative capacity—a power that is unique to God as a person (ŚrīB IV.iv.14–22). The view of the Dvaita school is that *mokṣa* consists in a likeness of one's nature to Brahman—a likeness that comes about by literally *entering* Brahman and having the use of Brahman's body to sense things—(MB IV.iv.4–5) though there are eternal gradations amongst liberated souls in how much they are like Brahman (MB IV.iii.16, and MT I.42–46,72–74). At any rate, all Vedāntins are in agreement that *mokṣa* consists in some kind of association with Brahman (ŚaṅB, ŚrīB and MB I.i.7).

12.3. Agency and the Problem of Evil

Arguably, one of the most intriguing aspects of Vedānta thought, which spans sectarian differences, is its platform view on the nature of the soul. The three major commentarial schools agree that souls are eternal existents. For (Ādi) Śaṅkara and Rāmānuja, this means that the soul has no origin to speak of (ŚaṅB II.iii.16; ŚrīB II.iii.18). For Rāmānuja, the originless nature of the soul is bound up with its essential role as a mode or constituent of Brahman's body.[2] Madhva's view is slightly different. While he holds that souls are eternal, yet he finds that it makes sense to talk about them as originating from God (MB II.iii.19).

A point of unanimity amongst the three major commentarial schools on the *Brahma Sūtra* is that the individual soul has, amongst other things, the property of being an agent (ŚaṅB II.iii.33,36–39; ŚrīB II.iii.33; MB II.iii.33–36). Hence, the official stance of the Vedānta group of systems is the Kriyāvāda position. However, the Kriyāvāda view is qualified in all three commentarial schools, for, according to the *Brahma Sūtra*, the soul's agency is dependent upon *Brahman* (ŚaṅB and ŚrīB II.iii.41; MB II.iii.42). Rāmānuja explains the view thus:

> The inwardly ruling highest Self [Brahman] promotes action insofar as it regards in the case of any action the volitional effort made by the individual soul, and then aids that effort by granting its favour or permission (*anumati*); action is not possible without permission on the part of the Highest Self. (ŚrīB. II.iii.41)

Similarly, Madhva states:

> As the carpenter is an agent under the master who causes him to work and is also an agent by himself, so in the case of the soul, there is the guidance of the Lord, as well as the soul's own capability of action .... And that capability of action is derived (by the soul) from the perfect Lord only ... the guiding of the Lord is according to the soul's previous works and his efforts or natural aptitude. (MB II.iii.40–42)

The dependence of the individual on Brahman for agency gives rise to the Problem of Evil (the problem of how a morally or axiologically perfect God could be responsible for giving rise to imperfect persons and an imperfect world). In some sense, the problem is most acute in the Vedānta context because the action of the individual is thought to be dependent upon Brahman. However, the Vedānta philosophies have a very unique solution to the Problem of Evil. The solution is a function of the view that individual souls are eternal. Brahman's regulative role consists in dispensing consequences for actions and choices. Since there is always some prior choice and action on the part of the individual according to which Brahman has to dispense consequences, at no point can Brahman be accused of partiality, cruelty, or, for that matter, making persons choose the things that they do (ŚaṅB and ŚrīB II.i.34; MB II.i.35,iii.42). Rāmānuja explains this thus:

> ... the assumption of his [Brahman] having actually created the world would lay him open to the charge of partiality, insofar as the world contains beings of high, middle, and low station—gods, men, animals, immovable beings; and to that of cruelty, insofar as he would be instrumental in making his creatures experience pain of the most dreadful kind. The reply to this is "not so ... on account of the inequality of creation depending on the deeds of the intelligent beings, gods, and so on, to be created ...." In the same way, the reverend Parāsara declares that what causes the difference in nature and status between gods, men, and so on, is the power of the former deeds of the souls about to enter into a new creation .... (ŚrīB. II.i.34)

Similarly, Śaṅkara states:

> No partiality or cruelty can be charged against God .... Had God created this erratic world by Himself, irrespective of other factors, He would be open to these charges of partiality and cruelty. But in His isolation (from these) He has no creatorship, for God makes this unequal creation by taking the help of other factors—"What factors does he take into consideration?" We say that these are merit and demerit. No fault attaches to God, since this unequal creation is brought about in conformity with the virtues and vices of the creatures that are about to be born.

> Rather, God is to be compared to rain. Just as rainfall is a common cause for the growth of paddy, barley, etc., the special reasons for the differences of paddy, barely, etc., being the individual potentiality of the respective seeds, similarly God is the common cause for the birth of gods, men and others, while the individual fruits of works associated with the individual creatures are the uncommon causes for the creation of the differences among the gods, men and others. (ŚaṅB II.i.34)

God, or Brahman, is cleared of responsibility for the moral problems of the world because the rewards and punishment that it awards (rewards and punishments that determine the unequal nature of life) are based on prior choices and deeds of individuals, which are without beginning.

12.4. Animal Sacrifices

A substantive moral matter in which there is only partial agreement among Vedānta authors is the propriety of animal sacrifices. Madhva is reputed, by tradition, to have made alternative arrangements so that real animals are spared in Vedic sacrifices. Specifically, he is reputed to have instituted gram flour replicas of animals as stand-ins for sacrificial animals.[3] The sectarian traditions of which (Ādi) Śaṅkara and Rāmānuja are heads (*ācāryas*) of have seemingly always practised vegetarianism (in the context of Vedic rituals and daily diet): or at least, nonvegetarianism has no part in the historical memories of these *sampradāyas* (orders). Yet, in their commentaries on the *Brahma Sūtra*, both the authors hold that the Vedānta position is that there is no wrong-doing associated with the practise of animal sacrifices. Specifically, they hold that the *Brahma Sūtra* states: "If it be argued that rites (involving killing of animals) are unholy, we say, no, since they are sanctioned by scriptures" (ŚaṅB and ŚrīB III.i.25; translation from ŚaṅB). (Ādi) Śaṅkara cashes out the issue thus:

> Opponent: It was argued that sacrificial actions are impure

> inasmuch as they are connected with animal-killing etc., and therefore their result can be inferred to be evil .... Vedāntin: That argument is being refuted. That is not so, for knowledge of virtue and vice is derived from the scriptures. The scriptures alone are the source of knowledge that such an act is virtuous, and another is not virtuous .... Opponent: By saying, "One should not injure any of the creatures", the scripture itself shows that injury done to any creature is unholy. Vedāntin: True; but that is only a general rule; and here is the exception, "one should immolate an animal for Agni and Soma". Both the general rule and the exception have their well-defined scopes .... Vedic rites are quite pure ... [and we know this to be so] since they are practised by good people and are not condemned by them. (ŚaṅB III.i.25)

It may seem that (Ādi) Śaṅkara's justification of animal sacrifices here is a repeat of the Pūrvamīmāṃsā view. However, both the Pūrvamīmāṃsā view and (Ādi) Śaṅkara's argument are a function of Vedic Foundationalism; a view embraced by both schools. If the Vedas have a sovereign validity, it follows that their pronouncements on matters of morality are also justified. The fact that the Vedic tradition (i.e. "good people") also practises animal sacrifices is an ancillary justification for it, which is ultimately based on the justificative force of the Vedas.

All Vedāntins, by virtue of their adherence to Vedic Foundationalism, are of the opinion that the fact that scripture prescribes something is sufficient justification for it. Yet, Rāmānuja offers a justification for the killing of sacrificial animals over and above it being sanctioned by the Vedas. Rāmānuja quotes the Vedas which assert that "The animal killed at the sacrifice having assumed a divine body goes to the heavenly world". He concludes that "an act which has a healing tendency, although it may cause a transitory pain, men of insight declare to be preservative and beneficial" (ŚrīB III.i.25). Rāmānuja's view here may be taken to imply Moral Rationalism, insofar as he seems to believe that certain reasons justify moral injunctions. However, Rāmānuja appears to be merely echoing the Pūrvamīmāṃsā sentiment, expressed in the Vedas itself; that dharma leads to *artha* (11.2. Dharma and Artha pp.288–291).

Madhva, in contrast to the other two principal Vedāntins, interprets the loci of the *sūtra* differently, so that the issue of animal sacrifices never comes up in his version of the *Brahma Sūtra*.

12.5. Advaita

As noted in his stand on animal sacrifices, (Ādi) Śaṅkara explicitly endorses the Vedic Foundationalism of the Vedānta and Pūrvamīmāṃsā group of systems. Yet, there is a wide gulf that separates (Ādi) Śaṅkara's Advaita thought on moral matters from that of other Vedic Foundationalists. (Ādi) Śaṅkara's thought on moral matters diverges from other Vedic Foundationalists from the point of view of his Error Theory, which is spelled out at the outset of his commentary on the *Brahma Sūtra*.

> It being an established fact that the object and the subject, that are fit to be the contents of the concepts "you" and "we" (respectively), and are by nature as contradictory as light and darkness, cannot logically have any identity, it follows that their attributes can have it still less .... [O]wing to an absence of discrimination between these attributes, as also between substances, which are absolutely disparate, there continues a natural human behaviour based on self-identification in the form of "I am this" or "This is mine" .... (ŚaṅB Preamble to I.i.1)

The confusion of the two categories, or "superimposition" of the category of objects on subjects (and *vice versa*), constitutes "*avidya*" or ignorance. This ignorance is the obstacle to achieving *mokṣa*. At the same time, this ignorance is the foundation of all cognition:

> Since a man without self-identification with the body, mind,

> sense, etc., cannot become a cognizer and as such, the means of knowledge cannot function for him ... therefore it follows that the means of knowledge, such as direct perception as well as the scriptures, must have a man as their locus who is subject to nescience. (ŚaṅB Preamble to I.i.1)

The implications of this theory of error are far reaching. One thing is for sure, the teachings of the Vedas themselves are brought into question, for they are sensible only to a person who is thoroughly mistaken about the way things are. If the Vedas are the ultimate source of teachings on dharma (as Ādi Śaṅkara holds) then dharma itself is founded on an error, or is sensible only to a person who is in error. Likewise, if only the radical separation of subjectivity and objectivity is true and accurate, it follows that *mokṣa* is the only real value, for all other values, such as dharma, *artha* and *kāma*, concern persons who are under the sway of *avidya*; persons who are able to cognize that they have a duty to do such and such a thing; that a certain action will bring them benefit or pleasure. In short, (Ādi) Śaṅkara's Error Theory implies Moral Irrealism: the view that morality rests on a mistake.

(Ādi) Śaṅkara's Moral Irrealism is expressed in his exposition of the *Bhagavad Gītā*. The *Gītā* is a philosophical poem that forms part of the epic, the *Mahābhāratha*. The *Gītā* depicts the dialogue between Kṛṣṇa (who is depicted in the poem as an incarnation of God) and his cousin Arjuna. The former agrees to be the latter's charioteer in a fratricidal war only to find Arjuna despondent prior to the battle. Arjuna is convinced that no good could possibly come out of a bloody battle that pits kin against kin; if riches and kingly fortunes are the only booty, it is better to abdicate the struggle than to kill for such vein results. In response, Kṛṣṇa argues that Arjuna has a duty, as a prince and a warrior, to participate in the impending battle, regardless of the consequences. One of the main themes of the *Gītā*, which runs through the whole text until the end (where it seems to be ironically retracted at *Gītā* 18:66) is that we ought to act and do our duty. Renunciation is a virtue, but real renunciation does not consist in forfeiting action, but the desire for consequences of moral action. In other words, the *Gītā* holds that ascetic renunciation consists in the perfection of a Deontological consciousness, which leads one to practise one's duty without thought of reward.

Instead of accentuating the *Gītā*'s theme of Deontology, (Ādi) Śaṅkara often makes remarks that criticize dharma; a direction in keeping with his Error Theory. (Ādi) Śaṅkara in his commentary on the *Gītā* writes:

> ... [R]ites and duties enjoined by the Vedas are meant only for one who is unenlightened and is possessed of desire. (Ādi Śaṅkara 1991 on *Gītā* 2:11 p.40)

> "Even dharma is injurious or harmful to a seeker of liberation as it causes bondage" (Ādi Śaṅkara 1989 on *Gītā* 4:21 p.143) or "... to one aspiring for Liberation, even righteousness is surely an evil because it brings bondage". (Ādi Śaṅkara 1991 on *Gītā* 4:21 pp.202–203)

> [T]he Lord Himself ... saw that the coexistence of Knowledge [*jñāna*] and rites and duties [*karma*] is not possible in the same person, they being based on the convictions of nonagentship and agentship, unity and diversity (respectively). (Ādi Śaṅkara 1991 on *Gītā* 2:11 p.39)

> In the case of the knower of the Self, since there has occurred a cessation of false knowledge, *karmayoga* [discipline of duties or actions], which is based on erroneous knowledge, will become impossible. (Ādi Śaṅkara's intro to *Gītā* 5 1991 p.235)

While the individual, on (Ādi) Śaṅkara's account, has obligations and is an agent, in reality, the whole conception of such an individual is an erroneous construct to be abandoned by those who wish to be free of error.

Given (Ādi) Śaṅkara's Error Theory and its Moral Irrealism, the question that naturally arises is whether (Ādi)

Śaṅkara has an ethic at all. Eliot Deutsch in his chapter on "Advaita Ethics" notes that "Advaita Vedānta in particular ... turns its back on all theoretical and practical considerations of morality ..." (Deutsch 1969 p.99). This is not quite true. (Ādi) Śaṅkara has a practical anthropology ethic, regarding our substantive obligations: this is laid out by the Vedas and *smṛti* literature. (Ādi) Śaṅkara also has a justificative ethic, by virtue of being a Vedāntin. The justificative ethic is Vedic Foundationalism, the view that the Vedas, which are the source of our knowledge of right and wrong, are independently valid, and constitute a sovereign authority on such matters (12.4. Animal Sacrifices (pp.311–312). He also offers another line for justifying morality, that has a pragmatic air to it. In his long commentary on *Gītā* 18:66,(Ādi) Śaṅkara writes:

> [Question] In this scripture, the *Gītā*, has Knowledge been established as the Supreme means to Liberation, or is it action, or both? ... [Advaitin] Knowledge of the Self ... is exclusively the cause of the highest good; for, through the removal of the idea of differences, it culminates in the result that is Liberation .... [A]ction does not constitute the means to the highest good. Nor do Knowledge and action in combination. Further, Knowledge, which has Liberation as its result, can have no dependence on the assistance of action, because, being the remover of ignorance, it is opposed (to action). Verily, darkness cannot be the despoiler of darkness. Therefore, Knowledge alone is the means to the highest good .... [F]rom this, it becomes proved that the absolute cessation of mundane existence is caused by steadfastness in Knowledge, accompanied by renunciation of all rites and duties .... [Yet] Vedic texts enjoining rites (and duties) etc. are not invalid, because they, through the generation of successively newer tendencies by eliminating the successively preceding tendencies, are meant for creating the tendency to turn towards the in dwelling Self. Although the means be unreal (in itself), still it may be meaningful in relation to the truth of the purpose it serves, as are the eulogistic sentences occurring along with injunctions. (Ādi Śaṅkara on *Gītā* 18:66 pp.740–759)

Finally, (Ādi) Śaṅkara also has a metaethical view: his Error Theory and its Moral Irrealism.

After suggesting that Advaita Vedānta turns its back on moral questions, Elliot Deutsch has the following to say: "The Advaitin does hold that one who has not yet attained self-realisation is very much bound up in the moral consequences of his action .... he is subject to ethical judgement, and he must accept a scale of values by which his own judgement may be informed" (Deutsch 1969 p.100). Again, I must disagree with Deutsch. The only way that the unrealized person can be "bound" by moral judgements, on the Advaitin's account, is by a psychological force of natural habit. It is precisely such judgements that Advaita Vedānta criticizes with its Error Theory.

That Moral Irrealism is something to which (Ādi) Śaṅkara's Advaita Vedānta is wedded may seem counter-intuitive to some. The disbelief is likely sustained by the impression that *mokṣa* is a good—the highest good—on Advaita reckoning, and hence a moral goal. This view is untenable, though. Not all goods or values are moral in nature. Considerable time was devoted, in Part II Chapter 2, to defining the nature of terms and statements that concern themselves with moral goals and values. An outcome of that investigation was the conclusion that a moral goal cannot be defined by being the highest or greatest good (2.3.3. Importance and Overridingness pp.43–47 p.184). While "*mokṣa*" is used often to define a value that is considered, in certain axiologies, to be the highest good, "*mokṣa*" itself is not a moral term (4.1. The Puruṣārtha Explanation of Indian Ethics p.181). In contrast, "dharma" has all the marks of being a moral term, and thus "dharma" is the term, out of the four *puruṣārthas*, which is a perfect translational match for "morality" and "ethics" (2.6.2. Traditional Meaning of "Dharma" pp.95–98). It follows from all this that there is nothing essentially moral about the concept of *MOKṢA*. This is not to say that the goal of *mokṣa* is never moral. For instance, in the context of Jainism, *mokṣa* denotes a goal that is *coextensive* with dharma, for its realisation consists in the perfection of dharma (8.4. Motion and

Mokṣa pp.251–254). Likewise, a case can be made that *mokṣa* is a moral goal for the Vedāntin Rāmānuja, for it is constitutive of the liberated state on his account, as we shall see. For (Ādi) Śaṅkara, however, the state of liberation is not *coextensive* with the moral state. On Advaita Vedānta's axiology, *mokṣa* is not a moral goal, for dharma is something that must be given up prior to liberation.

It would be a mistake to consider Advaita Vedānta's commitment to the view that *mokṣa* is not a moral goal as implying Moral Irrealism. Early Buddhism, in its literal interpretation of the Parable of the Raft, appears to be of the view that dharma is something that must be left off upon liberation (7.4. Early Buddhist Justificative Ethics pp.236–238). Likewise, the Sāṅkhya view appears to be that dharma has no essential role to play in the liberated state:

> Virtue (dharma) and the rest having ceased to function as causes, because of the attainment of perfect wisdom [the *puruṣa*] remains invested with the body, because of the force of past impressions, like the whirl of the (potter's) wheel (which persists for a while by virtue of the momentum imparted by a prior impulse). (SK 67)

Early Buddhist scripture, and the Sāṅkhya tradition, as codified by the *Sāṅkhya Kārikā*, do not explicitly state that dharma is a mistake: their view is that it has a limited scope of applicability. Advaita Vedānta, on the other hand, does use the language of error in connection with the topic of morality, both in stating that the Vedas are only operative as a means of knowledge for a person who is in error (ŚaṅB Preamble to I.i.1) and in (Ādi) Śaṅkara's comments on morality in the *Gītā* (Ādi Śaṅkara 1991 on *Gītā* 2:11, 4:21, 5:0). While some other schools of Indian thought agree with the Advaita view that liberation concerns an a-moral state of affairs, only Advaita Vedānta describes morality as a mistake, a sin, or, founded upon error. By definition, the view that morality rests on an error is Moral Irrealism; this is a logically distinct position from the view that certain value-theoretic goals are exclusively a-moral.

12.6. Viśiṣṭādvaita

In contrast to (Ādi) Śaṅkara, Rāmānuja has a very different attitude about the scope and importance of morality. We have seen that (Ādi) Śaṅkara believes that the *Gītā* is behind him in teaching that we ought to abandon our duties or action. While this is certainly not the content of the bulk of the *Gītā*, which concerns itself with cultivating an attitude of renunciation in conjunction with dutiful behaviour, the *Gītā* itself seems to state, towards the end, that one ought to abandon morality. The verse in question is *Gītā* 18:66, which states, in the voice of Kṛṣṇa, "Completely relinquishing all Dharmas, seek Me alone for refuge, I will release you from all sins. Grieve not" (translation from Rāmānuja 1991 p.598).

Rāmānuja cannot accept this statement, and offers two ways to interpret this verse to avoid the conclusion of Moral Irrealism.

On one interpretation, Rāmānuja argues, *Gītā* 18:66 can be taken to instruct us to abandon our sense of agency or possessiveness with regard to the *fruits* of actions. As Vedānta doctrine teaches, our agency is ultimately dependent on Brahman. Understanding this helps us devote ourselves to our duties in a nonsinful manner; a manner that leads us to abandon our claim to rewards of actions, and thus, to a practise of duties in accordance with the Deontological spirit that is characteristic of virtuous conduct. To support this view, Rāmānuja quotes the *Gītā* 18:11: "He who gives up the fruits of works is called the abandoner" (Rāmānuja 1991 on *Gītā* 18:66 pp.598–599).

Alternatively, Rāmānuja suggests, we can take *Gītā* 18:66 to be talking about the abandonment of expiatory ceremonies, which one performs to undo sins of the past:

> Bhakti yoga [the practise of our duties with a strict Deontological consciousness along with the knowledge that

> our power as agents is ultimately dependent upon God, who is in the ultimate analysis the real agent operative in the world, dispensing the fruits of our choices] is possible only for those people to whom the Lord is exceedingly dear and who are free from all evils. Those evils are so huge in some cases that the expiatory rites, which could wash them off, could not be performed in the limited time of one's life span. Arjuna therefore thought that he was unfit for commencing Bhakti Yoga. To remove this grief of Arjuna the Lord said: "Completely relinquishing all Dharmas, seek Me alone for refuge". Expiatory rites can be taken here as what is meant by Dharma .... (Rāmānuja 1991 on *Gītā* 18:66 p.599)

Under no circumstances, Rāmānuja holds, are we entitled to think that we can give up our duties. Even if it seems like God is telling us to give up morality, we cannot be hearing Him correctly.

Why is morality so important for Rāmānuja, and why are we guaranteed to be incorrect if we are under the impression that God wishes for us to give up our obligations? The answer to both the questions is the same: it has to do with God's nature. On Rāmānuja's account, moral perfection is central to God's divine nature.

Rāmānuja never tires of describing God's excellences. Yet, in his various expositions on God's nature, he invariably mentions something about Brahman's moral perfection. Generally, such mention takes the form of the statement that Brahman or the Ultimate Person (*Puruṣottama*) is opposed to or antagonistic to all evil.[4] Since *mokṣa*, the ultimate goal of Vedāntins, is achieved by approximating one's nature to Brahman, it would not be possible, on Rāmānuja's view, for an aspirant after liberation to give up morality. Moral perfection is part of rendering one's nature like that of God's, for God is morally perfect. It follows from all of this that dharma, on Rāmānuja's view, leads not merely to *artha* (as Pūrvamīmāṃsā authors hold) but to *mokṣa*. So, Rāmānuja urges that the acts enjoined in the Vedas, supplemented by the *smṛti* literature, "are the means for reaching Him and for pleasing Him" (Rāmānuja 1991 on *Gītā* 16:24 p.522). The conductivity of dharma to produce *mokṣa* is thus a distinct line of argument in Rāmānuja's justificative ethic.

Rāmānuja also has a second, practical, line of argument for justifying our adherence to dharma. In keeping with Vedānta tradition, Rāmānuja entertains the notion that the discipline of knowledge, or *jñāna*, constitutes a theoretically distinct means of attaining liberation. However, Rāmānuja argues that this means is perilous and doomed to failure. One's own dharma (*svadharma*) "is that which is suitable for performance by oneself". The practise of one's own duties constitutes *karmayoga* (the discipline of action). In contrast, the discipline of knowledge, or *jñāna-yoga,* "is liable to negligence, because it requires the control of the sense from the very beginning for its performance" (Rāmānuja 1991 on *Gītā* 18:47 p.583). In conclusion, Rāmānuja argues:

> [T]hough one is fit for *jñāna-yoga*, one should perform *karmayoga* only. All enterprises ... are indeed enveloped by imperfections, by pain, as fire by smoke. But there is this difference: *karmayoga* is easy and does not involve negligence, but *jñāna-yoga* is contrary to this (Rāmānuja 1991 on *Gītā* 18:48 p.582).

Before resting the investigation into Rāmānuja's stance on ethics, it is noteworthy that the term "dharma" has what is conventionally taken to be a technical use in the Viśiṣṭādvaita system. The term appears in the compound "*dharmabhūtajñāna*", which is often translated as "attributive consciousness" (Yamunāchārya 1988 p.65, Grimes 1996 p.113).[5] A seventeenth-century exponent of the Viśiṣṭādvaita system, Śrīnivāsadāsa, in his digest of the philosophy, *Yatīndramatadīpikā,* defines the term thus:

> Now, attributive consciousness [*dharmabhūtajñāna*] ... consists in being the subject (*viṣayin*, i.e., the objects are

> manifested by it) while it is a self-luminous, unconscious, substance. It is of the nature of substance–attribute (*dravya–guṇa*) like light while it is all-pervasive. Consciousness [*buddhi*, or intellect] is that which manifests the objects. These are the characteristics of attributive consciousness. (*Yatīndramatadīpikā* VII.1)[6]

The idea that is expressed by "*dharmabhūtajñāna*" is that of an epistemic state, which reveals knowledge that is cognitive in nature. By being cognitive, the state reveals that a certain quality or attribute inheres in a subject as its qualification. As a cognition is simply the application of a predicate to a subject, and a judgement is the very same thing, *dharmabhūtajñāna* is an epistemic state of forming a true judgement, or a cognition, that something is so. According to the Viśiṣṭādvaita this is an essential feature of all persons: in the case of God and eternals, it is unobscured, in the case of unliberated individuals, it is obscured, and in the case of those who are just liberated, it takes some time to become unobscured (*Yatīndramatadīpikā* VII.2).

How does *dharmabhūtajñāna* translate into "attributive consciousness"? The term breaks down into the terms "dharma", "*bhūta*" and "*jñāna*". "*Jñāna*" is an epistemic term, denoting a kind of comprehensive knowledge. "*Bhūta*" translates into "thing", "element" or "being". In this context, "dharma" denotes a quality or attribute. Hence, *dharmabhūtajñāna* is the knowledge (*jñāna*) of the quality/attributes (dharma) of things (*bhūta*) or "attributive consciousness".

The question now is: why are attributes morally significant for the Viśiṣṭādvaita system?

One of the chief aims of Rāmānuja's commentary on the *Brahma Sūtra* (particularly in his lengthy commentary on *Brahma Sūtra* I.i.1) is a refutation of Illusionist Monisms—versions of Advaita Vedānta that attempt to prove that there are no differences between things and God, and that there are no such things as attributes. The following is one of Rāmānuja's accounts of an argument of such a philosophy:

> Nor, in the second place, can *DIFFERENCE* be held to be an attribute (dharma). For if it were that, we should have to assume that *DIFFERENCE* possesses difference from essential nature; for otherwise it would be the same as the latter. And this latter difference would have to be viewed as an attribute of the first difference, and this would lead us on to a third difference, and so *ad infinitum*. And the view of difference being an attribute would further imply that difference is apprehended on the *apprehension of a thing distinguished by attributes* such as generic character and so on, and at the same time that the thing thus distinguished is apprehended on the apprehension of difference; and this would constitute a logical seesaw.—*DIFFERENCE* thus showing itself incapable of logical definition, we are confirmed in our view that perception reveals mere Being only. (ŚrīB I.i.1, Rāmānuja 1996 p.32, my italics)[7]

Rāmānuja in his commentary on the first aphorism of the *Brahma Sūtra* is keen to prove that there are important differences between things; that differences are not illusions, that differences consist in differences in attributes, and that attributes of objects are given in consciousness (ŚrīB I.i.1. Rāmānuja 1996 pp.39–156). The use of "dharma" by Rāmānuja to denote *ATTRIBUTE*, while describing his opponent's view, implies that what is at stake is a moral issue. The Illusionist agrees that attributes are morally evaluatable matters (hence the Illusionist uses "dharma" with the *extention* of *ATTRIBUTE*). Both agree that the reality of attributes entails the reality of difference. The question is, are attributes real or not. For the Illusionist, there are no distinct attributes—no morally evaluatable matters—and hence, no differences.

The concept of *dharmabhūtajñāna* in Viśiṣṭādvaita thought is a reaction to the Moral Irrealism of Illusionist Monism. The concept implies that the quality of things—their "dharma"—is a morally evaluatable matter, and moreover, that the quality/attributes (dharma) of a thing (*bhūta*) is epistemically apprehended in knowledge (*jñāna*). The concept of *dharmabhūtajñāna* is not simply a testament to the Moral Realism of the Viśiṣṭādvaita thought, but also to its over all metaphysical realism.

12.7. Dvaita

Compared to Rāmānuja, who regards dharma as a means to *mokṣa*, Madhva's view is that only *bhakti*, or devotion to God, leads one to *mokṣa*. *Bhakti*, on Rāmānuja's account, is a kind of refinement of the moral life, which adds to a Deontological consciousness the knowledge that one's agency is ultimately dependent upon God. Even if one did not have *bhakti*, Rāmānuja's view is that the practise of dharma is sufficient to lead one to *mokṣa*. Not so for Madhva: "Lord Viṣṇu [i.e. Brahman] will be pleased by *Bhakti* alone but not by any other means. He bestows liberation. *Bhakti* is the chief means for it" (MT I.117). More dramatically, Madhva states, "He who is not a devotee of the Supreme God will suffer even if he performs all prescribed duties. On the other hand, one who is a devotee will remain in the presence of God even if kills a Brāhmaṇa [which is a capital offence on Vedic reckoning]" (MT I.107). Dharma, from the point of Madhva's axiology, does not result in *mokṣa*.

Unlike (Ādi) Śaṅkara who ultimately rejects all moral concerns as founded on a mistake, Madhva is no Moral Irrealist. Moral concerns have an important part to play in his theory of eligibility for liberation. In Madhva's view, individuals are inherently graded in relation to others according to their moral character (MT I.17). The highest person is Brahman (*Puruṣottama*). There are three kinds of persons below Brahman: gods, humans and demons. Out of the three types, gods and humans of outstanding character are eligible for liberation. Middle-level humans transmigrate forever. The basest of humans go to hell, or a darkness, while demons go to an even lower hell or darkness. Moreover, on Madhva's account, "liberation and deep darkness are permanent; there is no return from these two positions" (MT I.85–88). Madhva thus appears to be the only thinker in the Indian tradition who is of the opinion that: (a) some persons will never attain liberation; and (b) that the moral character of persons is fixed, and cannot be changed.

Notes

1 There are several thinkers in the history of Indian philosophy with the name "Śaṅkara". To distinguish between these thinkers, sometimes, commentators refer to the Śaṅkara, the commentator on the *Brahma Sūtra*, as "Śaṅkarācārya". The problem with this convention is that there are also several Śaṅkarācāryas: Śaṅkara set up four monasteries in India, and those who are the leaders of these communities also go by the title of "Śaṅkarācārya". This naming convention has led to a lot of confusion; particularly in the matter of determining authorship. There are several works attributed to a Śaṅkarācārya that are presumed, often, to be written by the same Śaṅkara who is the commentator on the *Brahma Sūtra*, but which use language and stress doctrines that are not found in the commentary on the *Brahma Sūtra*. To avoid confusion, I refer to the commentator of the *Brahma Sūtra* as Ādi (*ANCIENT, FIRST*) Śaṅkara. On the question of what works are attributable to this single author, I defer to Hacker (1995 pp.27–57) who has identified a handful of works (including the famous commentary on the *Gītā*) as being works that we can be confident in being written by the author of the *Brahma Sūtra*. Characteristic of these works is a marked absence of reference to the concept of *MĀYA* or illusion, so frequently attributed to Śaṅkara, a latent Vaiṣṇavism and the reference to the author as "Śaṅkarabhagavatpāda" in the colophons.

2 Oddly enough, (Ādi) Śaṅkara seems to hold, at times, a similar position: that individual souls are parts of "God". This is his view in his commentary on B II.ii.43–47. What is not clear is whether it is "God" who is spoken of here, or Brahman. Many commentators on (Ādi) Śaṅkara hold that on his view there is a distinction to be drawn between a personal God and Brahman. However, (Ādi) Śaṅkara himself does not seem to pay much attention to the distinction, and often talks about Brahman as God, in personal terms. For more on (Ādi) Śaṅkara's closet theism, see Paul Hacker's (1995) "Relations of Early Advaitins to Vaiṣṇavism" pp.33–39.

3 According to one modern biographer, Madhva claimed that in "ancient days Vedic rituals did not allow animal sacrifices". See Tapasyānanda, 1990 p.115.

4 Translators are apt to use the term "evil" in their renditions of Rāmānuja's descriptions of what God is not. See Rāmānuja on B I.i.2 (1996 p.156) *Vedārthasaṁgraha* para.6 (1968 p.4) para.42 (1968 p.43) and Rāmānuja

on *Gītā* 18:42 (1991 p.579) and 18:73 (1991 p.604). In the *Gītā* the term that is translated into "evil" from Sanskrit is "*doṣa*"; a term that usually refers to something base, to be criticized and discarded. In the *Vedārthasaṁgraha*, the term translated into "evil" from the Sanskrit is "*heya*". Both terms are classic examples of *perfect, formal*, moral terms with *focus*.

5 According to Grimes, "What it illumines is always for another. It functions through the mind in all-knowing processes; thus, all objective knowledge is a modification of it. In perception, it goes out to the object, takes on the object's form, and as a result the object becomes known to the perceiving subject" (Grimes 1996 p.113).

6 The translation quoted, as always, is that of the translator's listed in the bibliography. The following is the original Sanskrit: *Atha kramaprāptaṃ dharmabhūtajñānaṃ nirūpyate. Svayamprakāśācetanadravyatve sati viṣayitva, vibhutve sati prabhāvadravyaguṇātmakatvam, arthaprakāśo buddhiḥ. tallakṣaṇam.* (*Yatīndramatadīpikā* VII.1.)

7 I believe that the following is the Sanskrit text that Thibaut has translated: "*Nāpi dharmaḥ; dharmatve sati tasya svarūpāt bhedaḥ avaśyāśrayaṇīyaḥ. Anyatha svarūpameva syat. Bhede ca tasyāpi bhedaḥ taddharmaḥ, tasyāpi iti anavasthā. Kim ca jātyādi viśiṣtavastugrahaṇe sati, bhedagrahaṇam; bhedagrahaṇe sati, jātyādi viśiṣtavastugrahaṇam, iti anyonyāśrayaṇam. Ataḥ bhedasya durnirūpatvāt sanmātrasyaiva prakāśakam pratyakśam*" (ŚrīB I.i.1, Rāmānuja 1985 p.46). "Dharma" is used several times to name the idea of an attribute in this passage.

Chapter 13

Cārvāka

13.1. Our Knowledge of the Cārvāka

No account of the history of Indian philosophy would be complete without a mention of the tradition of materialist and naturalistic thought present in the history of India. Materialism is the view that matter is the only substance. Naturalism is a slightly more robust doctrine that embraces materialism. Dale Riepe describes Naturalism as the conjunction of the following theses:

1) sense perception is the most important source of knowledge
2) knowledge is not esoteric, innate or mystical
3) the external world is mind-independent; i.e. it has an existence apart from individuals or their minds
4) the external world (with persons in it) is governed by predictable, invariable laws, which cannot be changed by thought, magic, sacrifice or prayer
5) there is no supernatural purpose to the world

Riepe concludes his description of Naturalism by adding the thesis: "The naturalist is humanistic. Man is not simply a mirror or deity or the absolute but a biological existent whose goal is to do what is proper to man. What is proper to man is discovered in a naturalistic context by the moral philosopher" (Riepe 1961 pp.6–7). On Riepe's description, Naturalism is the combination of materialism, empiricism and a humanistic outlook.

Riepe (1961) argues that there are naturalistic elements in many of India's philosophical systems. On his view, the Vedas, the Upaniṣads, Jainism, Early Buddhism, Sāṅkhya and the Vaiśeṣika systems all display aspects of naturalism. Our concern here is more specific. The present chapter is devoted to dealing with the ethics of India's school of materialist or naturalistic thought. Traditionally, this school has been designated by the names "Cārvāka", or alternatively, "Lokāyata". Traditionally, as well, this school is reputed to have regarded the sage Bṛhaspati as its founder.

Unfortunately, little is directly known about the Cārvāka or Lokāyata school. Most of our information on the Cārvāka comes to us indirectly. In general, secondary references to the Cārvāka or Lokāyata impute materialism and certain naturalistic doctrines to this school. The only work associated with the Cārvāka school that we have access to is Jayarāśi's *Tattvopaplavasiṃha*—which literally translates as "the lion upsetting of all principles". The doctrines adumbrated in this work foreshadow Hume's critique of inference and the *problem of induction*, but the work goes further. While Hume's thought ends with an empiricism and scepticism, the *Tattvopaplavasiṃha* rejects the validity of sense perception too. As K.K. Dixit notes, the doctrine of the *Tattvopaplavasiṃha* is that "everything is unreal and that we have no certain knowledge about anything whatsoever". Dixit goes on to note that "nobody [else] has ever attributed this doctrine to the Cārvākas, who are invariably treated as philosophers maintaining that everything is made up of four physical elements ... and that perception is the sole (or at least basic) means of valid knowledge" (Dixit, 1991 p.521).[1]

Prior to the discovery of the *Tattvopaplavasiṃha* Rhys Davids argued:

> Throughout the whole story we have no evidence for anyone who called himself a "Lokāyatika", or his own knowledge "Lokāyata". After the early use of the word in some such sense as Nature-lore, [or] folk-lore, there is a tone of unreality over

> all the statements we have. And of the real existence of a school of thought, or of a system of philosophy that called itself by the name, there is no trace. In the middle period the riddles and the quibbles of the Nature-lorists are despised. In the last period, the words Lokāyata, [and] Lokāyatika, become mere hobby-horses; pegs on which certain writers can hang the views that they impute to their adversaries, and give them, in doing so, an odious name. (Rhys Davids 1990 pp.375)

The relatively recent discovery of the *Tattvopaplavasiṃha* tempers Davids's findings. However, Jayarāśi's thought hardly counts as a token of Indian naturalism, or Indian materialism. This only adds to the suspicion that there never was a well-defined school of Indian naturalism or materialism that went under the heading of Cārvāka or Lokāyata, despite references to this school in the works of other philosophers.

13.2. Possible Cārvāka Axiology

If we turn to the Indian secondary accounts of the Cārvāka, and not simply the views of lone materialists like Pūraṇa Kassapa or Pakudha Kaccāyana examined earlier (pp.247–248) an unshocking view of Indian materialist, axiological, thinking emerges.

Haribhadra, the Jain author, in his work *Ṣaḍdarśanasamuccaya* (verse 80) states: "The Lokāyatas give their views as follows. There is neither god (*deva*) nor liberation. Dharma and adharma also do not exist. Nor is there any fruit of virtue and vice" (Haribhadra 1990 p.258). On this characterization, the Cārvāka are Moral Irrealists. Guṇaratna, in his commentary on Haribhadra's text, repeats this description of the Cārvāka view, but he also adds some intriguing and seemingly contradictory views regarding the Cārvāka position. Commenting on verse 86, Guṇaratna holds that the Cārvāka view is that "dharma is not superior to *kāma*". He continues to state that the Cārvāka view is that "*kāma* is the highest form of dharma ..." (Guṇaratna 1990 p.276). On this latter account, the Cārvāka are not only Moral Realists, but also subscribers to ethical hedonism: the view that the maximization of pleasure is solely what is morally good.

Mādhava's *Sarvadarśanasaṃgraha* takes the description of Cārvāka axiological thought in a different direction:

> The efforts of the Cārvāka are indeed hard to be eradicated, for the majority of living beings hold the current refrain—"While life is yours, live joyously; None can escape Death's searching eye: When once this frame of ours they burn, How shall it ever again return?"—The mass of men, in accordance with the *śāstras* [TREATISES] of policy [e.g. *arthaśāstra*, *nītiśastra*] and enjoyment [e.g. *kāmasūtra*] considering wealth and desire the only ends of man, and denying the existence of any object belonging to a future world, are found to follow only the doctrine of Cārvāka. Hence another name for that school is Lokāyata. (Mādhava 1967 p.228).

According to Mādhava's description, the Cārvāka hold that *artha* (material prosperity) and *kāma* (pleasure) are the values that ought to be maximized. This is the view attributed to the Cārvāka school in Śaṅkara's *Sarvasiddhāntasaṃgraha* (1967 pp.235) and the philosophical drama *Prabodhacandrodaya* (1967 pp.247–249). In contrast to Guṇaratna's account, none of these accounts depicts the Cārvāka concern with *artha* and *kāma* as constituting its moral thought. That is, the Cārvāka concern with *artha* and *kāma* is not depicted as constituting its conception of dharma.

Mādhava imputes to the Cārvāka the view that there is no final liberation (Mādhava 1967 p.233). This is in keeping with Haribhadra's and Guṇaratna's account. In contrast, Śaṅkara, the author of the *Sarvasiddhāntasaṃgraha*, attributes a belief in *mokṣa* to the Cārvāka. On Śaṅkara's account, the Cārvāka hold:

> The enjoyment of heaven lies in eating delicious food, keeping company of young women, using fine clothes, perfumes, garlands, sandal paste, etc. The pain of hell lies in the troubles that arise from enemies, weapons, disease; while *mokṣa* is

> death which is the cessation of life-breath. The wise therefore ought not to take pains on account of that [i.e. liberation]; it is only the fool who wears himself out by penances fasts, etc. (Śaṅkara 1967 p.234)

I have been duly reminded, however, by Prof. Priestley, that "the Cārvāka '*mokṣa*' is presented ironically, with grim humour: it is the '*mokṣa*' that everyone attains at death, since (in their view) there is no such thing as rebirth". This is one time when it seems appropriate not to take our Indian philosophers too literally, for they themselves apparently did not take the issue of liberation seriously at all.

13.3. Is the *Arthaśāstra* Materialist Ethics?

There are some grounds, in the literature, to presume that Kautilya's *Arthaśāstra*—the classic Indian work on politics—constitutes in some manner the expression of Indian materialist ethics. First, the aim of the work is the maximization of *artha*. Next, the *Arthaśāstra* favourably mentions Bṛhaspati, the legendary *ācārya* (MASTER) of the Cārvāka school (Kautilya I.i.4). As well, Kautilya lists "Lokāyata" as an analytic discipline *(ānvīkṣikī)* that comprises learning (*vidyātva*) (Kautilya I.i.9–10). Third, G. Tucci argues that the Lokāyata tradition is the forerunner of Indian political works like Kautilya's *Arthaśāstra*:

> The Lokāyatikas represent a reaction to this thought [that the greatest good is achieved in an after-life] as they teach that only that which can be perceived (*pratyakṣeṇa*) exists: direct experience is the only *pramāṇa* for men; what we cannot see is mere fancy .... Therefore, the interpretation we have to give to the name Lokāyata is quite different. It is but a science which has for its only object the *loka*, that is, this world .... Therefore this Lokāyata ... is the forerunner of *nīti* or *arthaśāstra*. (Tucci 1990 p.390)

Finally, David Kalupahana depicts Kautilya as putting forward a "teleological Utilitarian moral theory highlighting the fruits of the mundane life" (Kalupahana 1995 p.12). Such a theory would be consistent with the Cārvāka's metaphysics and Naturalistic world-view.

The problem with viewing Kautilya's *Arthaśāstra* as adumbrating the Cārvāka moral theory is that Kautilya defers to the Vedas on matters of morality. According to the *Arthaśāstra,* right and wrong in morals (*dharmādharmau*) is learnt from the Vedas (Kautilya I.i.11).

A case can be made that Kautilya does get into the game of justificative ethics, insofar as he argues that there are four branches of learning—(1) *ānvīkṣikī*, which includes the analytic or philosophical disciplines of Sāṅkhya, Yoga and Lokāyata, (2) the Vedas, (3) *vārta*, or the agricultural arts, cattle raising and trade and (4) *daṇḍanīti*, or political science—(Kautilya I.i.1) and that the common thread of these branches of learning (*vidyātva*) is that they are means to learning about the nature of dharma and *artha* (Kautilya I.i.9). While he refers to "Lokāyata" as part of the means of knowing dharma and *artha*, Kautilya's philosophical outlook is far from materialist, insofar as he recognizes the authority of the Vedas, and the philosophical schools of Sāṅkhya and Yoga. On the basis of Kautilya's justificative ethics, it cannot be concluded that Kautilya proffers the ethics of Indian Materialism.

Can Kautilya, as Kalupahana suggests, be viewed as putting forth a form of Utilitarian moral thought? Kautilya may in fact put forth a consequentialist political and economic theory, where the ends justify the means. However, this is not Kautilya's account of dharma, which he says comes from the Vedas. If his account of morality is Vedic, it is difficult to conceive how it could be a token of Utilitarianism.

13.4. Was there ever a Cārvāka Ethic?

The variety of axiological positions attributed to the Cārvāka makes it difficult to summarize their moral thinking. On Guṇaratna's account, the Cārvāka *darśana* held the position of ethical hedonism, by recognizing *kāma* as the highest dharma. Guṇaratna's account appears to be the minority view of the Cārvāka. Usually, moral views are not ascribed to the Cārvāka. Generally, we find a kind of Axiological Pragmatism attributed to them. When this wider pragmatic doctrine is ascribed to the Cārvāka, it is not defined as comprising its view on dharma.

Unfortunately, given the lack of primary texts associated with the naturalistic school of Cārvāka or Lokāyata, we have no solid information speaking to the positive moral doctrine of this school. We can only speculate that some Cārvāka held the position of ethical hedonism. We can also speculate that some Cārvāka held a more complex moral theory, which concerned itself not simply with pleasure, but with prosperous government, and the maximization of *artha* in general. However, these are simply speculations.

Notes

1 For more information on the *Tattvopaplavasiṃha*, see Eli Franco's "Studies in the *Tattvopaplavasiṃha*" (1983). Dixit notes, Jayarāśi is unusually friendly and approving in his references to Bṛhaspati; the legendary *ācārya* of Indian materialism (1991 pp.521–523). This supports the view that Jayarāśi is a Cārvāka philosopher. In conclusion, Dixit states: "Jayarāśi claims that he has been able to expose even such philosophical errors as were not taken into account by Bṛhaspati ... but a more honest ... claim on Jayarāśi's part would have been that he has been able to expose such philosophical errors as could make even Bṛhaspati their victim!" (1991 p.530). The relationship of Jayarāśi to the Cārvāka school is indeed baffling.

Chapter 14

Summary of Indian Ethics

14.1. Justificative Ethics

Attention was given to a group of *darśanas*: Buddhism (Early and Mahāyāna), Jainism, Cārvāka, Sāṅkhya, Yoga, Nyāya, Vaiśeṣika, Pūrvamīmāṃsā and Vedānta (Advaita, Viśiṣṭādvaita and Dvaita). Following Chatterjee and Datta (1960), Radhakrishnan and Charles A. Moore (1967), the three anti-Vedic and six pro-Vedic philosophical systems can be taken to comprise the Canon of systematic Indian philosophy. The exposition of these various schools attempted to bring to the fore the moral views of the *darśanas*. It was noted that there are several philosophical activities answering to the notion of ETHICS (5.2. On the Pursuits that Answer to "Ethics" pp.194–201).

Of these many activities, justificative ethics is the form of ethics to which Indian philosophers, on the whole, attended. Now we can summarize the contributions of Indian philosophers to justificative ethics.

The ultimate moral principle of Buddhism is *mediation or support*—an idea that is expressed in the Principle of Dependent Origination, (*Paticcasamuppāda*, *Pratītyasamutpāda*) (7.2. Dependent Origination and Dharma pp.229–230). On this view, something is moral, or a dharma, if it functions to mediate or support others. There are two distinct views in Indian Buddhism regarding how this moral principle is justified. One Buddhist view is that,

- morality, conceived in terms of the Principle of Dependent Origination, is justified by its usefulness in bringing about liberation.

This is the view that is characteristic of non-Mahāyāna Buddhist thought (p.238). A second Buddhist view is that,

- morality is the greatest of values, and is not justified because it is instrumental to other ends, but because it is intrinsically important and fulfilling. On this view, the moral life is the happy life.

This is the view of Dharma characteristic of the Mahāyāna (p.238).

For Jainism, our ultimate obligation is not to interfere with the well-being of others (p.256). Our normal, worldly, actions are those that interfere with, and violate, others. This is the state of moral imperfection, which consists in the state of immotility and adhesion to karma. Inculcating moral perfection releases us from the shackles of karma, and makes us motile. (p.251). Hence,

- morality is justified, on the Jain view, because it is Motion, or nonrestrictiveness, which, when perfected, constitutes a liberated state. On this view, moral perfection is our salvation.

For the Sāṅkhya philosophy, dharma, understood as virtue, leads one to the higher worlds (p.268). Hence,

- the justification of morality, on the Sāṅkhya view, is that it leads one to the heavens.

On the Yoga view, Dharma, in the form of the *yamas*, is part of the means to controlling one's thoughts (p.269), which is the goal of yoga. Hence,

- the Yoga tradition regards morality as justified because of its aid in controlling the mind.

Success in this direction results in the *dharmamegha samādhi.* (p.273). "*Samādhi*", though denoting a state of absorption where one retains body and mind, has strong soteriological implications: it constitutes a liberated state. The state of *dharmamegha samādhi*, in the Yoga tradition, appears to be something distinct, at least logically, from *mokṣa*, or *kaivalya* (p.276). Therefore,

- the Yoga view is that morality is also justified because its perfection—*dharmamegha samādhi*—constitutes an intrinsically rewarding and liberated state; distinct from *mokṣa*.

The Yoga philosophy also appears to depict final liberation, or *kaivalya*, as an aloneness that is a function of the *dharmamegha samādhi* (9.5. Dharmamegha Samādhi pp.273–274). Hence,

- dharma is also justified, on the Yoga account, because it directly leads to final liberation.

If one is not impressed with these lines of reasoning, the *Yoga Sūtra* cites a host of pragmatic benefits that follow the inculcation of *yamas* (p.270) that are additional justifications for living the moral life. According to the *Yoga Sūtra*:

> When [one] becomes steadfast in ... abstention from harming others, then all living creatures will cease to feel enmity in [one's] presence. When [one] becomes steadfast in ... abstention from falsehood, [one] gets the power of obtaining for [oneself] and others the fruits of good deeds, without [others] having to perform the deeds themselves. When [one] becomes steadfast in ... abstention from theft, all wealth comes ... Moreover, one achieves purification of the heart, cheerfulness of mind, the power of concentration, control of

> the passions and fitness for vision of the *Ātma* [self]. (YS II.35–41)

The Nyāya system, as a Hindu philosophical school, regards the Vedas as a source of teachings on moral matters. According to the Nyāya system, the validity of the Vedas is justified because of the reliability of the authors of the Vedas (p.280). Hence,

- the *Nyāya* view is that dharma, as specified by the Vedas, is justified owing to the reliability of the authors of the Vedas.

The Vaiśeṣika system proffers many lines of justification for dharma. One line holds that dharma is justified because it results in *abhyudaya* and *niḥśreyasa*. "*Abhyudaya*" appears to mean *EXALTATION*, but it also designates worldly success, or *artha*. "*Niḥśreyasa*", which means the *SUPREME / HIGHEST–GOOD*, is conventionally taken to designate *mokṣa* (p.282). Hence,

- dharma is justified, on the Vaiśeṣika system, because it results in *artha* and *mokṣa*.

The term "*abhyudaya*" is also susceptible to another interpretation: it designates the rise of a heavenly body. If the term is given this meaning then the Vaiśeṣika system appears to approximate Jain thought (p.281), for morality on this account would also be seen as giving rise to motion.

The Vaiśeṣika system also regards dharma as resulting in the knowledge of the predicables, knowledge of essences, or knowledge of truths (p.284). Hence,

- dharma is also justified, on the Vaiśeṣika system, by resulting in *jñāna* (*GNOSIS*), which is an appreciation of the essences of things.

In this last line of justification, the Vaiśeṣika system echoes the Sāṅkhya sentiment, that morality results in an epistemic virtue (which on the Sāṅkhya view is the *sattva guṇa*). However, the Vaiśeṣika view is that dharma directly facilitates liberation also, while the Sāṅkhya view is that dharma only leads to the higher worlds. On the Sāṅkhya account, it is nonattachment, and not dharma, which produces liberation (p.268).

Pūrvamīmāṃsā proffers a complex line of justification for dharma. On one level,

- Pūrvamīmāṃsā holds that dharma is justified because it gives rise to *artha*, understood as well-being (p.289).

However, the Pūrvamīmāṃsā also holds that we cannot determine the contents of dharma by reason, or by defining dharma as that which is conducive to well-being (11.4. Motive and Consequences pp.293–296). To know the contents of dharma we must turn to the Vedas, and the secondary literature based on the Vedas (the *smṛti* literature). The Vedas, in turn, are an independently valid source of knowledge, capable of justifying their contents and beliefs based upon them. Hence,

- the Pūrvamīmāṃsā system also holds that dharma is justified by the independent validity of the Vedas.

This view was identified earlier as part of Vedic Foundationalism (11.1. Vedic Foundationalism pp.287–288).

Vedānta authors typically agree with the Pūrvamīmāṃsā system in its two approaches to justifying dharma. The view that dharma leads to *artha* is presupposed in most Vedānta discussions. Vedic Foundationalism also plays an important part in the Vedānta school of thought (p.307). Hence, the view that dharma is justified because it is specified in the Vedas is also a line of justification taken by Vedānta authors (12.4. Animal Sacrifices pp.311–313). Vedānta authors also put forward views on ethics that go beyond the Pūrvamīmāṃsā account.

(Ādi) Śaṅkara has the distinction amongst Hindu, Buddhist and Jain, philosophers examined here (philosophers who hold that *mokṣa* is a real value) of putting forward the metaethical view of Moral Irrealism; the view that morality rests upon a mistake, or that in reality we have no moral obligations (12.5. Advaita pp.313–319). Yet, in conjunction with his Moral Irrealism, (Ādi) Śaṅkara offers a pragmatic justification for morality:

- while morality ultimately rests on a mistake, and is itself an error to be abandoned, based on the notion of individual agency, for (Ādi) Śaṅkara, morality is justified insofar as it leads a person to think about the Self (p.317).

This line of justification is proffered in addition to (Ādi) Śaṅkara's endorsement of Vedic Foundationalism as a means of justifying morality (pp.311–312).

Rāmānuja appears to provide two arguments for justifying dharma, over and above the Pūrvamīmāṃsā lines of justification. According to one line of justifying ethics,

- dharma, according to Rāmānuja, is justified because it leads directly to, and is constitutive of, *mokṣa* (pp.320–321).

Rāmānuja has a second line of argument for justifying dharma, which is dependent upon his first line of argument. According to Rāmānuja, the discipline of knowledge, or *jñāna-yoga*, is a theoretically distinct means to gaining liberation. Rāmānuja argues that this path is however doomed to failure. In contrast, the discipline of *karmayoga*, or attending to one's *deontic* obligations, is easy, and suitable to our individual constitutions, and a sure means to liberation (p.321). Hence,

- dharma is justified, for Rāmānuja, because it constitutes the easiest means to liberation.

Madhva in some respects is more conservative than Rāmānuja in his view on the relationship between dharma and *mokṣa*. For him, it is only *bhakti*, or devotion to God, and not dharma, that leads to *mokṣa* (p.324). Hence, Rāmānuja's two additional lines of justifying dharma play no part in the thought of Madhva. Unlike (Ādi) Śaṅkara, Madhva is no Moral Irrealist. Out of the three Vedāntins examined, Madhva's stance on justificative ethics, however, appears not to surpass the views articulated by the Pūrvamīmāṃsā (12.4. Animal Sacrifices pp.311–313).

14.2. Moral First Principles

Indian philosophers have given us different accounts of what they take to be the essence of Morality.[1] We might call such accounts of Morality "moral first principles".

In the Western tradition, we are accustomed to thinking of Morality as an ideal object, which is instantiated, indirectly, in things. This is the Platonic idea of Morality. Indian philosophers have given analogous accounts of the nature of Morality, but their accounts are quite different.

For the Buddhist, Dharma consists in being a mediator and being supportive: these features of Dharma imply that it is incapable of being reduced to one thing. Its nature is always tied with another. For this reason, Dharma is eventually called "Emptiness", or "Empty" in latter Buddhism. Such language could lead to the interpretation that latter Buddhism advocates Moral Irrealism. If Moral Irrealism is the view that Morality is a mistake, then, this is an inaccurate characterization of latter Buddhist thought on morality, for Dharma, or Emptiness, is the nature of things, on this latter account, and it is a manner of being that we ought to oblige. If Moral Irrealism is the view that Morality is not real, it would also be incorrect to attribute Moral Irrealism to latter Buddhist thought, for it recognizes the phenomena of dharma as something genuinely commendatory. On the latter Buddhist account, Dharma is called "Empty", for "Emptiness" is the closest way that we can come to speaking about Dharma as one, single, entity.[2]

There is another way to understand how it is that Dharma is Empty on Latter Buddhist thought: emptiness is a feature that pertains to the concept of *DHARMA*. On this account, *DHARMA* has no *extension*. This is not because *DHARMA* does not have *extentions* (things that we correctly apply the concept to) but, for the concept to have an *extension*, there need to be strictly definable individuals falling underneath it. The nature of Dharma is contrary to individuality, in latter Buddhism, for its nature is that of mediation and support. Thus, the concept of *DHARMA* appears to have no entities falling under it, and hence, it has no *extension*, rendering it *empty*. This emptiness of the concept *DHARMA* is a function, on the latter Buddhist account, of the truly moral nature of *DHARMA*.

The Earlier school of Buddhist thought appeared to avoid the Negative Theology approach to speaking about Dharma. Instead, it presented a principle as capturing the primary nature of Dharma (a principle operative in latter Buddhist thought on Dharma as well): the Principle of Dependent Origination. This principle of dependence implies the essence of Dharma as mediatory and supportive.

Jainism, in contrast to Buddhism, affirms the substantiality of Dharma. Dharma, on the Jain account, is an objective feature of the cosmos: it is Motion, considered as a substance.

This conception of Morality appears odd to many, but it has been pointed out to me (and I have Danny Goldstick to thank for this) that we often associate morality with progress, or betterment: the idea of Motion thus conforms to common intuitions that morality represents the possibility of concrete change in our lives.

In the context of Jain cosmology and metaphysics, the motile nature of Dharma is tied, intimately, with its disconnection with karma. *KARMA* means action. However, in the context of Jainism, this concept is treated with irony. Karma, in all instances of Indian thought, denotes worldly action. This is a false kind of movement (in the eyes of Jain ethics) which really constitutes a moral stagnation. By ridding ourselves of karma—by being Dharmic—we gain genuine movement in our lives, on the Jain account.

I am inclined to argue that the idea of Sacrifice is presupposed in many discussions of *DHARMA* in Hindu ethics, and moreover, that all Hindu speculation on Dharma can be subsumed under the idea of Sacrifice. In sacrifice, one forfeits a claim to something. In the various accounts of Dharma presented by Hindu thinkers, the idea of sacrifice appears to limit the moral. Such an idea of Dharma has its roots, ultimately, in the Vedic idea of Dharma as sacrifice to the Gods. This idea of Dharma is affirmed in the Yoga idea that dharma consists in an ascetic lifestyle, embodied in the *yamas*. The idea of Dharma as sacrifice is also affirmed in the Vaiśeṣika notion that knowledge of the Vaiśeṣika system constitutes a sagely forbearance, which is a particular dharma. As well, in affirming the Vedas as a source of Dharma, the Vaiśeṣika system, the Nyāya system, the Pūrvamīmāṃsā system and the Vedānta philosophies all affirm the idea of the essential connection between Dharma and sacrifice. The Pūrvamīmāṃsa system, of course, explicitly brings to the fore the connection between sacrifice and Dharma. The Sāṅkhya system, for its part, affirms the connection between sacrifice and Dharma in its view that the inculcation of dharma leads to the higher worlds—this is a classic feature of the Vedic, sacrifice account of Dharma. Thus, the Hindu first principle of Dharma is that of Sacrifice.

To summarize, the Buddhist first principle of ethics depicts Dharma as, essentially, mediating and supportive. The Jain first principle of ethics depicts Dharma as Motion. And, operative in Hindu schools of ethics is the notion that Dharma is ultimately of the nature of Sacrifice. These are, respectively, Buddhism's, Jainism's and Hinduism's most general characterizations of what they take to be the nature of Morality. Many lower level principles of ethics, asserted by the various schools of Buddhism, Jainism and Hinduism, can be understood as attempting to flesh out what counts, in a relatively concrete matter, as Mediating, Motion or Sacrifice.

14.3. Dharma and the Other *Puruṣārthas*

As noted *DHARMA* is only one of four values listed in the list of the *puruṣārthas*. The other value-theoretic concepts in this list are *kāma*, *artha* and *mokṣa*. The question of the relationship between the various spheres is complicated by the fact that these various terms are in fact *intentional* in nature. Thus, "*artha*" not only stands for a subdivision of the *puruṣārthas*, but for the *puruṣārthas* itself. Likewise, there is a specific *extention* of "*kāma*" which is that of worldly sensual pleasure. But *KĀMA* is really *ENJOYMENT*. Thus, *KĀMA* could subsume, conceptually, some philosophers' account of the *extension* of *MOKṢA* for they take it to be something blissful.

The question of the relationship of the *puruṣārthas* is thus made almost impossible to answer in any specific way if we consider the various values specified by the *puruṣārthas*, in themselves, for the corresponding concepts do not specify their *extentions* on their own. However, if we consider them within the context of what is identified as the *puruṣārthas* by classical writers, we see that they have relatively specific *extentions*. In this context, "*artha*" is used to refer to material prosperity, as *kāma* is used simply to refer to sensual enjoyment. In this context, the question of the relationship between the *puruṣārthas* is edifying, for the various schools of Indian philosophy have given us specific answers in light of these *extentions*.

There are major views on the relationship between dharma and the other *puruṣārthas*, which span *darṣanas*. These major views are that (a) dharma leads to *artha*, (b) dharma leads to *mokṣa*, and (c) dharma leads away form *artha*. Then there is the view that (d) dharma and *mokṣa* are identical. There are two versions of this view. In one view, *DHARMA* and *MOKṢA* are *coextensive*; that is, they have the same *extension*. In another view, there is an overlap of the *extensions* of *DHARMA* and *MOKṢA*.

Then there is the view that (e) dharma and *mokṣa* are utterly disparate. In this view, the *extension* of DHARMA and MOKṢA are mutually exclusive.

As noted, Vaiśeṣika, Sāṅkhya, Vedānta and Pūrvamīmāṃsā systems affirm that dharma leads to *artha*; the *Mīmāṃsā Sūtra* and the *Vaiśeṣika Sūtra* explicitly affirm this, and Sāṅkhya and Vedānta schools presuppose this aspect of dharma, insofar as they regard dharma as resulting in prosperity in this and other worlds. Buddhist thought frequently affirms that *artha* and dharma are consistent with each other, but it does not typically stress that dharma leads to *artha*. If anything, Buddhism's ascetic roots are critical of *artha*.

The view that dharma leads to *mokṣa* is to be found in Yoga, Viśiṣṭādvaita Vedānta (only), Vaiśeṣika and Buddhism.

The view that dharma leads away from *artha* is implicit in many of Jainism's criticisms of worldly wealth. The dharmic state on its account is one that is divorced from materiality. While dharma is an *artha* in its view, *artha*, when it refers to material prosperity, is mutually exclusive with dharma.

The view that dharma and *mokṣa* are identical, in some way, is affirmed by many schools of Indian thought. Jainism, Mahāyāna Buddhism, Viśiṣṭādvaita Vedānta and Yoga appear to affirm this thesis in various ways; the strongest proponent of this view is Jainism. As noted, there are two versions of the view that dharma and *mokṣa* are identical. The weaker version of the thesis holds that these two concepts have appropriate *extentions* in common; that their genuine *extensions* overlap. This is affirmed by Viśiṣṭādvaita Vedānta and Yoga, for both of these schools hold that liberation is a state of moral perfection, though they recognize that the sphere of morality extends to life outside of liberation. The stronger version of this thesis holds that the *extensions* of the concept DHARMA and MOKṢA are identical; that while the concepts DHARMA and MOKṢA have different meanings, they have the same genuine referents. This view is affirmed quite explicitly by Jainism, in its view that the only way to do the morally right thing is to be liberated from karma. This view also shows up in versions of latter Buddhist thought which regards *saṁsāra* (the world of bondage, or dharmas) as identical to *nirvāṇa* (or the state of liberation).[3]

The view that *DHARMA* and *MOKṢA* are utterly disparate is the view that their *extensions* (the class of entities that fall under them) do not overlap at all. This is a view that we find in Early Buddhism, insofar as it suggests that dharma is to be abandoned upon *mokṣa*, Sāṅkhya, which regards dharma to be inoperative the moment liberation is achieved, and Advaita Vedānta, which regards the concerns of dharma to be, in the final stages, inimical to the goal of liberation.

14.4. Reality of Morality

The noteworthy majority of Indian philosophical schools have affirmed the reality of Morality, as a sphere of value that is mind independently real; which we are obliged to indulge, for various reasons. A noteworthy minority position is that Morality is something less than real.

As noted, latter Buddhist thought appears to hold that Morality is something less than real. However, this philosophy has a very specific point in mind with this criticism. On its account, morality is something that we ought always to oblige; that we ought never to abandon it. What we need to abandon, on its account, is the view that morality is something substantial. Moral Irrealism—the view that morality is a mistake, or that it rests upon a mistake—has certain superficial similarities with latter Buddhist thought, but they are ultimately disparate positions, for latter Buddhism does not affirm that we are in error for being dharmic, or for attempting to do the moral thing. Our error with respect to morality consists, on its account, in the belief that it is a thing. In this respect, latter Buddhist thought appears to have some points of contact with *noncognitivism*, insofar as *noncognitivism* eschews the characterization of morality as consisting in certain facts, or moral states of affairs.

The view that the concept *DHARMA* has no genuine

extension—that there is nothing in reality that conforms to it—is also affirmed by Advaita Vedānta. While the latter Buddhist view is that it is correct to oblige Dharma, and to be dharmic, the Advaita position, as expounded by (Ādi) Śaṅkara, is that we are in error for obliging morality, for morality presupposes the notion that we are agents (on its account) and the truth of the matter is that our real, essential Self, is devoid of agency, and has the essential nature of being an observer. Moreover, the Advaita position as expounded by (Ādi) Śaṅkara is that moral conduct rests upon the conflation of the categories of object and subject, and the psychological construction of an ego. For the aspirant after Truth, such a conflation of logically distinct categories has to be renounced, and along with it, the conditions of morality.

14.5. Analysis of Moral Concepts

Moral philosophy, by definition, is *not* something that is necessarily bound up with the analyses of moral concepts. Moral philosophy is merely that which is regarded as being positively disposed towards wisdom about moral matters; such a discourse could never mention moral concepts, and still constitute moral philosophy, insofar as it is something that is regarded as being positively disposed towards wisdom about moral matters (Chapter 5, "Ethics in Philosophy" pp. 189–215). Yet, it is noteworthy that many schools of Indian philosophy involve themselves, explicitly, in an analysis of their substantive idea of *DHARMA*.

To understand what an analysis of a concept consists in, we need to understand what it is to analyze something. To analyze is to break something into components, or to identify its parts. The components of ideas or concepts are varied; they may be logical relationships. An analysis that concerned itself with this side of a concept would concern itself with providing an analysis of the *intension* of a concept. Also, amongst the components of a concept are the items that make up its *extension*. An account of the components of the *extension* of a concept—the objects that fall underneath the concept—constitutes an analysis of a concept.

Indian philosophers frequently concern themselves with analysing what they take to be the *extension* of *DHARMA*; such an analysis gives us an insight into what renders their moral theory substantively unique.

Early Buddhist philosophical texts consist in a persistent analysis of *DHARMA*. A few items were identified as central to the Buddhist analysis of *DHARMA*: (i) the Principle of Dependent Origination; (ii) the Four Noble Truths; (iii) the Eight-Fold Path; (iv) entities that are called "dharma". But the Early Buddhist analysis of *DHARMA* surpasses these items. Every early school of Buddhism has a corpus of texts that it calls the "*Abidharma*". It is an inventory of doctrinal matters, and it too constitutes an analysis of *DHARMA*, for Early Buddhism. Less explicitly, the *Vinaya* (*DISCIPLINE*) portion of Buddhist canonical literature, concerned with the rules of monastic life, also constitutes an analysis of *DHARMA*. The inventory of these items constitutes an analysis of *DHARMA*, for they all are regarded as making up the *extension* of *DHARMA*, on Early Buddhism's account.

The *Vaiśeṣika Sūtra* makes it clear that it concerns itself with an analysis of *DHARMA*. At the outset it informs us that Dharma consists in many things, including the contents of the Vedas, the teachings of the Vaiśeṣika system (particularly knowledge of its various ontological categories), which it regards as an elaboration on the contents of the Vedas, and a particular virtue, which is the knowledge of the Vaiśeṣika system. The remainder of the *Vaiśeṣika Sūtra* thus consists in an elaboration of the contents of its account of the concept *DHARMA* in the form of its elaboration on the contents of the Vaiśeṣika system itself.

The *Mīmāṃsā Sūtra* similarly makes an analysis of *DHARMA* its business. It surveys the various kinds of sacrifices and ordinances specified by the Vedas, which on its account, specifies what Dharma is.

An analysis of *DHARMA* is far more implicitly presented in the Yoga system. It explicitly analyzes *DHARMA* in its account of *dharmamegha samādhi*, but it implicitly analyzes it in its account of the *yamas*. I call the latter analysis "implicit", for the *yamas* are not explicitly cited as constituting dharma, though this can be inferred from the fact that the *yamas* are designated by moral terms (pp.269–272).

A text that is of foundational importance to the school of Vedānta is the *Bhagavad Gītā*. The text has relatively clear implications for an analysis of *DHARMA*; on its account, the *extension* of *DHARMA* consists in one's own duty ordained by the Vedas, one's own nature, and specified in the *smṛti* literature. Vedānta authors have typically deferred to this text for the analysis of their account of *DHARMA*.

Jainism, finally, provides an analysis of *DHARMA* at virtually every turn. Jainism regards its whole philosophy as Dharma. An explication of its contents, thus, constitute an analysis of the *extension* of *DHARMA* on its account.

Notes

1 The convention of capitalising some words is really one that is indigenous to Western languages; no such analogous orthographic convention exists in Sanskrit. Yet, there is a convention in the secondary literature on Indian thought of distinguishing between Dharma spelled with a "D" and dharma spelled with a "d". The only justification for this convention is that it helps clarify the *extention* of "dharma". When capitalised, "Dharma" stands for morality in general, while, when not capitalised, "dharma" stands for particular moral things. I shall thus employ this convention sometimes, when the distinction between morality as such, and individual moral things is important to emphasise in the current section.

2 Latter Buddhist thought on Morality is thus analogous to Negative Theology; speaking accurately about Dharma in the ultimate sense, on the latter Buddhist account, we can ultimately only note what it is not: it is not a single, self-sufficient entity. As self-sufficiency was taken as a metaphysical prerequisite to substantiality in latter Buddhist thought, the latter Buddhists were led to the conclusion that Dharma is less than a substance; that it is Empty of substantiality.

3 The identity of *saṁsāra* and *nirvāṇa* is a matter stressed by the Mādhyamika philosophy of Nāgārjuna, and stated explicitly at *Mūlamadhyamakakārikā* XXV.19; "*Na saṁsārasya nirvāṇat kiṁcid asti*

viśeṣaṇaṃ na nirvāṇasya saṁsārāt kiṁcid asti viśeṣaṇaṃ". Kalupahana translates this as "The life-process has no thing that distinguishes it from freedom. Freedom has no thing that distinguishes it from the life-process" (Nāgārjuna 1986 p.366). Garfield's translation of a Tibetan edition of this stanza is: "There is not the slightest difference between cyclic existence and *nirvāṇa*. There is not the slightest difference between *nirvāṇa* and cyclic existence" (Nāgārjuna 1995 p.75).

Part VI:

Conclusion

Chapter 15

On the Importance of Ethics to Indian Philosophy

15.1. Dharma Philosophy

So often in scholarship in the humanities we want to be able to hold up something concrete as the definition of some key category we are interested in. We want to be able to say "ethics is ..." and to point to something that ethics is as its definition. We want to be able to say that "philosophy is ..." and to point to something as a definitive token of philosophy. We think, often, that unless we have such a concrete, definitive, token, we are being neither specific, nor accurate; that our discussions remain indeterminate, and that they lack substance. Here is where many of our comparative impulses come from. We think we understand what tokens of such concepts as *MORAL–PHILOSOPHY* are in the West. By looking for like tokens in the Indian tradition we can settle the issue, we believe, of whether Indian philosophers pursued moral philosophy.

Such impulses are unfortunate, for they fail to appreciate the essence of the meaning of such key notions as *ETHICS* and *PHILOSOPHY.*

The key to deciphering what such philosophically ripe notions as *ETHICS* and *PHILOSOPHY* mean is in coming to terms with the *intentional* states that constitute their meanings.

The *intentional* meaning of "ethics" was the subject of a

prolonged investigation earlier. I argued that the *intentional* meaning of such a term is the inclination to get angry over some evaluative matter, should it be violated or not respected, in the absence of mitigating reasons. It is true that, in earlier history, terms like "ethics" and "moral" had more *substantive* meanings; designating matters of conduct or behaviour in their Greek and Latin incarnations as "*ethos*" and "*mores*". However, no sooner such terms began to represent a field of philosophical investigation, they lost their substantive meanings and retained their essential *intentional* meaning. The shedding of a substantive meaning was the flip side of their induction as terms to designate a field of philosophical investigation, for such terms must be key philosophical terms. For them to function as key philosophical terms, they must have no *substantive* elements as part of their meanings (2.2. Key Philosophical Terms pp.22–31).

The *intentional* meaning of *PHILOSOPHY* was subject to a far shorter investigation, because its etymological (historical) meaning lends itself to a purely *intentional* interpretation. Such an interpretation is fitting, for *PHILOSOPHY* is a key philosophical concept, over which there is substantive disagreement.

"Philosophy" breaks down into "philo" and "sophy". "Sophy" comes from the Greek "*sophia*", which stands for wisdom. If we need a definition of wisdom, I suggested that we would find its meaning in the notion of being epistemically revealing. As "wisdom" is an *intentional* term, over which we have intractable disagreements, we ought to define it as *WHAT–IS–REGARDED–AS–BEING–EPISTEMICALLY–REVELATORY*. The conventional translation of "*philo*" into English renders it as "friend" or "dear". I suggested that we could thus regard *PHILO* as translating as "friendly" or "dear". While this disjunctive account is accurate (for in disjunctive combination they define a concept whose meaning can be grasped without reference to *extentions*), the translation of *PHILO* as simply *FRIEND* is misleading, or is a poor translation, I would argue.

"Friend" is an *extentional* term. It is true that we apply the term to things that have a certain *intentional* disposition to other things—one of being supportive, and wishing well—but its meaning is still to be found in its *extentions*. Thus, "friend" is an *extentional* term after the manner of "intention", which is itself an *extentional* term, and subject to various *extentional* definitions (2.1. Extention and Intention pp.13–22).

FRIEND, by itself, is not a correct rendition of *PHILO*, I believe. For the very fact that lexicographers believe that it can be translated as *FRIEND* or *DEAR*[1] suggests that the meaning of *PHILO* can be grasped without reference to *extentions*, for *DEAR* is an *intentional* concept. To know what *DEAR* means, we cannot consider a list of things called "dear" its meaning. Rather, we need to grasp the *intention* behind the application of the term "dear" to things if we wish to know the meaning of the concept *DEAR*.

A better translation of "*philo*", thus, would be *A–THING THAT–IS–REGARDED–AS–FRIENDLY–OR–DEAR–TO–SOMETHING*. "Philosophy" is thus *THAT–WHICH–IS–REGARDED–AS–BEING–POSITIVELY–DISPOSED–TO–THAT–WHICH–IS–REGARDED–AS–EPISTEMICALLY–REVEALING*. For short, "philosophy" means *THAT–WHICH–IS–REGARDED– AS–AMENABLE– TO–WISDOM*.

On this understanding of *PHILOSOPHY*, moral philosophy, or philosophy about moral matters, philosophy need not objectify moral concepts and ponder them: it need only be regarded as well-disposed *towards* epistemic revelation about moral matters.

Our historical question is whether moral philosophy composes a part of the history of Indian philosophy. The only data we need, thus, to satisfy our definition of moral philosophy, in order to conclude that moral philosophy is a genuine part of the history of Indian philosophy, is the data that: Indian philosophers produced philosophies that they regarded as amenable to wisdom about dharma.

From the explications of the various schools of Indian philosophy, it is obvious that all Indian schools of philosophy addressed, in some manner, what they take to be dharma. This is the empirical proof that bears witness to the fact that Indian philosophers regarded morality as something they addressed in the context of their philosophies. The question asked thus is, "did Indian philosophers positively regard their writings as disposed towards wisdom about moral matters"? The answer to this question is, yes.

The objections to such an interpretation of Indian philosophy include claims like: what we mean by "moral philosophy", and even "moral" is something far more specific than what was relevant to "dharma". Once again, however, we find here the kind of concrete thinking that leads to mistaking tokens of *ETHICS* or *MORAL–PHILOSOPHY* with the meanings of these concepts. What "we" (conceived of very narrowly) call "moral philosophy" would very well be something far more specific and determinate than what many Indian philosophers regarded as the content of their moral philosophies: it would be a specific *extention* of the term "moral philosophy". But such things are not the meaning of the term "moral philosophy".

What renders the writings of Indian philosophers tokens of moral philosophy is that Indian philosophers themselves considered such writings as positively disposed to wisdom about moral matters. In one respect, thus, my efforts to summarize the contributions of Indian philosophers to moral philosophy may be misleading. I have stayed close to Indian philosophers' explicit treatment and use of the concept *DHARMA*. But moral philosophy is not restricted to an analysis of moral concepts, for it is that which is regarded as positively disposed towards wisdom about moral matters: moral philosophy can thus be removed, by several steps, from explicit questions about *MORALITY* itself. Thus, much important moral philosophy happens prior to any discussion of moral concepts, for here we have discussions of ancillary matters that are regarded by their authors as favourably disposed towards wisdom about moral matters. Thus, much of Indian moral philosophy is to be found in discussions on epistemological, metaphysical, and logical issues that do not mention or explicitly use moral concepts. However, as noted in this work, much of scholastic Indian philosophy concerned itself with the analysis of moral concepts as well.

15.2. Importance of Indian Moral Philosophy

Having presented the argument for the fact that moral philosophy constitutes part of the history of Indian philosophy, we might raise the issue of evaluating the significance or importance of Indian moral philosophy. Is moral philosophy an important part of the history of Indian philosophy?

Let us begin to answer this question by asking what could count against moral philosophy being considered an important part of the history of Indian philosophy? It is important to remind ourselves what renders Indian philosophy morally philosophical: its authors regard their texts as positively disposed towards wisdom about moral matters. Perhaps we would conclude that moral philosophy is an unimportant part of the history of Indian philosophy if Indian philosophers themselves were not so keen on the moral philosophical value of their works. But what would be the data here, which speaks against Indian philosophers being keen on moral philosophy? One might suggest that the data in question is the frequency (or infrequency) with which moral (dharmic) issues are explicitly raised or dealt with: we can interpret such objectively observable data as an indication of how important moral philosophy was for Indian philosophers.

The question of how frequently Indian philosophers raised issues of moral relevance takes us back into the vagaries of philosophy. How could we tell that a philosopher is not speaking about something morally philosophical? Perhaps we could make such a determination on the basis of whether moral terms appear in their discourse or not. But this approach is mistaken, for moral philosophy need not concern itself with an analysis of moral concepts, for it is that which is regarded as positively disposed *towards* wisdom about moral matters (including, moral concepts). If moral philosophy need not concern itself with an analysis of moral concepts, it follows that the absence of moral terms, or a relative infrequency in their appearance, cannot be taken as conclusive proof that the matters under discussion are not morally important for the author.

Perhaps we could determine the importance of moral philosophy, for Indian philosophers, on the basis of whether a position on moral matters is essential to their overall philosophical view, or *darśana*. If a *darśana* can be captured without employing moral concepts, then, we would be entitled to interpret the absence of moral concepts from the theory as speaking towards the unimportance of moral philosophy to its whole philosophy. This appears to me to be a reasonable way to determine whether moral philosophy is an important part of a philosophical project, for it does not reduce moral philosophy to the occurrence of moral terms in a discourse. Rather, it suggests that the presence of moral concepts within a philosophical *theory* is indicative of whether philosophical matters about morality is something important for the philosopher who proposes it.

If we are to determine the relative importance of moral philosophy to the Indian philosophical tradition on the basis of whether moral concepts figure in their philosophical theories, then we are led to the conclusion that moral philosophy is indeed an important part of the history of Indian philosophy, for a position on *DHARMA* is essential to the formulation of every school of the canon of Indian philosophy, for which we have primary material. Indeed, the difference between many *darśanas*, or versions of the same *darśana*, hinges on moral matters. For instance, the difference between Early and Mahāyāna Buddhism cannot be fully comprehended unless we take into account their differences on the justification of dharma. The controversy between the three prominent versions of Vedānta hinges largely on their respective views on the validity of dharma, and its relationship to liberation. Sāṅkhya and Yoga appear to be virtually the same philosophy unless we take into account their difference on the issue of whether persons are culpable agents or not. The two systems are also distinguished by their view on moral perfection. For the Yoga system, moral perfection constitutes a kind of liberated state, which produces final liberation. For Sāṅkhya, the maximization of dharma simply leads to higher worlds. With respect to Buddhism, Jainism, Pūrvamīmāṃsā and Vaiśeṣika, the analysis of *DHARMA* preoccupies these philosophical schools' explicit philosophical activity: the question of whether dharma is important to these schools does not arise owing to the presence of objective evidence that dharma is a central concern of these philosophical theories.

15.3. *Mokṣa* Philosophy

A prominent view in the secondary literature on Indian philosophy is that it is dominated by the value of *MOKṢA* or *FREEDOM*—as Karl Potter explains it (Potter 1963 pp.1–3). Even if we were to believe that this characterization of Indian philosophy is true, we would not be able to grasp, accurately, the particular views of the schools of Indian philosophy, on the nature of *mokṣa*, if we did not also know what their view on dharma is. For frequently, *MOKṢA* 's *extension* is defined in relation to, or is limited by, *DHARMA* (either *DHARMA* and *MOKṢA* are presented as mutually exclusive, *coextensive*, or partially overlapping in *extensions*). This is particularly true of a school of thought like Advaita Vedānta, which, on some readings, is the archetype of an a-ethical Indian philosophy (Deutsch 1969 p.99). In the case of (Ādi) Śaṅkara's view on *MOKṢA*, its *extension* is explicitly defined in relation to its mutual exclusivity to dharma. This aspect of the nature of *MOKṢA* is central to (Ādi) Śaṅkara's account. Hence, moral philosophy (wisdom about moral matters) is vitally important to his overall project.

The view that *MOKṢA* is the dominant concern of Indian philosophy is a twin thesis to the view that ethics plays little part in the history of Indian thought. Let us call this the "*MOKṢA* view of Indian Philosophy". The idea behind the Mokṣa View is that Indian philosophers were so preoccupied with the value of *mokṣa* that they neglected or were not interested in questions pertaining to *DHARMA*. But can this thesis be sustained in light of the fact that a view on *DHARMA* is essential to the definition of every *darśana* of the canon of Indian philosophy, for which we have primary material? What is the data that supports the view that *mokṣa*, to the exclusion, or domination, of other values, is the concern that has driven Indian philosophy?

The same considerations that are relevant to discerning whether Indian philosophers contributed to moral philosophy are relevant to determining the importance of *mokṣa* to Indian philosophers: the mere presence of the *intentional* term "*mokṣa*" cannot be taken as an indication of whether *mokṣa* to the exclusion of other values was being discussed, for moral philosophy, for instance, can consist in a discussion of *MOKṢA*, if such a discussion is regarded positively by the author as contributing to wisdom about *DHARMA*. Likewise, the absence of the term "*mokṣa*" cannot be taken as proof that a discourse of Indian philosophy is not an instance of soteriological philosophy, for being positively disposed towards wisdom about soteriological matters need not involve an analysis of the concept of soteriology, or *MOKṢA*.

There are also other textual considerations that are relevant to discerning the importance of soteriology to Indian philosophy. For instance, some Indian philosophers name *MOKṢA* as the highest good (for instance, the Vaiśeṣika school takes this position) but this is not the explicitly stated view of all Indian philosophers. As well, for many Indian philosophers, *DHARMA* and *MOKṢA* are *coextensive*. This is the case, I believe, with Jain thought, which defines the *extension* of *DHARMA* as Motion and the liberated state as a state devoid of the weight and inertia of karma. This is also the case, I think, for strands of latter Buddhist thought, which regard *saṁsāra* (the nonliberated state) as *coextensive* with the liberated state, or *nirvāṇa*. Here, liberation is frequently conceived not as a novel state, but an understanding with respect to the way things are: things are, in their nature, dharmic, on this view; *nirvāṇa*, or *moksa*, is liberation from ignorance about the dharmic nature of things.

Ultimately, the only way to discern whether soteriological philosophy is important for a philosopher, I believe, is to determine whether a view on soteriology is essential to the philosopher's overall philosophical view. In point of fact, soteriological matters are not part of every Indian philosophical theory. For instance, the early Pūrvamīmāṃsā has nothing to say about soteriological matters. However, for all other schools of Indian thought—even the Cārvāka—soteriological philosophy is part of their overall project, for they have something, philosophical, to say about *MOKṢA*. Recall, however, that almost the same thing can be said about moral philosophy: that a view on morality is essential to every school of Indian thought that is part of the canon of Indian philosophy, for which we have primary material. Hence, the question arises as to whether soteriological philosophy is more important to the Indian tradition than moral philosophy. On the basis of these considerations, it appears that there is no reason to conclude that soteriological philosophy is more important than moral philosophy to Indian philosophers. Certainly, with respect to some philosophers, we could say that they valued *MOKṢA* more than *DHARMA* or that *DHARMA* occupied a lesser place in their axiological scheme than *MOKṢA*; Advaita Vedānta, Sāṅkhya and Early Buddhism come to mind as examples of this view. However, this is not grounds for concluding that moral philosophy is any less important to the project of Advaita Vedānta, Sāṅkhya or Early Buddhism than soteriological philosophy. If anything, the scale tips in favour of the view that moral philosophy was, overall, more important to the history of Indian philosophy, for while not all schools of Indian thought have a view on *MOKṢA*, all schools of the canon of Indian philosophy (for which we have primary material) have an essential view regarding *DHARMA*.

With respect to the question of the importance of moral philosophy to the history of Indian philosophy, we can thus draw two conclusions. With respect to the history of Indian philosophy as a whole, moral philosophy constitutes an important part, for every school of Indian philosophy that we have primary source texts on has had something to say about *DHARMA*. With respect to individual philosophies and philosophers from the history of

Indian philosophy we can conclude that moral philosophy constitutes an important part of their particular philosophical projects, for each Indian philosophical theory or *darśana* is only definable with respect to a position on *DHARMA*. This is most exemplified in the case of philosophies that are critical of morality: a critical stance of morality in the case of the school of Advaita Vedānta is essential to a proper understanding of its idea of the value of liberation.

15.4. *Mokṣa* and Dharma

Could we conclude, as many have, that while soteriological philosophy is not more important to the history of Indian philosophy than moral philosophy, nevertheless, the value of *mokṣa* is more important to Indian philosophers than the value of dharma? I do not see how such a conclusion is supported by the facts.

Once we grant that moral philosophy is no less important to the projects of Indian philosophers than soteriological philosophy, how could we, consistently, believe that they however valued *mokṣa* more? We could draw such a conclusion if Indian philosophers themselves believed that the dictates of *mokṣa*, or the pursuit of this goal, ought to override the goals of morality. For then, we would have clear proof that Indian philosophers believed that *mokṣa* is more important than dharma. However, the facts do not support this view.

Few Indian philosophies explicitly state that the pursuit of *mokṣa* ought to override the pursuit of dharma. A relatively clear statement to this effect is found in Advaita Vedānta. But no such comparable statement is to be found in other schools of the canon of Indian philosophy.

Sometimes we find Indian philosophers calling *mokṣa* the "highest good", but this is not the universal opinion of Indian philosophers. For the early Pūrvamīmāṃsā thinkers, *artha* appears to be the highest good. For others, dharma itself is the highest good (Jainism, Mahāyāna Buddhism). For some, the talk of *mokṣa* makes little sense unless we understand its intrinsically moral nature (Viśiṣṭādvaita Vedānta, Yoga).

15.5. Moral Philosophy; East and West

The *historical* question of whether the Western or Indian tradition of philosophy has made greater contributions to moral philosophy is a meaningless question. For the very considerations that lead us to the conclusion that moral philosophy constitutes an important part of the history of Indian philosophy lead to the conclusion that moral philosophy cannot be said to be more important to either the Western or Indian traditions of philosophy.

Many a commentator's instinct is to conclude that the West has made the more significant contribution to moral philosophy, and Indian philosophers' contributions must be judged in relation to the Western yardstick. But what could go to this thesis once we have concluded that moral philosophy is an integral part of the philosophical projects of all the philosophies of the canon of Indian philosophy, for which we have primary material? Could we conclude that philosophies of the West have made the greater contribution to moral philosophy if, on the account of Western philosophical theories, morality is given greater weight than other values?

Let us assume, for the moment, that morality constitutes a sphere of value that is weighted more greatly in the West, in comparison to other values. How would this fact prove that moral philosophy was more important to the West? For moral philosophy is that which is regarded as friendly or dear to wisdom about moral matters. On this understanding of moral philosophy, one could have a moral philosophy about morality, and this philosophy could grant to morality a very low weighting, and yet, such a philosophy about moral matters could be very important to a philosopher's overall project. In other words, a philosopher might be a Moral Irrealist, and yet, moral philosophy is exceedingly important for such a philosopher, for wisdom about the low status of morality, on the philosopher's account, is something important. Thus, even if it were true that the West privileged the value of morality over other values, in a manner that we do not find in the Indian philosophical tradition, we could not conclude on the basis of this fact that moral philosophy was more important to the Western tradition.

In reality, however, the view that morality is the value that has been granted the greatest weight in the history of Western philosophy is not readily supported by the facts. We frequently have a black hole in our memory of the history of Western philosophy that swallows up the entire Mediaeval tradition. For philosophers like St. Augustine and St. Thomas Aquinus, the value of *mokṣa* is given at least equal importance to dharma (to the extent that such thinkers place the value of being a Christian over bare morality, it would appear that *mokṣa* is a more important value for them). Moreover, frequently, the Western tradition has coalesced its idea of the *extension* of dharma with its idea of the *extension* of *mokṣa*. This is true, I think, for Plato, the Neo-Platonic tradition, and for thinkers like Kant, who appear to regard morality, at times, as the instantiation of a divine order.

As noted, the Mokṣa View of Indian Philosophy, and the view that ethics plays little part in the history of Indian philosophy (let us call this the "Indian Ethics Deficiency View") are twin theses. In light of the view that Morality has been given greater importance in the tradition of Western philosophy than in the history of Indian philosophy, we can note yet another thesis associated with the twin theses. This additional, associated, thesis is that, while Mokṣa has dominated Indian philosophy, Dharma has dominated the history of Western philosophy. We could call this the "Mokṣa–India::Ethics–West Thesis".

Having concluded that moral philosophy is an integral part of the history of Indian philosophy, in light of the facts about the importance granted to *mokṣa* in the West too, and most importantly, in light of the fact that the weight granted to the values of dharma and *mokṣa* are irrelevant to the importance that moral or soteriological philosophy has for a philosopher's project, there is no sound historical basis for concluding that any particular philosophical tradition has exceeded the other in their contribution to moral philosophy.

Individual thinkers can have reasonable substantive views on the relative worth of Indian or Western moral philosophies. Such views could not aim to represent the history of philosophy, as a historian of philosophy might, but rather, such views would have the substantive validity of appraising contributions of philosophers from the perspectives of idiosyncratic, substantive, views on moral philosophy. This substantive mode of philosophical appraisal is indispensable to the activity of philosophy. However, the conscientious critic is fully aware that any such appraisal that they deliver is only a substantive appraisal of historical views of moral philosophers; not an account of what historical philosophers thought they were contributing to wisdom about moral matters. Our studies of the history of philosophy have been sullied by a failure to distinguish these two distinct approaches to the topic of moral philosophy.

Notes

1 Merriam-Webster 2002: "philo", *Collegiate Dictionary*. Merriam-Webster, <http://www.m-w.com/home.htm>. Oxford University, 2002: "philo-" *Oxford English Dictionary* 2nd edition (On-line). Oxford: Oxford University.

Bibliography

References have been split under "classical" and "contemporary" headings. Classical references consist mainly of canonical works in philosophy. Contemporary references include secondary literature. Anonymous canonical titles are designated at the outset of the reference, where the authors name would usually be. If an edited volume contains classical texts, it is listed first in the classical reference section. Edited works, and their publication information, are listed separately, with the editor's name marked at the outset.

Classical Sources

Ācārāṅga Sūtra. 1987. In *Jaina Sūtras*, 2 vols. Edited by H. G. Jacobi. Delhi: AVF Books, vol. 1 pp.1–216.

Amarakoṣa. 1934. Edited by Wāsudev Laxmaṇ Śāstrī Panśīkar. 7 ed. Bombay: Pāndurang Jāwajī.

Amritacandra Sūri. 1935. *Pravacanasāra of Kundakunda Āchārya together with the commentary Tattvadīpikā by Amritacandra Sūri*. Translated by B. Faddegon. Cambridge: Cambridge University.

Aṅguttara Nikāya. 1932–1936. Translated by F. L. Woodward and E. M. Hare, *Pali Text Society Translation Series; no. 22,* pp.24–27. London: Pali Text Society.

Aristotle. 1941. *Nicomachean Ethics* (*Ethica Nicomachea*), In *The Basic Works of Aristotle*. Edited by R. P. McKeon. New York, NY: Random House, pp.935–1127.

Arnauld, Antoine, and Pierre Nicole. 1964. *The Art of Thinking (La Logicque ou l'Art de Penser; Port-Royal Logic)*. Translated by J. Dickoff and P. James. Vol. 144, *The Library of Liberal Arts*. Indianapolis: Bobbs-Merrill.

Aśokā (Emperor). 272–223 B.C.E. *Seventh Aśokan Pillar Edict: Delhi-Topra*. Translated by N. K. Wagle of the University of Toronto.

Aṣṭasāhasrikā Prajñāpāramitā. 1958. Translated by E. Conze. Edited by R. Mitra. BI 1888.

Bhagavad Gītā. 1986. *(Śrīmad Bhagavad Gītā; the Scripture of Mankind)*. Translated by Swāmi Tapasyananda. Madras: Sri Ramakrishna Math.

Brentano, Franz Clemens. 1924. *Psychologie vom Empirischen Standpunkt*. Edited by O. Kraus. 3rd ed. 2 vols, *Der Philosophischen Bibliothek Bd.*. Leipzig: F. Meiner , pp.192–193 Original edition, Leipzig, 1874, 1911.

Chandrakānta. 1923. *Vaiśeṣika Sūtra (Gloss)*. Translated by N. Sinha. Allahabad: Sudhindra Nath Basu.

Chattopadhyaya, Debiprasad and M. Gangopadhyaya, eds. 1990. *Cārvāka/Lokāyata: an Anthology of Source Materials and Some Recent Studies*. New Delhi: Indian Council of Philosophical Research in association with Rddhi-India Calcutta.

Conze, Edward, ed. 1958. *Buddhist Wisdom Books, Containing the Diamond Sutra and the Heart Sutra. Translated and Explained by Edward Conze*. London: Allen & Unwin.

Diamond Sūtra. 1958. In *Buddhist Wisdom Books, Containing the Diamond Sutra and the Heart Sutra. Translated and Explained by Edward Conze*. Edited by E. Conze. London: Allen & Unwin, pp.21–72.

Dīgha Nikāya. 1995. Translated by T. W. R. Davids. Edited by C. A. R. Davids and T. W. R. Davids. 3 vols. Vol. 2–4, *Sacred Books of the Buddhists,*. London,: Pali Text Society.

Frege, Gottlob. 1966. *Translations from the Philosophical Writings of Gottlob Frege*. Edited by P. Geach and M. Black. 2nd ed. Oxford: Blackwell.

———. 1980. *Die Grundlagen der Arithmetik (The Foundations of Arithmetic : a Logicomathematical Enquiry into the Concept of Number)*. Translated by J. L. Austin. Oxford. Blackwell.

Gautama. 1930. *Nyāya Sūtra*. Translated by S. C. Viyabhusana. Edited by N. Sinha. 2nd rev. and enl. ed. Vol. 8, Sacred Books of the Hindus. Allahabad: Panini Office.

Guṇaratna. 1990. Tarkarahasyadīpika. In *Cārvāka/Lokāyata: an Anthology of Source Materials and Some Recent Studies*. Edited by D. Chattopadhyaya. New Delhi: Indian Council of Philosophical Research in association with Rddhi-India Calcutta, pp.266–278.

Hamilton, Edith, and Huntington Cairns, eds. 1966. *The Collected Dialogues of Plato, including the Letters, Bollingen Series 71*. New York: Pantheon Books.

Haribhadra. 1990. Ṣaḍdarśanasamuccaya. In *Cārvāka/Lokāyata: an Anthology of Source Materials and Some Recent Studies*. Edited by D. Chattopadhyaya. New Delhi: Indian Council of Philosophical Research in association with Rddhi-India Calcutta, pp.258–266.

Heart Sūtra. 1958. In *Buddhist Wisdom Books, Containing the Diamond Sutra and the Heart Sutra. Translated and Explained by Edward Conze*. Edited by E. Conze. London: Allen & Unwin, pp.77–108.

Hume, David. 1969. *A Treatise of Human Nature*. Edited by L. A. Selby-Bigge and P. H. Nidditch. Oxford; New York: Clarendon Press.

Īśvarakṛṣṇa. 1948. *Sāṅkhya Kārikā*. Translated by S. S. Suryanarayana-Sastri. Edited by S. S. Suryanarayana-Sastri. 2nd rev. ed, *Madras University Philosophical Series. no. 3*. Madras: University of Madras.

Jacobi, Harmann Georg, ed. 1968. *Jaina Sūtras*. 2 vols. Vol. 22, 45, *Sacred Books of the East*. Delhi: AVF Books.

Jaimini. 1923. *Mīmāṃsā Sūtra*. Translated by M. L. Sandal. Vol. 27, *Sacred Books of the Hindus*. Allahabad: Sudhindre Nath Basu.

Jayarāśi Bhaṭṭa. 1967. *Tattvopaplavasiṃha*. In *A Source Book in Indian Philosophy*. Edited by S. Radhakrishnan and C. A. Moore. Princeton, NJ: Princeton University Press, pp.236–246. Original edition, Sukhlalji Sanghavi and Rasiklal C. Parikh, *Gaekwad's Oriental Series*, vol.lxxxvii, Baroda: Oriental Institute1940.

Jha, Ganganatha. 1942. *Pūrva Mīmāṃsā in its Sources*. Translated by Jha, Ganganatha, *Library of Indian Philosophy and Religion*. Benares: Benares Hindu University.

Kaṇāda. 1923. *Vaiśeṣika Sūtra*. Translated by N. Sinha. Edited by N. Sinha. 2nd rev. and enl. ed. Vol. 6, *Sacred Books of the Hindus*.

Allahabad: Sudhindra Nath Basu, Panini Office.
Kant, Immanuel. 1956. *Groundwork of the Metaphysics of Morals.* Translated by H. J. Paton. New York: Harper Torchbooks.
Kaufmann, Walter Arnold, ed. 1975. *Existentialism from Dostoevsky to Sartre*. Toronto: Meridian.
Kautilya. 1951. *Arthaśāstra*. Translated by R. Shamasastri. 4rth ed. Mysore: Sri Raghuveer Printing Press.
Kierkegaard, Søren. 1985. *Fear and Trembling*. Translated by A. Hannay. Toronto: Penguin.
Kumārila. 1983. *Ślokavārtika*. Translated by G. Jha. Vol. 8, *Sri Garib Das Oriental Series*. Delhi: Sri Satguru. Original edition, 1909 Bibliotheca Indica. Calcutta: Asiatic Society.
Kundakunda (Ācārya). 1935. *Pravacanasāra of Kundakunda Āchārya together with the commentary Tattvadīpikā by Amritacandra Sūri*. Translated by B. Faddegon. Cambridge: Cambridge University.
Mādhava Ācārya. 1967. Sarvadarśanasaṁgraha. In *A Source Book in Indian Philosophy*. Edited by S. Radhakrishnan and C. A. Moore. Princeton, NJ: Princeton University Press, pp.228–234. Original edition, London: Kegan Paul, Trench Trubner & Co. 1904.
Madhva. 1904. *Vedānta Sūtras with the commentary of Śri Madhwacharya (Brahma Sūtra Bhāṣya)*. Translated by S. S. Rau. Madras: Thompson and Co.
———. 1993. *Mahābhāratātparyanirnaya*. Translated by K. T. Pandurang. Edited by K. T. Pandurang. Vol. 1. Chirtanur: Śrīman Madhva Siddhantonnanhini Sabha.
Majjhima Nikāya. 1957. Translated by I. B. Horner. 3 vols. Vol.29–31, *Pali Text Society Translation Series*. London: Published for the Pali Text Society by Luzac.
Manu. 1886. *The Laws of Manu (Manavadharmaśāstra)*. Translated by G. Buhler. Edited by M. Müller. Vol. xxv, *Sacred Books of the East*. Oxford: Oxford University Press.
McKeon, Richard Peter, ed. 1941. *The Basic Works of Aristotle*. New York, NY: Random House.
Mill, John Stuart. 1965. *Collected Works of John Stuart Mill*. Edited by J. M. Robson, F. E. Mineka, M. Filipiuk and J. O'Grady. 33 vols. Toronto: University of Toronto Press.

Moore, George Edward. 1903. *Principia Ethica*. Cambridge: University Press.

Nāgārjuna. 1934, 1936. Ratnāvali. In *The Journal of the Royal Asiatic Society of Great Britain and Ireland*, pp.308–325 (1934) and 252–435 (1936).

———. 1977. *The Philosophy of Nāgārjuna: as contained in the Ratnā vali*. Edited by H. N. Chatterji. 1 ed. Calcutta: Saraswat Library.

———. 1986. *Mulamadhyamakakārikā (Nāgārjuna: The Philosophy of the Middle Way)* (Sanskrit Edition and Translation). Translated by D. J. Kalupahana. Edited by D. J. Kalupahana. Albany: State University of New York.

———. 1995. *Mulamadhyamakakārikā (The Fundamental Wisdom of the Middle Way)*. Translated from Tibetan by J. L. Garfield. Oxford: Oxford University.

Patañjali. 1953. *Yoga Sūtra (Patañjali Yoga Sūtra)*(Edition and Translation). Translated by Swāmi Prabhavananda. Madras: Ramakrishna Math.

Plato. 1966. *Meno*. In *The Collected Dialogues of Plato, Including the Letters. Bollingen Series 71*. Edited by E. Hamilton and H. Cairns. New York: Pantheon Books, pp.353–385.

———. 1966. *Phaedo*. In *The Collected Dialogues of Plato, Including the Letters. Bollingen Series 71*. Edited by E. Hamilton and H. Cairns. New York: Pantheon Books, pp.40–99.

———. 1966. *Philibus*. In *The Collected Dialogues of Plato, Including the Letters. Bollingen Series 71*. Edited by E. Hamilton and H. Cairns. New York: Pantheon Books, 1086–1151.

———. 1966. *Republic*. In *The Collected Dialogues of Plato, Including the Letters. Bollingen Series 71*. Edited by E. Hamilton and H. Cairns. New York: Pantheon Books, pp.575–844.

Plotinus. 1969. *The Enneads*. Translated by S. Mackenna. 4th ed. London: Faber.

Prabhacandra. 1941. *Nyāyakaumudacarita*. Edited by M. K. Jain. Bombay.

Prabodhacandrodaya. 1967. In *A Source Book in Indian Philosophy*. Edited by S. Radhakrishnan and C. A. Moore. Princeton, NJ: Princeton University Press. Original edition, Originally published Bombay 1811, pp.19–22.

Radhakrishnan, S., and Charles Alexander Moore, eds. 1967. *A Source Book in Indian Philosophy*. Princeton, NJ: Princeton University Press.

Rāmānuja. 1968. *Vedārthasaṃgraha*. Translated by S. S. Ragavachar. Mysore: Sri Ramakrishna Ashrama.

———. 1985. *Śrī Bhāṣyam (Critical Edition)*. Melkote: Academy of Sanskrit Research.

———. 1991. *Śrī Rāmānuja Gītā Bhāṣya* (Edition and Translation). Translated by Svāmi Ādidevānanda. Madras: Sri Ramakrishna Math.

———. 1996. *Vedānta Sūtras with the commentary of Rāmānuja (Śri Bhāṣya)*. Translated by G. Thibaut. Vol. 48, *Sacred Books of the East*. Delhi: Motilal Banarsidass.

Śabara. 1933. *Śabara Bhāṣya*. Translated by G. Jha. Vols. 66, 70, 73, *Gaekwad's Oriental Series*. Baroda: Oriental Institute.

Śaṅkara. 1967. Sarvasiddhāntasaṃgraha. In *A Source Book in Indian Philosophy. Edited by* S. Radhakrishnan and C. A. Moore. Princeton, NJ: Princeton University Press, pp.234–235. Original edition, Calcutta, 1929.

(Ādi) Śaṅkara. 1983. *Brahma Sūtra Bhāṣya*. Translated by Swāmi Gambhirānanda. Calcutta: Advaita Ashrama.

———. 1989. *Śaṅkara's Teachings in his Own Words*. Translated by Swāmi Atmānanda. Bombay: Bharatiya Vidya Bhavan.

———. 1991. *Bhagavadgītā with the commentary of Śaṅkarācārya*. Translated by Swāmi Gambhirānanda. Calcutta: Advaita Ashrama.

Śaṅkara Misra. 1923. *Vaiśeṣika Sūtra Bhāṣya*. Translated by N. Sinha. Edited by N. Sinha. 2nd rev. and enl. ed. Vol. 6, *Sacred Books of the Hindus*. Allahabad: Sudhindra Nath Basu, Panini Office.

Sartre, Jean Paul. 1975. Existentialism is a Humanism. In *Existentialism from Dostoevsky to Sartre*. Edited by W. A. Kaufmann. Toronto: Meridian, pp.345–369. Original edition, This translation of Sartre's lecture L'existentialisme est un humanisme was originally published in 1964. London: Methuen and Co.

Śrīnivāsadāsa. 1978. *Yatīdramatadīpikā*. Translated by Svāmi Ādidevānanda. Madras: Sri Ramakrishna Math.

Sūtrakṛtāṅga. 1987. In *Jaina Sūtras*, 2 vols. Edited by H. G. Jacobi.

Delhi: AVF Books, Vol 2., pp.235–436.

Uttarādhyayana. 1987. In *Jaina Sūtras*, 2 vols. Edited by H. G. Jacobi. Delhi: AVF Books, Vol 2., pp.1–234.

Vālmīki. 1969. *Śrīmad Rāmāyana* (Edition and Translation). Gorakpur: Motilal Jalan.

Vasubandhu. 1923–31. *Abhidarmakośa*. Translated by Annoté L. de la Vallée-Poussin. 6 vols.

Visuddhimagga. 1967. In *A Source Book in Indian Philosophy*. Edited by S. Radhakrishnan and C. A. Moore. Princeton, NJ: Princeton University Press, pp.284–286, pp.289–292. Original edition, *Buddhism in Translations*, Cambridge, Mass: Harvard University.

Wittgenstein, Ludwig. 1922. *Tractatus Logico-Philosophicus* (Edition and Translation). Translated by C. K. Ogden. London: Routledge and Kegan Paul. Original edition, published in German by Annalen der Naturphilosophie, 1921 under title: Logisch-Philosophische Abhandlung.

———. 1958. *Philosophical Investigations*. Translated by G. E. M. Anscombe. 2nd ed. New York: Macmillan.

Contemporary References

Ammerman, R.R., ed. 1990. *Classics of Analytic Philosophy*. Indianapolis: Hacket.

Audi, Robert, ed. 1995. *Cambridge Dictionary of Philosophy*. Cambridge: Cambridge University.

Audi, Robert, and William J. Wainwright, eds. 1986. *Rationality, Religious Belief, and Moral Commitment; New Essays in the Philosophy of Religions*. London: Cornell University Press.

Ayer, A.J. 1946. *Language Truth and Logic*. New York: Dover Publications.

Bharadwaja, V.K. 1984. A Non-Ethical Concept of Ahimsa. *Indian Philosophical Quarterly*. xi (2): pp.171–177.

Bilimoria, Puruṣottama. 1991. Indian Ethics. In *A Companion To Ethics.*. Edited by P. Singer. Cambridge, Mass.: Blackwell Reference.

Bratman, Michael E. 1995. Intention. In *Cambridge Dictionary of Philosophy*. Edited by R. Audi. Cambridge: Cambridge

University, pp.43–57.

Buitenen, J.A.B. van. 1957. Dharma and Mokṣa. *Philosophy East and West* 7: pp.33–40.

Byrski, M Christopher. 1976. Trivurga: the Threefold Sphere of Indian Ethics. *Dialectics and Humanism* (3–4): pp.17–31.

Calhoun, Cheshire. 1989. Responsibility and Reproach. *Ethics* 99: pp.389–406.

Castaneda, H.N. , and G. Nakhnikian, eds. 1963. *Morality and the Language of Conduct*. Detroit: Wayne State University.

Chaterjee, Satischandra, and Dhirendramohan Datta. 1960. *An Introduction to Indian Philosophy*. Calcutta: University of Calcutta.

Chisholm, Roderick M. 1952. Intentionality and the Theory of Signs. *Philosophical Studies* 3: pp.56–63.

Cohen, Stephen. 1977. Distinctions among Blame Concepts. *Philosophy and Phenomenological Research* 38: pp.149–166.

Conze, Edward. 1967. *Buddhist Thought in India; Three Phases of Buddhist Philosophy*. Ann Arbor: University of Michigan.

Cooper, Neil. 1970. Morality and Importance. In *The Definition of Morality*. Edited by G. Wallace and A. D. M. Walker. London: Methuen and Co, pp.91–97.

Copleston, Frederick C. 1977. Ethics and Metaphysics: East and West. *Proceedings of the American Catholic Philosophical Association; Ethical Wisdom East And/Or West* 51: pp.75–86.

Couture, Jocelyne, and Kai Nielsen. 1993. Introduction—On Construing Philosophy. In *MetaPhilosophie; Reconstruing Philosophy?*. Edited by J. Couture and K. Nielsen. Calgary: University of Calgary, pp.1–56.

———, eds. 1993. *MetaPhilosophie; Reconstruing Philosophy?* Vol. (Supplementary) 19. Calgary: University of Calgary.

Crawford, S. Cromewell. 1974. *The Evolution of Hindu Ethical Ideals*. Calcutta: Firma K. L. Mukhopadhyay.

Creel, Austin B. 1977. *Dharma in Hindu Ethics*. Calcutta: Firma KLM

Danto, Arthur Coleman. 1972. *Mysticism and Morality: Oriental Thought and Moral Philosophy*. New York: Basic Books.

Darwall, Stephen, Allan Gibbard, and Peter Railton. 1992. Toward "Fin de siecle" Ethics: Some Trends. *Philosophical Review* 101 (1): pp.115–189.

Dasgupta, Surama. 1961. *Development of Moral Philosophy in India.* New York: Frederick Ungar Publishing Co.

Dasgupta, Surendranath. 1975. *A History of Indian Philosophy.* Delhi: Motilal Banarsidass.

Davids, Rhys. 1990. On Lokāyata. In *Cārvāka/Lokāyata: an Anthology of Source Materials and Some Recent Studies.* Edited by D. Chattopadhyaya. New Delhi: Indian Council of Philosophical Research in association with Rddhi-India Calcutta1, pp.369–376. Original edition, *Dialogues of the Buddha*, London 1889, pp.66–172.

Davidson, Donald. 1980. *Essays on Actions and Events.* New York: Clarendon Press.

———. 1982. Paradoxes of Irrationality. In *Philosophical Essays on Freud.* Edited by R. Wollheim and J. Hopkins. London: Cambridge University Press, pp.289–305.

———. 1984. *Inquiries into Truth and Interpretation.* New York: Oxford University Press.

———. 1984. Introduction. In *Inquiries into Truth and Interpretation.* New York: Oxford Univ Press, xvii.

———. 1985a. Donald Davidson Responds. In *Essays on Davidson: Actions and Events.* Edited by B. Vermazen and M. B. Hintikka. Oxford: Clarendon Press, pp.195–252.

———. 1985b. A New Basis for Decision Theory. *Theory and Decision* 18: pp.87–98.

———. 1986. A Coherence Theory of Truth and Knowledge. In *Truth and Interpretation: Perspectives on the Philosophy of Donald Davidson.* Edited by E. Le Pore. Cambridge: Blackwell, pp.307–319.

———. 1987. Problems in the Explanation of Action. In *Metaphysics and Morality: Essays in Honour of J.J.C. Smart.* Edited by P. Pettit, R. Sylvan and J. Norman. Oxford, UK; New York, US: B. Blackwell, pp.35–49.

———. 1990a. Representation and Interpretation. In *Modelling the Mind.* Edited by K. A. M. Said. Oxford; New York: Clarendon Press; Oxford University Press, pp.13–26.

———. 1990b. The Structure and Content of Truth. *Journal of Philosophy* 87 (6): pp.279–328.

Davis, Donald R. Jr., 2004. Being Hindu or Being Human: A

Reappraisal of the Purusarthas. *The International Journal of Hindu Studies* 8: pp.1–27.

Deleuze, Gilles, and Félix Gauttari. 1994. *What is Philosophy?* Translated by H. Tomlinson and G. Burchell. New York: Columbia University.

Dennett, Daniel C. 1995. Intentionality. In *Cambridge Dictionary of Philosophy*. Edited by R. Audi. Cambridge: Cambridge University, p.381.

Derrida, Jacques. 1974. *Of Grammatology*. Translated by G. C. Spivak. 1st American ed. Baltimore: Johns Hopkins University Press. Original edition, *De la Grammatologie*.

Deutsch, Eliot. 1969. *Advaita Vedānta: a Philosophical Reconstruction*. 1st ed. Honolulu: East-West Center Press.

Devaraja, N.K. 1962. *An Introduction to Śaṅkara's Theory of Knowledge*. Delhi: Motilal Banarsi Dass.

Dewey, John, and James H. Tufts. 1929. *Ethics*. New York: Henry Holt and Co.

Dixit, K.K. 1990. The Ideological Affiliation of Jayarāśi—The Author of the Tattvopaplavasiṃha. In *Cārvāka/Lokāyata: an Anthology of Source Materials and Some Recent Studies*. Edited by D. Chattopadhyaya. New Delhi: Indian Council of Philosophical Research in association with Rddhi-India Calcutta, pp.520–530. Original edition, *Indian Studies: Past and Present*, Calcutta, vol.iv, pp.98–104.

Dummett, Michael. 1967. Frege, Gottlob. In *The Encyclopedia of Philosophy*. Edited by P. Edwards. New York: Macmillan and the Free Press, pp.225–37.

Dundas, Paul. 1992. *The Jains*. New York: Routledge.

Edwards, Paul, ed. 1967. *The Encyclopedia of Philosophy*. 8 vols. New York: Macmillan and the Free Press.

Falk, W. D. 1963. Morality, Self and Others. In *Morality and the Language of Conduct*. Edited by H. N. Castaneda and G. Nakhnikian. Detroit: Wayne State University, pp.25–66.

Foot, Philippa. 1995. Morality as a System of Hypothetical Imperatives. In *Meta-Ethics*. Edited by M. Smith. Aldershot; Brookfield, USA: Dartmouth, pp.89–100.

———. 1995. Recantation 1994. In *Meta-Ethics*. Edited by M. Smith. Aldershot; Brookfield, USA: Dartmouth, pp.100–02.

Foulk, Gary J. 1973. The Relationship between Normative Ethics and Metaethics. *Personalist* 54 (3): pp.171–175.

Franco, Eli. 1983. Studies in the Tattvopaplavasiṁa. *Journal of Indian Philosophy* 11 (2): pp.147–166.

———. 1989. Mahāyāna Buddhism—An Unfortunate Misunderstanding? *Berliner Indologische Studien* (4/5): pp.39–47.

Frankena, William K. 1963. Recent Conceptions of Morality. In *Morality and the Language of Conduct*. Edited by H. N. Castaneda and G. Nakhnikian. Detroit: Wayne State University, pp.1–24.

———. 1973. *Ethics*. 2nd ed. Englewood Cliffs NJ: Prentice Hall.

Gadamer, Hans-Georg. 1996. *Truth and Method*. Translated by J. Weinsheimer and D. G. Marshall. 2nd (Revised English Language) ed. New York: Continuum.

Gewirth, Alan. 1960. Meta-Ethics and Normative Ethics. *Mind* 69: pp.187–205.

———. 1968. Metaethics and Moral Neutrality. *Ethics* 78: pp.214–225.

Goldstick, Danny. 1998. Mores. Draft/Unpublished.

Goodwin, William F. 1956. Mysticism and Ethics: An Examination of Radhakrishnan's Reply to Schweitzer's Critique of Indian Thought. *Ethics* 67: pp.25–41.

Green, G.H. 1982. The Doctrine of Metaethical Neutrality. *Metaphilosophy* 13 (2): pp.131–137.

Grimes, John. 1996. *A Concise Dictionary of Indian Philosophy*. Albany: State University of New York.

Hacker, Paul. 1995. *Philology and Confrontation*. Edited by W. Halbfass. Albany: State Universisty of New York.

Halbfass, Wilhelm. 1988. *India and Europe: an Essay in Understanding*. Albany, NY: State University of New York. Original edition, *Indien und Europa: Perspektiven ihrer geistigen Begegnung*. Basel; Stuttgart: Schwabe, 1981.

———. 1991. *Tradition and Reflection : Explorations in Indian Thought*. Albany, NY: State University of New York.

Hale, Susan C. 1991. Against Supererogation. *American Philosophical Quarterly*: pp.273–285.

Hare, R.M. 1955. Universalizability. *Proceedings of the Aristotelian Society*: pp.295–312.

———. 1971. *Freedom and Reason*. London: Oxford University Press.
Hart, H.L.A. 1961. *The Concept Of Law*. Oxford: Clarendon Press.
Inden, Ronald B. 1990. *Imagining India*. Cambridge, Mass.: Blackwell.
India; Government of. 1950. *Glossary of Technical Terms, Constitution of India*. New Delhi.
India; Ministry of Education, Government of. 1962. *A Consolidated Glossary of Technical Terms (English – Hindi)*: Central Hindi Directorate.
Kalupahana, David J. 1995. *Ethics in Early Buddhism*. Honolulu: University of Hawai'i.
Kane, Pandurang Vaman. 1990. *History Of Dharmaśastra: Ancient And Mediæval Religious And Civil Law In India*. 2nd rev. and enl. ed, *Government Oriental Series. Class B. no. 6*. Poona: Bhandarkar Oriental Research Institute.
Klostermaier, Klaus. 1986: Dharmamegha samādhi: Comments on Yogasūtra IV.29. *Philosophy East and West* 36 (3): pp.253–262.
Koehn, Donald. 1974. Normative Ethics That Are Neither Teleological Nor Deontological. *Metaphilosophy* 5: pp.173–180.
Larson, Gerald James. 1972. The Trimurti of Dharma in Indian Thought: Paradox or Contradiction? *Philosophy East and West* 22: pp.145–153.
———.1987. The History and Literature of Sāṃkhya. In *Samkhya : a Dualist Tradition in Indian Philosophy.* Edited by G. J. Larson and R. S. Bhattacharya. Princeton, NJ: Princeton University Press.
Larson, Gerald James and Bhattacharya, Ram Shankar. 1987. *Sāṃkhya; A Dualist Tradition in Indian Philosophy.* Princeton, NJ: Princeton University Press.
Le Pore, Ernest, ed. 1986. *Truth and Interpretation: Perspectives on the Philosophy of Donald Davidson*. Cambridge: Blackwell.
Leslie, John. 1972. Ethically Required Existence. *American Philosophical Quarterly* 9: pp.215–224.
Lingat, Robert. 1973. *The Classical Law of India*. Translated by J. D. M. Derrett. Berkeley,: University of California Press.
MacKinnon, Catharine A. 1989. Pornography: On Morality and Politics. In *Toward a Feminist Theory of the State*. Cambridge, Mass.: Harvard University Press, pp.195–124.

Mahadevan, T.M.P. 1951. The Basis of Social, Ethical, and Spiritual Values in Indian Philosophy. In *Essays in East–West Philosophy; an Attempt at World Philosophical Synthesis*. Edited by C. A. Moore. Honolulu: University of Hawaii Press.

Matilal, Bimal Krishna, ed. 1989. *Moral Dilemmas in the Mahābhā rata*. Shimla; Delhi: Indian Institute of Advanced Study in association with Motilal Banarsidass, Delhi.

———.1989. Moral Dilemmas: Insights from the Indian Epics. In *Moral dilemmas in the Mahābhārata*. Edited by B. K. Matilal. Shimla; Delhi: Indian Institute of Advanced Study in association with Motilal Banarsidass, Delhi, pp.1–19.

McDowell, John. 1995. Are Moral Requirements Hypothetical Imperatives. In *Meta-Ethics*. Edited by M. Smith. Aldershot; Brookfield, USA: Dartmouth, pp.103–120. Original edition, *Proceedings of the Aristotelian Society*, (1978) 52: pp.13–29.

McKenzie, John S. 1929. *A Manual of Ethics*. 6th ed. London: University Tutorial Press.

Melden, Abraham Irving, ed. 1958. *Essays in Moral Philosophy*. Seattle: University of Washington Press.

Mellema, Gregory. 1996. Is it Bad to Omit and Act of Supererogation? *Journal of Philosophical Research* 21: pp.405–416.

Moody, Ernest A. 1967. William of Ockham. In *The Encyclopedia of Philosophy*. Edited by P. Edwards. New York: Macmillan and the Free Press, pp.306–317.

Moore, Charles Alexander, ed. 1951. *Essays in East–West philosophy; an Attempt at World Philosophical Synthesis*. Honolulu,: University of Hawaii Press.

Moore, Charles Alexander, and Aldyth V. Morris, eds. 1967. *The Indian Mind : Essentials of Indian Philosophy and Culture. Papers presented at the four East-West Philosophers' Conferences held at the University of Hawaii in 1939, 1949, 1959 and 1964*. Honolulu: East-West Center Press.

Müller, F. Max. 1861. *Lectures on the Science of Language*. London: Longman. Original edition, Delivered at the Royal Institution of Great Britain in April, May and June of 1861.

Nadler, Steven. 1995. Port Royal Logic. In *Cambridge Dictionary of Philosophy*. Edited by R. Audi. Cambridge: Cambridge University, p.632.

Nute, Donald. 1995. Intention. In *Cambridge Dictionary of Philosophy*. Edited by R. Audi. Cambridge: Cambridge University, p.379.

Outka, Gene H., and John P. Reeder. 1973. *Religion and Morality; a Collection of Essays*. 1st ed. Garden City, NY: Anchor Press.

Paton, H.J. 1956. Analysis of the Argument. In (Immanuel Kant's) *Groundwork of the Metaphyics of Morals*. New York: Harper Tourchooks, pp.13–52.

Pettit, Philip, Richard Sylvan, and Jean Norman, eds. 1987. *Metaphysics and Morality : Essays in Honour of J.J.C. Smart*. Oxford, UK; New York, NY, USA: B. Blackwell.

Potter, Karl H. 1963. *Presuppositions of India's Philosophies, Prentice-Hall Philosophy Series*. Englewood Cliffs, NJ: Prentice-Hall.

———, ed. 1970–1992. *Encyclopedia of Indian Philosophies*. 5 vols. Princeton NJ; Delhi: Princeton University Press; Motilal Banarsidass.

Potter, Karl H., and Sibajiban Bhattacharya. 1977. *Indian Metaphysics and Epistemology: The Tradition of Nyāya–Vaiśeṣika up to Gaṅgésa*. Edited by K. H. Potter, *The Encyclopedia of Indian Philosophies*. Princeton NJ: Princeton University.

———. 1992. *Indian Philosophical Analysis: Nyāya–Vaiśesika from Gangeśa to Raghunātha Śiromani*. Edited by K. H. Potter. 1st ed, *The Encyclopedia of Indian Philosophies*. Princeton NJ: Princeton University.

Putnam, Hilary. 2002. *The Collapse of the Fact/Value Dichotomy and Other Essays*. Cambridge, MA: Harvard University Press.

Quine, Willard Van Orman. 1960. *Word and Object*. Cambridge: Technology Press of the Massachusetts Institute of Technology.

———. 1990. Two Dogmas of Empiricism. In *Classics of Analytic Philosophy*. Edited by R. R. Ammerman. Indianapolis: Hacket, pp.196–213. Original edition, *Philosophical Review* 1950.

Quinn, Philip L. 1986. Moral Obligation, Religious Demand, and Practical Conflict. In *Rationality, Religious Belief, and Moral Commitment; New Essays in the Philosophy of Religions*. Edited by R. Audi and W. J. Wainwright. London: Cornell University Press, pp.195–212.

Quinton, Anthony. 1993. Morals and Politics. In *Ethics* (Royal Institute of Philosophy Supplement: 35). Edited by A. P. Griffiths. New York: Cambridge Univ Pres, pp. 96–106.

Radhakrishnan, S. 1940. Mysticism and Ethics in Hindu Thought. In *Eastern Religions and Western Thought*. London: Oxford University Press, ch.3. Original edition of specific essay was delivered as the *Sir George Birdwood Memorial Lecture*, given at the Royal Society of Arts, London, on April 30, 1937.

Raju, P.T. 1967. Metaphysical Theories in Indian Philosophy (1949). In *The Indian Mind: Essentials of Indian Philosophy and Culture. (Papers Presented at the Four East-West Philosophers' Conferences held at the University of Hawaii in 1939, 1949, 1959 and 1964)*. Edited by C. A. Moore and A. V. Morris. Honolulu: East-West Center Press, pp.25–28.

Rangaswami Aiyangar, K(umbakonam) V(iraraghava). 1952. *Some Aspects of the Hindu View of Life According to Dharmaśāstra, Sayaji Row Memorial Lectures, 1947–48*. Baroda: Director Oriental Institute.

Rawls, John. 1971. *A Theory of Justice.* Cambridge, Mass.: Belknap Press of Harvard University Press.

———. 1996. *Political Liberalism*. Paperback ed, *John Dewey Essays in Philosophy; no. 4*. New York: Columbia University Press.

Riepe, Dale Maurice. 1961. *The Naturalistic Tradition in Indian Thought*. Seattle: University of Washington Press.

Said, Edward W. 1978. *Orientalism*. 1st Vintage Books ed. New York: Vintage Books.

Said, K. A. Mohyeldin, ed. 1990. *Modelling the Mind.* Oxford; New York: Clarendon Press; Oxford University Press.

Sare-McCord, Geoffrey. 1995. Fact-Value Distinction. In *Cambridge Dictionary of Philosophy*. Edited by R. Audi. Cambridge: Cambridge University, p.260.

Sastri, D.R. 1990. A Short History of Indian Materialism. In *Cārvā ka/Lokāyata: an Anthology of Source Materials and Some Recent Studies*. Edited by D. Chattopadhyaya. New Delhi: Indian Council of Philosophical Research in association with Rddhi-India Calcutt, pp:394–431.

Schmitt, Richard. 1967. Husserl, Edmund. In *The Encyclopedia of Philosophy*. Edited by P. Edwards. New York: Macmillan and the Free Pres, pp.96–99.

———. 1967. Phenomenology. In *The Encyclopedia of Philosophy.* Edited by P. Edwards. New York: Macmillan and the Free Press, pp.135–151.

Schweitzer, Albert. 1936. *Indian Thought and its Development.* Translated by C. E. B. Russell. New York,: H. Holt and Company.

Sen, Sanat Kumar. 1967. Indian Philosophy and Social Ethics. *Journal of the Indian Academy of Philosophy* (1/2): pp.63–74.

Seth, James. 1928. *A Study of Ethical Principles.* 8th ed. London: W. Blackwood and Sons.

Seuren, Pieter A.M. 1998. *Western Linguistics.* Oxford: Blackwell.

Sharma, I. C. 1965. *Ethical Philosophies of India.* London: George Allen and Unwin.

Singer, Peter ed. 1991. *A Companion To Ethics.* Cambridge, Mass.: Blackwell Reference.

———. 1993. *Practical Ethics.* 2nd ed. Cambridge: Cambridge University.

Skorupski, John. 1993. The Definition of Morality. *Philosophy* 35(Supp): pp.121–144.

Smith, Michael, ed. 1995. *Meta-Ethics, International Research Library of Philosophy; 12. The Philosophy of Value.* Aldershot; Brookfield, USA: Dartmouth.

———. 1995. *The Moral Problem.* Oxford, UK; Cambridge, Mass., USA: Blackwell.

Sogani, Kamal Chand. 1975. Jaina Ethical Theory. *Indian Philosophical Quarterly.* 2 (2): pp.177–183.

Solomon, R. C. 1970. Normative and Meta-Ethics. *Philosophy and Phenomenological Research* 31:97–107.

Sprigg, T. L. S. 1970. Definition of a Moral Judgement. In *The Definition of Morality.* Edited by G. Wallace and A. D. M. Walker. London: Methuen and Co., pp.119–145. Original edition, *Philosophy* (1964): pp.301–22.

Stevenson, Charles L. 1944. *Ethics and Language.* New Haven: Yale University Press.

Strawson, P. F. 1962. Freedom and Resentment. *Proceedings of the British Academy* 48: pp.187-211.

Swoyer, Chris. 1995. Leibniz on Intension and Extension. *Noûs* 29 (1):96–114.

Tapasyānanda. 1990. *Bhakti Schools of Vedānta*. Madras: Ramakrishna Math.

Trianosky, Gregory W. 1986. Supererogation, Wrongdoing, and Vice: On the Autonomy of the Ethics of Virtue. *Journal of Philosophy* 83: pp.26–40.

Tucci, G. 1990. A Sketch of Indian Materialism. In *Cārvāka/Lokāyata: an Anthology of Source Materials and Some Recent Studies*. Edited by D. Chattopadhyaya. New Delhi: Indian Council of Philosophical Research in association with Rddhi-India Calcutta, pp.384–393. Original edition, *Proceedings of the First Indian Philosophical Congress* (1925).

Upper, John. *Davidson's Three Versions of the Principle of Charity* 1995 [cited. Available from http://qsilver.queensu.ca/~3jku/mypapers/dd3pc.pdf.

Urmson, J.O. 1958. Saints and Heroes. In *Essays in Moral Philosophy*. Seattle,: University of Washington Press, pp.185–216.

Vermazen, Bruce, and Merrill B. Hintikka, eds. 1985. *Essays on Davidson: Actions and Events*. Oxford: Clarendon Press.

Vetter, Tilmann . 1992. On the Authenticity of the *Ratnāvali*. *Asiatische Studien* (Zurich) 46 (1): pp.492–506.

Vireswarānanda (Swāmi). 1986:. Introduction. In *Brahma Sūtras; With Text; English Rendering, Comments According to Śri Bhāṣya of Śri Rāmānuja, and Index*. Calcutta: Advaita Ashrama, xxvii–lxxix.

Waligora, Melitta. 1991. Das Tal der Sachlichkeit: Albert Schweitzer uber Indien. *Conceptus* 26 (65): pp.47–56.

Wallace, Gerald , and Arthur David McKinnon Walker, eds. 1970. *The Definition of Morality*. London: Methuen and Co.

———. 1970. Introduction. In *The Definition of Morality*. Edited by G. Wallace and A. D. M. Walker. London: Methuen and Co, pp.1–25.

Whicher, Ian. 1998. *The Integrity of the Yoga Darśana*. Albany: State University of New York.

Williams, Bernard. 1985. *Ethics and the Limits of Philosophy*. Cambridge: Harvard University Press.

Wilson, N.L. 1959. Substance Without Substrata. *Review of Metaphysics* XII (4): pp.521–539.

Wilson, W.Kent. 1995. Equivocation. In *Cambridge Dictionary of*

Philosophy. Edited by R. Audi. Cambridge: Cambridge University, p.235.

Wollheim, Richard, and James Hopkins, eds. 1982. *Philosophical Essays on Freud*. Cambridge; New York: Cambridge University Press.

Wood, Allen. 1991. Marx Against Morality. In *A Companion To Ethics*.. Edited by P. Singer. Cambridge, Mass.: Blackwell Reference, pp.511–524.

Yamunācārya, M. 1988. *Rāmānuja's Teachings in his Own Words*. Bombay: Bharatiya Vidya Bhavan.

Yandell, Keith E. 1984. On Classifying Indian Ethical Systems. *Journal of Indian Council of Philosophical Research* II (1): pp.61–66.

Zimmerman, David. 1980. Meta-Ethics Naturalized. *Canadian Journal of Philosophy* 10: pp.637–662.

Zimmerman, Michael J. 1997. A Plea for Accuses. *American Philosophical Quarterly* 34 (2): pp.229–243

Index

A

B

C

D

E

F

G

H

I

J

K

P

Q

R

S

T

U

V

294, 312, 315, 316, 318, 329, 336, 338, 348
viṣāda 264
Viśiṣṭādvaita Vedānta 96, 221, 306, 308, 319, 321, 322, 323, 324, 335, 345

W

Wagle, N.K. 10, 111
Walker, A.D.M. 43, 44
Wallace, G. 43, 44
weak supererogation 65
Whicher, Ian 262, 266, 273, 275, 277
Wilson, N.L. 116
Wittgenstein, Ludwig 126, 149, 150, 151, 152, 153, 196, 208, 209
wrong 37, 38, 45, 47, 48, 49, 50, 51, 52, 53, 55, 58, 59, 83, 84, 85, 88, 89, 131, 137, 156, 164, 171, 189, 196, 234, 236, 238, 248, 255, 258, 259, 271, 295, 311, 316, 332

Y

yama 269, 270
Yandell, Keith E. 186
Yoga 102, 124, 221, 222, 223, 224, 253, 260, 261, 262, 263, 264, 265, 267, 268, 269, 270, 271, 272, 273, 274, 275, 276, 277, 279, 315, 319, 320, 321, 332, 335, 336, 337, 340, 343, 345, 348, 358, 363
Yoga Sūtra 262, 263, 264, 267, 269, 271, 272, 273, 274, 277, 337

Z

Zimmerman, David 201
Zimmerman, Michael J. 48